OUTSIDE AND INSIDE

ADVISORY BOARD

David Evans, General Editor
Barry Jean Ancelet
Edward A. Berlin
Joyce J. Bolden
Rob Bowman
Susan C. Cook
Curtis Ellison
William Ferris
John Edward Hasse
Kip Lornell
Bill Malone
Eddie S. Meadows
Manuel H. Peña
Wayne D. Shirley
Robert Walser

OUTSIDE AND INSIDE

Race and Identity in
White Jazz Autobiography

REVA MARIN

University Press of Mississippi / Jackson

The University Press of Mississippi is the scholarly publishing agency of
the Mississippi Institutions of Higher Learning: Alcorn State University,
Delta State University, Jackson State University, Mississippi State University,
Mississippi University for Women, Mississippi Valley State University,
University of Mississippi, and University of Southern Mississippi.

www.upress.state.ms.us

The University Press of Mississippi is a member
of the Association of University Presses.

Copyright © 2020 by University Press of Mississippi
All rights reserved

First printing 2020
∞

Library of Congress Cataloging-in-Publication Data

Names: Marin, Reva, author.
Title: Outside and inside: race and identity in white jazz autobiography / Reva Marin.
Other titles: American made music series.
Description: Jackson: University Press of Mississippi, 2020. | Series: American made music series | Includes bibliographical references and index.
Identifiers: LCCN 2020014525 (print) | LCCN 2020014526 (ebook) | ISBN 9781496829979 (hardback) | ISBN 9781496829986 (trade paperback) | ISBN 9781496829993 (epub) | ISBN 9781496830005 (epub) | ISBN 9781496830012 (pdf) | ISBN 9781496830029 (pdf)
Subjects: LCSH: Jazz musicians, White—United States—Biography—History and criticism. | Jazz musicians—United States—Biography—History and criticism. | Jazz—History and criticism. | Music and race—United States.
Classification: LCC ML3508 .M3 2020 (print) | LCC ML3508 (ebook) | DDC 781.65089/09—dc23
LC record available at https://lccn.loc.gov/2020014525
LC ebook record available at https://lccn.loc.gov/2020014526

British Library Cataloging-in-Publication Data available

CONTENTS

Preface vii

Acknowledgments xiii

Introduction xv

1 The Authenticating Collaborators of White Jazz Autobiography 3

2 Bob Wilber, the Westchester Kid: White Privilege
and Perspectives on Jazz Belonging 37

3 Race and Place and the Construction of Jazz Authenticity:
New Orleanian Autobiographers Tom Sancton
and "Wingy" Manone 59

4 Representations of Identity in Jewish Jazz Autobiography 82

5 Don Asher's Fictional-Real Jazz World 122

6 "Straight Life": The Jazz Journey of Art Pepper 149

Conclusion 177

Notes 183

Works Cited 211

Index 221

PREFACE

On an August afternoon in 1994, the Stanley H. Kaplan Penthouse at New York's Lincoln Center was the site of a highly charged debate between Wynton Marsalis—the famed trumpeter, composer, and artistic director of Jazz at Lincoln Center (JALC)—and James Lincoln Collier—the prolific but controversial jazz historian and biographer.[1] The fireworks had started months earlier with the publication of Marsalis's letter in the *New York Times Book Review*, in which Marsalis vented his outrage over the paper's favorable review of Collier's recent book, *Jazz: The American Theme Song* (1993). Describing Collier as "a pompous social scientist who for too long has passed as a serious scholar of jazz music," Marsalis expressed consternation over the reviewer's failure to recognize the contempt that some jazz people held for Collier—"this viper in the bosom of blues and swing" ("Letter" 31).[2]

For his part, Collier had plenty of his own grievances against Marsalis. He and other critics had already voiced their concern with Marsalis's programming decisions at Lincoln Center, suggesting that under the influence of his mentors—the prominent African American authors and cultural critics, Albert Murray and Stanley Crouch—Marsalis had adopted a program based on nepotism, racism against white musicians, and antagonism toward the jazz avant-garde. Collier also took issue with Marsalis's promotion of an Afrocentric teaching of jazz history, which he and others believed overlooked the contributions of white musicians to jazz.[3] In his response to Marsalis in the *New York Times*, Collier offered a blistering assessment of Marsalis's inadequacies as a jazz scholar while eagerly accepting his challenge to a public debate ("Jazz Mythology" 90).

Before the debate had even begun, the high level of acrimony between Marsalis and Collier overwhelmed any chance of a constructive or thoughtful discussion of their differences. Although the men agreed to focus first on Collier's musical interpretations in his biographies of Louis Armstrong and Duke Ellington before turning to Marsalis's role at Jazz at Lincoln Center, the tenuous distinction between music and race quickly evaporated. Marsalis, armed with copies of Collier's books, read aloud passages that he attempted to demonstrate (with considerable success) as factually incorrect. Among them were Collier's explanation of Louis Armstrong's chronic difficulties with his embouchure, which Collier attributed in part to the size of Armstrong's lips, and his emphasis on illiteracy and impoverishment as defining characteristics of the African American community of New Orleans in which Armstrong was raised in the early decades of the twentieth century (and Marsalis, a half century later) (Marsalis et al., "Jazz People" 144–46, 174–76). In his scathing critique of Collier's biography of Ellington, Marsalis targeted Collier's disparagement of the bandleader's intellect and lack of formal musical training and identified numerous errors in Collier's harmonic analysis and interpretations of Ellington's methodology (147–55).

Forced back on his heels, Collier defended his scholarship, insisting that his prodigious reading of books, interviews, and oral histories of jazz musicians gave his work an authority and credibility that no firsthand accounts (including Marsalis's own) could match. Although Marsalis succeeded in getting him to acknowledge (and agree to correct in future editions) some specific errors of musical analysis, Collier refused to yield on other points, even as the audience's frequent applause and jeering made clear whose side they were on. Despite Marsalis's attempt to stick to a fact-based analysis of Collier's work, on several occasions, his emotions overcame him—no more so than when he felt that his own New Orleans's cultural heritage was under attack. "These were poor people and humble," Marsalis insisted, "but they have a lot of dignity and pride and soul. And when you say these things, they're hurtful, and they're not true and—I'm gonna collect myself—but it's incorrect" (157, 147–48, 174).[4]

The atmosphere was no less explosive when the discussion turned to Collier's charges against Marsalis, including the degree to which Marsalis's own musical preferences had or should determine the programming of a major cultural institution. Although Marsalis had some success in defending his record, the discussion disintegrated into bitter exchanges marked by an inflexible adherence to terminology such as "whites" and "blacks" (from Collier) and "United States negro culture" (from Marsalis) that only served to highlight the gaping cultural chasm between them (162, 165, 166, 170).

So how was it that two people who had devoted their lives to playing, teaching, and writing about jazz—and who in fact shared many of the same stylistic and aesthetic preferences—could be so helplessly incapable of communicating with each other across the racial and cultural divide? How could Collier fail to grasp the insensitivity of his obsession with the size of Armstrong's lips or Ellington's supposed intellectual deficits—subjects that fed into some of the oldest and most pernicious stereotypes about African Americans? How are we to interpret his vehement denials of racism in light of the racist, or at least racialist, imagery and language that pervade his biographies of Armstrong and Ellington? Could Marsalis have done a better job of explaining his distinction between "black culture" and "United States negro culture" to Collier? Or was the onus on Collier, as a white man, to seek common ground with the intellectual work that underlay Marsalis's distinction, even as Collier's own animus toward those views was widely known? (Gennari 361–62, 364).

While I propose these questions for consideration, I'd like to jump forward twenty-four years to January 2018, when Marsalis was again at the center of a public airing of issues of race in jazz. The occasion was the inaugural Jazz Congress, a two-day event hosted by JALC featuring performances, workshops, and panel discussions that sought to address some of the key concerns of musicians, educators, and industry insiders today. That the congress chose to open with the panel discussion "Jazz and Race: A Conversation" offers compelling evidence that fundamental questions posed by musicians, critics, and scholars about twentieth-century jazz—many of them on vivid display in the earlier Marsalis-Collier debate—remain no less relevant today.[5] The contentious issues of racism in jazz, appropriation and exploitation, and the Afrocentric bias of mainstream jazz historiography—as worn and seemingly exhausted as they may seem—continue to reveal themselves as potent and divisive forces on the US jazz scene. Whose music is jazz, anyway? Whose jazz stories have been told, and whose stories have been left out? Who has a right to tell these stories? What does the history of jazz say about the history of race relations in US society more broadly?

Joining Marsalis on stage that January day were Ethan Iverson—the acclaimed white pianist, composer, and educator from Wisconsin who came to prominence in the early 2000s with his all-white trio, the Bad Plus, and who has since performed and recorded with African American luminaries such as Billy Hart, Ron Carter, and Albert "Tootie" Heath—and the moderator Andre Guess, African American author and cultural critic. The sharp contrast between the mood of this recent "race and jazz" conversation and the earlier debate cannot be overstated; in place of the intense animosity of the former was an atmosphere of mutual respect that signaled the participants' awareness of a shared, or at least overlapping, worldview.

Even so, a palpable tension and awkwardness accompanied the conversation, along with the heightened displays of deference and politeness that mark even the most sympathetic discussions of race in an interracial setting. Guess attempted to set the tone for the discussion with his promise that it would provide "a safe place" for participants to express themselves without fear of judgment, to articulate their differences in a search for "some common ground." Iverson thanked Marsalis "for inviting me into your house," admitting that his friends had questioned the wisdom of his decision to participate in a public discussion on race. In his response, Marsalis sought to reassure

Iverson, echoing Guess's promise of civility and cordiality in a manner that also established his position of authority in the Lincoln Center setting; as Iverson had acknowledged, Marsalis was truly the host of the gathering.

The specific questions posed by Guess mattered less than the opportunity they gave the musicians to articulate their views on race and authenticity as shaped by their own cultural backgrounds and experiences. Iverson responded with respectful deference to the olive branch that Marsalis and Guess had extended; he acknowledged his own accomplishments in the world of European art music ("I'm not at Wynton's level at dealing with that stuff, but I've dealt with it") before eagerly pronouncing his view of jazz as "the best music of the twentieth century," adding that "almost always the best musicians of this greatest music were black, that's for sure, end of story."

Marsalis took the occasion to once again promote his neoclassicist spin on jazz, race, and American society that he learned as a young, rising star on the New York jazz scene of the 1980s from Murray and Crouch, and that he has since honed in his thirty-plus years as the most famous jazz musician and educator on the planet. He riffed on race as a social construct used by the ruling class to create "a permanent underclass to be exploited for social reasons" and the role of jazz as a unifier through its cultural inclusivity. In this way, he was signaling his respect for the white musician Iverson, describing attempts to separate the different streams that have come together in jazz as akin to "punching water." Later, Iverson offered his own perspective on Marsalis's thesis, suggesting that even as jazz culture shows the confluence of multiple cultural influences, white musicians bear the responsibility to "deal with black music," that is, to acknowledge its centrality to the jazz tradition. By doing so, he added, "I can love myself as a white Wisconsin boy better, you know what I mean? I can have some pride in where *I'm* from.... It's American music... stand tall."

But just beneath the civilities and mutual complements were the real divisions that discussions of race were sure to expose. Marsalis admitted, under Guess's prodding, that his goal "to make America swing again" had met with considerable resistance, opining that "there's something in the swing rhythm that the nation has been against"—something surely related to its roots in black vernacular musical practices. The reality of race as a social construct, he explained later, does not negate the fact that these constructs have real and devastating effects on the lives of oppressed people. For all of Marsalis's polished phrases about jazz as the great cultural unifier, then, we see him moving seamlessly into an account of his conversations about race with the baritone saxophonist Gerry Mulligan, in which the two would tease each other about their decisions to maintain segregated bands; in Marsalis's words, "sometimes you can get to an honesty of discussion."

But an honest discussion might surely want to acknowledge the confusions, ambivalences, and contradictions that discussions of race—including this one and the earlier Marsalis-Collier debate—frequently expose. Thus, we find Marsalis and Iverson insisting that jazz is both a melding of disparate cultural influences and at the same time essentially "black"; that the false theories of racial difference uncover the truth that anyone, irrespective of skin tone, is capable of playing jazz, but that the contributions of African Americans have been without question most consequential to the music's development; moreover, that challenges to this thesis are essentially racist in nature.

There have been many other public airings—some in recent years—of contentious issues pertaining to race and jazz over the music's century-plus history; later chapters of this book will consider particular debates in jazz magazines from the 1930s to the 1960s as useful historical context for analysis.[6] But I chose to focus on these two JALC debates because I believe they illuminate in a powerful and relatively concise way many of the themes, attitudes, and perspectives—as well as the confusions and contradictions—on display in the autobiographies of the jazz musicians who are the focus of this book.

Collier and Iverson—the white participants in the two JALC debates—reveal a range of white engagement with African American jazz culture that also emerges in the accounts of white jazz autobiographers. Collier's embrace of the "white resentment narrative" (more on this in the introduction) is reminiscent of attitudes that we will find in some of their accounts. In some cases, these attitudes emerge in the response of white jazz autobiographers to particular interracial experiences or because their insecurities leave them unable or unwilling to acknowledge the historical context framing their participation in black jazz culture. Other autobiographers display attitudes closer to those of Iverson, the twenty-first-century white jazzman who goes out of his way to pay homage to the African American roots of jazz and to the African American jazz masters—past and present—who have been central to his own development as a jazz musician.

But it is equally important to reflect on the differences between the Wynton Marsalis who showed up to debate James Lincoln Collier and the one who participated in the recent conversation with Ethan Iverson and Andre Guess. While there is evidence that Marsalis's views on jazz interracialism have softened in the twenty-plus years that separated these two jazz conversations, his beliefs regarding the importance of jazz in relation to African American culture and society have remained fundamentally consistent.[7] I would suggest, then, that the contrasting tones of sympathy and animosity that animate the respective conversations account in large part for the difference in Marsalis's own stance and demeanor. In the first, Marsalis came prepared to battle a jazz critic antagonistic to his vision of jazz music and culture and its relationship to the history of black-white relations in the United States; in the second, Marsalis saw his vision affirmed and supported by a younger white musician.

This is not to suggest that Marsalis is beyond reproach for his own conduct and demeanor in his role as jazz's most influential and powerful spokesperson nor that his aesthetic and cultural vision for jazz and for American culture more broadly—ones that he has imprinted with such success on the institution he directs—are undeserving of the scrutiny and criticism they have received.[8] Nor is my intention to suggest that any one culture is inherently more empathic or expansive than any other or that one's cultural background absolves one of responsibility to try to reach across the barriers erected to separate people based on differences of culture, gender identity, political beliefs, and religion. Indeed, our perspective is limited if we fail to take into account the personal conduct of the individuals involved in interracial interactions, wherever these interactions take place—on the bandstand or in debates in the pages of jazz magazines or at JALC. As this study aims to show, the response of participants matters: are they empathetic or close-minded, defensive or expansive in their responses to the tense and sometimes explosive conditions that mark interracial and intercultural exchanges?

But in agreement with theorists of white privilege, I see that discussions of jazz and race are much more likely to break down when white participants are unwilling to recognize the sociohistorical conditions that inform them—when they attempt to isolate discussions of white participation in jazz as simply a matter of musical achievement detached from its social and historical context, or when they elevate book-learning over insider perspectives in order to make judgments about African Americans and their culture. This is, of course, what happened in the Collier-Marsalis debate, and the results are clear. By contrast, the recent discussion at JALC went in quite another direction, one perhaps best illustrated by the panel's response to an audience member who asked them how they would have responded if the session had instead been called "Jazz and Racism." Iverson jumped in first, admitting that he would "have had less trepidation" about participating in the discussion "because racism is a very real situation." But Guess and Marsalis both pushed back, arguing that the word "racism" was too polarizing and ultimately unhelpful for their goal to advance constructive dialogue and, as Guess repeated, to "find some common ground."

I offer this brief look at these two "jazz and race" discussions as an introduction to the types of racialist attitudes and beliefs that will emerge in the chapters that follow, as we turn our attention to the accounts and descriptions of interracial jazz experiences in texts authored by white jazz musicians. I have also intended my analysis of the debates to provide a model of the methods that inform this study, with the insider perspectives (the words and texts) of these autobiographers serving as the foundational material against which I consider the historical and cultural conditions that shaped them, always mindful, as the Lincoln Center debates forcefully remind us, of their relevance in our own time.

ACKNOWLEDGMENTS

Outside and Inside is the culmination of my decision to return to school as a middle-aged graduate student and become a jazz scholar. My love of jazz, however, goes back many decades, when, as a teenager in the late 1970s, I began to study jazz guitar and then, a few years later, the alto saxophone. The many teachers I've had the privilege of studying with, including Roy Patterson, the late Mike Roberts, Jane Fair, and Jerry Bergonzi, were my first, and in many ways my most important, inspirations; their dedication to their music and their eagerness to pass on their knowledge became a model for my own life path.

I'm immensely grateful to Marlene Kadar for encouraging me to return to school and for her continuing support and friendship. I'm also thankful for my York community, in particular Leslie Sanders, Art Redding, and Michael Coghlan, who were engaged with my project at every stage and went out of their way to provide helpful comments and suggestions. Warren Crichlow was incredibly generous to me with his time and suggestions, directing me to jazz scholarship and music and always remaining open and receptive to whatever I was working on. Graduate seminars led by Bob Witmer (African American music), Andrea Davis (black women writers in the African diaspora), and Leslie Sanders (African American poetry) greatly enriched my own thinking about race and jazz culture. For several years, I also had the pleasure of being a teaching assistant in Andrea Davis's Cultures of Resistance in the Americas: The African American Experience.

Many thanks to Sherrie Tucker, for her extremely detailed and thoughtful response to an earlier version of this project. Similarly generous were the anonymous readers who wrote detailed critiques of the manuscript and whose suggestions for revision substantially improved the earlier draft. For their generosity in sharing their photographs and giving me permission to reprint them here, I'm very grateful to Laurie Pepper and Tom Sancton and to Rich Falco, director of the Jazz History Database, who spent considerable effort in tracking down photographs of Don Asher and obtaining permissions for their use here.

At the University Press of Mississippi, I've received kind and expert guidance from everyone involved in this project through its various stages of revision and production. Thanks in particular to Craig Gill, Laura Strong, Emily Bandy, and Carlton McGrone; and to Camille Hale, for her meticulous copyediting of the final draft.

My friends have offered their encouragement and support to me at many critical points of this journey. Thanks especially to Janet Zweig, Ann Lau, Bessie Goldberg, Sol Goldberg, and Patrick Taylor. And finally, to Matthew Clark, my life partner and friend, for his love and support, his wisdom and his humor. And to my sister and ex-wombmate, Bayla Marin, whose devotion to her music and teaching inspires me daily. It is to Matthew and Bayla that I dedicate this book.

An earlier version of chapter 4 was published in the *Canadian Review of American Studies* 45, no. 3, 2015.

INTRODUCTION

From 1926, with the publication of Paul Whiteman's *Jazz*, to the end of the first decade of the twenty-first century, somewhere in the range of eighty US jazz musicians published their autobiographies and memoirs;[1] taken together, this body of work offers valuable firsthand accounts of jazz from the music's infancy to the present day, allowing important insights into changing musical, cultural, and social landscapes that tie the history of jazz to the history of the United States in the twentieth century. While many of these autobiographies were published by trade presses, in the 1980s and 1990s university presses greatly accelerated the publication of jazz autobiographies, clearly hoping to preserve the life stories of aging musicians whose careers represented a wide sweep of jazz history, including the early music of New Orleans and Chicago, big band swing, bebop, West Coast jazz, and various postbop and free jazz communities of the 1960s and beyond.

Although many jazz autobiographies published between the 1920s and 1950s attracted considerable public interest—promoted as celebrity or entertainment biography in jazz magazines and general-interest publications—it is only since the 1980s that critics began to turn to forms of self-inscription such as oral history and autobiography as legitimate sources for scholarly investigation (Stein, "The Performance" 173). Since then, a number of studies have appeared that examine jazz autobiography through the lens of cultural and social history, ethnomusicology, and literary criticism in order to explore the autobiographical form itself or to illuminate historical discourses around race, gender, culture, and politics in twentieth-century American life. The work of these critics, which I engage throughout this study, has been invaluable for shaping my own approach to the study of jazz autobiography.

Essays by Kathy J. Ogren (1991), William Howland Kenney (1991), and Christopher Harlos (1995) established the foundation for scholarship on jazz autobiography; all three critics emphasize the performative nature of jazz autobiography and draw analogies between jazz musicians' construction of their literary and musical identities. Ogren finds evidence of the black vernacular practices of "storytelling, bragging, and humor" ("Jazz Isn't Just Me" 113) in both the music and autobiographical texts of jazz musicians, stressing the participatory nature of jazz performance and the ways in which the written texts reflect this concern for and interaction with audience (118–19). Kenney considers the significance of the collaborative process in Louis Armstrong's four "autobiographical statements," noting Armstrong's conscious manipulation of racial and social expectations and his use of these documents to further his career and position as a leading African American entertainer (Kenney, "Negotiating"). Harlos also examines the issue of authorial control in coauthored or multivoiced jazz autobiographies.[2]

Since then, critics have continued to elaborate on the performative elements of jazz autobiography and on analogies between jazz music and jazz literature. Daniel Stein, who has emerged as a leading scholar of music autobiography theory, examines a number of jazz autobiographies for "the narrative strategies the musicians mobilize to fashion autobiographical selves that echo the complexities and dynamics of jazz practices" ("The Performance" 174). Stein suggests (in agreement with Ajay Heble) that the fluidity and lack of predictability of jazz improvisation is analogous to the fluid, changing constructions of self in jazz autobiography (181).[3] It is hardly surprising that the focus of much of this critical attention has been on texts written by African American jazz musicians or that African Americans comprise the majority (by a significant margin) of jazz autobiographers.[4] It is, after all, commonly understood that the various styles of music that came to be known as "jazz" evolved from black vernacular forms (as they combined with Euro-American practices), and African American jazz musicians are widely acknowledged to be among its most prominent practitioners, innovators, and composers.

Outside and Inside: Race and Identity in White Jazz Autobiography seeks to fill a gap in scholarship on jazz autobiography as the first full-length study of autobiographies of white jazz musicians. It begins with the claim that white jazz autobiographers display attitudes and themes on issues pertaining to race, ethnicity, and gender identity that cut across stylistic and historical difference and that reveal crucial aspects of their self-identifications as white musicians in a predominantly black art form. These attitudes offer important evidence that over the first six decades of the twentieth century white musicians from a wide range of musical, social, and economic backgrounds looked to black music and culture as a central (although not exclusive) model on which to form both their personal and musical identities. The insistence with which these autobiographers approach and revisit this subject is in notable contrast to other important studies of the jazz-learning process that involve at least some nonblack musicians as participants or subjects; among them is Paul Berliner's groundbreaking 1994 ethnography on jazz improvisation, in which there is for the most part the *assumption*, rather than the *exploration*, of the primacy of black music and culture in the jazz tradition.[5]

The term, "white," of course, requires further explanation. Simply put, in *Outside and Inside*, white jazz autobiographers are those who self-identified as white—at least in certain contexts and over a significant period of their lives—and who were regarded as such by the general public, including their audiences, fans, collaborators, and critics. The significance of their white identification will be taken up in detail in the chapters that follow, especially in relation to those Jewish, Irish, or Italian autobiographers who, due to the fluidity of legal and social definitions of whiteness in the United States over the course of the twentieth century, spent much of their childhood inhabiting "not-quite-white" or "inbetween" identities (Brodkin 60; Roediger passim). To varying degrees of detail, *Outside and Inside* considers the work of sixteen of these autobiographers; all of them are men, and all of them are instrumentalists. (Many of them are, in addition, arrangers, composers, and bandleaders.)

The notably disproportionate representation of male autobiographers and collaborators in this study is a reflection of the general marginalization of women in jazz throughout much of the twentieth century,[6] a marginalization that is clearly illustrated in the dearth of jazz autobiographies authored by women; those that do exist do not fit comfortably within the parameters of this study, either because the autobiographer is not white, or is not an instrumentalist, or was not raised in the United States, or some combination of the above.[7] For these reasons, I was especially pleased to discover Laurie Pepper's autobiography following its publication in 2014; her brilliant and perceptive account of her own life, and particularly of her relationship with Art Pepper, is critical to my analysis of Pepper's autobiography, *Straight Life* (see chapter 6).

With the exception of Mezz Mezzrow and Tom Sancton, all of the autobiographers under discussion here were born within the first three decades of the twentieth century (Mezzrow was born in 1899; Sancton in 1949), yet they represent a remarkable diversity in respect to their socioeconomic, geographical, and cultural backgrounds. Bob Wilber and Charlie Barnet came from wealthy East Coast families, Mezz Mezzrow from a respectable middle-class Jewish family on Chicago's Northwest Side. Many of the others came from working-class or lower-middle-class immigrant families who faced economic hardship and social and cultural disruption as they adjusted to their new lives in America. Among them were Sicilian American trumpeter Wingy Manone; second-generation Jewish Americans Benny Goodman, Artie Shaw, and Max Kaminsky; and Russian-born and Chicago-raised pianist, Art Hodes. Several of them—including Goodman, Kaminsky, Shaw, and Hodes—were making important contributions to their family's finances through their income as professional musicians from the time they were teenagers.

Many of these jazz autobiographers grew up in or near one of the urban centers of jazz—New Orleans, Chicago, New York, or Los Angeles; those who did not set out in search of urban jazz centers at a young age.[8] Their descriptions of this process of discovery help to illuminate the ethos of a particular city's jazz culture; as well, they provide important insights into the emergence and development of particular jazz styles. Manone gives a glimpse of the complex and highly stratified racial and cultural environment of New Orleans during the early decades of the twentieth century, as jazz music was first emerging into public consciousness; Sancton offers a nuanced history of race in New Orleans in his account of his experiences as a white youngster in interracial jazz communities during the 1960s, during the final years of the traditional jazz revival there. Wilber documents the heyday of that revival on the East Coast during the 1940s and 1950s. Bud Freeman, Benny Goodman, Art Hodes, Max Kaminsky, Mezz Mezzrow, and Eddie Condon describe their jazz-learning experiences on Chicago's South Side during the 1920s and in Harlem in the 1930s. California-born Art Pepper recalls his experiences on Central Avenue, the heart of Los Angeles's black jazz community, during the late 1930s and 1940s, as the music went through dramatic restructurings of form and content in the shape of big band swing, bebop, and postbebop styles. Don Asher details his experiences in jam sessions in predominantly black clubs in Boston in the early 1950s.

As a result of specific thematic considerations, some white jazz autobiographies receive closer attention than others, while others are left out entirely. Simple questions guided my selection process: To what degree had a particular autobiographer associated in his career and personal life with black music and culture, and to what degree was he willing or able to consider these experiences?[9] Notably absent is Paul Whiteman's *Jazz* (1926)—the earliest and perhaps best-known jazz autobiography by a white musician. Although Whiteman quickly establishes the African and slave origins of jazz—his imagery steeped in the essentialist language of his time—he is almost silent on the topic of the historical or contemporary contribution of Africans or African Americans to jazz (3, 4). Instead, his autobiography functions as his *apologia* for jazz—his attempt to counter the widespread view of jazz in the 1920s as a musical and cultural practice associated with tawdry and immoral practices and activities (Ogren, *Jazz Revolution* 139–61). During his career, Whiteman strove to make popular dance music respectable to middle-class white Americans by removing it from its association with brothels and speakeasies and bringing it into the concert hall, by hiring formally trained musicians, and by emphasizing its connection to European art music.

In the few instances in which Whiteman does acknowledge the black contributions to American popular music, as he does when he refers to the origins of ragtime in "negro syncopated dance" (Whiteman 177), he dwells on the accomplishments of formally trained musicians such as W. C. Handy and Scott Joplin while failing to credit the black oral traditions that were essential to their own musical development. The implication of Whiteman's well-known desire "to make a lady of jazz" is that jazz will be saved by white musicians with European music training who will sanitize the primitive and unrefined jazz that sprang from black sources.

Undoubtedly, Whiteman is *sui generis* among jazz autobiographers; some others not included in this study are perhaps easier to categorize. Briefly, they all represent a type of musician who flourished in jazz and popular music environments from the 1920s through the 1950s, who played primarily in Dixieland bands or in large dance or swing bands, or in the white territory bands in the West or Southwest or in the studios of New York or Los Angeles. For many of these musicians, it was possible to pass their entire careers with relatively little personal contact with black musicians or African American musical traditions more generally. For this reason, there is notably little discussion in their autobiographies of the role of race in jazz or of the degree to which their own playing was shaped by African American music and culture.[10]

My decision to focus on autobiography follows in the wake of scholarship of recent decades that has insisted upon the value of insider perspectives—including forms of self-inscription such as oral history and autobiography—for historians, literary critics, and scholars of popular culture.[11] Scott DeVeaux makes this point in his monumental social and musical history of bebop (1997), in which he distinguishes his own work from the "largely suprapersonal" approach of earlier jazz history writing in which "the real agents of change are abstractions to which individual will is subordinated" (*Birth of Bebop* 28). Although DeVeaux grants the benefits of this approach, noting that historical trends "are often larger than individuals," he believes that "telling history this way sacrifices the complexity and ambiguity of lives lived in a particular historical moment" (28).

With only slight revision, DeVeaux's observations may serve as a concise explanation of this study's focus on autobiography as a way to uncover aspects of jazz history through "the complexity and ambiguity of lives lived in ... particular historical moment[s]." This is not to deny, of course, the inherent limitations of the autobiographical form; rather, this study proposes, following Daniel Stein, to adopt "a theoretical lens through which jazz autobiography can be read productively, without either accepting the basic 'untruth' of autobiographical narrative, as poststructuralist critics might advocate, or damning the texts to the status of simple eye-witness accounts" ("The Performance" 174). My approach to these texts, in other words, is both respectful and skeptical, as I attempt to honor the accounts of these jazz people while holding them up to rigorous scrutiny.

The Search for a Jazz Identity

Beyond the sense of identity as shaped by racial or ethnic affiliation, there is another, equally important, sense of the term in *Outside and Inside*, one that addresses its specific resonance in a jazz context. As Bruce Raeburn notes in his discussion of early twentieth-century New Orleans jazz communities, "jazz musicians shared an expectation of developing a unique 'voice,' a musical identity that fused talent and personality" ("Stars of David" 127). Here Raeburn is referring to the jazz musician's search for a distinctive sound and approach to playing that involves much hard work and a myriad of choices, including those related to rhythmic, harmonic, and melodic expression as well as timbre, intonation, and vibrato. Raeburn's comments, of course, need not be restricted to the purpose and methods of early New Orleans jazz musicians; throughout the music's history and irrespective of style, jazz musicians have foregrounded their unique musical personalities as central to their value as creative performers.

While white jazz autobiographers describe their immersion experiences in African American jazz communities as a necessary part of their search for jazz authenticity, their legitimacy as jazz musicians, in other words, depends ultimately on their ability to forge their own jazz voice—one that reflects the full extent of their musical and cultural experiences and that, in the context of the multiethnic, multicultural clamor of twentieth-century urban jazz communities, goes beyond strict ethnic or racial affiliation. With varying degrees of candor and self-awareness, all of the white jazz autobiographers under discussion here describe this search for a jazz identity. For many of them, this search involves a process of exposure first to white, and then to black, jazz bands and their star instrumentalists and arrangers. The euphoria of discovery and immersion in black jazz communities is followed by a period of reassessment in which autobiographers describe their efforts to find a place for themselves in jazz as white musicians who have paid their dues—who have undergone, that is, rigorous schooling in black vernacular practices but who also have their own unique contributions to make.

I am particularly concerned with exploring the spirit in which these autobiographers articulate this process of discovery, immersion, and search for a jazz identity—the tone, tenor, and reflectiveness of their individual accounts. How do they describe the dramatic political and social upheavals in US society that formed the backdrop against which they learned to play and later to establish themselves as professional jazz musicians? How willing are they to acknowledge the racial dynamics and inherent tensions in their participation in black music environments or to recognize the limitations or dangers in their desire to don the black mask, either literally or figuratively? What insights may be gleaned from their depictions of particular interracial relationships or encounters?

Reading the "White Resentment Narrative" in White Jazz Autobiography

In *Freedom Sounds: Civil Rights Call Out to Jazz and Africa* (2007), Ingrid Monson provides a valuable entrée to discussions of the spirit or tone of white jazz autobiography through her consideration of the "white resentment narrative" in the work of some jazz historians and critics (16). This tendency—especially as articulated in various essays and full-length studies over the past three decades and in public debates within jazz circles that go back much further—makes use of "liberal, individualist ideology to argue for a colorblind or race-neutral perspective that views music itself as above and beyond politics" (*Freedom Sounds* 16). Central to this colorblind perspective is its insistence that the history of jazz has been unfairly represented as the exclusive or primary domain of black music and culture, and that, as a result, the contributions of white jazz musicians as creators, innovators, and stylists have been obscured or deliberately misrepresented.[12]

Among the most controversial of these "race-neutral" studies are Richard M. Sudhalter's *Lost Chords: White Musicians and Their Contribution to Jazz, 1915–1945* (1999) and Randall Sandke's *Where the Dark and the Light Folks Meet: Race and the Mythology, Politics, and Business of Jazz* (2010).[13] In *Lost Chords*, Sudhalter argues that a "black creationist canon" has dominated jazz's written record and prevented the recognition of "a distinct, significant, and creative white presence" within jazz since its beginnings (xviii). Like Sudhalter, Sandke attributes racialist attitudes both to the dominant jazz historiography, which he holds largely responsible for creating an inaccurate and distorted view of white jazz musicians and their contribution to jazz, and also to the music industry itself, which he believes has promoted African American musicians at the expense of deserving non–African American musicians.[14]

The studies by Sudhalter and Sandke provoked heated debate in jazz circles in the months and years following their publications. Many reviewers applauded them for providing what they saw as important correctives to the Afrocentric perspectives on jazz history that have dominated jazz writing and the teaching of jazz at US colleges and universities and for illuminating the careers of many relatively obscure (as well as famous) white jazz musicians.[15] Many others, however, were fiercely critical of the authors' assumptions and methodologies; they pointed to Sudhalter's misreading of important theories of African American vernacular culture (such as Albert Murray's work on the blues) (Berry 122); Sandke's charge that jazz historiography and teaching have largely insisted on the insularity of black culture removed from external influences (Johnson 139); and the tendency of both authors to highlight the skills and accomplishments of white musicians through unnecessary comparisons with black musicians (Sager 510; Nelson 3).

Underlying these specific points of contention is a fundamental sense of unease with Sudhalter and Sandke's lack of sensitivity to the *perceptions* of racism in their colorblind versions of jazz history. Several critics have identified the lack of nuance in the authors' views of race relations in jazz history as a central flaw of their studies (Nelson 2; Johnson 144; Berry 3), and even some of their most enthusiastic supporters make efforts to defend Sudhalter and Sandke against charges (real or anticipated) of malice or racism (Gridley 127). Significantly, following the publication of their studies, both authors defended themselves from charges of racism while insisting on their respect for the black jazz tradition and its centrality to jazz history.[16]

There is no doubt that the claims of Sudhalter and Sandke, as well as those of other critics who have challenged dominant Afrocentric perspectives of jazz history, are echoed by some of the autobiographers under discussion in these pages. Indeed, as we will see, the spirit or tone of the "white resentment narrative" is apparent in Art Pepper's description of the hostility he perceived within black jazz circles during the 1960s and in the account of Bob Wilber, who angrily insists on a universalist rather than particularist approach to jazz. At other times, however, they and other white jazz autobiographers challenge fundamental aspects of this narrative, portraying their immersion in black music and culture as both critical to their own identity formation and a source of deeply moving experiences by which their jazz skills are tested and affirmed.

White Jazz Autobiographers as Outsiders and Insiders

In many respects, the trope of outside and inside carries powerful, multivalent meanings within the texts of white jazz autobiographers. Many of them describe their status as outsiders in respect to African American music and culture; as professional jazz musicians, some of them also inhabited an outsider position in respect to the values of mainstream American society. Furthermore, as published authors who—with few exceptions—lack literary training or credentials, they are also outsiders to the literary world on which they made claims. The effort of white jazz musicians to become insiders, or conversely to justify their outsider status, assumes great significance within their narratives.

I have already noted the significance of their immersion in African American musical and cultural spheres as a necessary part of their jazz education and their status as professional musicians. These accounts of immersion reinforce the notion of jazz as one of the few spheres within US society in which cultural authority has been granted to African Americans (albeit under specific conditions and with obvious limitations), and in which white musicians, as Burton W. Peretti suggests, "innovated and rebelled by willingly becoming musically subordinate to a socially and culturally subordinated group" (Peretti 96–97). Through their descriptions of this process, white jazz autobiographers reveal that the playing of jazz created and necessitated interracial and interethnic mingling to a degree rarely seen in the mainstream society out of which these stories emerge. Yet these accounts also reveal the sharp boundaries that marked interracialism in the jazz worlds they describe; in this respect, these autobiographies provide a fertile source for considering the limitations of culture—and more importantly, the limited willingness or ability of individual cultural producers—to disrupt, challenge, or circumvent entrenched notions of racial difference and separation.

White jazz autobiographers also reveal a deep concern with claiming versions of masculinity that have been shaped by their immersion experiences. In their accounts of themselves as young white men learning jazz from and alongside African American men, they illustrate a process by which they don masculine identities in emulation of the black musicians who are their idols and teachers. Manifestations of this impulse may be seen in their descriptions of listening to and learning to play jazz, descriptions in which they convey a physical as well as an emotional attraction to African American men; in this respect, white jazz autobiographers fit into a long and well-documented tradition of white fascination with black masculinity, a subject that I will return to later in this introduction and throughout the book.

In more general terms, white jazz autobiographers give a vivid impression of the hypermasculinity of the jazz communities in which they live and work.[17] Sherrie Tucker and other contemporary jazz scholars have identified the role of mainstream jazz historiography—including popular jazz histories, college textbooks, and biographies of great musicians—in encouraging a particular "masculinist focus" (*Swing Shift* 20). In the autobiographies of white male jazz musicians, we discover the same impulse toward erasure of women, or at least the tendency to restrict them to the domestic or sexual realm, or to their role as singers, while making them mainly invisible as instrumentalists or bandleaders.

In these environments, a deeply troubling sexism or blatant misogyny sometimes flourishes, emerging in depictions of girl singers in the big bands, wives or sisters or mothers, mistresses or girlfriends, one-night pick-ups or adoring fans. In *Trumpet on the Wing*, Wingy Manone rails against musicians' wives who "hold 'em back and ruin their success" by preventing them from going on the road where "musicians must keep going on to make a bigger success" (209). In *Drew's Blues: A Sideman's Life with the Big Bands*, Texan reeds player Drew Page describes women as vultures who pursue men in order to lure them into sex or marriage, or both (26–27). In *We Called It Music: A Generation of Jazz,* Eddie Condon recalls that during his summer experience at Lake Delavan resort in Wisconsin, he and his buddies "drove to town every day in the Wills St. Clair and checked our trap line for new girls" (116). In *The Trouble with Cinderella: An Outline of Identity,* Artie Shaw notes his considerable surprise when, as a young man, he discovered that "a fellow could actually go to bed with a 'nice' girl and still continue to like her" (185). In *Straight Life: The Story of Art Pepper,* Pepper describes in graphic detail his difficult and sometimes abusive relationships with women.

It is indeed rare, particularly in the earlier jazz autobiographies, to find accounts in which women (other than Bessie Smith and Billie Holiday) are depicted as serious musicians worthy of the respect of male musicians, or in which women are collaborators or friends. On the other hand, it is not unusual to find misogynistic outbursts interspersed with portraits of affection and devotion toward the particular woman who has brought stability to their lives and nudged them into blissful domesticity (Condon with Sugrue; Barnet). To be clear, in addition to the overt sexism evidenced in many of the autobiographies under examination in *Outside and Inside,* there are also nuanced and sensitive accounts of musicians' personal relationships with women, both personal and professional.

In some respects, the absence or invisibility of women in these texts is as significant as are particular examples of misogyny, for it allows many of these autobiographers to avoid serious discussion of their interpersonal relationships with women inside and outside of the jazz world, including their dependence on their wives and partners for the financial stability that allowed them to pursue their careers in jazz. By contrast—and this is a critical point for the focus of this study—these same musicians are unable to avoid at least some discussion of the impact of race on their lives and careers as white jazz musicians. Thus, we find misogynistic rants and crude objectification of women appearing side by side with emotional pleas for racial tolerance or descriptions of happy interracial sessions (Barnet 70). The contrast between white jazz autobiographers' efforts to address racial inequity and their seeming acceptance of the misogyny that prevailed within jazz culture is striking; it seems likely that at work here were societal pressures that encouraged at least a degree of reflection about race while at the same time leaving gender inequity relatively unchallenged.[18]

My analysis of these narratives is informed by a broad and interdisciplinary body of work on jazz over the past three decades from cultural and social historians, ethnomusicologists, political scientists, and literary critics. While these scholars display a range of critical approaches and methodologies, their analyses of performance practices, stylistic developments in jazz, and relationships between musicians and their audiences and critics at pivotal moments of twentieth-century jazz history reveal a common concern with uncovering the significance of jazz in American cultural and social life—in particular, the ways that jazz culture reflects and sometimes anticipates attitudes toward race, ethnicity, gender, and conceptions of regional and national identity.[19]

In a related way, many recent studies on jazz have embraced the insights of geographical particularity by exploring the history and development of a particular city or region's jazz culture.[20] As these studies illustrate, knowledge of prevailing laws and customs that shaped the racial history of a particular city or region is critical for understanding the development and evolution of its interracial jazz scene. These studies help to contextualize and historicize white jazz autobiographers' firsthand and often emotionally charged accounts of their own interracial jazz experiences, giving us greater insight into the decisions of individual musicians to comply with or challenge local customs or traditions against the backdrop of heightened racial tension, the increasing assertiveness of African Americans, and federal and local resistance to desegregation and civil rights.

Texts by US race historians, critical race theorists, and film studies scholars have also contributed to my interpretation of white jazz autobiography: among them are studies that focus on the historically fluid and mutable concepts of race, ethnicity, and whiteness in the United States;[21] white fascination with African Americans from minstrelsy to the present day in American music, literature, and film;[22] and white privilege as a legacy of socially and legally constructed white hegemony in the United States.[23] Although some of these studies fall outside the immediate historical and cultural circumstances that frame the lives and careers of the white jazz autobiographers, they offer valuable context against which to interpret (and sometimes distinguish) the particular expressions of whiteness, white fascination with blackness, and white privilege that emerge from these autobiographies.

Studies on US race history inform my discussions of autobiographers born and raised in New Orleans (Manone and Sancton) or associated with early New Orleans jazz styles (Wilber); they also help to clarify the shifting racial and ethnic identities of the four Jewish jazz autobiographers examined in chapter 4, as do studies that focus specifically on the racialization of Jews in nineteenth- and twentieth-century American legislative, political, and cultural life.[24] More detailed references to this scholarship will follow in later chapters; briefly, however, I would like to situate *Outside and Inside* in relationship to two of the central concerns of the cultural criticism outlined above—namely, white people's perceptions of African Americans and white privilege.

White Fascination with African Americans

White jazz autobiographers provide valuable insider perspectives on a topic that has dominated cultural studies of jazz and popular music in recent decades—that is, the relationship of non-African Americans to African Americans and their culture, a relationship described by Eric Lott as "love and theft" in his seminal 1993 study, or more generally, as emulation and appropriation, desire and ridicule (Lott, *Love and Theft* 4, 6). Lott and other critics have provided historical context by which to consider white jazz autobiographers' fascination with and attraction to African Americans (particularly African American men) and their culture. While Lott focuses on minstrelsy in the antebellum North, Ingrid Monson (1995) addresses "the problem with white hipness" in jazz in the period following the Second World War, yet both cast a broad view on this phenomenon, outlining its presence in American culture from minstrelsy to the present day (Monson, "The Problem" 398; Lott, *Love and Theft* 4, 54, 248). Krin Gabbard's seminal work on representations of jazz in American film and literature provides additional insights on the racialized and gendered aspects of white participation in black jazz culture (*Black Magic*; *Jammin'*).

Several themes dominate the work of these critics. One is the perpetuation of racist stereotyping and the commodification of black cultural forms that takes place when white people desire and perform (that is, imitate and emulate) their *perceptions* of black people and black cultural forms (Monson, "The Problem" 421; Lott, *Love and Theft* 31). Another is the centrality of gender in white fascination with blackness. Lott examines "homosocial relationships" within minstrelsy, concluding that fear of the all-powerful black male body combined with "homosexual fantasies, or at the very least envy, of black men" (*Love and Theft* 55, 120, 126). Gabbard updates these fantasies with his examination of Hollywood biopics in which white musicians achieve sexual maturity or prowess through their association with African American musicians, while they are simultaneously portrayed as their musical and intellectual superiors (*Jammin'* 82–83). Monson insists that in order to understand the racial and gendered aspects of hipness in the context of jazz (specifically bebop) following the Second World War, one must understand its preoccupation with "the sartorial display and bearing of black men" ("The Problem" 401).

The same kind of questions that these scholars pose about antebellum blackface minstrels, white bebop musicians, and portraits of jazz in American cinema might also be asked of these white autobiographers. To what degree, for example, do their descriptions of their interracial jazz experiences also reveal racialist and stereotypical views about the African American jazz musicians who are their teachers or peers? What evidence is there of homosocial or homoerotic attraction in their descriptions of their immersion experiences in black jazz communities?

For many contemporary critics, the figure of "the white Negro" holds particular resonance, representing the complex ambiguity inherent in the white attraction to and appropriation of black masculinity and African American cultural forms more generally. On this topic, no essay has generated more intense scrutiny and outright acrimony than Norman Mailer's "The White Negro" (1957), in which Mailer describes the white hipsters' critique of mainstream America values and embrace of the music, language, and sexuality of black men.[25] Aspects of Mailer's depiction of the white hipsters' attraction to the black male are also recognizable within the accounts of these autobiographers. Like Mailer and other young white males of his generation, many white jazz musicians were drawn to an urban black cultural aesthetic and a longing to be black themselves—that is, to assimilate and perform the musical as well as extramusical aspects of black cultural expression that they identified in the black men who were their teachers and role models. Yet their accounts also provide an excellent opportunity to test Mailer's more extreme claims and, ultimately, I will argue, to differentiate their attitudes and experiences from those of Mailer's white hipsters or from Lott's blackface minstrels.

Monson provides the beginnings of this comparison when she contrasts Mailer's views toward black men with those of Mezz Mezzrow—the most famous white Negro jazz musician. In her view, Mezzrow's autobiographical depiction of African Americans illustrates what she describes (by way of James Baldwin) as the proximity of "[a]dmiration and the reinforcement of stereotype" ("The Problem" 402). Although she claims not to doubt Mezzrow's devotion to a black masculinist identity, she suggests that his mythologizing of black culture at times resembles Andrew Ross's description of a "romantic version of racism" (403; Ross 85). Despite this, Monson finds Mezzrow's mythologizing "relatively benign" in comparison with Mailer's, concluding that they "occupy contrasting points along a spectrum of gendered white hip identification with African American culture" ("The Problem" 404).

Monson's characterization of Mezzrow's mythologizing as relatively benign is perhaps because "Negrophilia," rather than resentment or ridicule, underlies his essentialist and stereotypical views about African Americans. Yet if Mezzrow's attitudes are benign in comparison with Mailer's, they must surely be considered among the most extreme of those considered in this study. In fact, only Art Pepper and Don Asher match or surpass him in their hyperbolic depictions of African Americans; indeed, at times, their accounts reveal the more sinister features of white identification with blackness noted by Lott, including "fear of and fascination with the black male" and "ridicule and racist lampoon" (*Love and Theft* 18, 25). While "romantic version[s] of racism" are also apparent in the accounts of other white jazz autobiographers investigated in these pages, it is fair to say that, on the whole, their depictions are considerably less extreme than those of Mailer's or the other autobiographers noted above.

White jazz musicians, in other words, are not minstrel men, or "not *exactly* minstrel men," as Gabbard asserts about Benny Goodman and Mick Jagger in his analysis of their performances of black masculinity (*Jammin'*

45, emphasis added). For unlike the nineteenth-century minstrel men, twentieth-century jazz musicians and popular entertainers had direct and easy access to live performances and recordings "of real African Americans" and went to great efforts to learn their music, thus leaving them more heavily invested in their own personal relationships with black men (45). Gabbard's observation is consistent with my reading of the accounts of white jazz autobiographers, who describe their close and sometimes enduring relationships with the black musicians who are their teachers, mentors, and colleagues on the bandstand.

Gabbard also notes that expressions of masculinity by black male jazz musicians are considerably more nuanced and varied than are the ubiquitous images of the modern "athlete, the rock star, or the white suburban teenager with baggy shorts, a turned-around baseball cap, and a loping walk" (*Black Magic* 249). Although he maintains, in agreement with many other critics, that forms of white male emulation of black masculinity have persisted long past minstrelsy, he notes that a musician such as Hoagy Carmichael seemed genuinely more interested in the musical accomplishments of the black musicians he met when he was learning to play than in their "physical and sexual prowess" (*Jammin'* 258–59). Gabbard's point here is also consistent with my own interpretations of white jazz autobiographers, for whom the gendered and racialized aspects of their attraction to black men exist alongside their universal fascination with and respect for black music.

Kimberly Chabot Davis's recent reception study, *Beyond the White Negro: Empathy and Anti-Racist Reading* (2014), offers another model through which to clarify my own interpretative approach to reading white jazz autobiography. Although there is little overlap in respect to the subject material or methodologies of our respective studies—Davis's focus is on white reception of "African American literature, film, theater, and music in the late twentieth and early twenty-first centuries" (Davis 2)—I sympathize with her appeal for a more expansive interpretation of white involvement in black culture. As she suggests, a view of white engagement in black culture that sees only appropriation and exploitation—"the White Negro paradigm"—does not do justice to the "varied politics of cross-racial identification" that she identifies in her study, including "the potential of some instances of crossover to function as radical acts of 'race treason' against white privilege" (2, 28).

With perhaps the exception of Tom Sancton's experience with the aging New Orleans musicians (see chapter 3), the interracial experiences described in the chapters that follow rarely rise to the level of "radical acts of 'race treason' against white privilege"; nonetheless, like Davis, I am interested in rooting out "both the promise and failures of cross-racial empathy" (17) that are discernable, to lesser or greater degrees, in the accounts of all the white jazz musicians under investigation in these pages. Throughout *Outside and Inside*, in other words, I search for interpretative approaches that best illuminate the nuanced, conflicted, and contradictory expressions of white association with black culture, that grant the evidence of racist or racialist thinking without dismissing other, more positive aspects of their interracial relationships.

Valuing the Less-Than-Heroic Narratives of White Jazz Autobiographers

In his brilliant and provocative study, *The Possessive Investment in Whiteness: How White People Profit From Identity Politics*, George Lipsitz offers a moving account of the origins of his own realization of white privilege—that is, the "social structure that gives value to whiteness and offers rewards for racism"—through the story of Bill Moore, the white Baltimore postal worker who was murdered in 1963 during his solitary march from Tennessee to Mississippi to protest the violent resistance to school desegregation in Mississippi (*Possessive* viii–ix). According to Lipsitz, Moore's death as a result of his stand against white supremacy changed his own life. "It made me look into myself and provoked me to think about what I was willing to risk for my own beliefs" (xii–xiii). Lipsitz was struck by Moore's decision to do more than simply oppose "white supremacy in principle" but rather to take action, even at the risk of losing his own life (xiii). Through this distinction, Lipsitz offers a critique of white liberal paternalism, in which he believes lip service to antiracist principles often substitutes for individuals taking a stand—acting, that is, to oppose white supremacy (xiv).[26]

Lipsitz's scholarship reflects his extraordinary command of the legal and social frameworks of racism and resistance to racism in the United States, including its manifestations in the realm of popular culture; as such, it has had a strong influence on my own thinking, forcing me to clarify and sometimes to reevaluate my own stance in respect to the white jazz autobiographers in my study. In particular, his biography of and various collaborations with Johnny Otis provide invaluable sources for explorations of a white person's immersion in black music and culture.[27] Otis—the pioneering rhythm and blues and rock and roll drummer, bandleader, record producer, and community activist—was undoubtedly among the most successful race-crossers in twentieth-century American popular culture. The son of Greek immigrants, he began his life in 1921 as John Veliotes in a multiracial neighborhood in Berkeley, California, where he quickly gravitated to black music and culture; he attended black churches, had black friends, and was attracted to blues and jazz. From an early age, Otis began to think of himself as "Black by persuasion"; later, he married a black woman and raised a family with her (Otis, *Listen* x–xi; Lipsitz, *Midnight* xviii).[28] Like Bill Moore, Otis was willing to take significant personal risks—as a newspaper columnist, radio show host, and prominent civil rights campaigner—to stand up to white supremacy (*Midnight* 72, 80–81).[29]

It is fair to say that none of the white jazz autobiographers under consideration in this study risked their lives for their involvement in black music and culture (except, as we will see, as a consequence of their own naïve or impulsive acts of defiance concerning interracial behavior in segregated locations); nor were they inclined to be on the frontlines of civil rights campaigns or active at demonstrations. Moreover, while many white jazz musicians, including the leading white bandleaders of the Swing Era—Benny Goodman, Artie Shaw, and Charlie Barnet—took important steps when they integrated their bands and initiated interracial recording sessions and public performances, they had established sufficient leverage in the music world when they did so to withstand any serious backlash against their actions. In comparison with Bill Moore's one-man march or Otis's fiery denunciations against white supremacy and his bold efforts to ensure artistic and economic control for African American artists, the efforts of these jazz musicians might strike many as cautious at best, or perhaps even as self-serving.

By many measures, then, white jazz autobiographers would fail to meet the bar established by Lipsitz and other scholars of white privilege, who see the inability of individual white people to acknowledge their privilege as implicit in the system of white hegemony that has served as the basis for American social, legal, and political structures throughout its history. In the accounts of these musicians, we will find many examples of white privilege by which they benefitted in their lives and careers, yet with few exceptions these examples seem unexamined and even beneath their consciousness. As these autobiographers detail their engagements in white dance bands, or in recording studios, or on network radio shows, or in the most popular and best-paid white big bands of the Swing Era, they frequently reveal their indebtedness to the African American musicians and bands who comprised their most important influences, yet rarely do they acknowledge, let alone attempt to redress, the economic and social advantages they enjoyed over them. Moreover, for the dozens of descriptions in these autobiographies of white youngsters trekking to the South Side or Harlem or Central Avenue, there is rarely mention that interracialism almost always went in one direction; that is, that white musicians were allowed to visit African American neighborhoods and clubs, but that segregation—both by law and by custom—kept African American musicians out of white neighborhoods and clubs, either as audience members or as performers.

Yet in Lipsitz's tribute to Bill Moore, he also acknowledges that solutions to racism will not come simply from "dramatic moments of individual heroism" but also from white Americans acknowledging and working to change "the structural and cultural forces that racialize human rights, opportunities, and life chances in our country" (*Possessive* xv). With this comment, Lipsitz seems to be recognizing the limited usefulness of the heroic/nonheroic binary as a way to account for the tremendous variety and complexity of interracial involvement and communication and the potential within them for promoting positive societal change.

There is little doubt that white jazz musicians' frequent and often intimate presence in black social and cultural spaces gave them greater opportunity than most white people of their time and place to influence "the structural and cultural forces that racialize human rights, opportunities, and life chances." To decide that these musicians are unworthy of serious attention because they fall short of the standards of heroism exemplified by Otis or Moore, in other words, would be to miss many occasions to highlight the contributions of jazz culture to positive changes in American society. Conversely, white jazz autobiographers also describe interracial experiences that end in dismal failure, sometimes because of their own inability to appreciate the dynamics of power and authority in their relationships with the black musicians who are their teachers and associates—because of their failure, that is, to recognize their own privilege. In the interest of achieving a deeper understanding of twentieth-century jazz culture and the larger cultural and social forces that contributed to shaping it, we need to investigate the full range of these interracial experiences, wherever they lead us.

With this aim in mind, I have chosen a thematic approach to the chapters that follow, arranging groupings of autobiographies for comparative purposes. Chapter 1 considers the role of the collaborator and other collaborating voices in shaping the process of authentication that I have identified as central to these texts. Drawing on previous studies of African American jazz autobiography and recent scholarship on the history of jazz criticism, I examine brief appended introductory materials—prefaces, forewords, and introductions—in the autobiographies of Charlie Barnet, Bud Freeman, Art Hodes, and Steve Jordan; more extensive collaborative contributions in the autobiographies of Benny Goodman and Eddie Condon; and the collaboration between Mezz Mezzrow and Bernard Wolfe on *Really the Blues*.

The remaining five chapters of *Outside and Inside* consider immersion experiences in African American and Creole jazz communities from the perspective of the white autobiographical subjects themselves and the impact of these experiences on their racial and gender identification and representation. Chapters 2 and 3 examine three autobiographies of musicians closely linked to early New Orleans jazz communities, interpreting their accounts of their interracial jazz experiences against an extensive body of scholarship on the racial and social history of early New Orleans jazz, biographies of early New Orleans jazz musicians, and other studies on the midcentury New Orleans jazz revival.

The focus of chapter 2 is Bob Wilber's *Music Was Not Enough*, in which Wilber, a respected jazz instrumentalist and bandleader, offers a detailed account of his experience in New York during the mid-1940s as a student and protégé of the renowned New Orleans musician Sidney Bechet and the effect of that experience on his life and career. Wilber's colorblind perspective on jazz history stands in contrast to the accounts of interracialism offered by New Orleanian-raised musicians Wingy Manone and Tom Sancton, whose jazz autobiographies I consider in chapter 3. Although separated by two generations and sharply contrasting socioeconomic and cultural backgrounds, Manone and Sancton both foreground the significance of their immersion experiences in New Orleans's complex multiracial and multicultural environments in shaping their views on race and jazz authenticity; for Manone and Sancton, in other words, race *and* place are central to their constructions of their jazz selves.

Chapter 4 turns to the fluid and multifaceted representations of identity in the jazz autobiographies of Artie Shaw, Benny Goodman, Mezz Mezzrow, and Max Kaminsky, whose accounts illuminate the disparate paths to belonging of second-generation Jewish Americans in early twentieth-century American life. Chapters 5 and 6 examine the autobiographies of two musicians whose experiences in bop and postbop jazz communities provide important evidence of the growing strains on interracial alliances in jazz against the rising tide of black-nationalist expression in postwar America. In chapter 5, I consider the autobiography of Don Asher, who studied with pianist Jaki Byard before embarking on a career as a New England society band and honkytonk pianist and later as a nightclub pianist in San Francisco. But Asher was also a novelist, short-story writer, essayist, and collaborator, and my comparison of selected works of his fiction and nonfiction seeks to highlight recurring themes, characterizations, language, and plot structures that reveal his enduring—and at times transgressive—fascination with African American music and culture.

The focus of chapter 6 is saxophonist Art Pepper's *Straight Life: The Story of Art Pepper*, which I read against an extensive body of work that has emerged over the past three decades detailing the social, political, and cultural history of Los Angeles' Central Avenue, as well as more general studies of West Coast jazz. As the only jazz autobiography under consideration here coauthored by a woman, *Straight Life* also opens pathways for considering women's resistance to the misogyny and rigid gendering that has dominated jazz culture through most of its history. Laurie Pepper's accounts of her role as coauthor of *Straight Life* and her steady management of her husband's personal care and business affairs in the final decade of his life illuminate the authority and influence of a jazzwoman in a study of texts in which women's voices are generally on the periphery or absent entirely.

OUTSIDE AND INSIDE

1

The Authenticating Collaborators of White Jazz Autobiography

In the final pages of Mezz Mezzrow's *Really the Blues* (published in 1946),[1] Mezzrow describes meeting Bernard Wolfe one night at a Greenwich Village jam session, when "this young white fellow who tells me he don't know much about music, he's a writer, but he likes my records fine" approaches him about the idea of doing a magazine piece (Mezzrow 333). Soon, Wolfe begins spending time with "Mezz" in Harlem, convinced that his story requires more than just an article to do it justice:

> "Listen Mezz," he says, and I know there's a hype coming. "You know you've got a pretty interesting story to tell—nobody could do justice to it in one lousy article, and besides, if we told the truth, no magazine in the country would dare to print it, they'd be so scared of corrupting the morals of the young. It needs a book, a hell of a long book, and you've got to write it. It's more important than you think." (334)

A similar scene is depicted in the first chapter of Eddie Condon's autobiography, *We Called It Music: A Generation of Jazz* (published in 1947), as Condon describes the role of his friend, the journalist John McNulty, in convincing him to write his autobiography.[2] Although Thomas Sugrue received credit as Condon's official collaborator, according to Condon it was McNulty who first coaxed from him the random memories and associations by which he would begin to capture a version of his life on paper. Initially, though, Condon was reluctant, asking McNulty, "How am I going to do it and what am I going to write about?" (Condon with Sugrue 4). McNulty asked him to produce a typewriter, into which he inserted a piece of paper before turning to Condon:

"Where and when were you born?" he said to me. I told him. On the sheet he typed: Goodland, Indiana, November 16, 1905. He spaced and wrote another line: Present address, Washington Square North, New York City. "Now all you've got to do," he said, "is put down on paper what happened between those two lines. Try it. What do you remember?" (4)

It is hardly surprising to discover, as in the examples cited above, that a majority of jazz autobiographers have collaborated with a professional writer or amanuensis in the process of writing their autobiographies; most of them, after all, had little prior experience as writers.[3] For this reason, most white jazz autobiographies credit at least one other author, or collaborator, in addition to the autobiographical subject.[4] It is rare, however, to find the collaborative process explained and even dramatized as it is in the passages above; more typically, collaborators make their presence known in paratextual additions—that is, in introductory or concluding materials or through insertions in the body of the text itself.[5]

In a study that is centrally concerned with notions of authentication and identity, this chapter will consider the contributions of these additional voices to this process of authentication. How and for what purpose do these other authors—the collaborator, amanuensis, or explainer—attempt to legitimate the autobiographical subject, to convince the reader of his worthiness as a jazz musician, and also as a figure of historical, cultural, and sometimes even literary, significance? While undoubtedly one of the primary roles of all collaborators of autobiography is to vouch for the significance of the individual whose life is being represented, white jazz autobiographers presented a unique set of challenges for their collaborators, who responded to these challenges by employing particular authenticating strategies. As they did so, they established ideological positions that resembled (with variations) those drawn by the contestants of the jazz wars of the 1930s to the 1960s, those fiery debates that divided the jazz community into various ideological camps, pitting proponents of traditional New Orleans style against the bebop modernists, big band swing against small improvising ensembles, and mainstream against the so-called free jazz of the 1960s. Central to all of these ideological expressions was an extraordinary concern with race, in particular with contesting the origins, meanings, and performance of jazz along racial and ethnic lines.

In addition to their own personal enthusiasms, collaborators brought with them a wide range of professional writing credentials that help to illuminate their association with particular jazz autobiographers. Among them, only Irving Kolodin (1908–1988) and Stanley Dance (1910–1999) were prominent music critics: Kolodin was music critic for the *New York Sun* when he collaborated with Benny Goodman on *The Kingdom of Swing* (1939); at the time of their collaboration, Kolodin—known chiefly as a classical music critic—had fallen under the influence of John Hammond, who was a central influence in Goodman's career (Kolodin, "Number One" 431–40). Dance, who collaborated with white bandleader Charlie Barnet on *Those Swinging Years: The Autobiography of Charlie Barnet* (1984), was an influential British jazz critic who moved to the United States in 1959 and became a key proponent of the "jazz mainstream"—a term he coined that embraced a range of jazz performance practices, from Armstrong's small ensembles of the late 1920s to the big bands of the Swing Era, but which vehemently rejected later developments in jazz, such as bebop and the "post-bop avant garde" (Gennari 208). As we will see, Dance's views on jazz authenticity are critical for understanding his significance as Barnet's collaborator.

Other collaborations considered in this chapter may be understood as the result of shared regional, as well as musical, connections. Thomas Scanlan and guitarist Steve Jordan, who collaborated on *Rhythm Man: Fifty Years in Jazz* (1984), became acquainted as longtime residents of the Washington, DC, area; Jordan was an active member of the jazz scene there, Scanlan an avid jazz fan and amateur guitarist. Longtime Chicago radio host and oral historian Studs Terkel wrote the introduction to fellow Chicagoan Bud Freeman's *Crazeology*. Former University of Illinois professor Chadwick Hansen collaborated with Chicago pianist Art Hodes on two volumes: Hodes's autobiography, *Hot Man: The Life of Art Hodes* (1992), and *Selections from the Gutter: Jazz Portraits from "The Jazz Record"* (1977). In the latter volume, Hansen explains that his musical connection to Hodes goes back to the 1940s, when Hodes performed at his high school in Bronxville, New York (Hodes and Hansen, *Selections* xi).[6]

The other collaborations examined here, however, seem motivated by rather different kinds of attraction between collaborator and autobiographical subject. Thomas Sugrue, who collaborated with Eddie Condon on *We Called It Music*, was no authority on jazz; rather, it is likely that their mutual interest in their Irish Catholic working-class background and Sugrue's journalistic bent for conversation and interviewing were the basis for their collaboration.[7] Bernard Wolfe, a writer associated with the New York intellectuals, found in Mezz Mezzrow a fascinating subject through which to explore his own deepening interest in race relations in American society; in particular, his curiosity about white America's obsession with blackness as it played out in the figure of the hipster.

While a diverse range of interests and ideological commitments guide the contributions of these various collaborators, for the most part, they seem to share the assumption that white jazz musicians are outsiders to the predominately black jazz communities in which they work and sometimes live and to the elite cultural and intellectual communities of their collaborators. Moreover, even when a collaborator challenges particular aspects of the model of black primacy in jazz—as Tom Scanlan does in his collaboration with Steve

Jordan—he nonetheless shares with these other collaborators a heightened self-consciousness about the racial dynamics within jazz that leaves the white jazz musician on sometimes insecure footing. One of the key functions of these collaborators, then, is to convince the reader that autobiographical subjects who in some crucial sense do not seem to belong in the communities to which they are making claims are nonetheless deserving of recognition (and even authority) in them.

A deep cultural anxiety, in other words, underlies the efforts of collaborators to authenticate their autobiographical subjects, an anxiety that reveals itself primarily through a notable preoccupation with issues of race and ethnicity; in this way, the autobiographical subject as a racialized being becomes a dominant theme within their collaboration. Various permutations of the racialized subject are permitted, even required, by the unique circumstances of each autobiographical subject; this allows collaborators to construct portraits of white jazz musicians that stress the significance of their white or white-ethnic heritage or of their relationship to blackness through their diligent attention to African American musical and cultural forms, or various combinations of the above. Common to all of them, however, is the collaborators' construction of a racial-ethnic consciousness that grants these autobiographical subjects access to particular kinds of knowledge and understanding, all of which contribute to their legitimacy and authenticity as white jazz musicians.

Among these various strategies, collaborators most frequently strive to legitimate their white jazz subjects by emphasizing their diligence in learning and mastering African American musical and cultural practices. By so doing, collaborators both implicitly (and often explicitly) recognize the African American origins of jazz, as well as the primacy of African American jazz musicians as teachers, composers, bandleaders, and performers. In several of these texts, however, the authenticating strategies are considerably more convoluted, as the collaborator attempts to frame the white jazz musician within both African American and Euro-American intellectual and cultural spheres. Underlying all of these strategies are ambivalence and insecurity, as the collaborator works to construct an autobiographical subject who appears to belong in many worlds at once, but who seems totally secure in none; that is, neither in the African American jazz communities nor in the literary and cultural spheres in which he has been positioned by his collaborator. It is worth asking, of course, whose ambivalence is reflected here—that of the collaborator or of his autobiographical subject? As much as it is possible to untangle collaborations that yield only glimpses of their actual workings, the discussion that follows will propose some answers to this question.

Earlier, I cited previous studies of jazz autobiography by Kenney, Ogren, and Harlos, all of which direct attention to the literary function and significance of the autobiographer's collaborator. With few exceptions, the focus of this previous work is on autobiographies by African American jazz musicians, in which issues of authorial control are clearly central to the text's impact and reception; for this very reason, these studies provide valuable material for comparing the role of collaborators in white jazz autobiography.[8] An important theoretical source for these studies is Robert Stepto's seminal 1979 text, *From behind the Veil: A Study of Afro-American Narrative*, in which Stepto builds a model for investigating the collaborator/autobiographer relationship in eighteenth- and nineteenth-century slave narratives. Stepto describes "three phases of narration" by which the slave narratives may be grouped (5); the first phase of narration, or "eclectic narrative form," as he designates it, provides the specific model for these previous studies of jazz autobiography:

> In their most elementary form, slave narratives are full of other voices which are frequently just as responsible for articulating a narrative's tale and strategy.... Their primary function is, of course, to authenticate the former slave's account; in doing so, they are at least partially responsible for the narrative's acceptance as historical evidence. (3)

In his analysis of Louis Armstrong's autobiographies, Kenney applies Stepto's eclectic narrative form in his analysis of four documents for which Armstrong received credit as author or coauthor in order to investigate the extent of his authorial agency ("Negotiating" 40). Kenney examines voices in addition to Armstrong's in his earliest autobiography, *Swing That Music* (1936), noting that all of them are white, and that all serve to explain, translate, or vouch for the integrity of the autobiographical subject (40).[9] In his view, *Swing That Music* "offers a sort of conversation between whites that frames the black jazz star's narrative, recreating the structural characteristics of the nineteenth-century former slave narratives that were similarly surrounded by the comments of white abolitionists" (40). Kenney goes further, suggesting that the narrative structure of *Swing That Music* replicates "the power structures that had dominated Armstrong's relations with the owners and customers of South Side Chicago's black and tans" (44).

Christopher Harlos also invokes Stepto's narrative model in his analysis of the paratextual material of a number of jazz autobiographies; his intention is to uncover the ways in which the collaborator or other textual voices serve to diminish the authority of the autobiographical subject. It is striking, of course, that both Kenney and Harlos consider the authenticating strategies of the slave narratives an appropriate model for describing the relationship between black jazz autobiographers and their white collaborators, including celebrated jazz musicians such as Louis Armstrong, Dicky Wells, and Pops Foster (Kenney, "Negotiating" 40; Harlos, "Jazz Autobiography" 151–58).

Clearly, the disparity of power and authority that they identify in these relationships finds no analogy in relationships between *white* jazz autobiographers and their *white* collaborators—relationships often characterized by mutual admiration and sometimes even friendship. In other respects, however, I would argue that there is a clear resemblance between them, a resemblance with an inversion, if you will: for just as African American jazz musicians are authenticated by their white collaborators as subjects worthy of the European literary tradition of autobiography, so too are white jazz autobiographers authenticated by their collaborators and editors, but in a reverse way—as possessing the musical skills and cultural familiarity that grant them legitimacy within African American jazz traditions.

This "reverse authentication" is also apparent in a related theme in white jazz autobiographies, in which some collaborators invoke an extreme essentialism to authenticate their autobiographical subjects, constructing portraits of them that emphasize their natural or instinctive musicality, reminiscent of the "twenties vogue of primitivism" in jazz criticism and literature that was still discernable in later criticism (Ogren, *Jazz Revolution* 146).[10] As these collaborators foreground their white autobiographical subjects' gifts for rhythm (see Sugrue on Condon) or their emotional (rather than intellectual) intelligence (see Hansen on Hodes), they replicate the collaborator/autobiographical subject roles of black jazz autobiography, but, once again, with a significant twist, with white-on-white primitivism replacing the white-on-black primitivism of the latter.[11]

My use of the term "reverse authentication" in the following discussion serves two distinct but related functions: first, it emphasizes the primacy of black music and culture in white jazz autobiography; and, second, it describes the pattern by which the collaborators of these texts attempt to demonstrate the "blackness," and therefore the authenticity, of these white autobiographers within the black jazz worlds described in their accounts. In musical and cultural terms, African Americans are almost without exception the authorities in these autobiographies, possessing the key to authenticity that white jazz musicians try to unlock through study and emulation.

Authenticating Prefaces, Forewords, and Introductions

Earlier, I remarked on the degree to which the ideological positions of the collaborators considered in this chapter reflect those of the central participants in the jazz wars; among them, however, only British jazz critic Stanley Dance was prominent in those wars, with his views about race and jazz central to his mission to promote the careers of African American swing musicians. John Gennari names him as one "of a handful of critics" in Europe who "determined which jazz records were available to the public and hence made a critic-centered, black-dominated jazz canon a virtual *fait accompli*" (Gennari 94–95).

In this context, I would like to consider Dance's collaboration with Charlie Barnet on *Those Swinging Years*. Before their collaboration, Dance had compiled an impressive list of publications written with or about African American jazz musicians and had overseen important recording dates featuring them for several different labels.[12] In addition, Dance's lengthy biographical study, *The World of Swing*, is devoted almost entirely to the achievements of African American musicians, with Barnet receiving only parenthetical mention.

In his obituary of Dance in *The Independent*, Steve Voce argues that Dance's belief in the superior musical abilities of African Americans, although never stated directly, was demonstrable in his writings and public comments. According to Voce, Dance used his term "mainstream" to distinguish jazz played by African American musicians from "swing," which he reserved for the music played by white bandleaders such as Benny Goodman and Artie Shaw. Although mainstream and swing were similar in terms of "the music and its roots," the racial origins of the players seemed key to the distinction he made between them, and although Dance "never spoke of the matter or engaged in racial politics, [he] felt that black players made superior music to their white counterparts" (Voce). In light of his primary interests, then, his decision to collaborate with Barnet is particularly intriguing.

Dance, in fact, begins his preface with an acknowledgment that this particular collaboration is a step in a different direction for him: "In previous books I have primarily been concerned with the big band era as viewed by black musicians. In this case the perspective is that of one of the most successful white bandleaders" (Barnet xv). Why did Barnet's life and career warrant attention from someone who had invested so deeply in promoting African American jazz musicians? Precisely, according to Dance, because of Barnet's significant yet overlooked role in swing as an employer of black musicians. Although Benny Goodman received accolades for his decision to integrate his band, Dance points out that Barnet hired many more African American musicians "than Goodman or any other white bandleader ever did," and this "without fanfare" (xv). Quiet activism accompanied by a modest demeanor, Dance seems to be suggesting, is at the core of Barnet's significance as a Swing Era bandleader.

Key to Dance's authenticating strategy, then, is his focus on Charlie Barnet's supposedly progressive stance on racial matters, as well as on the African American musical sources that shaped Barnet's playing. Dance supports his claim for Barnet's progressive stance in various ways: he gives a statistical breakdown of the black and white players employed by Barnet in his career as bandleader (xv); he includes a complimentary quote about Barnet from vocalist Lena Horne, whose racial consciousness and activist stance have been well documented (see Horne and Schickel); and he notes Barnet's frequent references to the music of Duke Ellington as his "greatest source of inspiration" and to saxophonists Johnny Hodges and Coleman Hawkins as his primary instrumental influences (Barnet xvi).

Admittedly, Dance does refer to other aspects of Barnet's life that contribute to the shaping of his autobiographical persona, including his prodigious drinking and tumultuous relationships with women. Yet Barnet's misogyny and bad-boy image are compatible with the overall construction of the white male subject that we will see in many of these texts—a subject who is more attuned to the racial discrimination and inequality of his day than is the mainstream of white America but who is generally unreflective on the relationship among racial, gender, and class inequality. By establishing a narrow lens for viewing Barnet's accomplishments, Dance manages to sidestep some of the more controversial aspects of the bandleader's character.[13]

In *Hot Man: The Life of Art Hodes* (1992), collaborator Chadwick Hansen also attempts to authenticate his autobiographical subject—like Dance in his collaboration with Barnet—by compiling a sort of resume of black credentials to which Hodes may lay claim. But if Dance looks to the black swing-band tradition as the standard by which to judge Barnet's value as a white bandleader, then Hansen must look elsewhere to find Hodes's central music influences: specifically, to the small-ensemble, "hot" jazz styles that found their way from New Orleans to Chicago, Hodes's hometown, beginning in the late 1910s,[14] as well as to the "downhome" black blues-piano tradition that Hodes learned as a young man in the 1920s in working-class joints on Chicago's South Side. Yet Hansen begins his preface by admitting the difficulty of categorizing someone whose playing falls in between styles commonly demarcated along racial lines; for although Hodes's "roots are partly in the Chicago style, . . . his playing is blacker than that of most of the white Chicagoans, and his "strongest roots are in the blues" (Hodes ix). Among white blues pianists, then, Hodes stands out precisely for his ability to sound "black," a claim that Hansen makes clear is widely shared: "One critic remarked as early as 1939 that he was the only white pianist who could play the blues convincingly, and many others have echoed that judgment since" (ix).

Hansen thus establishes his strategy to convince the reader that Hodes's life and career are worthy of attention because he has passed the test of black authenticity. At the same time, he seems anxious to clarify his own contribution to the writing of *Hot Man*, stating that his role as editor and sometimes-biographer was necessary because of Hodes's tendency to write "anecdotally rather than historically" and to offer sometimes-contradictory versions of events. Furthermore, Hodes's natural modesty seems to have left him reluctant to say things that Hansen believes were worth saying (x).

Pianist Art Hodes at Ole South, New York, ca. Oct. 1946. With George Luggi, trombone; Henry Goodwin, trumpet; Cecil (Xavier) Scott, clarinet; George "Pops" Foster, bass. Drummer Baby Dodds is behind Luggi. William P. Gottlieb/Ira and Leonore S. Gershwin Fund Collection, Music Division, Library of Congress.

The goal of Hansen's rather detailed explanation seems to be to justify his frequent insertions (set in italics) in the body of the autobiography itself; the purpose of these insertions, which appear between passages set in Hodes's first-person narrative voice, seems to be to provide biographical or contextual information for the reader. Yet the more Hansen says about the collaborative process itself, the more one senses his significant role in shaping the particular version of Art Hodes that we will come to know in *Hot Man*. In Hansen's words, "The reader should be warned, then, that although when Art is speaking the words are always his, the sentence structure is often mine and the larger narrative structure is always mine" (xi–xii). Nonetheless, Hansen assures the reader that the *voice* captured on these pages is that of Hodes, and he insists on the connection between Hodes's style as a storyteller and his style as a musician:

> Art once said about his piano playing that he was "part schooled and part primitive," and the same might be said of his language. Both the music and the language have rich rewards for the attentive listener. The music is suffused with the blues, and in many ways this book is itself a blues—a lament for and a celebration of a music that has been here and gone. (xii)

Hodes's "part schooled and part primitive" way of talking and playing is proof of his mastery of an authentic black musical and cultural tradition that he learned back in 1920s Chicago; yet the qualities of that tradition most worthy of praise, Hansen suggests, require an "attentive listener," or perhaps a skilled collaborator, to make them accessible to those less-than-attentive listeners (readers). In this, his explanation of his role as collaborator, the white academic Hansen seems to borrow a page from the white collaborator of black autobiography in order to explain and authenticate Art Hodes, the white jazz and blues pianist. From this perspective, the collaboration between Hansen and Hodes provides a rich example of white-on-white primitivism, with Hansen paying homage to a black musical history with a "part primitive" white musician at its center.

Thus, although Hansen praises Hodes's ability to talk and write for himself, his insertions often seem to contradict these claims; they appear (like anxious hiccups) in the middle of Hodes's own narrative, offering information or explanation that Hodes is seemingly incapable of conveying himself. "*Art has a style that is his and no one else's*," Hansen explains in an insertion that immediately precedes a chapter in which Hodes details his jazz education on Chicago's South Side. "*How he developed that style is something he can't describe or define, except to say that it's his way of speaking the musical language of jazz, of telling his own story*" (19). Hansen, by contrast, has no difficulty in proposing the influences that shaped Hodes's unique style: "*One can hear something of Lil Hardin in the way he drives a band with his left hand, something of Earl Hines in an occasional right-hand phrase, and something of the many pianists he followed on Chicago's South Side in the blues that suffuse much of his playing*" (19). Once again, Hansen has taken this opportunity to remind the reader of Hodes's link to African American jazz and blues-piano traditions.

While Stanley Dance cites Charlie Barnet's progressive stance in hiring black musicians for his big band as part of his larger authenticating strategy, Hansen stresses Hodes's role—in his career as jazz radio host and editor of *The Jazz Record*—in the preservation of important aspects of black jazz history and the honoring of some of its important but overlooked contributors (56–57). In more personal terms, he emphasizes Hodes's desire to push the boundaries of interracialism in jazz, noting that he often led interracial bands and that during his tenure at *The Jazz Record* from 1943 to 1947, he would alternate the cover stories, "*black musicians scrupulously alternating with whites*" (59). These small details add up to a carefully constructed autobiographical subject, a white jazz musician whose life and music have been principally shaped by his dual commitments to racial equality and to African American cultural expression. Perhaps it is to make this point one final time that Hansen notes that although Hodes has received praise from well-known critics Virgil Thomson, John S. Wilson, and Whitney Balliett, he "*values even more the praise of fellow musicians, especially the praise of black pianists: Little Brother Montgomery, who told him, 'You're blacker than 90 percent of black piano players'; Horace Silver, who said, 'If there was no Art Hodes there'd be no Horace'*" (109).

Another very brief contribution to this idea of reverse authentication may be found in Bud Freeman's as-told-to autobiography, *Crazeology*; it is not Freeman's amanuensis, Robert Wolf, however, who performs this task, but rather Studs Terkel—the Chicago-based radio host, oral historian, and author—who introduces the reader to Freeman in a short foreword. Terkel's credits as an author and well-known public figure on the subjects of oral history, jazz, and race give him an authority, not unlike Dance's in his collaboration with Barnet, by which he may argue for Freeman's significance as a jazz musician and as a storyteller about the jazz community from which he came.[15] Yet Terkel, unlike Dance and Hansen, is less concerned with compiling specific evidence that Freeman, the white jazz saxophonist, modeled his sound after particular black instrumentalists or with listing the many ways he participated in black jazz culture and interracial sessions; rather, he focuses on Freeman's general appreciation and respect for African American musical and cultural values and the extent to which those values have become part of an American cultural mainstream.

Freeman, who was eighty-two when *Crazeology* was published in 1989, was one of a group of young white Chicagoans who learned to play jazz in the 1920s, in the years following the beginnings of black migration to Chicago from New Orleans. He and the other youngsters—known as the Austin High Gang after the Chicago suburban high school they attended—spent their waking hours memorizing the recordings of early New Orleans jazz bands on the wind-up Victrola at their local soda parlor; later they were introduced to the black music environments of Chicago's South Side, where they received their real jazz education.

It is the latter influence that Terkel focuses on in his introduction, claiming that Freeman's life was forever changed by his visits to Chicago's South Side to hear African American musicians such as Louis Armstrong, King Oliver, and Bessie Smith (Freeman xii). But Terkel goes further, arguing for the potential

Bud Freeman on tenor saxophone with trumpeter Marty Marsala at Jimmy Ryan's in New York, ca. July 1947. William P. Gottlieb/Ira and Leonore S. Gershwin Fund Collection, Music Division, Library of Congress.

of black music to transform American society more generally; from this perspective, *Crazeology*'s most important contribution is its acknowledgment of "the everlasting debt we owe the black jazz artists for enriching our lives" (Freeman xii). With the political conservatism of the Reagan-Bush era of the late 1980s as his backdrop, Terkel contrasts Freeman's desire to highlight the generosity of his black teachers and the black jazz communities in which he came of age as a musician with "the shallow, 'profound' commentary on race that we hear these confabulating days" (xii). Terkel's foreword helps to shape a specific expectation for readers of what kind of jazz autobiography we are about to experience: while Freeman's legacy is rooted in the white Chicago jazz school of the 1920s, his most important apprenticeship took place in the smoky clubs of the city's South Side, where he absorbed the musical influences of the black masters of jazz and blues, including Armstrong, Oliver, and Smith.

As noted earlier, authentication is also an important element of Tom Scanlan's brief introduction to Steve Jordan's *Rhythm Man*, and yet there is a critical distinction to be made between Scanlan's manner and purpose of authentication and the examples discussed above.[16] In contrast to these others, Scanlan stresses that the rhythm-guitar tradition from which Jordan emerged was dominated by white players and that these white players were in fact important influences for some of the most important African American rhythm guitarists. Scanlan's discussion, in which race is only mentioned parenthetically, relies on the reader's knowledge of jazz guitar history to construe its heavily racialized undertones.

Although Scanlan acknowledges the relative obscurity of his autobiographical subject, he introduces him by emphasizing his superlative skills as a jazz rhythm guitarist. Jordan is, in Scanlan's words, "a musician's musician and one of the best rhythm guitar players in jazz history" (Jordan 2). Significantly, the stories Scanlan chooses to demonstrate Jordan's excellence place him in direct comparison with three African American jazz guitar legends: Freddie Green, Wes Montgomery, and Charlie Christian. In the first one, Scanlan compares Jordan to Green, rhythm guitarist in the Count Basie band for fifty years. Noting that both Jordan and Green "were schooled in the George Van Eps fingering system as taught by Allan Reuss"—Van Eps and Reuss were both white—Scanlan offers a brief summary of their respective styles and playing techniques before suggesting that the question of who was the superior player was simply "a matter of taste" (2). While Scanlan never claims that Jordan was better than Green, he argues that Green's chief claim to fame was his association with Basie, without which, he "would be, like Jordan, a great player known only to those inside the world of jazz" (1).[17]

Next, Scanlan sounds his belief that the rhythm guitar has suffered from a general lack of critical attention (largely due to its background role), and as a result few writers and even many guitar soloists know little about the rhythm guitar tradition (2). As evidence of the latter, Scanlan recalls his own experience of witnessing guitar legend Wes Montgomery studying Jordan as he played in order to try to figure out his chord voicings. Scanlan seems convinced that Montgomery "was clearly impressed" but also perplexed by Jordan's playing, telling him, "It sounds great, but I don't understand what you're doing!" Scanlan's response—"And I'm sure he didn't"—is a harsh indictment of Montgomery's supposed shortcomings as a rhythm guitarist, particularly since Montgomery's remarkably innovative and influential soloing style was based in part on his use of block chords and octaves as a way of building interest and intensity.

Finally, while Scanlan acknowledges the pioneering role of Charlie Christian in the development of the electric guitar in jazz, he feels compelled to point out that Christian's shortcomings as a rhythm guitarist forced

Christian's big-band employer, Benny Goodman, to hire someone else to fill those duties (3). Although Scanlan presumably has chosen to compare Jordan with these particular guitarists in order to illustrate Jordan's rarity *and* excellence, his tone and manner leave the impression of authentication through derogation. Clearly, he believes that Jordan deserves to be better known and more successful, and he concedes that at least part of the reason for his relative obscurity is that he was strictly a rhythm guitarist rather than a soloist. But lurking just beneath his comparison of Jordan's obscurity with the fame of these three African American jazz guitarists hovers the suggestion of Crow Jim, the idea that Jordan's whiteness prevented him from getting the attention and recognition he might have had he been black.[18]

In the other collaborative pairings we have considered to this point—Stanley Dance and Charlie Barnet, Art Hodes and Chadwick Hansen, and Studs Terkel and Bud Freeman—the ideological positions established by the collaborator in his paratextual contributions seem generally consistent with those expressed by the autobiographical subject within the body text. By contrast, Steve Jordan's own discussion of the jazz guitar tradition and of particular African American guitarists differs in important respects from that set forth by Scanlan in his introduction. In particular, Jordan is notably effusive in his praise of other musicians and refers to his close friendships with many African American jazz musicians. He, like Scanlan, traces the rhythm guitar lineage to the white guitarists George Van Eps and Allan Reuss, but he does so without the competitive edge that marks Scanlan's account (Jordan 137–38). In a chapter, "Memorable Recording Sessions," he recalls that he "felt complimented to be the only white musician" at two different sessions in which he was in the company of leading African American jazz musicians (84, 87). In these examples, Jordan conveys his awareness of the struggles over interracialism in jazz and of the ongoing systemic racism in the United States that forms the backdrop to his stories about mixed studio sessions. In its entirety, his account stresses his presence within highly integrated jazz communities marked by respect and friendship rather than competition and animosity.

The seeming inconsistency between the voices of collaborator and autobiographical subject in *Rhythm Man* may be better understood with a brief look at another text authored by Scanlan, *The Joy of Jazz: Swing Era, 1935–1947* (1996), a slim volume of swing history published a few years after his collaboration with Jordan, in which Scanlan presents an ambivalent and often contradictory analysis of racial issues within jazz communities of the 1930s and 1940s. In his chapter "White, Black, Brown, and Beige," Scanlan discusses "racial problems" that have "bedeviled America from the beginning" and the harmful effects of Jim Crow during the Swing Era before turning abruptly to consider the heroic efforts of white bandleaders Benny Goodman and Charlie Barnet to integrate their bands (Scanlan 55–61). His belief that jazz ought to be—and sometimes succeeded in being—a site that promoted universalist, colorblind ideologies is clear. Yet he writes as if talking to the unconvinced, and a defensive tone frequently marks his explanations. Concluding that "[i]t is pointless and almost impossible to rehash or explain with any degree of certainty all the slippery slopes of racial thinking then," he warns against the tendency toward "presentism" when judging the racial attitudes and behavior of white Swing Era musicians (62).

Just who Scanlan holds responsible for this "presentism" in jazz discourse becomes more apparent later in the chapter, in which he reveals his discomfort with the Afrocentric attitudes expressed by a younger generation of jazz musicians and critics (71). He disputes the contention that jazz is "a black art, or African-American art" and that "contributions to jazz by white players have been meager," insisting that such positions have their roots in a "racial militancy unrelated to music" and concluding that "[j]azz is not defined by race but by artistry" (71).[19] By the end of the chapter, his anger is palpable, and his summation of his argument reads like a list of grievances against the critics and musicians who have gotten jazz history all wrong. Although Scanlan is less well-known than the central figures associated with the white resentment narrative, in important respects, his views resemble theirs. In his introduction to *Rhythm Man*, Scanlan writes that one of the readers of the manuscript had noted Jordan's "uncynical, open-minded, unenvious outlook" (Jordan 5); the same, it seems, cannot be said about his collaborator.

The Authenticating Collaborators of Eddie Condon's *We Called It Music*

At the beginning of this chapter, I briefly considered the passage from *We Called It Music* in which John McNulty encourages Eddie Condon to write his autobiography. Written from Condon's perspective, the passage establishes his modest, even self-deprecating, evaluation of his own writing abilities, just as it secures McNulty's own position of authority as a writer. Condon's portrayal here is consistent with other accounts he offered of his limitations as a writer and his need to seek the assistance of a skilled coauthor, or collaborator, for the various writing projects he undertook in his life.[20]

Condon's self-representation as an author must be viewed as one aspect of his carefully constructed public persona, one in which his credentials as a guitarist and bandleader were less significant than his role as *the* chief spokesman and ardent promoter and proselytizer for Chicago Dixieland style, a small-ensemble jazz style developed by an extended community of young white musicians living in Chicago in the late 1920s and featuring "hot" improvisation and "head"—rather than notated—arrangements. For the next four decades, Condon and his peers presented themselves as a righteous alternative to the commercialism of big-band swing music, as well as to the hyperintellectual, highbrow modern jazz of Charlie Parker, Dizzy Gillespie, and others. His quick wit and verbal agility were legendary in jazz circles, and his most cherished quotes became, in Gary Giddins's words, "part of jazz lore" (Condon with Sugrue vi).

Although I do not doubt that Condon, like most authors, stood to benefit from the assistance of editors, it is worth asking why such a gifted raconteur would rely so heavily on voices other than his own in his published works. It is notable, for instance, that *We Called It Music* has not one, but two authenticating voices; one belongs to McNulty, whom we have briefly met (and will consider in greater detail below), and the other, to Thomas Sugrue—the person who receives credit as coauthor on the book's title page and who undoubtedly provides the chief collaborative voice in Condon's narrative.

In his introduction to a 1992 edition of *We Called It Music*, Giddins defines Sugrue's role quite specifically, stating that he "was responsible for the book's strictly historical italicized passages" (ix). These passages, which total approximately forty pages of the almost three-hundred-page autobiography, are divided into four separate chapters called simply "Narration." Giddins's use of the term "historical" to describe Sugrue's contribution leaves considerable leeway for interpretation, particularly since Giddins himself challenges the historical accuracy of some of the content within Sugrue's "Narration" (ix–x). Since Sugrue had no expertise or previous writing credentials on jazz, one might ask how he formed the views of jazz history that made their way into his "Narration."

Clues may be found in an essay written by Condon, "This Is Jazz," originally published in *Holiday* magazine in 1953 and later revised and reprinted in *Eddie Condon's Treasury of Jazz* (Condon and Gehman 21–32). Much of the essay is taken up with Condon's condemnation of "the jazz cultists"—the mid-twentieth-century writers, critics, and record collectors whose intellectualizing approach to the analysis of jazz music and culture rankled him.[21] We will consider specific details of Condon's and Sugrue's respective accounts below, but for now it is sufficient to say that they are in many respects alike and that they both also reflect and contest many of the dominant views of contemporaneous jazz criticism. Although Sugrue's italicized chapters are in the voice of an omniscient third-person narrator (in contrast to the body text that is in Condon's voice), I suspect that Condon and Sugrue collaborated on the "Narration" *as well as* on the body text of the autobiography.[22] Yet a decision was made, so it appears, that an authoritative voice (Sugrue's) would contextualize and shape Condon's first-person narrative by juxtaposing the history of jazz against the personal family history of the autobiographical subject. But what benefit, we might ask, is it to Condon to have these extra narrative voices of McNulty and Sugrue participating in the construction of his life story? To what extent is their authenticating function distinct or similar? What could these collaborators say or convey about Condon that he could not say himself?

Near the end of *We Called It Music*, we learn that Condon and McNulty had become friends at Costello's saloon at Forty-Fourth Street and Third Avenue in New York, described by Condon as "a watering place for writers, newspapermen, Irishmen, and residents of the neighborhood" (Condon with Sugrue 258). McNulty was, according to the saloon owner's brother, "a chronicler" in the Irish tradition, whose job it was "to keep a record of important events and to make sure that a few legends grew up along the way." Condon took pleasure in McNulty's company, describing him as "fine company for me and he never seemed busy" (258).

In his essay "Eddie Condon in Illinois: The Roots of a 'Jazz Personality,'" William Kenney suggests that Condon—whose own father ran saloons in Indiana and Illinois while being pursued by Prohibition activists—was drawn to "the American version of the old Irish pub," where the convivial atmosphere encouraged "male solidarity and avuncular loyalty" and which "continued to supplement the church and family in providing ethnic cohesion" (Kenney, "Eddie Condon" 262). This desire for "ethnic cohesion"—and by extension a more general desire for male bonding in the social setting of urban nightlife—stayed with Condon as he made his way east and settled in New York City; it was undoubtedly an important element in his fondness for the smoke-filled clubs in which he spent much of his adult life, including the eponymous nightclubs he successfully operated in New York from 1945 to 1967.[23]

In this largely male world, Condon formed close friendships with some of the most prominent American writers, critics, and actors of his generation, many of whom, including collaborators McNulty and Sugrue, shared Condon's Irish American heritage. McNulty's visit to Condon's apartment on New York's Washington Square North that forms the backdrop to the first chapter thus also serves to position Condon, the Chicago-style jazz performer, club owner, and raconteur, within New York's literary and cultural establishment. In fact, McNulty uses his own recently announced book publication as the special inducement to urge Condon to write his own autobiography.[24] McNulty's endorsement of Condon as a worthy subject for autobiography gives Condon legitimacy within the world of New York's cultural elite.

As Condon's memory is stirred by McNulty's questions, prominent figures from this world are named, sometimes by Condon himself, sometimes by his wife, who passes through the room while the men are talking. The reader learns, for example, that Irish American authors John O'Hara, Joe McCarthy, and George Frazier were guest speakers on Condon's radio program (Condon with Sugrue 2); that John Steinbeck dropped by Condon's club one night to urge Condon to return to playing the banjo (5); that Condon was offered a

Eddie Condon at his New York nightclub, Condon's, ca. June 1946. Front row, from left: Condon, guitar; Tony Parenti, clarinet; "Wild" Bill Davison, cornet; Arthur Bradford "Brad" Gowans, trombone. Second row, from left: unidentified drummer and Jack Lesberg, bass. William P. Gottlieb/Ira and Leonore S. Gershwin Fund Collection, Music Division, Library of Congress.

part in a proposed theatrical production of Dorothy Baker's *Young Man with a Horn*, in which another friend, Burgess Meredith, was offered the role of Bix Beiderbecke; and that when the proposal fell through, Meredith and Tyrone Power offered financial backing for Condon to open a jazz club (7–8). This is nothing else if not deliberate name-dropping, and details about Condon's precise relationship to the individuals are neither given nor really necessary. The purpose of these impressionistic recollections is to situate Condon—and even to show him as a figure of some significance—in this world.

But people from a community a world apart from the New York cultural elite are also named: musicians associated with the Chicago style of jazz that Condon played throughout his career, including Mezz Mezzrow, Bud Freeman, and Condon's musical idol, Beiderbecke. Significantly, Condon's recollections of these musicians are interspersed with those of the authors and actors named above. In other words, in the dialogue between McNulty and Condon, there is no distinction made between these two communities, and the people that inhabit them share equal ranking as Condon's companions and associates. Perhaps most striking about the memories and associations that Condon recalls in this first chapter is the absence of references to African

American musicians or to jazz as a music with roots in black culture; to the contrary, the world portrayed here is strikingly white, or white-ethnic, with its focus on Condon's Irish heritage.

By contrast, the narrated chapters attributed to Sugrue reveal a sharply different perspective, one that highlights the complex, multiracial and multi-ethnic influences that shaped Condon's musical and cultural worldview. These chapters appear to have several aims: to construct an elaborate, heroic family narrative that foregrounds Condon's ancestors' moral rejection of slavery and their flouting of middle-class respectability; to demonstrate Condon's ties to African American music and culture, and therefore to legitimize his claim as a jazz musician who made a significant contribution to the "hot" Chicago style jazz; to establish jazz as the only true art produced in America and an art deserving of a place on the European concert stage; and finally, to position Condon within broader American and Irish American cultural realms. In making these claims, the "Narration" demonstrates its familiarity with the central battleground positions of contemporary jazz criticism, all of which share—despite their diverse preoccupations and biases—an overarching concern with demonstrating jazz authenticity through the language of race, ethnicity, class, and nation.

Sugrue's first chapter begins with a portrait of Condon's Irish grandparents, who came to America to escape the Great Famine, but quickly the focus shifts from Condon's Irish heritage to his grandfather's experience with the music of African Americans on the levees of New Orleans, where he had found employment. In a letter to his wife, David Condon wrote that "*the city ... had a great deal of music, which would please her. The Negroes ... sang especially well, and had many songs and dances of their own*" (Condon with Sugrue 13). Later, we learn that Eddie's grandparents and most of their children sang and played instruments. The juxtaposition of these two storylines illustrates the process by which the "Narration" links the Irish Condons to the music and culture of African Americans. More specifically, the Condons' music, like the singing that David heard on the levees of New Orleans, is represented as the pure, natural music of the folk—an expression of joy and vitality amidst the hardships and toil of daily life (16–19).

Following a more general discussion of black and Irish folk music, the narrator offers a brief, emotional description of the history of jazz, beginning with the music of African Americans in the US South in the years "*following the war in which* [David Condon] *refused to take part*" (19). The narrator stresses the innate ability of African Americans to communicate feeling through music; moreover, this particular form of musical expression that came to African Americans in a "*natural way*" was "*something new. It was jazz*" (19). With the musical history of the Condon family still fresh in the minds of readers, it is no huge leap to see that the ground is being laid to establish

Eddie Condon's own connection to jazz music; this pattern of authentication through linkage will continue throughout Sugrue's "Narration."

In a passage that describes David Condon's refusal to join the Confederate army, the "Narration" seeks to establish an ethical as well as aesthetic connection between Eddie Condon's family history and the history of African Americans. Using language that stresses David's humanity as it evokes the imagery of the Underground Railroad, the narrator explains that he "*had no desire to fight for slavery against a government which guaranteed his freedom. To avoid the Confederate draft he walked home. He traveled by night, hiding in cornfields and canebrakes during the day. He was fed by slaves who smuggled food to him 'hidden in their bosoms.' He arrived home barefoot*" (14). The heroic, near-mythical imagery of these passages, characterized by Sugrue's overwrought prose, lends gravity to Condon's personal history that stands in sharp contrast to the dry wit and one-liners of Condon's own first-person account.

The views on African American music and culture expressed in the "Narration" must be seen not in isolation, of course, but rather in their relationship to the language and attitudes of the wider jazz discourse of the day. The following passages elaborate upon these attitudes, constructing an ideological template for the origins of jazz, its central and defining stylistic features, and its moral force, into which the white jazz musician, Eddie Condon, may be positioned. The narrator refers to the "fratricidal warfare between the Fundamentalists and the Modernists," as the modern jazz of the beboppers threatened to push into oblivion the traditional jazz with which Condon was associated. He condemns jazz scholars who insist on judging authenticity based on racial and geographic origins, and who use the technical language of European art music to describe a music which, as the earlier passages argued, was a natural expression of feeling, not thought (19–20).[25]

Yet the narrator proceeds to do what he has just condemned, that is, to use race and geography as the central criteria by which to form his own evaluations regarding authenticity in jazz. The key difference between the West African musical tradition of the slaves and European art music, he argues, had nothing to do with "*color or culture*," but rather with "*consciousness*" (20). Whereas European culture strove toward individual attainment based on "*reason*," the "*Negro . . . showed no desire to go away from what the European called the unconscious or subconscious mind*" (21).[26] And while European music was guided by a theoretical understanding of "*melody and harmony*" and reproduced sounds that could be represented through musical notation, the Negro had the ability to hear "*all the sounds*" and to imitate them, with the result that his music was rhythmically and tonally more complex (21).

The essentialist views expressed here—for example, the belief in the superior ability of black people for mimicry, emotional response, intuition, and passion; and conversely, of white people for intellect and reasoning—echo those of many contemporaneous jazz histories. The "Narration" also reflects prevailing contemporary views that traced the origins of jazz to black New Orleans (see Ramsey and Smith) while attributing the music's development (or evolution) to a synthesis of African and European musical influences in America (Condon with Sugrue 23–25).[27] The latter view is hardly surprising, of course: for all the reverence that Sugrue and the other collaborators of white jazz autobiographers pay to African American cultural expressions, they are also concerned with establishing the unique contributions of white musicians to jazz.

The focus of the second narrated chapter, then, turns to these white Chicagoans—the *"white boys gathered around the bandstands at the Dreamland and Lincoln Gardens, some of them startlingly young* [who were] *discovering the new music and listening to its masters"* (100). The narrator has now set the table to introduce Condon and to place him within this group of eager youngsters, as well as to convey information about him in a manner that could not be conveyed by the autobiographical subject himself: *"They knew the Condon kid from Chicago Heights, too; he was small, quick-moving, clothes-conscious, sharp-tongued, seldom still, and forever organizing parties, dates, and excursions to the south side"* (101). Here, Sugrue directs the reader's attention to Condon's role as a bridge between the white and black jazz communities in late-1920s Chicago; by organizing trips to the South Side, Condon was responsible for introducing many of the young white Chicagoans to the music of the great New Orleans musicians, among them King Oliver and Louis Armstrong (103).

But the anxiety that was apparent in the collaborators' accounts discussed earlier in this chapter also reveals itself in Sugrue's "Narration," primarily through the narrator's effort—or perhaps struggle—to validate these white jazzmen while he continues to highlight the social and musical differences between them and their black peers; for example, in his comment that *"Jazz was not considered a proper profession for well-bred young white men"* who were forced to work in establishments operated by the likes of Al Capone and his associates, or his claim that the different upbringing and musical backgrounds of these white musicians was reflected in a different sensibility toward the playing of jazz, including a rushed and "nervous" approach to rhythmic and melodic construction that stood in sharp contrast to *"the unhurried, effortless, relaxed mood of Negro jazz"* (104). The narrator's explanation, guided by stereotypical assumptions about the social and cultural backgrounds of jazz musicians, is at once apologetic—the white players are not capable of producing the easy, "relaxed" mood of the black players—and boastful in its implication that the "fresh expression" and "new voice" of these white jazz musicians offered a significant development for jazz.[28]

Later, Sugrue attempts to illustrate Condon's accomplishment in absorbing crucial elements of black music in his own playing before turning to his attempts to bring his hot, Chicago-style jazz to New York's concert halls (162, 165–66). In Sugrue's portrayal, we see Condon driven by seemingly contradictory impulses, with his contempt for the highbrow snobbery of the classical music world standing alongside his persistent efforts to present jazz in venues traditionally associated with that world. It is possible, of course, that Condon's goal was to encourage the highbrow patrons of European art music to change *their* attitudes toward jazz, to have them see it for what he insisted it was—not "low-brow music" but rather "music for everybody" (Condon and Gehman 27). Yet in Sugrue's depiction of Condon's battle to win Town Hall—and in so doing to win over the hearts and minds and physical spaces of New York's highbrow music communities—we find his success as a jazz musician measured by the very standards of mainstream propriety and respectability that he had consistently challenged for most of his career.

The ambiguity seen here seems an accurate reflection of Condon's own conflicting views, evident not only in his own musical aspirations but also in his relationship to the world of the cultural elite, including the literary men, jazz writers, and celebrities from the world of entertainment and business whom he counted among his friends. We have already considered the contradictory impulses that Condon reveals in his self-deprecating representation as an author, a representation challenged by his many publications and his close friendships with New York's literary elite. In a similar way, his scorn for professional jazz critics (a scorn related to a broader anti-intellectual stance) must certainly be read against his public efforts as an author and spokesperson to historicize jazz and to propose answers to many of the same questions that drove the jazz debates—including questions regarding the music's origins, racial aspects, and stylistic features.

Sugrue ends his "Narration" with an attempt to establish Condon's artistic significance, both within the United States and on the world's stage. In his scenario, Condon is leader of a vanguard standing in opposition to the nation's elitist establishment, an establishment that has failed to recognize the genius of jazz, an art form born within its own doors. The final passage recounts Condon's failed attempts to book Washington's Constitution Hall for a jazz concert under his direction. They were turned down, according to the "Narration," because the owners of the hall—the Daughters of the American Revolution—feared that a jazz audience might cause damage to their hall (Condon with Sugrue 296). In his response to this incident Sugrue introduces a remarkable simile, comparing the reception of Condon and his associates by mainstream America to that of James Joyce within Ireland; in so doing, the narrator grants Condon's music the stature of high art while he simultaneously denigrates those critics and members of the general public who were unable to recognize it as such (296–97). The pretension of the passage notwithstanding, Sugrue's final image provides a neat reprise of the first chapter, in which Condon attempts to establish his credentials as an autobiographer by placing himself within an elite circle of American writers.

I have devoted considerable attention to the historical and cultural forces behind the portrait of Eddie Condon that emerges in his autobiography because they are key, in my view, to understanding the authenticating strategies at work here. Although Condon was not an extraordinary instrumentalist *or* bandleader, his career as instrumentalist and bandleader was long and prosperous. Sugrue's task in his "Narration" is to convince the reader that Condon's success was deserved; he does so by establishing Condon's significance within the contemporary historical jazz discourse that emphasized jazz's origins in black music as well as the particular contributions of white jazz musicians to its stylistic development. When Sugrue traces the development of white Chicago-style jazz as played by Eddie Condon and his associates to the influence of King Oliver and Louis Armstrong, he is making more than just a musical claim; he is also claiming jazz as a progressive site of multiracial and multiethnic cultural blending, with Condon assuming a leading role.

Similarly, although Condon was not considered a writer of particular significance, he enjoyed a long and varied career as a published author, a career that he constructed in large part with the help and encouragement of some of the best-known American writers of his generation. Both Sugrue's "Narration" and the first chapter featuring Condon's extended dialogue with McNulty serve the function of authenticating Condon within this elite literary community; his ease with this community is portrayed in part as an extension of his Irish American upbringing, with an emphasis on mainly male camaraderie within New York's nightclub environment.

The tone and manner of these collaborators, as I suggested earlier, are as important as what they say. John McNulty's is light, warm, and humorous; Sugrue's is lofty and ponderous. McNulty appears as Condon's kindred spirit in the dialogues between the two men; they are Irish American drinking partners exchanging stories and banter, directing barbs at respectability and convention. By contrast, Sugrue stands outside the drama; his distance is appropriate for his heroic, near-mythologizing portrait of Condon, and for his claims regarding Condon's significance in jazz history and his unappreciated genius. Yet despite their seeming incompatibility, these two authenticating voices succeed in creating a coherent and convincing autobiographical subject, one whose deepest attachments came from the diverse musical and cultural worlds of Chicago-style jazz and the Irish American saloon, and whose closest friendships were with the writers, actors, and critics who patronized them.

Benny Goodman and Irving Kolodin's *The Kingdom of Swing*[29]

If Sugrue's "Narration" may be situated within the framework of jazz writings of the 1930s and 1940s, another obvious model for him and Condon was Benny Goodman's 1939 autobiography, *The Kingdom of Swing*, written at the height of the bandleader's popularity with the assistance of his collaborator, Irving Kolodin.[30] In particular, there are notable similarities in the content and language of Sugrue's and Kolodin's paratextual insertions: Kolodin, like Sugrue, offers a concise but far-reaching history of jazz that establishes the significance of his autobiographical subject; his history also includes lengthy digressions on the New Orleans origins of jazz, the unique contributions of black and white players, and the particular importance of 1920s Chicago to the music's development. In addition, Kolodin identifies instinct as a necessary ingredient of the best jazz, and his descriptions of black music and musicians display a similar tendency toward essentialist language and imagery.[31]

But if ambivalence is evident in Sugrue's construction of Condon's relationship to the highbrow/folk art worlds in which he traveled, Kolodin's insecurity runs much deeper, as he displays an almost-obsessive fixation on judging and evaluating American jazz traditions in relation to European art music. Since Kolodin was primarily a classical music critic and author, it is not surprising that his explanations of jazz history and stylistic development are framed within the formal language and pedagogy of the European art music tradition.[32] Yet, in the period in which Kolodin was collaborating with Goodman, he was also involved, as a spokesperson and writer, in introducing swing music to the wider American public. According to Goodman biographer Ross Firestone, Kolodin—"a Goodman fan"—became involved with the bandleader when preparations were underway for Goodman's 1938 historic Carnegie Hall concert. With the intention of elevating the tone of Goodman's jazz concert, Kolodin received a commission to write program notes "addressed to those whose knowledge of swing is limited," with detailed explanations of the music and "analysis of each selection in the erudite style of classical concert guides" (Firestone 208–9).

In Firestone's view, Kolodin's role as Goodman's collaborator on *The Kingdom of Swing* was intended to serve a similar function, "assuring that the project would have a certain quality and be taken seriously as something more than mere public relations flackery" (257–58). And yet, despite Kolodin's apparent respect for Goodman and his commitment to understanding the contemporary jazz scene, a palpable discomfort underlies his evaluations of the bandleader and his music, as well as his explanations of the central characteristics of jazz performance. In his foreword, Kolodin suggests that the "virtuoso performer of popular dance music" (of which he names Goodman as an example) deserves the respect and attention given to classical musicians; he lays the blame for the music's bad reputation in part on the less-than-respectable venues in which it had typically been heard (Goodman 11). Moreover, he adds that jazz should be judged "*according to its own standards*"; in his attempt to define what these particular standards might be, he refers to Benny Goodman's jazz as "a *player's music*, created out of the instinct, and only in a secondary sense out of the training of the performers themselves" (12; emphasis in original). A player's interpretation of a particular tune, he argues, is the key factor in judging a jazz performance (12).

Kolodin's defensiveness here is striking. He seems to suggest that the readers of Goodman's autobiography are somehow unsympathetic to his music and that it is his (Kolodin's) job to convince them otherwise; furthermore, he will teach them to admire Goodman's popular dance music through a comparison to European art music—that is, to the music with which they are presumably familiar and for which they have sympathy. On the one hand, then, Kolodin seems to appeal to Goodman's readers to withhold their own judgment regarding Goodman's swing music; on the other hand, his own judgments seem to dominate. As great as his effort is to convince readers that Goodman and his music are deserving of serious attention and respect, he will frequently resort to stereotype to distinguish popular music rooted in African American culture from the training and requirements of European art music.

In Kolodin's first interpolation, he offers a brief and didactic account of jazz history with New Orleans as the music's original source, but with Chicago (the main focus of the chapter) as the clear center of jazz during the period of its northern migration. Although Chicago was an important center of white culture and finance, Kolodin notes that "Goodman's Chicago was none of these" (46); rather, his was "the close-packed West Side" (where he lived) and "the even more closely-packed South Side," where "a staggering number of [African Americans] lived in squalor and filth" but still managed to produce a vibrant music scene that encouraged "some of the most original musicians in jazz" (46–47). Here Kolodin establishes Goodman's roots in Chicago's working poor, while at the same time he shows his specific connection to the city's black South Side, where he and many other young white musicians would receive their formative jazz education.

Kolodin's jazz history continues as he sketches the path by which Goodman and other white Chicagoans learned to play swing music, focusing on the cultural origins of the music and the extent of white imitation and borrowings of an African American art form. In brief biographies, he introduces the central figures of New Orleans—"both colored and white"—who left the city and made the trek northward, settling in Chicago where they contributed the key "element in jazz which . . . became known as swing" (50–51). But since jazz lacked a formal "written history" or pedagogical system, students were left to learn the music through emulation, that is, by listening to records or hearing live bands in performance (51–52). In this way, the white musicians who came of age in 1920s Chicago (Kolodin lists Goodman and many others) were lucky enough to learn directly from their favorite musicians and to become "outstanding white players" with "unique qualities of genius" (52). Kolodin's description here is strikingly similar to Sugrue's regarding Condon and the other white Chicagoans quoted earlier (Condon with Sugrue 104). It is easy to imagine that his term "unique" and Sugrue's terms "new" and "fresh" to distinguish the white Chicagoans from their African American counterparts are simply euphemisms for "superior."

Kolodin then illustrates the interactions between these black and white musicians, with the white players making the trek to the Lincoln Gardens and other jazz venues on Chicago's South Side, where they learned about approaches to improvisation and rhythm that stood in marked contrast to the sweet music played by the contemporary white bands. Here Kolodin is quick to insist that the benefits from these interracial mixings went both ways: for while the white drummer, Dave Tough, first brought Earl Hines to the attention of Louis Armstrong, it is also possible to trace Zutty Singleton's influence on Gene Krupa (who was introduced to Singleton by Mezz Mezzrow) and to find Singleton "climbing over a wall at the Southmoor Hotel to peer in at a window just to see a white boy whose playing on records had been the talk of his band—a white boy named Benny Goodman" (Goodman 58). Thus, Kolodin's brief history of jazz—in which he has managed a clever dance between homage to the black sources of American jazz and insistence on the significant contributions of white musicians—ends with a vivid image of black New Orleans drummer Singleton scaling a wall to catch sight of the teenaged Benny Goodman.

Later, Kolodin turns to focus specifically on the swing phenomenon of the mid-to-late 1930s that would cast Goodman, above any other American popular musician, black or white, in the leading role. Notably, he identifies race as one of the central factors in the enormous popularity of swing music, observing that for the first time there was "the concentration of enough fine jazz musicians in a single white band to direct attention to it that no colored band, however good, could hope to attract" (171). Here he pauses to identify the defining characteristics of Goodman's band, which had absorbed the influences of the dance bands of the 1920s, with their emphasis on formal training and the use of arrangements, but which insisted on translating "the resources of part-writing, voicing and instrumentation *into jazz terms*" (172, emphasis in original). So what exactly does Kolodin mean by "jazz terms"? Precisely those attributes that Goodman and other white musicians learned originally from black sources; that is, music that placed a premium on "vitality and independence" and that stressed individual improvisation within group interaction. In this context, then, the use of formal elements such as arrangements only contributed to strengthen the music, "to make it more orderly, more integrated, more unified" (172).

But when Kolodin attempts to give a more precise definition of swing, he is forced to abandon analogies to European art music and return to examples from the leading black bands, whose playing contained "an element" that defied strict notational translation (174). For many years, Kolodin continues, only a limited number of white musicians had been playing in this style:

> It was only when an attempt was made to transfer this atmosphere and enthusiasm to a large white band (which eventually succeeded in the perfected Goodman organization) that a large public became aware of the particular stimulation and interest that *authentic* jazz, in its straightforward, undiluted form possesses. (175, emphasis added)

Circular as Kolodin's argument seems, his overall intention is clear: to emphasize the authenticity of Benny Goodman's swing music by establishing, once again, its links to black music; and to insist that Goodman's astonishing popular success—which he achieved without sacrificing his musical integrity—is proof of his unique and far-reaching contribution to jazz.

Later, Kolodin revives his comparison between swing and European art music with the suggestion that the former had evolved to a point at which the technical language of the latter—including terms such as "inflections, accents, intonation and phrasing"—might be appropriately applied to it, as well (177). These words have barely escaped from his pen before he anticipates the outrage of those European art music critics who question the serious attention given to jazz musicians, with their presumed substandard technical abilities (178). The key element, according to Kolodin, is intention. Swing musicians do not lack technical ability; rather, the decisions they make regarding tone quality and vibrato, melody and rhythm, all have to do with cultivating an "individual style," the hallmark of the best jazz playing (178-79). But, once again, Kolodin seems to qualify his praise, suggesting that the key ingredient which distinguishes them from their classical counterparts has to do with opportunity, or, more precisely, the lack of it:

> Who is to say what accomplishments a Beiderbecke, an Armstrong or a Teagarden might not have achieved had his talent been directed along more conventional lines? Their backgrounds in Iowa, Louisiana and Texas inclined them to the most convenient outlets that came to hand—bringing them eventually to a jazz band rather than a Philharmonic, to Fifty-second Street (in New York) rather than Fifty-seventh Street. (180)

With this final comparison, any pretense at objectivity seems to unravel, and Kolodin's true feelings about jazz are unmasked. In his primitive-turned-highbrow fantasy, jazz musicians become world-class symphony players, finding homes for themselves in the Philharmonic, rather than in a jazz band. Moreover, Kolodin's concerns for cultural uplift extend to the ardent fans of swing music as well, as he speculates that some of them might also turn their considerable listening skills to European art music (182).[33]

In his account of Goodman's music and career, Kolodin walks a precarious tightrope between elevating jazz as America's only true art form and apologizing for its inadequacies. As we saw earlier, this impulse was also apparent, if to a lesser degree, in Sugrue's "Narration" in *We Called It Music*, in which Sugrue's ambivalence about jazz and its relationship to European art music was in general an accurate reflection of Condon's own. By contrast, Goodman's views on this topic in his autobiography differ in important respects from those of his collaborator. While Kolodin's stentorian voice resounds in his explanations of music history, wide-eyed naïveté and modesty mark Goodman's descriptions of his early experiences with European art music and his impressions of that music in relation to swing. By his own admission, he lacked even the most basic knowledge of classical music until John Hammond asked him to participate in a performance of the Mozart Clarinet Quintet at the Hammond family mansion on Ninety-First Street,[34] and his recollection of his preparation for the concert is striking for its simple language and unassuming tone:

> Naturally, I had a tough time at first adapting myself to this sort of thing, getting the right reed to play with a nice soft tone quality, but the music did appeal to me. There were such marvelous melodies in it, and the way it all worked out, with one instrument changing parts with the others, and the wonderful way in which the composer gives you a terrific climax when some simple idea works out into a different thing altogether—that was an experience I never had in music before. (Goodman 167)

At least briefly, Goodman's description seems to support Kolodin's portrayal of the primitive jazz musician who seeks a higher level of intellectual and cultural experience through immersion in European art music. But if Kolodin insists on a hierarchical relationship between jazz and classical music, there is no such suggestion in Goodman's account. To the contrary, his descriptions of his early classical music performances and recordings stress the similarities between the two musical worlds; for example, in his comparison of his trio with Teddy Wilson and the Mozart string quartet with which he played, as well as in his later account of his experiences with the Hungarian violinist Josef Szigetti and the Budapest String Quartet (186, 242–44). Moreover, in his intriguing comments about his 1938 Carnegie Hall performance, Goodman provides an oblique critique of highbrow snobbery, insisting that "if the stuff is worth playing at all, it's worth playing in any hall that presents itself" (232–33). Like Eddie Condon, Goodman seems eager to use the concert hall as an opportunity to present jazz on an equal footing with European art music.

If this is indeed one of the central points of Goodman's account—to insist that jazz has a validity and worthiness equal to the European art music tradition—then it must be seen as a direct challenge to Kolodin's Eurocentrist music history. That the perspectives of autobiographical subject and collaborator should appear to differ so fundamentally in *The Kingdom of Swing* is in itself intriguing, perhaps a reflection not only of Goodman's and Kolodin's individual experiences and perspectives but also of the larger debate that was taking place in American society in the late 1930s on the meaning and significance of jazz and its place in American culture (Denning 323–61).

By his own account, Benny Goodman's newfound engagement with classical music was not a contradictory endeavor; he could still be the most popular swing bandleader in America even as he performed and recorded Mozart and Bartok. For his collaborator, however, the chasm between the art forms seems to have been too wide to bridge. What Kolodin's analysis reveals above all, in other words, is his own discomfort with elevating jazz to high art, even as he calls upon others to do so. Yet Kolodin's discomfort is not simply the expression of a Eurocentric music critic but also a reflection of the skepticism with which jazz was still regarded in the late 1930s by a generous segment of the American public, including the highbrow readers of Kolodin's prolific writings on European art music.[35]

If—as Firestone suggests—Kolodin approached his role as Goodman's collaborator and as the author of the program notes for the Carnegie Hall concert with the purpose of using his highbrow credentials to give the bandleader's life and music greater legitimacy, then his efforts ought to be viewed a success. In his interpolations, as in his earlier program notes, Kolodin manages two distinct authenticating strategies: he illustrates Goodman's commitment to the African American musical influences that were central to the creation and development of his own swing band, while at the same time he shows Goodman's striving toward loftier musical achievements through his study of European art music.

It is worth asking if Goodman's loyal young fans required the explanations and justifications of a highbrow critic such as Kolodin to guide their response to Goodman and his music; reviews of the Carnegie Hall concert suggest not. *Down Beat* reported that "the audience included 'adolescent schoolboys ... who applauded everything, including the klinkers' and 'boggy-eyed pseudo sophisticates who applauded nothing'" (qtd. in Erenberg 68). In Lewis Erenberg's interpretation, "The night belonged to the young," who had "no need for elaborate program notes to appreciate the music [and] reacted as if the music was entirely theirs and not for music critics" (68). Catherine Tackley offers further evidence of this point, noting accounts from both *Down Beat* and *Melody Maker* that "the balcony and gallery audience went into complete disregard for Carnegie Hall etiquette and amused itself by throwing small paper aeroplanes through the hall and, in general, turning the occasion into a Mardi Gras atmosphere" (qtd. in Tackley 165). The icing on the cake, as she explains, was that the paper planes "were likely made from Kolodin's program notes, adding to the subversion of this activity" (165).

The fascinating clash of cultures apparent at Goodman's Carnegie Hall concert has its analogy in the widely contrasting voices of *The Kingdom of Swing*, with Goodman's simple and straightforward style—likely aimed at his loyal young jitterbug fans—providing a marked contrast to the lofty tone of his collaborator. Viewed from this perspective, it was more likely Kolodin's highbrow associates, rather than Goodman's true fans, who required the guidance of his interpolations in *The Kingdom of Swing* in order to be convinced of the bandleader's talents and achievements.

The Authenticating Collaborator in Mezz Mezzrow's *Really the Blues*

As noted earlier, Mezzrow's *Really the Blues* is the only autobiography under discussion in this chapter in which the collaborator's voice is not revealed in intertextual or paratextual insertions, but rather at the end of the text's final *chapter*, and then by the autobiographical subject himself, when Mezzrow breaks away from his narration to tell the reader how the book came to be written. Until this point, Mezzrow's autobiography is written entirely in his first-person voice and has given no clues as to the specific editorial intervention of his collaborator, Bernard Wolfe.[36]

These final passages in *Really the Blues* bring the question of authorial control to the forefront, forcing the reader to consider the degree to which Mezzrow's lengthy first-person narration is in fact biography rather than autobiography. In his afterword published in the 1990 Citadel Press reissue of *Really the Blues* (and in subsequent editions), Wolfe refers to "the experience of writing the Mezzrow book" (Mezzrow 391). Critic Scott Saul persuasively argues for the substantial role played by Wolfe, referring to him as Mezzrow's "literary midwife and probably the one who gave the edge to Mezzrow's sociological analysis and the blinding gloss to his jiving spiel" (Saul 345, fn. 30); my reading of the collaboration between Mezzrow and Wolfe is consistent with Saul's position.[37]

Despite Mezzrow's colorful attempts to convince Wolfe that he's not up to a literary undertaking, Wolfe insists on Mezzrow's place among other significant storytellers of his time, writers about whom Mezzrow claims ignorance,

Mezz Mezzrow, in his office in New York, ca. Nov. 1946, celebrating the publication of *Really the Blues*. Photos of his wife and son are pinned on the wall behind him, as well as records from his own label, King Jazz. William P. Gottlieb/Ira and Leonore S. Gershwin Fund Collection, Music Division, Library of Congress.

including André Gide, B. Traven, Céline, Henry Miller, "and guys like that" (Mezzrow 334). The common thread within this perhaps seemingly disparate group of writers is that they all functioned, to varying degrees, as outsiders reporting on the societies in which they lived and worked; in Wolfe's view, this would also be Mezzrow's chief contribution to American letters. Wolfe says to Mezzrow,

> Mezz, you've got a story to tell just like those writers did, and it deserves to get down on paper. Look: you've been lying flat on your back for a quarter of a century, almost, watching the screwy kaleidoscope of American life jiggle and squirm over your head.... It's a real American success story, upside down: Horatio Alger standing on his head. (334)

But then Wolfe warns Mezzrow not to expect the commercial or popular success from his story that "hammy poets" and others achieve, for his tale, unlike theirs, does not lend itself to "sloganizing verse" or recitation "over the radio on patriotic occasions" (334). Yet its very lack of commercial appeal would, according to Wolfe, highlight its chief value: namely, its "authentic" portrayal of "the plight of the creative artist in the U.S.A.—to borrow a phrase from Henry Miller, that writer I told you about" (335).[38]

Mezzrow's response of tongue-in-cheek humility—"I sure never suspected I was living a saga and an odyssey.... Now it turns out I was *significant!*"—leads, in the book's final paragraph, to his agreeing to participate in this joint venture with Wolfe: "We put our heads together hard, . . . and we finally wrote that book" (335, emphasis in original). This "conversation" between Mezzrow and Wolfe within the final pages of Mezzrow's autobiography offers yet another example of the authentication of a white jazz autobiographer by his collaborator, but it is a notably different kind of authentication from those uncovered in the other autobiographies discussed in this chapter. Mezzrow, in Wolfe's creation, is the quintessential hipster, standing by choice and inclination on the outside looking in, "a real American success story, upside down" (334).

In Mezzrow's hipster world, marijuana and hard drugs take the place of whiskey, and the African American/European art music dichotomy fades into the background. And while references to jazz musicians and writers abound in his first-person narration, notably absent are references to the literary figures mentioned, under Wolfe's influence, in these final pages of his autobiography. In this respect, then, this final section tells the reader more about Wolfe's literary interests and associations than about the cultural circles in which Mezzrow himself traveled.[39] Nonetheless, Wolfe's namedropping creates a place for Mezzrow within various American and European bohemian literary circles and at the same time establishes his importance as a storyteller. In so doing, Wolfe seems to have found an effective authenticating strategy, convincing the enthusiastic readers of *Really the Blues* that Mezzrow—the high school dropout who was as well-known as a supplier of high-quality marijuana as he was for his abilities as a jazz musician—was a worthy literary subject (Saul 41).

In his seminal study of jazz criticism, John Gennari identifies a number of themes in the histories of jazz written from the 1930s to the 1960s that are striking for their similarity to those articulated by many of the collaborators whom we have considered in this chapter. The first theme is "jazz's history as a hidden, occluded history of the United States writ large" (Gennari 121). In Gennari's view, the writings of early jazz historians amount to "a historiography of American culture," meriting serious attention from scholars of US history for their contribution "to the study of the lives and cultural practices of American common people" (121). More specifically, Gennari adds, "this body of work sought to uncover the African American foundations of American culture" (121). Yet, at the same time, these writings also debated the question "of *how* and *to what extent* African cultural orientations and practices insinuated themselves into other cultural streams that were shaping American civilization" (121, emphasis in original). These multidirectional paths of inquiry comprise the second theme, which Gennari identifies as "the contact, interaction, and exchange between African and European cultures in the development of jazz" (121). The third theme examines jazz "as a cultural form and practice that develops within the context of larger historical narratives: migration, modernization, industrialization, and urbanization" (121).

As we have seen, collaborators of white jazz autobiography also display a strong impulse to historicize jazz, proposing their own versions of jazz history in the process of illuminating the life and career of a particular white jazz musician—a custom-made jazz history, if you will. While the most detailed and expansive histories emerge in Irving Kolodin's interpolations and Thomas Sugrue's "Narration," other collaborators focus on a particular aspect of jazz history: for example, Tom Scanlan's history of the jazz guitar in his introduction to *Rhythm Man*, and Dance's history of swing in his introduction to *Those Swinging Years*. In these histories, collaborators attempt to situate their autobiographical subjects within the vibrant, multiracial and multiethnic landscape of urban America in the first decades of the twentieth century, emphasizing these subjects' encounters with cultures outside their own as a necessary and rewarding part of their development as jazz musicians. Like the jazz historians in Gennari's study, many collaborators are especially concerned with showing the primacy of African American musical and cultural forms in the development of jazz. As I have argued, their effort to demonstrate white jazz musicians' comfort with these forms becomes their central authenticating strategy, a strategy I call "reverse authentication" for the way it inverts the literary conventions that marked the slave narratives as well as some black jazz autobiographies, in which black subjects are legitimized by demonstrating their worthiness in relation to white European cultural traditions.

Nonetheless, collaborators of white jazz autobiography still face the challenge of proving that white jazz musicians had something special to contribute to jazz. Not surprisingly, then, they expend considerable energy—again like the jazz critics of Gennari's study—in illustrating "the contact, interaction, and exchange between African and European cultures." My contention that anxiety accompanies this endeavor is, in fact, another way in which the accounts of these collaborators resemble those of the mostly white subjects of Gennari's study, whose focus on issues of race and class in jazz often seems an expression of their own anxiety as white writers working in a field dominated by African American musicians. Finally, many of these collaborators also map the development of jazz "in the context of larger historical narratives"; thus, we see a focus in their writings on the migration of jazz from New Orleans to Chicago and other urban centers, and the effect of "modernization, industrialization, and urbanization" on the development of Chicago-style hot jazz, for example, or on swing music as a national phenomenon.

Gennari urges cultural historians of the United States to include as source material the works of criticism and history that dominated jazz discourse in the mid-twentieth century (121). I would suggest that the work of the collaborators of white jazz autobiography are also worthy of the attention of these historians, contributing as they do to an understanding of "jazz's history as a hidden, occluded history of the United States writ large" (121). In particular, they deserve attention for the ways in which they allow the stories of individual musicians to illuminate aspects of interracial contact and shifting attitudes toward race and culture in the periods in which the texts were published and also in those on which they are primarily focused.

In each of the autobiographies discussed in this chapter, the collaborator seems guided by two distinct goals: first, to convince the reader that such an unlikely subject as a white jazz musician—doubly an outsider by virtue of his playing a style chiefly created by African Americans and lacking any clear credentials as a literary figure—is worthy of our attention as a jazz autobiographer; and second, to legitimate the autobiographical subject's participation in African American or Euro-American musical and intellectual spheres. In the following chapters, the focus shifts from the authenticating strategies of the collaborators of these texts to those of the autobiographical subjects themselves, as they describe interracial experiences central to their jazz education and careers as professional musicians, and, in the process, deepen our understanding of attitudes regarding race, ethnicity, and gender identity in a wide range of twentieth-century urban jazz centers.

2

Bob Wilber, the Westchester Kid: White Privilege and Perspectives on Jazz Belonging

"Mine was such a privileged childhood, with so many nice things about it," Bob Wilber states in the opening pages of *Music Was Not Enough* (1987), an account of a white musician's experience in jazz that is at turns unreflective and illuminating. Wilber, a highly respected clarinetist, saxophonist, and bandleader, rose to prominence while he was still in his teens in New York during the mid-1940s as a gifted student of the great New Orleans jazz musician Sidney Bechet, and his account of his jazz education with Bechet and his subsequent professional career suggest immersion experiences in New Orleans and East Coast traditional and swing jazz communities as rich and complex as any considered here. Yet the colorblind lens through which Wilber filters these experiences serves to deemphasize, or even negate, the significance of race in the interracial experiences he describes. My aim here is to try to understand the apparent contradictions in Wilber's account, in particular his simultaneous closeness to and distance from New Orleans's jazz culture, which I ascribe in part to the privilege of his life and to his geographical and social distance from New Orleans itself.

Wilber was born in 1928 in Greenwich Village into upper-middle-class prosperity. His father was a partner in a small firm that published college textbooks; his stepmother's father was treasurer and vice-president of US Steel (Wilber 3, 6). Their next-door neighbor was John Hammond, the Vanderbilt heir who would go on to become one of the most influential promoters, critics, and producers of American popular music in the twentieth century. About this coincidence, Wilber writes, "I have often wondered if the first jazz I ever heard was from John's phonograph next door as I lay in my crib" (4).

Wilber's early memories of visits with his stepmother's parents include a formal Victorian lifestyle of house servants, "household schedules and social arrangements" (6). Wilber was fascinated by the family's black butler and chauffeur, Madison, who loved Bill Robinson and would show Wilber simple tap-dancing moves, thus providing him with one of his earliest experiences with African American cultural expression (6). In 1931, the family moved to New York's Gramercy Park, but a couple of years later to Scarsdale, a lily-white "Ivy League enclave" north of Manhattan, where Wilber describes a life "of wealth and privilege, of country clubs and gracious socializing" (4).

Wilber's father was an enthusiastic amateur ragtime pianist whose nightly playing sessions encouraged his son's own emerging musical interests (5). His privileged childhood exposed him to a wide variety of music—his fifth-grade "music appreciation group" tuned in to the classical music classes on Walter Damrosch's radio program for children—but Wilber was particularly drawn to the popular swing bands of the day (6). He began his career as an instrumentalist by playing along with big-band records on tin flute; by the time he reached junior high school, he had switched to clarinet and had also learned some boogie-woogie piano (7). His first exposure was to the white big bands of Glenn Miller, Benny Goodman, and Harry James, but his friends soon introduced him to the recordings of the best-known black swing bands, as well as to the earlier jazz styles of New Orleans, Kansas City, and Chicago. "The more I listened," he explains, "the more excited I became. The music seemed to contain something that was flesh and blood and reality" (8). By his early teens, when Wilber became a regular at the jam sessions at Jimmy Ryan's in New York, jazz had become the center of his world, providing him with "an escape from a environment I didn't like and an alternative to the problems of growing up" (9).

For while "privileged" aptly describes the genteel upper-middle-class prosperity that was Wilber's experience of childhood, "nice things" fails to convey the insecurity and anxiety that accompanied his privileged life and which forms a central theme of his narrative. Early on, Wilber admits to his "feelings of sexual inadequacy," feelings that he claims stem from his relationship with his father, who was "a ladies' man" and an extremely successful businessman. "In truth, I desperately needed an area in which I could do something as well as he. I found it in music, in which I knew I really could outshine him" (16).

A notable aspect of Wilber's account of his early musical experience is his depiction of the symbiotic relationship between the world of Scarsdale affluence and New York's black jazz community. His father's fascination with pianist Teddy Wilson led him to take his family to see Wilson and his band at Café Society Uptown in 1941 (8); the family also attended Ellington's premiere performance of *Black, Brown and Beige* at Carnegie Hall in 1943, "a black-tie affair with the proceeds going to the Russian War Relief Fund" (10). Wilber recalls that his grandmother—a lifelong church organist—turned to him as trombonist Tricky Sam Nanton performed one of his renowned plunger solos and exclaimed, "'He's trying to tell us something.' Clearly, the message of this music had even reached her!" (10). In these anecdotes, Wilber offers evidence of the attitudes of liberal paternalism with which he was raised and which are reflected throughout his narrative, most notably in his account of his relationship with Sidney Bechet.

The relationship between New York's black jazz community and its suburban admirers became significantly more personal when Wilber's school friend made arrangements for weekly lessons at his Scarsdale home with Willie "the Lion" Smith, the great Harlem stride pianist (9). Following the lessons, the family and their friends gathered for drinks while Smith "would entertain them. He loved to perform and could mesmerize any audience" (9). Wilber embraced the opportunity "to play with the great Willie Smith and be coached by him—'the Lion' was our professor!" he comments, thus marking this experience as an important part of his early jazz education (9). He and drummer Denny Strong formed the Hot Club of Scarsdale, and Wilber's father gave him permission to host jam sessions at their house (Burke 188; Rowe 4).[1] For a final school concert before summer vacation, the youngsters recruited an interracial group of "all-star musicians" from New York, including Art Hodes, Pop's Foster, and Mezz Mezzrow. Generating great enthusiasm at the school, the concert made instant "heroes" of Wilber's "jazz gang" (Wilber 11).

But Wilber soon faced the limits of his parents' support of his musical endeavors, as they made clear their expectations that he would embrace the Scarsdale career path of Ivy League school training for a career in a profession such as law or medicine. Yet not only did Wilber reject the Ivy League route, he lasted only briefly at the Eastman School of Music in Rochester, where he had agreed to go as a compromise, repelled by its coldness and focus on European classical music (13). His decision to move to New York shortly afterward was in part an escape from the stifling conventionality and expectations of his family, and Wilber dwells on his own rebellious impulses and those of his suburban companions. His stories of their adolescent behavior, however, serve mainly to demonstrate that theirs was a rebellion of rich kids slow to part with the privileges of their affluence.[2] Unkempt and wild, they lived for their music and "immersed" themselves in Mezz Mezzrow's *Really the Blues*—"our Bible" (15). Their antics attracted the attention of the jazz press, who referred to them as "the Westchester Kids" (15).

With his parents' permission, Wilber rented a small apartment at 112th and Broadway with pianist Dick Wellstood and another musician friend (17). At a time when bebop had become the dominant language of expression within jazz, these youngsters—some, including Wilber, still in their teens—were obsessed with keeping the old music alive. In 1945, Wilber joined forces with several of them to form the Wildcats, a New Orleans revivalist band that aimed for fresh interpretations "in the context of the New Orleans idiom"; soon, the Wildcats were playing at dances and small clubs throughout Westchester County, Connecticut, at Nick's in Greenwich Village "and all points in between" (15, 18).[3]

Wilber and his friends steeped themselves in a mid-1940s New York jazz scene that included the traditional (or Dixieland) jazz revival, Harlem stride and boogie-woogie piano, small swing combos, and big-band swing—a scene Wilber remembers as welcoming to those who showed due respect for the music, regardless of their racial or ethnic background. "All my feelings about the musicians of that generation are, without exception, good ones," he insists,

> I can't remember a single instance where any musician put me down or sloughed me off.... The musicians took me seriously because I took their music seriously. They didn't feel threatened because there was work for everybody. I never felt any racial antagonism from that generation of black musicians. Maybe I was seeing the world through rose-colored spectacles, but I never had any feeling of, "Hey, white boy, what are you doing here?" (21)

Wilber formed significant friendships with many of the older and more established black musicians on the New York scene. He recalls going up to Willie "the Lion" Smith's flat in Harlem for lessons in jazz harmony, but he also describes a social friendship with Smith, who would take him to Father Divine's in Harlem for some soul food following the lessons (20–21).[4] Wilber and his friends became a fixture at Jimmy Ryan's on Fifty-Second Street, where Sidney Bechet began working steadily in 1947. Every night Bechet would invite Wilber to sit in with him, and after closing time, they would go "uptown to Creole Pete's to get some gumbo, or to friends of his up on Sugar Hill" (21). Other musicians also befriended and encouraged Wilber; among them were the great trumpeter and bandleader Hot Lips Page as well as Bechet's pianist, Sammy Price, who would invite Wilber to Sunday dinners at his family's home, where Wilber experienced the wonderful home cooking of "Mamma Price," a "ladies' room attendant" at Ryan's who would occasionally "come out and sing the blues" (21). On Mondays, Wilber and the Wildcats would venture up to the Hollywood in Harlem for "piano night," featuring "cutting sessions when all the stride cats came by," and where Wilber again paints a picture of interracial accord: "The three of us would be the only white people in the place. Sometimes they invited us to play and we were accepted and applauded" (22).

There is truth to Wilber's portrait of Fifty-Second Street in the 1940s, or at least *some* truth, as Patrick Burke details in his comprehensive history of

The Wildcats, the teen New Orleans revivalist band, at Jimmy Ryan's in New York, ca. December 1946. From left: Johnny Glasel, trumpet; Bob Wilber, soprano saxophone; Charlie Traeger, bass; Dick Wellstood, piano; Ed Phyfe, drums. William P. Gottlieb/Ira and Leonore S. Gershwin Fund Collection, Music Division, Library of Congress.

Fifty-Second Street—commonly referred to as "The Street" by the musicians and audiences who made it their second home for more than a decade, beginning in the mid-1930s (Burke 3). While clubs on Fifty-Second Street were at the forefront of interracialism in jazz, "among the first in New York to feature racially integrated bands and to allow integrated audiences," blatant "racial discrimination and stereotyping" was a persistent reality of life on Fifty-Second Street (4). Moreover, while Wilber's account might lead one to conclude that "mixed" or integrated bands were the norm, they were in fact the rare exception to the segregated bands that performed on Fifty-Second Street (147). As Burke explains, far more common sources of interracial contact in this period occurred when musicians "sat in" with the regular band or appeared on the bandstand together for the public jam sessions that many of the clubs featured (147); indeed, this seems to match Wilber's own descriptions of "playing the whole of the last half of the evening with Sidney" at Ryan's or attending the Sunday afternoon jam sessions there (Wilber 21; Rowe 7).[5]

In 1946, Wilber began lessons with Bechet, who had recently opened a music school in his "old, ramshackle, three-story house" on Quincy Street in Brooklyn (Wilber 23). According to Wilber, he was Bechet's "first and, for a while, his only pupil," adding that Bechet had a keen interest in teaching and even "wanted to write a book on jazz improvisation because he felt that so many young musicians didn't understand what it was all about" (23).[6] Wilber's lessons with Bechet were, in his words, "everything I had hoped for" for he found Bechet to be "a marvelous teacher and a wonderful man" (24).

When Bechet discovered that Wilber was unemployed and low on funds, he proposed that Wilber live with him and his mistress on Quincy Street—an arrangement Wilber's parents formalized after a meeting with Bechet at Ryan's jazz club in Harlem, at which time they quietly arranged to pay their son's expenses. "Such was my rebellious nature at that time," Wilber admits, "they were probably afraid that I would find out and fling the money back in their faces" (24). The meeting went well, in Wilber's view, because Bechet "had a way of making meaningful contact and being at ease with all sorts of people from all walks of life and all stratas [sic] of society, many of whom might never have had much contact with a black man or a jazz musician" (24).

The paternalistic tone of this passage continues with Wilber's explanation that he has included a reproduction of a letter that Bechet wrote to his father, in which Bechet explains his role as Wilber's teacher, in order to offer "the reader a feel for the gentle, kindly side to Sidney's nature. . . . Although his lack of formal education is evident from spelling mistakes, his charm and dignity shine forth from the page" (24). His father insisted that Bechet had written him another letter in which he stated, "I've taught Bobie everything I know and now he's teaching me," although Wilber admits that he never saw the letter himself (24). One wonders at his motive for including this footnote: Did he find humor in Bechet's stiff formality with his parents, in which politeness and propriety mattered more than telling the truth? Or was his ego sufficiently stroked by his teacher's flattering description that he could not resist including it?

In either interpretation, it is clear that an intense awareness of race underlies Wilber's analysis of his parents' negotiations with Bechet; in his telling, his parents gave him permission to live with Bechet because, "[b]eing Christian and very liberal in their outlook, they saw nothing wrong with my being taken under the wing of this black man" (24). Noting that there was a historical precedent in the family for "this kind of understanding attitude," Wilber recounts that his great-grandmother, on behalf of the Ladies' Guild of Cincinnati, had put up Booker T. Washington in her home when he came to address the women's group and it was discovered that no plans had been made "for his accommodation. A hotel, of course, was out of the question" (24). The family story becomes a source for outright boasting, with Wilber explaining that during his visit, "Mr Washington" requested

> some writing facilities, as he had a deadline drawing near. He was provided with a writing desk in the comfort and privacy of the drawing room. It was not very long after this event that Washington's famous book *Up from Slavery* was published. The family always liked to think that some of its pages might

have been written there in great-grandmother's drawing room. It was no different from the courteous way in which my own parents were now dealing with Sidney. (24–25)

Although Wilber is ostensibly describing the attitudes of paternalistic benevolence of his upper-crust family, the manner of his telling suggests the degree to which he had internalized these attitudes himself. Yet it is only after an extensive and sometimes technical account of his lessons with Bechet that Wilber stops to consider the interracial aspect of their relationship—even then his discussion is somewhat circumspect.[7] In 1947, he explains, when Bechet got an offer for a recording date with Columbia Records, he proposed that the Wildcats accompany him for half of the session, an offer that Wilber credits to Bechet's sincere desire to help the youngsters gain a toehold in the New York traditional jazz scene. Understandably, the Wildcats were thrilled but anxious about recording with "the master" Bechet, and they prepared with marathon practice sessions "in the front parlor at Quincy Street. Musically we weren't in the same league as Bechet; he couldn't really fly in his customary fashion with our stiff rhythm section. Nevertheless, he enjoyed having these young admirers around him, and instead of dominating us all, he played a true ensemble role" (31).

To this point, Wilber has focused on the disparity of age, experience, and talent that separated him and the other Wildcats from Bechet, but when he opens the door to consider the racial dynamics of their relationship, there is a dramatic shift of meaning and significance to their collaboration. In Wilber's view, Bechet gave so much time and attention to the Wildcats because "[t]he musical ideals that he had stood for all his life were under attack and being ignored by young musicians of his race. Bop was all the rage, and Ryan's was the only traditional-jazz spot left on Fifty-Second Street. Sidney felt all this very acutely, and I think he believed that through this group of young, willing pupils he could perpetuate his musical message" (31).

Wilber's assessment of Bechet's response to the white musicians who came to study with him is an accurate representation of the tensions and unexpected alliances that formed during the jazz wars of the late 1930s and 1940s. Like many of the great New Orleans musicians, Bechet was bewildered to find his style of jazz dismissed as outdated by the various modernist jazz communities. Wilber recognized that Bechet's willingness to play and record with a group of white adolescents was because of their reverence for him and their devotion to the music he loved; in his words, Bechet "was very flattered by my interest in him and my desire to play the clarinet and soprano in his style. I was his protégé and he was proud of me, but of course he never felt threatened by me musically, nor indeed should he have been; he was still at the height of his powers and I was just beginning" (33).[8]

Burton Peretti reaches a somewhat more cautious conclusion when he suggests that many African American musicians of Bechet's generation responded to their ardent white followers "with a mixture of avuncular pride and circumspection, proud of their hard-won artistic status but aware of the continuing precariousness of their economic and social positions." When these musicians referred to their "white disciples" as "my boys" or "cubs," Peretti adds, "they expressed as black men a degree of mastery and authority rarely matched in American race relations" (Peretti 208).[9]

In a later passage, Wilber pauses to consider Bechet's own racial self-representation, one that he apparently finds peculiar. "Funnily enough," he comments, "Sidney never thought of himself as a black man. He was a Creole, the product of the fusion, generations before, of French and negro [sic] blood. Creoles like Bechet and Jelly Roll did not see themselves as black, yet they were not accepted as white men" (Wilber 48). His inability to be seen as he saw himself, Wilber suggests, led Bechet to make "strange statements" in which he expressed his animosity toward African Americans for behaving in ways that reflected badly on folks such as himself—or, as Wilber quotes Bechet, "Them Goddam niggers, doin' this and doin' that, and givin' us all a bad name" (48). When Wilber attempted to challenge Bechet for praising the racist Mississippi politician, Theodore Gilmore Bilbo, Bechet brushed aside the criticism, maintaining that Bilbo was "doin' a fine job" (48).

A critical point here is that Wilber also thinks of Bechet "as black" and repeatedly refers to him as such; Wilber's anecdote about Booker T. Washington in the same passage in which he describes arrangements for his lessons with Bechet is clearly intended to display the tolerant attitude of his family toward African Americans. Significantly, then, Wilber's discussion shows him to be either unwilling or unable to consider the cultural and social history of New Orleans Creoles of Color that might help to contextualize Bechet's comments about race (48). In fact, his teacher's insistence on distinguishing his own Creole heritage from that of the "Negro" culture of New Orleans—and his expressions of contempt for non-Creole blacks that accompanied this—was not strange at all, but rather expressive of the attitudes he had learned in the highly stratified New Orleans society from which he came.

Sidney Bechet's Creole Identity and Its Shaping of His Jazz Persona

Studies by Charles Hersch (2009) and David Ake (2002) have examined the particular complexity of racial classification in New Orleans history as a result of the city's significant Creole of Color population, and the impact of their changing social and legal status on the development of jazz in New Orleans at the turn of the twentieth century. A stated goal of these scholars is to challenge the binary racial view that had influenced much of previous jazz historiography (Ake 11–14; Hersch 6–7). Hersch begins his introduction with a discussion of Homer Plessy, the "octoroon" Louisiana Creole of Color and plaintiff in the landmark 1896 *Plessy v. Ferguson* decision that upheld the "separate but equal" doctrine enforcing segregation and the implementation of Jim Crow laws in the US South. Not only would *Plessy* provide an important legal basis for the rights and restrictions that affected the daily lives of US citizens for more than half a century (until 1954, when the decision of *Brown v. Board of Education* began the slow erosion of *Plessy*'s influence), but as Hersch notes, it also served to entrench the binary racial classification in the United States that remains largely unchallenged to the present day (4).

Bechet was born in 1897 (a year after the *Plessy* decision) into a middle-class Creole family in Downtown New Orleans, and the impact of these changing racial definitions and laws on him and the wider Creole community from which he came cannot be overstated. As we will see, Bechet's views concerning his Creole heritage—as he expressed them in his 1960 autobiography, *Treat It Gentle*, and in interviews from various sources—were complex and inconsistent, in part the result of competing generational influences that caused him to revise and reevaluate his own self-representation as a New Orleans Creole of Color and as a musician. My investigation of his views here is not intended to gloss over their complexity but rather to try to understand them against the historical reality of Jim Crow in which Bechet emerged as one of the leading figures of New Orleans jazz.

Most of Bechet's relatives earned their livelihood in the skilled trades and professions for which the Louisiana Creoles had earned their reputations, and Bechet's insistence on forging a career in music and his particular attraction to the rough, unschooled sounds of the city's Uptown black musicians may be viewed as gestures of defiance and rebellion against some of the core values of his Creole upbringing (Chilton 9–10; Hersch, *Subversive* 104; Ake 26–27). As Ake and Hersch point out, the "third-race" status that Creoles had experienced in New Orleans for most of the nineteenth century before the advent of formal, institutionalized segregation allowed them the possibility to define themselves primarily through their European, rather than their African, heritage (*Subversive* 99; Ake 18). Language and geography were important markers by which the Creoles distinguished themselves; for example, many of them spoke French and lived in Downtown New Orleans, thus putting physical, as well as cultural, distance between themselves and New Orleans's black Uptown population (*Subversive* 64).

In addition, New Orleans Creoles—including Bechet's own family—embraced European musical traditions that elevated formal musical training, skill in reading music notation, development of pitch and tone control based on European musical aesthetics, and extensive knowledge of European art music, including opera. "Holding on to a European identity," Hersch writes,

"Creoles thus at first resisted African-based music. Older and wealthier Creoles of Color in particular opposed the new music and looked down on younger musicians who embraced the new style" (*Subversive* 67).[10] John Chilton, Bechet's biographer, notes that even after Sidney began to contribute some of his earnings to his family, "no amount of money compensated the family for the fact that Sidney was working regularly in 'the District'; such employment was thought of by them as a stigma" (Chilton 16–17).[11]

In a 1949 interview with Alan Lomax, Sidney's brother, Leonard, revealed his own discomfort with New Orleans Uptown musicians, describing them as "naturally always rough, ignorant," and without the benefits of "a background like the . . . Creole people." By contrast, he used words such as "prestige" and "respect" to describe Creole musicians, who "never played jazz—played nice music." Yet, as he admitted, in the end "the pull of the music was too strong" (qtd. in Hersch, *Subversive* 102–3). The contrasting attitudes of the Bechet brothers support Ake's contention that Sidney "maintained a decidedly more Uptown, even Afrocentric, position than the one taken by most Creoles of his day" and that "this stance extended beyond music" and included Bechet's decision to move to France because, as he explains in his autobiography, it brought him "closer to Africa" (Ake 25; Bechet 45).[12] Bechet's Afrocentrism also reveals itself in a passage in which he suggests that despite the effort of "white musicianers" to emulate the black New Orleans "style as best they could," their efforts were ultimately unsuccessful, for "it's awful hard for a man who isn't black to play a melody that's come deep out of black people" (114).

Burton Peretti has suggested that Bechet's statements about race in *Treat It Gentle* justify a characterization of "the older Sidney Bechet" as "passionately separatist" (Peretti 192). Perhaps it is not surprising, then, that Bechet devotes little space in his autobiography to Wilber, undoubtedly his most famous white student and someone with whom he performed frequently in New York during the late forties (Wilber 29; Balliett, "Westchester Kids" 305). His few references focus mainly on his role as Wilber's teacher and his impressions of him as a talented but insecure musician; although his evaluation is not without kindness or praise, his tone is gruff and at times even distant. Wilber's parents commissioned him "to look after" their son, he explains, but although "he could read very good" when he first came to him, "it was the instrument he didn't know. . . . He wanted to play but he couldn't" (Bechet 185).[13] In order to ensure that Wilber would keep coming for lessons, he decided "to tell him a lie—I said, 'That's it, Bobbie, that's it. Now you're coming,'" as he worked with Wilber on putting more air through the clarinet and on producing "different tones and growls" (185). While Bechet admits that Wilber made excellent progress during his studies, he sensed that Wilber's confusion regarding his own musical direction was holding him back, despite his ability (185–86).

Here Bechet correctly identifies the source of Wilber's unhappiness as his inability to find his own voice. He recalls that Wilber "played so close to me that it began to annoy him, because people used to say, 'Oh, that boy, he plays just like Bechet'" (186). Indeed, the revivalist press frequently described their relationship as that of a master passing on the torch to his devoted apprentice.[14] As I discuss below, Wilber's struggles to find a musical identity free from Bechet's influence emerges as a dominant theme of his own autobiography.[15] By the late 1950s, the period in which Bechet was working on his autobiography, he had clearly lost touch with his former student: "I haven't seen him in a good while now," he remarks, adding almost parenthetically, "and I hope he's doing all right because he was a fine boy and a good musicianer" (186).

If the above examples point to Bechet's embrace of an Afrocentric worldview, we are still left with his impulse to distance himself from certain *types* of black people and to support certain white supremacists, as in his comments to Wilber discussed earlier. On this point, Ake suggests that "Bechet's position on his racial heritage was neither unremittingly Afrocentric nor uncomplicated. In spite of his apparent Uptown ties, he never disavowed his Creole-French roots" and would "occasionally revert to the virulent racism that characterized Downtown attitudes" (Ake 25). Bechet's seemingly contradictory views about race and his own racial self-identity exemplify the continuing struggles of New Orleans Creoles of his generation to negotiate their place in a society in which, as Hersch argues, "race rather than place now defined them: to become Americans, Creoles had to become black." But even as they did so, Hersch insists that "the transformation in their legal and social status was much more gradual, the ambiguity much more prolonged, than most jazz histories have indicated" (*Subversive* 99). Bechet's negotiation of race, nation, and self-identity is a clear example of the prolonged struggle to which Hersch refers, as Creoles sought to define themselves within the increasingly rigid binary of black and white.

More Than Just Sounding like Bechet

If Wilber is candid about his emulation of Bechet's musical style, there is also a strong suggestion of sexual emulation in the relationship between student and teacher. This aspect of their relationship emerges in Wilber's account of an incident involving the actor Tallulah Bankhead, Bechet's longtime mistress, who called Bechet one night at Ryan's in New York and demanded that he come up to her hotel room.[16] According to Wilber, Bechet asked him, "You wanna have some laughs? Pick up your horn and come along with me" (Wilber 29). When they arrived, they were met at the door by the "stark naked" Bankhead, who commanded them to play as she crawled back into bed with a "gentleman friend"—later, Wilber learned that he was her "leading

Bob Wilber, sitting in with Sidney Bechet at Jimmy Ryan's, New York, ca. June 1947. William P. Gottlieb/Ira and Leonore S. Gershwin Fund Collection, Music Division, Library of Congress.

man" in a production of *Private Lives* then being staged on Broadway, and the play's producers had assigned him the task "of keeping Tallulah sober between performances" (29–30). When Bankhead's lover left the room, Bankhead took the opportunity to demand several refills of her drink as she "carried on a non-stop monologue, mostly about how absolutely horrible everybody else was in the play." When her thirst and desire for the blues had been quenched, she dismissed them, and "still naked, led us to the door. She bid us goodnight and we left" (30).

Even more striking than the story itself is Wilber's lack of commentary about this scene he recalls in such vivid detail decades later, not only here in his autobiography but also in an interview with Bechet's biographer that he gave in the same period (Chilton 193, 303, fns. 11 and 12); instead, he makes an astonishing leap into a story about Bechet's passion for motorboats (Wilber 30–31). It's certainly possible to imagine that Wilber—still in his teens at the time of the incident with Bankhead, and by his own admission "painfully shy and insecure with the opposite sex" (23)—would have had some kind of reaction to the open display of sexuality that he witnessed. This suggestion is supported by Wilber himself, who in his interview with Chilton referred to Bechet's explicitly sexual stage performances at Ryan's, during which "[h]e'd point his soprano at a woman he liked and push it up slowly like a giant phallus. It was like the work of a snake charmer, and he had plenty of conquests" (qtd. in Chilton 193). Wilber does not say in what position their sopranos were pointed as he and Bechet serenaded Bankhead and her leading man.

On another occasion, Bechet was away for the afternoon, and Wilber and Bechet's mistress, Laura, were alone together in the house in Brooklyn. According to Wilber, Laura became very drunk and finally "enticed me into bed with her," an experience about which he expressed shame, offering it as evidence of his inability to reject any opportunity to bolster his precarious sense of his own masculinity and his struggle "to deal with normal youthful lust" (Wilber 32). He confesses his terror at the prospect that Bechet might discover what had happened, knowing as he did that his teacher had a short fuse, particularly when he had been drinking, and that he always carried a switchblade with him (32–33). Although Wilber's anxiety and shame about the incident seem genuine, his reluctance to reveal more about how he felt at substituting for Bechet in an explicitly sexual performance is regrettable; since Wilber is quite candid about his early desire to sound like Bechet, it is not a huge leap to imagine that at some level he also wanted to emulate Bechet's sexual prowess, particularly in light of his own admission of sexual insecurities.

Life after Bechet

Following his detailed examination of his studies with Bechet, Wilber spends much of the remainder of his narrative explaining his effort to free himself from his "identification with Sidney Bechet," an effort that involved finding not only a new musical identity, but also a version of masculinity independent of his teacher's (50). By the late 1940s, he admits, he had become increasingly discontent with "living in Sidney's shadow and always being known as his protégé." He realized that "[l]arge numbers of fans were coming, not to hear Bob Wilber, but to hear someone who sounded like Bechet," an experience that left him feeling "like some sort of freak show, and there came a time when I just had to break away from it" (50). Here Wilber's discomfort with the racial dynamics inherent in his position as Bechet's "protégé" is more obvious; he recalls that after performing at the Nice jazz festival in 1948, he returned to New York "with an enhanced reputation and found myself referred to in some quarters as 'the great white hope of jazz.' It was all very flattering, but I didn't approve of the description" (43).

In light of the discussion of Bechet's "passionately separatist" views discussed above, it is ironic that Wilber uses this opportunity to express his extreme discomfort with the particularist arguments for jazz that he encountered upon his return to the United States, which saw white jazz musicians as second-rate imitators of "the black man's music" (43). Remarkably, he claims that "never heard this idea expressed before, but I recognized it at the time as racial bullshit, just as it is racial bullshit today" (43). Later he offers this summary of his own position: "Jazz is American music, only nowadays we have musicians from all over the world, of every nationality and color, who can play it" (44).

While Wilber effectively conveys his sincerity and disappointment, he seems unwilling to consider explanations for jazz's long history of contestation along racial lines. Although he has spent his entire career playing earlier styles of jazz, he was in fact a contemporary of many of the bebop and postbebop stylists whose music was strongly linked to the growing mood of African American assertiveness and nationalist impulses that he so adamantly rejects. Later in his narrative, Wilber repeats his colorblind argument for jazz in his account of a four-concert Ellington retrospective organized by George Wein in the 1970s. When Wein told Wilber that he would have to hire a black pianist because there were not "enough black players in the band," Wilber reluctantly agreed, although he insisted that the replacement was not as good as his first choice and that Wein's demand was another instance of "that old racial bullshit" (132).

Wilber's colorblind perspective dominates the remainder of his narrative. His criticism of the jazz studies programs that were initiated at universities in the United States "during the black studies craze" of the 1960s resembles the white resentment narrative examined earlier, including his charge that the programs presented a distorted view of jazz history "as the black man's music, totally ignoring the white musician's involvement right from the beginning" (173).[17] There is truth to some of Wilber's complaints here; other critics have also observed the selective biases of jazz studies programs, and the tendency—as Scott DeVeaux observes—for "textbooks aimed at the college market" to depict jazz "as a coherent whole, and its history as a skillfully contrived and easily comprehended narrative" ("Constructing" 525).[18] Yet in his criticism of bebop and the avant-garde jazz of the 1960s, Wilber reveals he is as prone to bias and stylistic exclusion as the jazz educators who draw his ire (Wilber 194). More to the point, he readily admits that the focus of his own university teaching (and he has taught widely) is on the classic jazz and swing era that he favors (174–76).[19]

At times, Wilber's insistence on the colorblind argument for jazz leads to a rigidity and tunnel vision that in its more extreme articulations resembles a kind of paternalistic racism, as in his suggestion that black studies programs were successful until "it was soon discovered that the black students' interests in their cultural roots were quite superficial." In Wilber's view, "what black students wanted were the tools and skills to make it in the white man's world, to be a part of that upwardly mobile American middle class. They really wanted to forget the past and be part of the American Dream—a wife and kids, two homes, two cars and a pocketful of credit cards" (173). A generous interpretation of Wilber's comments here might be that African American students are just like any other students; yet the overt racism and paternalism of his analysis is inescapable (the world is the domain of the white man), as well as its rigid view of gender roles and assumption that a desire for financial security precludes an interest in one's "cultural roots." Wilber seems unable to imagine a world in which middle-class respectability is not a universal goal, irrespective of one's cultural background; despite his efforts to leave the influence of his Scarsdale upbringing behind him, more than a trace of it remains, seemingly permanent and inerasable.[20]

Wilber's views on race resist definitive conclusions because they are, in my view, so fundamentally unexamined and contradictory. He readily acknowledges that his own musical voice was largely shaped by African American jazz musicians and grants the inequity in the jazz world that left them earning less and having fewer employment opportunities than their white counterparts (Wilber 48). Often, he goes further, sharing particular stories that reflect racism in the jazz world and in the broader society (104, 107, 144–45). Yet Wilber also displays his insensitivity to the dynamics of particular interracial situations and to the nuances of US race history more generally.[21] More specifically, he has difficulty separating his own struggles (and the struggles of other white musicians) from his more general examination of racism and discrimination, with the result that his critiques on race seem to break down or become merged with the difficulties of being an artist in American society.

Early in his autobiography, Wilber acknowledges the role of racial discrimination in destroying "so many good people," including Lester Young and Coleman Hawkins, who "finally realized that, with all his ability and talent, nothing was going to happen—he was just another black saxophone player" (48). Later, Wilber returns to the topic of great jazz musicians who died disillusioned and broken; once again, he mentions Hawkins and Young, but this time the white trombonist Jack Teagarden joins the list. Despite his earlier suggestion that systemic racism had tragic consequences for Hawkins and Young, here he seems to attribute their difficult lives and tragic deaths not to racism but rather to America's inability to grant jazz the "status of high culture"; this revised explanation allows for the inclusion of Teagarden—a tragic white jazz musician (149). The turning point for Young ("Pres"), in Wilber's view, was his military experience, following which "he was never the same again" (150). Wilber would surely have known that Young served in the still-segregated US army and that racism was at the heart of Young's brutal military experience, but he does not mention it directly; instead he makes a more general reference to Young's vulnerability and his inability "to cope with the lack of feeling and sensitivity of the outside world" (150).[22]

There is only one overt reference to racism in this passage, when Wilber considers the case of Will Marion Cook, the classical violinist whose career in the United States was stopped short by discrimination and who was forced "to endure the indignity of writing coon songs for some white publisher in order to finance his classical studies and then find that it had all been in vain" (151). Wilber's indignation here is undoubtedly sincere, and yet he is unable to sustain his focus but instead turns in the next breath to himself—"The swing era also gave me false expectations"—thus creating the impression that his own disappointments were on a par with those of the black jazz musicians whose struggles he had just documented. "It takes a strong person to survive in such an insecure world," he concludes, "to be able to feel at ease, to conduct their life with stability and dignity, to have a normal relationship with a woman, to raise a family and to do all the things that normal people do" (151). Since Wilber's own lack of confidence as a musician and difficulty in establishing positive and enduring relationships with women has formed the central preoccupation for the first half or more of his autobiography, it is easy to read his concluding comments as directed primarily at himself.

This impression is reinforced by a new section and chapter—titled respectively "Happiness" and "At Last"—that follow on the heels of the passage discussed above; in it Wilber describes his transformation to a life of greater joy and contentment, a transformation which he attributes largely to his relationship with the English vocalist Pug Horton, with whom he has enjoyed (to this day) a significant musical, as well as personal, collaboration. The chapter opens with Wilber informing the reader that he and Pug purchased their first house "in Brewster on Cape Cod, an area I had known all my life"; The description that follows, of their first "idyllic summer" there that included "beautiful sunny days with the sparkling water and warm beaches" and a gig at "the most beautiful inn on the whole of the Cape," reinforces the impression of privilege in Wilber's life that stands alongside his struggles and insecurities (153).

The Burden of Privilege

In various interviews, Wilber has made statements concerning the racial origins of jazz and the contributions of black and white musicians to its development that seem to contradict the colorblind position that emerges in his autobiography. In a 1946 interview in *American Jazz Review*, Wilber opined that jazz was "a Negroid music, based up[on] ... his amazing rhythmic sense, his great sense of humor, and his continual search for freedom" (qtd. in Burke 191). And in a 1977 interview with Whitney Balliett, Wilber argued that the New Orleans revival was proof of the division of racial roles in jazz history whereby "the museum work, the musical anthropology . . . has been done by middle-class whites [who] have gone back and exposed the roots of what began as a black music, while black musicians have almost exclusively practiced the cult of the hip. We have been the conservatives and they have been the revolutionaries" ("Westchester Kids" 309). In these interviews, Wilber appears to embrace the "black origins" perspective of jazz history as well as the belief that whites and blacks had played fundamentally different roles in jazz history, leading Patrick Burke to suggest that Wilber "still held a conventionally essentialist view of black musicianship despite extensive exposure to an idiosyncratic individualist such as Bechet" (Burke 191).

Wilber offers insight into the origins of these attitudes and beliefs—as well as the contradictions contained in them—in an interview from the late 1990s, in which he was asked to describe the difference between the music of the Wildcats and the Chicago-style ("Condon-style") jazz of the white musicians who came from or flocked to Chicago in the late 1920s and then later to New York and whose chief influence, like the Wildcats, was the music of the early black New Orleans bands. In his reply, Wilber explains that "the Condon style was a group of musicians who were kids growing up in Chicago in the '20's, listening to King Oliver, Armstrong, the Dodds brothers, and being totally knocked out and inspired by that music." By contrast, "what we kids were doing, *we were inspired by the records of the same musicians that they had heard in person*. . . . So we thought of ourselves as the new Austin High gang" (Rowe 7–8, emphasis added).

Wilber's response here is key: while most of the white jazz autobiographers considered in this study identify their direct immersion in African American jazz spaces as central to their jazz-learning experience, Wilber and his Westchester associates first learned to play in their comfortable living rooms in suburban New York, playing along with the recordings of their favorite musicians or listening to the live performances of Willie "the Lion" Smith, who entertained his students and their families as they reciprocated with plentiful food and whiskey. Wilber and his friends, in other words, were considerably more removed from the original sources of their veneration than were these other white jazz musicians, and, as a result, they developed notions of authenticity less wedded to geography.[23] This impression is reinforced by Wilber's recollection that the appearance of Bunk Johnson and his band in New York in 1945 was "the first time I had heard authentic New Orleans jazz in person, and it thrilled me to the core" (Wilber 32).

There is also evidence of Bechet's influence in shaping Wilber's attitudes regarding authenticity and New Orleans jazz. In his autobiography, Wilber states that Bechet "saw no reason for trying to keep jazz the same as it was played in New Orleans in the early days," noting his harmonic sophistication in comparison with "most players of his generation" (25, 27). He reinforced this point in a *Downbeat* interview in the late 1980s, observing that "Bechet was not a New Orleans player in quotes. He was very much a swing era player; loved Art Tatum, Kenny Clarke, Sid Catlett, and wasn't interested at all in Preservation Hall" (Helland 51). Authenticity, in other words, was judged neither by proximity to New Orleans nor to precise emulation of early New Orleans recordings.

An impression of distance is also evident in Wilber's account of his trips to New York when he was a teenager, trips which, as I have already suggested, held particular resonance for him, for they represented his move away from the wealth and privilege of Scarsdale toward the excitement and stimulation of the New York jazz world. Yet by his own account there was an element of fantasy to this experience, which he likens to Dorothy's in *The Wizard of Oz* as she passed

> from the real world of black and white into the fantasy world of Technicolor. This is exactly what I felt when I traveled into the city on the New York Central railroad. Even the name of the branch line that Scarsdale was on, the Harlem Division, had an exciting appropriateness to it. There was a magic line between Scarsdale and New York, and every time the train approached the 125th Street station in Harlem I crossed the line and passed from black and white into color, and vice versa. (Wilber 9)

Wilber's comparison of his spatial and temporal move—from Scarsdale to Harlem to the fantasy world of Hollywood—has the effect of distancing himself from his own recollections of interracialism in jazz, leaving the reader to imagine Wilber watching (perhaps on a large screen in Technicolor) his own experiences of Harlem and Fifty-Second Street and the African American jazz musicians he listened to and learned from there. Moreover, his reference to fantasy here is reminiscent of another image, discussed earlier—the "rose-colored spectacles"—through which he remembered interracial relationships in New York's traditional jazz community of the mid-1940s and which seems to have prevented him from perceiving those less-than-rosy aspects of jazz interracialism, such as those noted by Bechet in his autobiography.

Wilber, in other words, creates this impression of distance, of being removed at least to some degree from the daily struggles of the working jazz musician, including the negotiations over interracial interactions that figure so prominently in the accounts of other white jazz autobiographers. By his own admission, his family's affluence played a large role in sheltering or keeping him—Wilber offers both perspectives—from certain experiences typically associated with the life of a jazz musician. In the early fifties, he lived for some period on a generous inheritance left to him by his grandmother, and later he borrowed money from his mother for a house in Rockland

County that he ruefully admits "ended up as a gift because of my inability to keep up the repayments" (55, 78–79).

Significantly, he describes the inheritance as a "handicap" for he "was never forced to face up to the realities of the day-to-day struggle of making a career, of making a reputation or name that would stand me in good stead in future years" (55). Instead, he withdrew into a solitary lifestyle that involved endless practice sessions, "secure in the knowledge that household bills were the least of my problems, requiring nothing more than a periodic withdrawal from the band or a phone call to my stockbroker" (55). He notes the irony of his rebellion "against the wealth and privilege of Scarsdale," admitting that it was Scarsdale that "kept coming back to bale me out of my difficulties" (79). Wilber's discomfort here is obvious; he acknowledges that although he was grateful for the help, his dependence on his family was detrimental to his self-esteem, and he "sank deeper and deeper into this fantasy world, living the life of the country squire but without having any solid position in my career" (79).

But Wilber also had a very different kind of experience in the early fifties, when he was drafted and spent two years in the army, serving as an instructor in The Ninth Army Band School (57). He recalls the benefits of the arduous basic training he underwent for it gave him the opportunity to mix "with a cross-section of America . . . with men from rural areas, from the ghettos, with different racial and ethnic backgrounds. . . . I saw how other people thought and lived," Wilber explains, "and it jolted me out of that dream world I had been living in" (56). It is indeed astonishing that Wilber presents his military experience as his first encounter with men of different cultural backgrounds from his own. He had, after all, been a professional jazz musician for several years at the time of his army experience, performing and recording with many of the black musicians who played in the older New Orleans style—all in addition to his intense personal and professional relationship with Bechet, Smith, and others. Once again, Wilber creates an impression of his life in jazz as distant from the intense experiences of interracialism that we will encounter elsewhere in this book.

From "The Rotten Club" to Jazz at Lincoln Center

There is perhaps no better illustration of the complex and sometimes surprising workings of interracialism in jazz than Wilber's contrasting experiences with Wynton Marsalis and Stanley Crouch, as glimpsed through his involvement with Francis Ford Coppola's *The Cotton Club* and his subsequent collaboration with Marsalis and JALC. The well-publicized friendship between Marsalis and Crouch (see my preface) makes their divergent responses to Wilber all the more intriguing: if Wilber's mideighties feud with Crouch in the pages of the *Village Voice* illuminates the still-vigorous debates around the meaning of authenticity in jazz and white appropriation and exploitation of black culture more generally, then his significant role in Marsalis's repertory projects over the past two decades—including tribute concerts to Sidney Bechet, Benny Carter, and Benny Goodman—might well be seen as the triumph of a shared artistic vision over racial and cultural difference.

In *Music Was Not Enough*, Wilber details the complicated history of his involvement with Coppola's movie that led to his last-minute hiring as musical director to replace Ralph Burns, whom Coppola had abruptly fired and who had already "recorded a complete score" (178–79). He acknowledges the backlash over his decision to use white musicians for the *Cotton Club* soundtrack album (winner of the Grammy Award for Best Jazz Instrumental Performance, Big Band in 1986), which featured the music of two great African American bandleaders, Duke Ellington and Cab Calloway. In his elaborate explanation, he insists that his sole intention was to hire "who I thought were the best musicians for the job regardless of color"; that the diminished technical ability and stamina of "the original players" left them unable "to re-create the music" for the soundtrack; and that young black musicians were not interested in or qualified to play jazz styles prior to bebop (187). He ends with his defense of his decision to hire young black musicians to pose as if they were actually playing the recorded music. "Naturally the band that was assembled for the visual shots had to look like the Ellington and Calloway bands of the period," he explains. "They looked right, but they just couldn't play that music" (187). Even so, he adds, he hired almost a dozen black musicians who *were* qualified to play on the soundtrack. While Wilber is certainly not alone in his belief that black communities have been largely indifferent to jazz since the 1960s, his failure to anticipate the response to his hiring decisions is striking, particularly in light of the long history of discrimination against African American musicians in the movie industry and in Hollywood studios. His incomprehension at the backlash seems genuine, reminiscent of his earlier admission of surprise to learning about the black-origins theory of jazz history.

In Crouch's blistering review of the film, "The Rotten Club," he takes aim at its depiction of black life in Harlem in the late 1920s and early 1930s, its reduction of the African American characters to "black caricatures," and the complexity of interracial relations at the Cotton Club to broad stereotype (Crouch 59). He is no kinder to the film's soundtrack, describing it as "a piece of modern minstrelsy" as he outlines the missed opportunities to hire outstanding African American jazz musicians Benny Carter and Sy Oliver—until finally, as if dragged up from the bottom of a deep, dark well, "they ended up with Bob Wilber" (57). But Crouch was not finished, declaring that the "white" sound of the band (as judged by its "timbre and attack") was obvious from the moment Duke Ellington's "The Mooche" was heard over the opening credits; surely the film's budget was sufficient, he argues, "to get a band of authentic

Ellingtonians who could have given the score the 'idiomatic nuance' . . . the soundtrack is so decidedly missing" (57).²⁴

In his response that appeared in the *Voice* later that month, Wilber acknowledged the "validity" of some of Crouch's charges, reiterating his own disappointment "that Coppola's passion for authenticity in sets, costumes, and music did not extend to the storyline"; yet he also expressed disappointment that Crouch's "views on the music are so distorted by an obvious racial bias" ("Letters" 3). Insisting that his hiring decisions were based entirely on the musicians' expertise "in early Ellington," Wilber pushed back against the unnamed musician quoted by Crouch who referred to them as "a bunch of white boys," calling it "a racist comment" from someone "whom Crouch uses as a mouthpiece for his own sentiments" (3). Pointing to his own "reputation as an authority on early jazz," he asserted the position he would reiterate so forcefully in his autobiography: "to disqualify people's contributions because of their color is racist bullshit. And racism, no matter which side of the fence it comes from, is still racism" (3).²⁵

The *Voice* also printed Crouch's response to the letters, in which he appeared to back down slightly, insisting that he did not say that Wilber was "unqualified to play jazz because he's white" but rather that the generous budget for the film would have enabled the film's producers to hire the best African American musicians of the Ellington era ("Letters" 39). As a gesture of reconciliation, however, it was mainly unconvincing; not only did Crouch fail to address his use of the phrase "a bunch of white boys," he repeated his essentialist beliefs concerning "tonal color" and racial difference before ending his letter with a personal jab at Wilber and Horton (39).²⁶

If Crouch's review and the responses it provoked illustrate the potential for interracial exchanges in jazz to break down amidst charges and countercharges of racially offensive behavior and language—or more generally a lack of empathy and goodwill (on both sides)—it is also important to identify instances of interracial resilience in which musicians and critics weather the fallout from these debates and seek new opportunities for intercultural common ground. In their various collaborations since the 1990s with the Lincoln Center Jazz Orchestra (LCJO), Wilber and Marsalis appear to have done just that, finding through their repertory projects a comfortable place to express their shared veneration of the jazz tradition and their insistence on the importance of keeping that tradition alive for new generations of jazz musicians and audiences.²⁷

There is, in fact, significant accord between Wilber and Marsalis in their views about jazz and its significance to American culture, including their belief that the pulse and rhythm of swing is central to the best jazz since the 1920s and that the jazz avant-garde's valorization of European art music over swing represents a tragic turn away from the music's essence. There is no evidence, in other words, that Marsalis has found Wilber's playing and arranging lacking in the "idiomatic nuance" identified by Crouch (via Murray) in his *Cotton Club* review; to the contrary, Wilber's work with the LCJO over the years is proof of Marsalis's regard for him as an authority on early jazz and on swing figures such as Goodman and Ellington.[28] Indeed, Marsalis's relationship with Wilber offers compelling evidence of the softening in his stance on jazz interracialism that I noted earlier; by contrast, Wilber's work with the JLCO may be seen to validate the colorblind and meritocratic positions he argues most strenuously in his autobiography.

Over his long career, Wilber has proved his skill and dexterity as a performer and bandleader in a variety of interracial jazz contexts, yet his attempts in his autobiography and elsewhere to construct a cohesive analysis of these experiences have been less successful. His long struggle to achieve a sense of self-worth as a musician and as a man has left him with seemingly little desire or energy to develop a consistent or nuanced philosophy of race relations in jazz or in US society more generally. The recognition he received as a skilled practitioner of early jazz styles when he was a young man served to solidify his impression that talent and hard work, rather than one's ethnic origins, was the most significant factor for success as a jazz musician. The close relationship he formed with Bechet, and his obvious talent in emulating a style that originated in a cultural environment so remote from his own, only strengthened that impression. These experiences, in my view, left Wilber susceptible to the colorblind narrative of jazz history that he embraces with reactionary zeal in his autobiography while he remained—in large part due to the support of his wealthy family—at a safe distance from the daily conflicts and tensions that were at the heart of the color controversy in jazz. By the same token, his distance from the fray appears to have left him unconcerned with expressing seemingly contradictory views, such as those sympathetic to the black origins model of jazz considered earlier.

Wilber's general de-emphasis on the significance of race in jazz history and in his own personal experience as a jazz musician is in sharp contrast to the experiences of interracialism portrayed by white jazz autobiographers Wingy Manone and Tom Sancton, whose musical foundations lie, like Wilber's, in traditional New Orleans jazz. As we will see in the next chapter, for New Orleanians Manone and Sancton, the place itself and the multiracial and multiethnic communities that were at the heart of New Orleans's music culture were central to shaping their views on jazz authenticity.

3

Race and Place and the Construction of Jazz Authenticity: New Orleanian Autobiographers Tom Sancton and "Wingy" Manone

Lessons in Music and Life: Tom Sancton's Homage to His Fathers, "Black and White"

If *Music Was Not Enough* reveals Bob Wilber's difficulty in sustaining a clear and consistent perspective on the complex issues around interracialism in jazz, then Tom Sancton's *Song for My Fathers: A New Orleans Story in Black and White* may be seen as the author's attempt to do just the opposite: that is, to offer a comprehensive and introspective meditation on race and interracialism in various New Orleans jazz communities in the 1950s and 1960s.[1] Sancton seems well-positioned for this task, for it is fair to suggest that few middle-class white New Orleanians at that time experienced a more intimate or sustained relationship with New Orleans's black jazz community than did Sancton, who served his musical apprenticeship in that community for several years, beginning when he was barely a teenager.[2]

But Sancton's memoir is more than just an account of his own personal experience; his training as a historian and lengthy career as a professional journalist and author are reflected in his examination of New Orleans's racial history, a subject that he engages in earnest in his memoir as he attempts to understand the complex cultural histories of the old New Orleans musicians—African American and Creole—who are central to his story. In this respect, his memoir stands alongside the studies on New Orleans racial history discussed in the previous chapter; perhaps more significantly, it also serves as an important contrast to the colorblind perspective on jazz history that dominates Wilber's narrative.[3]

Although Sancton had been working on *Song for My Fathers* for several years prior to Hurricane Katrina, it was that disaster that prompted his return to New Orleans and opened the way to his decision to live again in the city in which he was raised (Sancton, *Song* 9). Although his primary purpose was to find out if his parents' house was still standing, he found himself drawn to the French Quarter, and specifically to Preservation Hall, the famed jazz landmark where he spent so much of his adolescence and which at that time "had seemed like the very heart of New Orleans and the passionate center of my existence" (8).[4] As Sancton reached the front entrance of the hall, he was flooded with memories of "that hot summer night when my father first took me there, more than forty years earlier, and opened the door to the most profound experience of my life" (9):

> Thus began my apprenticeship alongside some of the city's legendary old black jazzmen. They became my idols and mentors. They taught me about their music, of course, but more than that. They taught me about their world, their neighborhoods, their humor and anger, their fears and disappointments, their courage in the face of poverty and prejudice, sickness and death. Most of all, they taught me their humanity. They called themselves "the mens." (9)

Sancton dedicates his book to "my fathers—the white one who sired, raised, and coached me, and the black ones who inspired and encouraged me, and enriched my life beyond measure"; he also stresses the importance of New Orleans itself to his story, calling it "perhaps the central player," for the particular jazz journey he recounts "could not have taken place in any other city in the world" (9).

Sancton's first encounter with New Orleans's jazz culture supports this claim. In 1954, when he was five years old, he and his family attended the funeral of the famed trumpeter Papa Celestin. Over his mother's objections, his father decided that they would go, explaining that "[i]n New Orleans, . . . a jazz funeral is a cultural event" (11). As Sancton's family walked alongside the Eureka and Tuxedo Brass Bands, his mother recognized the clarinetist George Lewis, who acknowledged her greeting "with a smile like a sunburst, then put his horn in his mouth and continued playing" (14). Sancton recalls that Lewis's sound—"like a woman singing, or crying, or both"—made a great impression on him. "Who could have known," he wonders, "that this little man would one day become my idol, my friend, my teacher? And that many of the men playing alongside him would fill my world with joy, wonder, and a sense of purpose" (14).[5]

But as Sancton's dedication makes clear, the influence of Thomas Sancton Sr., the father "who sired, raised, and coached me," was also incalculable; for it was Sancton Sr.—a radical Southerner who in his early career had written passionately in defense of the rights of African Americans and other poor and marginalized groups—who showed him a path from his own middle-class white world to the world of "the mens." Sancton expends considerable energy in his narrative trying to make sense of his father's strange career, one marked by early success and great promise followed by repeated disappointments. Although Sancton Sr. flourished as a young reporter with the *New Orleans Times-Picayune*, the racial codes of the South prevented him from writing openly in the white press on the topic of "race relations," a subject that, according to his son, interested him above all others. "Growing up poor and half-orphaned in a working-class neighborhood," Sancton explains, his father "had a deep and instinctive sense of kinship with what W. E. B. Du Bois called 'the souls of black folk'" (42).[6]

Motivated by a sense of moral indignation, Sancton Sr. began "contributing articles to the so-called Negro press, passionately exposing the travesty of segregation, denouncing the Southern caste system, and cheering on the early civil rights movement" (43).[7] It took some time for whites to discover these pieces, for, as Sancton notes, "[n]o white people in New Orleans ever read the Negro press, . . . so his writings remained underground"—that is, until "a black postman proudly showed my grandmother a piece her son had written." As his grandmother later told Sancton, "I almost died. You see, he was *for* the colored people!" (43, emphasis in original). Sancton Sr. quickly developed a reputation as "a radical, a Communist, and—worst of all—a 'nigger lover'" (43).

Soon after this, Sancton Sr. left New Orleans and moved to the Northeast, where by the early 1940s he was attracting considerable attention as a social critic, author, and editor; he attended Harvard on a Nieman Fellowship, and when he was twenty-eight, he was hired by the *New Republic* as managing editor. Before long, his articles on race had earned him a reputation "as one of the country's most outspoken and radical voices in favor of racial equality" (5–6).[8] At the same time, he developed relationships with some of the leading African American writers of his generation, including Langston Hughes and Ralph Ellison, as well as with other progressive-minded whites (43). In a letter to W. E. B. Du Bois published in 1924, Sancton Sr. asked, "What white men now alive or in recent years . . . do you think have really understood, have really felt, have really helped the progress of Negroes to the decent things of life?" According to Sancton, no response from Du Bois has been found, "but this was clearly the role Tom Sancton hoped to play" (43).

But the spectacular success that Sancton's father experienced in his early career was short-lived. A promising opportunity to write essays on "race relations" for *Life* magazine fell through due to apparent disagreements between Sancton Sr. and the magazine's editor, and the essays were never published (44). On the heels of this setback, Sancton Sr. abruptly gave up on his promising career in the North and returned to New Orleans with dreams of becoming "a great Southern author. That didn't happen. His career went off the rails then, and he never really got back on track" (5–6).[9]

Against this backdrop of unrealized potential, Sancton describes his father at forty-five, with "two failed novels behind him, three kids to feed, and no job," walking aimlessly through the French Quarter in 1962 and pausing outside Preservation Hall to listen to the music filling the night air (49–50). Stepping inside, he saw George Lewis, Jim Robinson, and Alcide "Slow Drag" Pavageau on the bandstand—musicians he had gotten to know in New York during the heyday of the traditional jazz revival there in the 1940s (50). "My father spoke to them during the break," Sancton writes, "feasted on their warmth, their humor, and the instinctive folk-genius of their music. In the midst of the most devastating spiritual storm of his life, he had found a haven of humanity" (50). Sancton Sr. returned home "euphoric" and convinced his wife and young son to accompany him to Preservation Hall the following night (50–51). For the next several years, Preservation Hall and the musicians who played there would be the Sanctons' closest community and the center of their social lives, providing them with the rare opportunity to steep themselves physically, emotionally, and intellectually in the cultural life of black New Orleans.

Life Lessons in New Orleans's Racial History

Soon after Sancton became a regular at Preservation Hall, he received a clarinet as a gift and began lessons with George Lewis, a featured performer at the hall and one of a number of New Orleans jazzmen whose careers had been revitalized during the New Orleans jazz revival of the 1940s. "Like most black people in the South," Sancton writes, Lewis "had lived most of his life against the constant backdrop of poverty and discrimination"; he attributes Lewis's determination and perseverance to his religious faith, which "was never far from George's thinking about his music" (*Song* 86).[10] Lewis had played clarinet on the famous recording that Bill Russell made of trumpeter Bunk Johnson in 1942, a recording that revived Johnson's career after decades of obscurity (90–91; Bethell 93, 122–40). Just as bebop was becoming the dominant new expression in jazz, "Bunk's rediscovery launched a nationwide revival of interest in traditional jazz," and for several years he and his band traveled widely, bringing the sounds of New Orleans jazz to new fans throughout the United States and Europe (Sancton, *Song* 91). When Johnson died in 1949, Lewis became the leader of the band—renamed the George Lewis Ragtime Band—and for many years his band toured almost constantly and recorded frequently (92).

By the time Sancton began his studies with Lewis in the early 1960s, Lewis's career was in decline, and he rarely toured anymore.[11] In Sancton's view, Lewis and other traditional New Orleans musicians were grateful for the opportunity to play regularly at Preservation Hall, which became for them "a ticket out of obscurity and unemployment" (92).[12] For Sancton, Lewis's regular presence at the hall "allowed me to spend a lot of time learning at George's feet.... It was the apprenticeship method: you learn by doing, in the presence of a master" (92).[13] Whereas Bob Wilber describes a rigorous regimen of scales and exercises as an important aspect of his lessons with Sidney Bechet, Sancton discovered that "George's teaching method was hands on, master to apprentice. No scales, no theory, no fingering exercises, no sheet music. George, in fact, didn't know anything about all that. He barely knew the names of the notes" (77). In fact, Lewis presented his lack of formal music training as an asset, teaching Sancton the distinction between "readers" and "spellers" and pronouncing his own position on the matter: "Folks don't pay nobody to read.... They pay 'em to *play*." Choosing his teacher's model for his own, Sancton also became a "speller," learning how to read notation "from a method book, but never developing any great facility with written music" (77, emphasis in original).

Lewis's musical practices and attitudes about jazz seem consistent with those often attributed to New Orleans Uptown black musicians, with an emphasis on a process of learning by ear and emulation rather than by formal music notation. Yet Lewis's biographer, Tom Bethell, insists that Lewis "did not give any credence to the uptown-downtown distinction" adding that Lewis, who "would have to be classified in the hot, untutored school, lived all his life in the downtown Creole section" (Bethell 23).[14] According to Sancton, Lewis was quiet and reserved, and he and his teacher had few direct conversations on the topic of race in general or Louisiana race history more specifically. Yet one time he recalls that he asked the dark-skinned Lewis about his relationship with Alphonse Picou, the famed Creole clarinetist. On this occasion, Lewis's answer was blunt and direct: "Picou didn't talk to people like me.... Picou didn't like you unless you had silky hair" (Sancton, *Song* 117).

It was only after Sancton began to study with the Creole banjoist George Guesnon that he came to appreciate the significance of Lewis's remark about Picou, for it was Guesnon who opened his eyes to the rich complexity of Louisiana racial history. "I went to George Guesnon for music lessons," he recalls, "but I wound up getting much more than that" (115). For on the question of identity,

> George Guesnon knew who he was. It was written right there on his red mailbox..."Creole George Guesnon," it said, in crudely painted letters, along with a few notes of music. Creole *and* musician. Those were the fundamental,

inseparable, pillars of his identity. And no visitor ever entered his door without learning that. (115, emphasis in original)

Sancton had barely arrived for his first lesson when Guesnon challenged him to say what he knew "about the Creoles." When Sancton responded with the version he had learned at school—"the Creoles were the descendants of the original French and Spanish settlers"—Guesnon corrected him, insisting that he was "talkin' about the *real* Creoles, the Creoles of color. That's *my* people, the *gens de couleur*. We're a race within a race, a mixture of French, Spanish, and Negro" (116, emphasis in original). He explained their origins as free people and their status as slaveholders; he noted their professional skills, education, and wealth, before ending with the challenge, "They didn't teach you that in your Jim Crow school, did they?" (116). By Guesnon's account, it was "the envy on the part of the whites that wound up pushin' the Creoles into the same ghettos with the blacks" (116).

As a direct result of his lessons with Guesnon, Sancton developed a respect for the nuanced complexity of New Orleans's racial classification system in a way that Wilber seemingly never did, despite his close association with Bechet: "To most people on the white side of the color line, Negroes were Negroes and that was that," Sancton writes. "But on the other side, as George explained, there was a hierarchy—a caste system—with the Creoles at the apex and the 'Africans' below them" (117). This notion of a hierarchy or scale of "blackness" helped Sancton to understand "the attitudes some of the musicians had toward one another," including the Creole Picou's apparent scorn for the dark-skinned Lewis.

Moreover, Sancton understood that Guesnon's explanation of his Creole heritage was not "an idle history lesson" but rather "who he was; unless a person grasped his superiority as a man and an artist, he believed, there was nothing he could teach them about music" (117). Sancton's choice of the word "superiority" here is instructive, reflecting attitudes within Creole society on such diverse matters as skin tone and hair texture, education, professional status, and cultural traditions. As we saw earlier, Bechet also conveyed that sense of his own superiority through his insistence on distinguishing his cultural values and his music from non-Creole African American musicians. While Sancton acknowledges that he found Guesnon's skin-tone prejudice both "distasteful" and "fascinating," he credits him with opening his eyes to "the complex fabric of New Orleans culture and society" (126).

Guesnon's lessons were not restricted to Creole history but also included a more general consideration of racism in the United States. One day, he read Sancton a description of a lynching in Mississippi from Herbert Aptheker's *History of the Negro People* and told him about the 1900 Robert Charles race riot in New Orleans (123).[15] When Sancton told Guesnon that he didn't believe that such things could happen in present-day New Orleans, Guesnon offered a sharp refutation, comparing New Orleans to a "pressure cooker that can blow at any moment" (124).

But as happens so often in his narrative, Sancton balances the influence of "the mens" with the influence of his father. When in his junior year of high school his class was given an assignment on Louisiana history, his father urged him to write on *Plessy v. Ferguson*, telling him that the Plessy case "affected the whole history of race relations in this country" (181). Sancton Sr. had a personal connection with the family, having interviewed Antoine Plessy, a cousin of the plaintiff, Homer Plessy, for a newspaper article on the sixtieth anniversary of the decision (182). To Sancton's complaint that he would rather write about the history of jazz, his father retorted, "This case will teach you more about the roots of jazz in this city than anything else you could do" (181).

Sancton conveys the casual intimacy of their meeting with Antoine, a "retired carpenter and contractor," at his home in downtown New Orleans (182). Through Antoine's stories, which centered on his famous relative's fight for Creoles to retain their distinctive place in Louisiana society, Sancton came to understand that the primary objective for both Plessy "and his fellow committee members was to defend their own rights—not those of the colored population in general" (183). In Antoine's description of his cousin's beliefs, and by extension those of the Creole community from which he came, we hear echoes of the attitudes and worldview expressed by the Creole Guesnon; among them the belief in Creole superiority over "the American-speaking colored" based on class distinctions and contrasting histories as slaves and freemen (183).

It was precisely to maintain the distance between their two cultures that Creoles erected separate cultural institutions—including "social clubs and dance halls"—throughout New Orleans (183). Antoine's memories of these Creole institutions stirred recollections of the leading Creole musicians who figured so prominently in them, including Plessy's childhood friends Freddie Keppard, Alphonse Picou, and Lorenzo Tio Jr. (183). Suddenly Sancton understood why his father had insisted on a connection between the Plessy case and the history of jazz in New Orleans: the early jazz musicians whose lives and accomplishments had been so vital to his own jazz education were also "part of [Antoine's] and Homer's world." They, too, in other words, experienced the dramatic consequences of the Plessy case, which over time erased the legal and cultural distance between Creoles and the "American-speaking colored" population of New Orleans. Through this intricate entanglement of institutional laws and cultural practices, Sancton saw "how this music, which would later have such a huge impact on America's cultural history, had coalesced like a rich gumbo on the back streets of New Orleans" (183).

Sancton's father encouraged him to continue his research by consulting two other prominent New Orleans legal authorities: A. P. Tureaud Sr., a famed civil rights lawyer and Creole of color; and Judge John Minor Wisdom, a white southerner and a power in Louisiana's Republican party (184–86).[16] It is indeed remarkable that Sancton, while still in high school, had the opportunity for private meetings with these brilliant legal authorities; moreover, his account suggests that they treated him with respect, discussing at length particular aspects of the Plessy case and the nineteenth-century history of Creoles in Louisiana. Through the prodding of his radical father and the musician George Guesnon, Sancton worked hard to understand the complex history of Creoles in Louisiana, a history that allowed him to see that they "were anything but 'color blind,'" and that gave him important insights into "the complex world of the mens" (188). By the end of this process, Sancton would come to the realization that "[h]istory was present in every note, every word, every glance exchanged on the bandstand" (188).[17]

Meditations on Interracialism in 1960s New Orleans

It is hardly a stretch to view Sancton's interest in the history of Creoles and African Americans in Louisiana as an aspect of his own search for self-understanding, to see how it provided a path for him to explore his own history as a white Southerner in a society founded on slavery, and in which racism and discrimination continued to flourish. His interest in Southern history was closely tied to a central aspect of his narrative: his attempt to learn the possibilities and limitations of interracialism in the still deeply segregated New Orleans of the early 1960s, during which time his passion for jazz was bringing him into frequent, intimate contact with the city's black and Creole musicians. Noting that "black people and black culture had no place in my school," Sancton quickly came to recognize the sharp division that existed between his life as a teenager attending a segregated New Orleans high school and his life with "the mens" (102–3). He dwells on the overtly defiant aspects of his relationships with the musicians, noting, in his succinct summary of his experiences, that "it was technically illegal for the races to 'consort' together," and "[f]or a white kid growing up at the tail end of the Jim Crow era, the world of these old musicians was an unlikely fraternity" (55).[18]

Although Sancton does not shy away from examining the racial gulf that separated him from "the mens," he also tries to show the willingness, even eagerness, of both sides to bridge the divide. There is no pretense, however, that these interactions were without tension or awkwardness. He recalls that his first lesson with Lewis took place at the Sanctons' house and was "a big event" for the family; that his mother served coffee for their guest; and that Lewis was "very polite" and "almost deferential," a response which Sancton attributes to "[t]he primordial survival instincts of southern blacks" which would have prevented "a man of George's generation to be entirely at ease in the home of a white man—even a dyed-in-the-wool liberal like my father" (76).

Sometimes he and his father would go to visit Punch Miller, an accomplished New Orleans trumpeter and teacher who led "informal Sunday jam sessions" at Preservation Hall with young, up-and-coming musicians (93).[19] Miller lived in a "rough black quarter" in a New Orleans neighborhood where white people, as Sancton observes, were rarely to be found (96–97). The "curious or hostile stares" he and his father got from Miller's neighbors is reminiscent of the reception experienced by other white jazz autobiographers when they attempt to cross over into rigidly segregated spaces. Sancton began to appreciate the profound impact of his whiteness on these interracial experiences, that his family's "sympathies on the race question, or my father's track record as a crusader for civil rights" mattered little to Punch Miller's neighbors. His description of his family's self-identification here is instructive: "We didn't have the word liberal tattooed on our foreheads." Their visits always included a stern warning from Miller to Sancton's father, "Don't come 'round here after dark, Tom" (97).[20]

On one occasion, Fred Ramsey, the coeditor of *Jazzmen* (1939), a seminal early history of New Orleans jazz, came to visit Sancton's father, whom he had befriended as a result of their shared progressive values and love of jazz.[21] While Ramsey was there, he used the Sanctons' living room as his studio to record Dora Bliggen, known throughout the neighborhood as "the blackberry woman," whose "haunting chant" could be heard for blocks around as she sold the fruit that she had just recently picked (24–25).[22] As Sancton points out, Bliggen's mere presence in their house was a challenge to Louisiana's segregation laws, which prohibited blacks and whites from being "under the same roof—except if the blacks were working for the whites" (25).

As should be clear, Sancton's father played a central role in these interracial experiences, both through his physical presence (Sancton Sr. was there for many of his son's most memorable experiences with the New Orleans musicians) and through his intellectual and moral guidance. Furthermore, Sancton stresses the significance of his father's independent relationships with the musicians, noting the mutual feelings of "affection and respect." As one player told Sancton, "Me and your daddy, we admires to be 'mongst one another" (194). He notes George Lewis's "special bond" with his father, a bond that stemmed from "his realization that my dad respected him as an exceptional man and a great artist" (81). In his summary of the musicians' attitudes toward his father, Sancton writes, "To them, he was just Tom Sancton, a decent-hearted white man, an avid jazz fan, and a faithful friend who was there when they needed him. He was always helping them out—driving them home, taking them to the hospital, slipping them a few bucks when they were having hard times" (194).[23]

Punch Miller, one of the venerable New Orleans musicians, instructing the young Tom Sancton at his weekly jam session at Preservation Hall. Photo by Dan Lehrer, used with permission of Tom Sancton.

But along with Sancton's desire to highlight the friendship and collegiality that existed between his family and "the mens" are moments of self-examination in which he pauses to consider the motivations of his white Southern family in seeking these interracial relationships. He admits that his high school girlfriend accused him of condescension in his anecdotes about "the mens," of portraying them "like clowns and buffoons" and paying attention to them because it 'flattered our sense of class superiority' and allowed us to 'flaunt our white liberal magnanimity'" (230). Her charges clearly distressed

Sancton, causing him to wonder if his family's relationship with the old black musicians resembled Huck Finn's with "nigger Jim" (230).

Notably, Sancton turns first to his father's life and career as proof of his family's sincerity on the question of race. He was able to dismiss his girlfriend's charges, he explains, because of his father's antiracism commitment in his career as a journalist and his ability to forge personal friendships across "the color line" with the old musicians (230–31). When he paused to consider his own motivations ("What strange force drove a white middle-class teenager down that road with such passion and single-mindedness?") he was forced to admit that he and his mother were in part "following daddy's lead" (231). Not satisfied to leave it at that, Sancton digs deeper, questioning if his attraction was a result of the beauty of the music itself, the desire for his father's approval, or the possibility that he viewed "the mens themselves as father figures and role models." His answer combines self-critique with self-forgiveness: "Our motivations were varied and complex, but they did not include condescension. . . . Even the ones who clowned around the most always kept their human dignity. And we felt privileged to be around them" (232).

There is little reason to doubt Sancton's sincerity on this last point. He had been studying with Lewis for some months when his teacher started inviting him to sit in with his quartet at Preservation Hall. By 1964, Sancton had joined the black local of the Musicians' Union—a public proclamation of his identification with New Orleans's African American and Creole music communities—and was sworn in by Louis Cottrell, the "elegant Creole clarinetist and the no-nonsense president of the colored Musicians' Union" (135).[24] When Sancton was still in high school, Harold Dejan, the leader of the Olympia Brass Band, invited him and some of the other young musicians "to sit in with the Olympia on parades and funerals," providing Sancton with his first opportunity to experience the life of a working New Orleans jazz musician (141). Sancton emphasizes the rarity of this opportunity, one "that very few local white people could have in those days: marching, playing, and watching from the inside of a brass band as it wound its way through the heart of the old black neighborhoods. . . . This was more than music. This was life. I wanted to drink it all in" (141–42).

One time the Olympia band was hired to play a parade "for the Tremé Sports, one of the city's wildest, baddest marching clubs" (143). When gunfire erupted around Sancton as they marched, the other musicians tried to reassure him that violence among local gangs was a common occurrence in Tremé, but that it rarely involved the musicians themselves (146–47). But as the hours passed and the "second liners" and the musicians themselves grew increasingly inebriated—the parades in the intense New Orleans heat were accompanied by frequent beer breaks at the local bars—Sancton experienced an increasing sense of vulnerability, a feeling reinforced by a musician's warning to him not to "hang around the bar when the musicians leave. You go on home, you hear me? This ain't your neighborhood" (149).

Sancton's anxiety was not misplaced; as he left the bar, two drunken young men confronted him, demanding to know the contents of his clarinet case. To Sancton's reply, one of them identified himself as the nephew of the clarinetist and saxophonist Israel Gorman, insisting, "I bet he play better than you" (149).[25] Sancton attempted to ingratiate himself with the young men, declaring that he knew Gorman and "even had one of his records," but his words only served to inflame his antagonists, one of whom accused him of lying—"You don't know nothin' about no motherfuckin' record" (149).

In response, Sancton took out his clarinet and played Gorman's solo on a recording of "St. Louis Blues" by heart, even attempting "to imitate Gorman's shrill, eerie tone." The performance had its intended effect: the young man's expression softened as he declared, "You proved yo'self, man. You sure did. Ain't gotta say another word." Offering Sancton "a high five," he referred to him as his "soul brother, baby—even if you *is* the wrong color'" (149, emphasis in original). Sancton's apparent good humor in the face of this challenge to his cultural authority is notably different from the response of some other white jazz autobiographers to their interracial experiences; rather than becoming defensive, he turns immediately to a consideration of New Orleans pervasive and systemic racism, detailing the destruction of Tremé—"the heart of the city's jazz and Creole culture"—in the late 1960s as a result of decisions made by greedy and corrupt city officials (149).

With these comments, Sancton acknowledges the discrimination that has stymied efforts toward a more democratic and just society in his native city. In many respects, his response here is consistent with his descriptions of his relationships with the old musicians, descriptions that reveal his empathy for their hard lives and respect for their perseverance and humanity. But the goodwill and empathy that Sancton displays cannot, of course, eliminate the gulf that exists between him—with his life of privilege and boundless opportunity—and "the mens," whose lives are played out against the backdrop of racism and deprivation. At times, as Sancton is forced to admit, the legacy of Southern history casts its long shadow over his relationships with the musicians.

On one such occasion, the Creole musician Albert Burbank offered to take him and the German trombonist Frank Naundorf to his "fishing camp on the north shore of Lake Pontchartrain" (238–39). Burbank took enormous pride in his ability as a fisherman, and he spent a long day with the youngsters, at the end of which they had a generous haul of crabs that Burbank prepared to cook in a large tub (140). As Sancton and Naundorf watched the crabs die in the mixture of boiling water and "Zatarain's spicy crab-boil," Naundorf, in a snide aside to Sancton, remarked on its resemblance to Dresden. Burbank interpreted Naundorf's "sardonic smile" as evidence of his derisive attitude toward Creole culture and later expressed his anger over the incident to Sancton. "We live kinda rough over there," he admitted, "but we ain't no low-lifes. That tub was clean. Weren't nothin' wrong with them crabs, man" (141). Sancton tried to explain Naundorf's reaction, but Burbank "didn't want to know about Dresden. We had insulted him, scorned his hospitality, and hurt his Creole pride" (241).

Sancton's experience with Burbank is a poignant demonstration of the opportunities that interracial contact provides for the historical wounds of racism to open and fester, no matter the goodwill of the parties involved. Despite Sancton's many successes in crossing cultural boundaries, he would always be to some degree an interloper, an earnest white kid with a passion for learning jazz and the cultural traditions from which it sprang. That he would choose for the most part to highlight the positive aspects of his own and his family's experiences with the old musicians is hardly surprising, nor his insistence that the respect and admiration went both ways and sprang from shared values and beliefs.

Yet Sancton's implicit claim that the bonds between his family and "the mens" trumped racial and cultural difference at times strains credulity. Sancton insists that his father's closeness with the old musicians was not simply "the knee-jerk rhetoric of a political liberal" but because of "a sense of shared poverty and precariousness"; in his father's words, "I've lived in jeopardy all my life. And that is the real basis of my brotherhood with the men" (231). By the standards of an educated white Southerner of his day, Sancton Sr. did indeed live a precarious and impoverished life, but one that was a direct result of his own decisions and choices. For the black New Orleans musicians of his generation, "choice" was a far more restricted concept that did not include opportunities for fellowships at Harvard or respectable positions as editors and journalists.

And what of Sancton's choices and possibilities for his own life and career? Unlike most of the other jazz autobiographers in this study, Sancton claims that he did not have a single-minded desire to pursue a career as a professional jazz musician. Although music was his "passion," he was also a gifted and engaged student, and he shared his father's desire that he would end up at an Ivy League school and follow a more secure path "even as [he] dreamed of becoming a great jazz musician" (264). In 1967, he went to Harvard and then to Oxford as a Rhodes Scholar, where he completed his PhD in history before embarking on a highly successful career as a writer, editor, and foreign correspondent for *Time* magazine; in doing so, he admits that he was "fulfilling, perhaps unconsciously, the career that my father had abandoned to write his novels" (289).[26] Significantly, for twelve years, Sancton stopped playing music, but since then he has toured and recorded extensively in the United States and Europe with traditional New Orleans–style jazz bands (289).[27]

Being There: Experiencing New Orleans's Jazz Culture Firsthand

It is significant that Sancton has continued to perform regularly in his hometown, consistent with his declaration early in his narrative that the city itself is the thread—"the central player"—of his narrative (9). His intimate and detailed descriptions of New Orleans—its neighborhoods, its climate, the cultures and languages and worldviews of its residents—form a significant aspect of his memoir and stand in sharp contrast to Bob Wilber's geographical and cultural distance from New Orleans.

I noted earlier that Sancton emphasizes the rarity of his experience in black and Creole New Orleans communities, explaining that he "was about the only white middle-class kid of my generation who came from within the local culture" (108).[28] These comments come in the context of his discussion of the "jazz pilgrims," the young white musicians who came to New Orleans from every corner of the world, driven to experience the "Mecca of traditional jazz," moved—like Sancton—"to come drink at the source, learn firsthand from the old sages, practice the rites of initiation, and in time, pass the flame along to others" (104).[29] Sancton's depiction of his own authenticity as a New Orleans-style jazz musician is hugely invested in this "origins" narrative: his own history of learning the music and culture of New Orleans directly from the source and over a long period of time, and the ways these experiences (along with his family's influence) shaped his attitudes and perceptions about race and interracialism in and beyond the jazz world.

Yet his status as a local person, Sancton suggests, grants him a privileged relationship to the music and culture of "the mens," akin to that of "an Afrikaner boy from Johannesburg" going "to a black village to learn tribal drumming." Although a foreigner would also be capable of learning in that environment, "a white kid born within the system would see things differently—and be seen differently by his black teachers" (108). Echoing the explanation offered by Wilber and other white jazz autobiographers of the racial composition of traditional jazz enthusiasts at midcentury, Sancton notes that few young black New Orleanians came to Preservation Hall during "the dawn of Black Power," viewing the old music as "degrading, servile, Steppin Fetchit stuff. . . . For reasons that are as understandable as they are regrettable, they cut themselves off from their own heritage" (108–9). In light of this, he argues, the old New Orleans musicians were grateful for the attention of young whites, from wherever they came, who expressed an interest in the jazz tradition. "By default, perhaps, but with the fervor of converts, we became the anointed keepers of the flame" (109).[30]

Sancton returns to this imagery near the end of his memoir, when he recounts his move back to New Orleans in 2007 and the opportunities he found for playing traditional jazz, including a regular gig at his old haunt,

Preservation Hall (314). In a passage saturated with nostalgia, Sancton attempts to explain and to justify his role in carrying on the New Orleans jazz tradition. He notes his feelings of surprise to find himself seated "on the bandstand, possibly on the same chair George [Lewis] occupied the first night I heard him," and to realize that the audiences were now "looking at me and my fellow bandsmen. The torch has been passed. Now *we* are the mens" (315, emphasis in original).

Here, as elsewhere, Sancton interrupts his account to examine the racial implications of the situation he is describing. The idea that he had now come to think of himself and his bandsmen as "the mens," he admits, at first "seemed absurd, almost sacrilegious":

> How could I possibly claim to be an authentic New Orleans jazzman? I was a white, middle-class boy who went to an elite college in the North, spent more than half his adult life in France, and never even made his living as a full-time musician. The lessons with George, the sessions with Punch Miller, the parades and funerals with Harold Dejan's brass band—all that was a long way back. (315)

As in the passage described earlier, when Sancton defended his family's attitudes toward the old musicians against his girlfriend's charges, his self-questioning here seems largely rhetorical, providing him with another opportunity to reflect on his relationship to the New Orleans jazz tradition. "If the old men embraced me as an aspiring musician," he suggests, "it was not just to humor a young white boy. They were preparing a succession, someone to carry on the tradition when they were gone." For that reason, it was not simply Sancton's "right but a duty to take what they gave me and hand it on, just as they had passed it down from an earlier generation of jazzmen" (315).

In this passage, as in many others that I have examined in this chapter, Sancton foregrounds both race and place in a formula that looks something like this: the New Orleans jazz tradition was developed and nurtured within the African American and Creole communities of New Orleans; Sancton was mentored by some of the leading musicians from these communities; Sancton derives his own sense of authenticity from his proximity to the people and the place at the center of jazz history.[31] In many respects, these views resemble those posited by Joseph Matthews "Wingy" Manone, another New Orleans jazz musician and autobiographer. Half a century before Sancton began sitting in with Lewis and "the mens" at Preservation Hall, Manone was busy learning to play jazz in the vibrant, multiracial, and multicultural neighborhoods of New Orleans, an experience that he details in his 1948 autobiography, *Trumpet on the Wing*, as he offers his own perspective on race and place in early twentieth-century New Orleans.

Tom Sancton, with Sammy Rimington (left) and Dr. Michael White, in a tribute to George Lewis at the 2008 Jazzfest in New Orleans. Photo by Julian Sancton, used with permission of Tom Sancton.

"Those Colored Boys across the Levee... Really Taught Me to Play": "Wingy" Manone's New Orleans's Jazz Experience

If Sancton's memoir may be characterized by its careful attention to historical, cultural, and geographical specificity, Joseph Matthews "Wingy" Manone's *Trumpet on the Wing* (1948) is by contrast impressionistic and breezy, its vernacular, anecdotal style seemingly aimed at jazz lovers in search of kicks from an authentic, jive-talking New Orleans jazzman. Topics such as Jim Crow, the cultural traditions of black New Orleans, and highbrow versus lowbrow attitudes toward music learning are all present in *Trumpet on the Wing*, but more often through hints and allusion than commentary or analysis. Manone (1900–1982),[32] who was given his nickname after he lost his right arm in a streetcar accident in New Orleans when he was a child, has little to say about himself as an ethnic minority in New Orleans's early jazz communities; he refers to himself as "of Italian descent" but does not mention his Sicilian heritage, and his discussion of the neighborhood where he grew up and other parts of the city where he rambled during his childhood is evocative but notably short on detail (Manone 14–15, 18).[33] We learn that his father, Vincent Mannone, was a fruit distributor on the docks in New Orleans and that his mother's name was Rosie Lopez, although he gives no details about her family background (10).

Manone was born and raised in New Orleans, but by the early 1920s he was traveling widely in search of playing opportunities and would never again live for any extended period in his hometown.[34] Whereas Sancton's narrative focuses almost entirely on his life in New Orleans, Manone's account of his

Wingy Manone, posing in the office of the famed jazz photographer William P. Gottlieb. New York, between 1946 and 1948. William P. Gottlieb/Ira and Leonore S. Gershwin Fund Collection, Music Division, Library of Congress.

New Orleans childhood comprises only the first few chapters of his memoir. There is nonetheless a remarkable "likeness" in their perspectives on the musical and cultural traditions of black New Orleans, which they depict as a source of deep spiritual nourishment and as central to the development of their own musical personas.

In "Stars of David and Sons of Sicily: Constellations beyond the Canon in Early New Orleans Jazz," Bruce Raeburn traces the contribution of Jewish and Italian musicians to the early development of jazz in New Orleans (124). In part, his essay is a response to Michael Paul Rogin's contention that "racial 'cross-dressing' enabled Jewish immigrants such as Al Jolson to become 'white,' and therefore 'American,' via blackface" (124). By contrast, Raeburn stresses the development of "neighborhood-based jazz scenes" in New Orleans in order to "explore an alternative model by which Jews and Italian-Americans (as well as Latinos and Afro-French Creoles) were able to create

'American' identities for themselves by assimilation to black vernacular musical practices through jazz" (124).[35]

Raeburn situates his discussion of ethnic minorities in early twentieth-century New Orleans jazz through a detailed analysis of patterns of settlement within the city's mixed neighborhoods, in which the "multi-cultural demographic conditions . . . created opportunities for interaction among those who were receptive to experimentation across racial and ethnic boundaries" ("Stars of David" 126). Manone grew up in one such neighborhood, the Irish Channel, an "uptown, mostly white working-class community" that Charles Hersch notes produced "many important white jazz musicians" and fostered "interracial interactions centered on jazz" (*Subversive Sounds* 83). Notably, Manone makes no mention of the Irish Channel in his autobiography; rather, he claims to have lived with his working-class Italian family "near the French Quarter, and Storyville, where jazz was born in the houses of joy, wasn't far from our house" (Manone 10–11). Manone's claim here likely serves a mythologizing function, linking him to the black neighborhoods so closely associated with the origins of jazz.

Perhaps it might more accurately be said of Manone that all of New Orleans was his playground, an impression confirmed by his declaration that he and his friends "were all over town—'back o' town' (which was north of Rampart Street), 'uptown,' 'downtown,' and 'front o' town' (where the river ran)" (17). Manone's ebullience and love of adventure emerge in his descriptions of his exploration of the streets and back alleys of New Orleans, his fishing trips to Lake Pontchartrain, and his feats as a swimmer (17–18). The festivals, cooking and eating, music and dance that Raeburn notes as a prominent aspect of daily outdoor life in New Orleans's racially and ethnically mixed neighborhoods are described in vivid detail by Manone, who emphasizes the cross-cultural contact that these interactions provided. He recalls the tradition of the fish fry, in which the host would hang "a red lantern" to indicate "a fish fry was going on and everybody was welcome," and where "[e]verybody would be happy, eating that delicious fish and doing the mess-around to the jamming of some neighborhood cats" (18). The African influences of "the mess-around" are obvious in Manone's description of "a kind of dance where you just messed around with your feet in one place, letting your body do most of the work, while keeping time by snapping your fingers with one hand and holding a slab of fish in your other" (18).

Manone also describes his participation in the "second line" that followed along when there was "a party, a parade, or a funeral going on"—or, in his evocative language, a "planting party"—and where he "caught that righteous jazz. For they really played jazz at funerals, and no foolin'" (19). A rite of passage for him was his transition from "tagging along with the second line" to participating, "[a]s I got older, and played better, . . . in that second line myself" (22). Less formal experiences also brought him in close contact with African American musical traditions, including the "hollers" of the "blackberry woman" and the "crawfish boys" he heard in the French Quarter (see Sancton's account of the "blackberry woman" earlier in this chapter), and the singing of the "colored boys who toted the girders" when Manone worked "as water boy on a grain-elevator construction job" (11, 24).

It is notable, however, that Manone's stories of his music learning also highlight the daring and transgressive impulses that led him in search of the black music traditions of New Orleans. He studied cornet when he was eight years old with a woman who tried to teach him "the rudiments," but before the year was up, he told her, "I would like to take you someplace and let you hear the kind of stuff I want to learn" (12). His teacher agreed, so Manone "took her way up on the river in New Orleans, and we went across on the other side of the levee. . . . When we got there I showed her all the colored people, waitin' to hear some music. We were the only two white people in about a thousand colored folks" (12–13).

Although the music was beyond the understanding of his teacher—she referred to the black musicians as "a bunch of fakers" because they played by ear—Manone challenged her to admit that "it sounds good, don't it?" His teacher reluctantly agreed, adding that if he wanted to learn music that was "not in the book," she would "disown" him (13). Manone's replied that she "better start disownin', 'cause I done took my last lesson" (13). With this experience came the realization that the music education that really mattered would come from "those colored boys across the levee . . . who really taught me to play" (13).

The scene that Manone depicts here is not one of interracial immersion but rather one of cautious and respectful observation; although "white folks" were not welcome, his presence was tolerated "as long as I stayed on the boundary line. . . . So I picked my spots to stand on" (13). Manone's description supports Hersch's observation that "[o]utdoor performance—'the street as theater'"— was critical to the development of early jazz in New Orleans, providing "white ethnic groups like Sicilians and Jews" exposure to musical traditions across the color line. "Not only did a variety of races and classes hear the music, they often listened in close proximity to one another" (Hersch, *Subversive Sounds* 79).

Manone's account of his experience "on the other side of the levee" also exemplifies Raeburn's contention that New Orleans's Italian Americans in the early years of the twentieth century were experiencing the same kind of generational conflicts over competing cultural traditions—European versus vernacular African American—as were the city's Creoles ("Stars of David" 146). In his stories, Manone frequently conveys his pride in his skills as an "ear" player and improviser and his disdain for reading music notation or for formal music schooling more generally—this even as his impulse to explore beyond the cultural traditions of his own Sicilian American community contributed to tensions within his own family (Manone 27–28).

Yet Manone's multicultural outreach did not erase his sense of proprietorship regarding his own community; he recalls that he and his pals would hurl rocks at Louis Armstrong and Zutty Singleton when they rode by on their bicycles "delivering for Max Sampson's drugstore. . . . Of course, when we got into Louis's or Zutty's territory they rocked us too, and I don't mean with music" (19).[36] Territorial, rather than racial or ethnic, tensions seem to be at play here; on the whole, Manone conveys his considerable ease with interracial mixing, both during his childhood and later as a professional musician. Raeburn credits him with participating in an integrated recording session on August 15, 1934, "made nearly a year before the oft-cited Benny Goodman Trio sides that supposedly shattered the color line in jazz" ("Stars of David" 150).[37]

Manone describes his developing personal friendship with Armstrong when the two were in Chicago in the late 1920s, recalling that Armstrong invited him and Art Hodes "to latch onto some barbecue with him" after they had come to hear him play at an after-hours joint (Manone 62–63) and that, on another occasion, he and Earl Hines accompanied Armstrong to a music store when Armstrong was in the market for a new trumpet (63–64). Although he offers no explicit commentary about these friendships in relation to his own self-identity as an ethnic minority, there is evidence that he was driven by a strong sense of class-consciousness that was established early in his interactions with other working-class residents of New Orleans and that these attitudes remained even after he became a famous and successful jazz musician. An illustration of these attitudes may be found in the passage discussed earlier, in which Manone conveys his delight at participating in the Friday night fish fries. "Of course, this was poor folks' fun," he comments. "If you wanted to see Mr. and Mrs. Society Stuff, you hung around the corner of Baronne and Canal streets" (19).

Bruce Raeburn, in agreement with other critics, suggests that the precarious social position of Louisiana's minority populations in the early jazz period had a significant effect on their relationships with the local Creole and African American populations. "Under segregation," he notes, "Sicilians, Jews, and Latinos could be perceived as marginally white," especially those raised in the "crazy quilt" neighborhoods where "parochial cultural eccentricity [blended] with racial ambiguity"; the result of this was "more fluidity of social interaction than was possible between black and white polar extremes under segregation" ("Stars of David" 133, 140–41). Central to his argument, then, is the evidence that "both jazz and racism created incentives that brought Sicilians and blacks together" (137).[38]

Perhaps no Sicilian-American jazz musician from New Orleans was more closely identified with black culture than was the trumpeter-bandleader Louis

Prima, who came from the downtown neighborhood of Tremé, where he absorbed the style of the black and Creole musicians there (Raeburn, "Stars of David" 133). Raeburn sees compelling similarities between Prima and Manone: both became jazz celebrities when they moved away from New Orleans, thus "serving as cultural ambassadors for New Orleans attitudes and eccentricities in much the same way that Louis Armstrong did" (150–51). Moreover, like Prima, Manone "recognized the benefits" of both his "Italian heritage" and "the black vernacular" in his persona as a professional musician (151). A clear illustration of this was Manone's "jive talk," which was an important aspect of his public persona and which he insists originated "in New Orleans, on bawdy Basin Street" (Manone 143). Clearly relishing his role as cultural interpreter, he explains that "[p]eople kept writing into the papers asking for an interpretation, and finally I gave a reporter an interview and set him straight on the meaning of 'git-box,' 'riff,' 'killer-diller,' 'lick,' and words that are now well known to anybody except a square from Delaware" (143). According to Manone, his "way of talking soon began to be imitated by others" (144).

Patrick Burke examines Prima's and Manone's engagements at the Famous Door and other Fifty-Second Street clubs beginning in the mid-1930s, crediting them with extending "notions of authentic black music prevalent among 52nd Street's original circle of white musicians" (Burke 10, 41–51). Burke, like Raeburn, emphasizes the racial malleability of these Italian American jazz musicians, suggesting that "Manone's popularity, like Prima's, was linked to his ability to perform a black identity while still remaining acceptably 'white'" (51). The central influence for both men was undoubtedly Louis Armstrong, an influence that Burke detects in their instrumental, vocal, and rhythmic styles, as well as in their blending of hot New Orleans-style polyphony and Tin Pan Alley repertoire (42–44, 50). Burke suggests that Manone's and Prima's racial ambiguity—an ambiguity that encompassed their physical appearance and mannerisms as well as their speaking and singing styles—allowed audiences "to safely indulge" their fantasies about black male sexuality (48).[39] As evidence of Manone's racial ambiguity, Burke refers to a 1935 article in *Down Beat* that details Manone's marriage to a woman who waged a bet with her sister that Manone was not black. "In the end," Burke concludes, "although Manone was unambiguously 'white' enough to settle a bet, his performances alluringly exceeded the supposedly definite boundaries of fixed racial categories" (51).[40]

As stated earlier, Manone was one of a large number of musicians to leave New Orleans in the teens and 1920s. By the mid-1930s, he had become a "jazz celebrity" in New York with his hit recording "The Isle of Capri" (Raeburn, "Stars of David" 150; Burke 50–51), but he never forgot his New Orleans roots or his veneration for the black musicians, particularly Louis Armstrong, who had such a profound influence on his own musical persona (Hodes 21). In *New Orleans Style and the Writing of American Jazz History*, Bruce Raeburn proposes an argument for viewing the early jazz of New Orleans as "the functional music of a people and a place, not blacks or whites but Orleanians, which replaces racial explanations with cultural and environmental ones" (43). This is perhaps another way of stating the "race and place" emphasis that I observed in Sancton's analysis of his own experience with the music and culture of New Orleans and that also emerges in Manone's account, in which the musical influences of his hometown are just one aspect of a broader cultural immersion that shaped his views in and beyond the musical sphere.

It is from the perspective of a New Orleans cultural insider that Manone describes his experience of watching Louis Armstrong's performance in the 1932 Paramount short film *A Rhapsody in Black and Blue* in a Chicago movie theater. Manone begins the story by explaining a New Orleans tradition about which he clearly assumes his readers would be unfamiliar: "Down in New Orleans," he writes, "whenever a cat buys himself a new garb, he goes down on the main drag so everybody will see it. He doesn't say nothin', but struts up and down with his thumb hooked under the lapel of his coat, so everybody will catch on that he has a fine new suit" (Manone 127).

In the movie, Armstrong, who was outfitted in "a tiger skin, and wearing a hat with horns on it," began to sing "Shine," the popular 1910 "plantation song" by Ford Dabney and Cecil Mack (Raeburn, "I'll Be Glad" 67), "and when he got to the part about being 'all dressed up in the latest style,' he stuck his thumb under the lapel of that tiger skin and started to strut" (Manone 127). Manone, who got the cultural reference immediately, "laughed so much" that he was kicked out of the theater. The other members of the audience also began to laugh, but as Manone points out, "they didn't dig" (127). When Manone tried, without success, to explain the joke to the theater manager, he concluded that "it was one of those private jokes that you have to be hipped to, to dig" (127).

Critics have noted Armstrong's subversion of white racism in this early film through the sheer brilliance of his musical performance, his powerful masculinity and sexuality, and his masterful deployment of black vernacular practices such as signifying.[41] Manone's story conveys his understanding of these elements of Armstrong's performance; moreover, it illustrates the degree to which his sense of himself as a New Orleans jazz musician is bound not just to the music but also to the *customs* of New Orleans (Raeburn, "Stars of David" 126). From Manone's perspective, the music and the customs are intertwined and inseparable, and they work together to produce an authentic New Orleans jazz personality. Although he lived for a time in Chicago and New York, he admits in his autobiography that he would return to New Orleans "[w]henever I am sad or brought down" (Manone 98).[42] His book ends on this note of homage to his hometown, in particular to the black music of New Orleans as the foundation from which his own playing sprang: "I ain't never been sorry that I went up over the levee and listened to the only kind of music that's really solid, and caught it. And kept on playin' it all my life" (239).

Manone's experience in New Orleans in the early decades of the twentieth century provides our first glimpse of the impact of black cultural practices on the lives of second-generation Americans—that is, the children of southern and eastern European immigrants who were arriving in the United States by the thousands from the end of the nineteenth century. The next chapter continues the exploration of white-ethnic jazz autobiographers with a focus on four Jewish American jazz musicians who, like Manone, found their way into American culture through jazz.

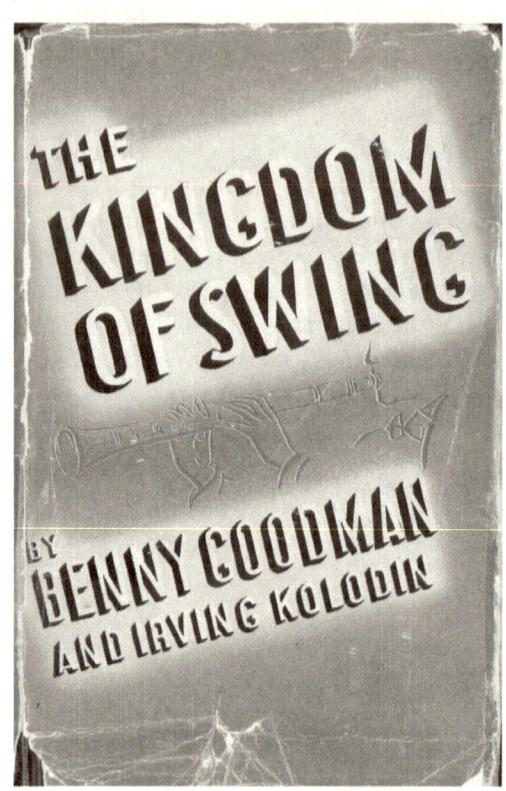

First edition of *The Kingdom of Swing* (1939), by Stackpole Sons, and the Armed Services Edition published the same year. A Horatio Alger tale for Goodman's jitterbug fans at home and abroad.

Eddie Condon, musician and raconteur. First edition of *We Called It Music* (1947), published by Henry Holt.

Tracing the path from Arthur Arshawsky to Artie Shaw. 1992 Fithian Press reprint, originally published by Farrar, Straus, and Young (1952).

A jazz life, starring Max Kaminsky and an interracial cast. Harper and Row first edition, 1963.

The swing bandleader, Charlie Barnet. His collaborator, Stanley Dance, emphasized Barnet's progressive stance on race and the African American influences that shaped his style. 1992 Da Capo Press reprint, originally published by Louisiana State University Press, 1984.

Beginning in the 1980s, university presses accelerated the publication of jazz autobiographies, hoping to preserve the life stories of aging jazz musicians. The autobiographies of Bud Freeman (1989) and Art Hodes (1992), published by University of Illinois Press, exemplify this trend.

Steve Jordan, a master of the rhythm guitar. University of Michigan Press, 1991.

Bob Wilber's conflicted tale of a jazz life lived at a distance from the tensions of interracialism he describes. MacMillan Press, 1987.

Without Laurie Pepper, there would be no *Straight Life*, a searing coauthored autobiography of the great saxophonist, Art Pepper. 1994 Da Capo Press reprint, originally published by Schirmer Books, 1979.

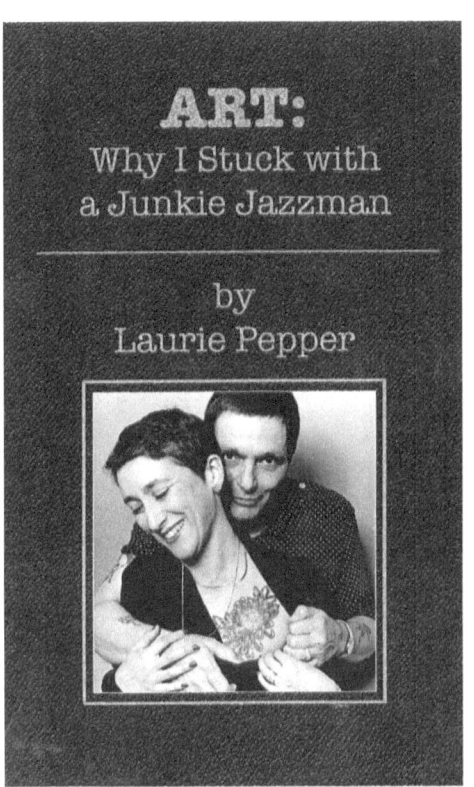

Laurie Pepper's moving account of her relationship with Art Pepper and her own experiences as a jazzwoman. Arthur Pepper Music Corporation. Cover photo of Laurie and Art Pepper by Phil Bray, courtesy of Laurie Pepper.

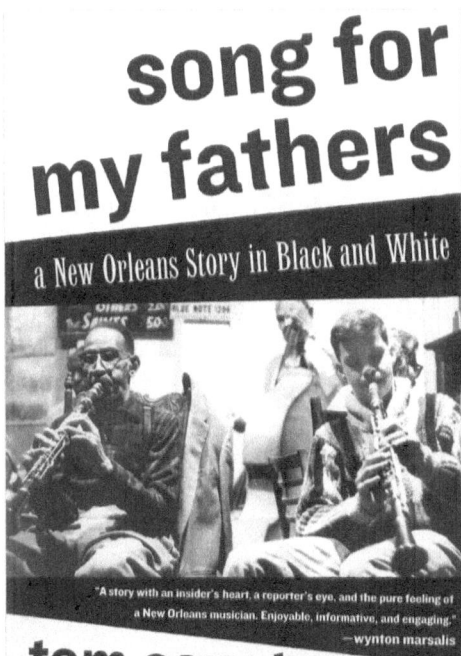

Bringing jazz autobiography into the twenty-first century: Tom Sancton's passionate meditation on race and jazz culture in the highly segregated New Orleans of the 1950s and 1960s. Other Press, 2010.

4

Representations of Identity in Jewish Jazz Autobiography

This chapter examines the autobiographies of Artie Shaw, Benny Goodman, Mezz Mezzrow, and Max Kaminsky, focusing on their portraits of their complex and multifaceted identities as second-generation Jewish Americans whose lives and careers brought them into close contact with African American music and society. In many respects, these autobiographies offer a particularly rich palette for comparison: all four autobiographers were born within about a decade of one another—from the end of the nineteenth century to the close of the first decade of the twentieth—during a period in which Jewish Americans were considered, as Karen Brodkin notes, "'not-quite-white,' 'not-bright-white,' or perhaps 'conditionally white'" (Brodkin 60).[1] All four were the children of Russian Jewish immigrants who had come to America in the 1880s and 1890s, settling eventually in urban centers—Mezzrow's and Goodman's families in Chicago, Shaw's on New York's Lower East Side, and Kaminsky's in Brockton, Massachusetts and then Roxbury, a Boston neighborhood.[2] With the exception of Mezzrow, whose family was middle class, the others were all from working-class families who struggled to stay afloat with the types of low-wage, often menial occupations available to them as newly arrived eastern European immigrants.

It is no great surprise, then, that these autobiographers expend considerable energy recounting childhoods in which their experience of being Jewish and living at a distance—both geographically and psychologically—from Protestant white America seems central to their identity formation. And yet the language and imagery of these texts suggests that their identities are far from fixed or static; that their intense focus on themselves as ethnic Jews—as "other"—is complemented by, or even in some instances replaced by, a more general self-identification as "white," and then, to varying degrees, by a longing to be black, or at least to experience immersion in African American culture. This process is facilitated by their experiences of city life and their attraction to jazz music and the jazz nightlife—all of which exposes them to the racial, ethnic, and socioeconomic diversity of American life.

Over the past two decades, scholars of Jewish and whiteness studies have made important contributions to our understanding of the historically fluid and mutable concepts of race, ethnicity, and whiteness in the United States, including the changing ways in which Jewish Americans—along with other European immigrants—were designated and designated themselves with respect to whiteness, and the implications of that designation on relationships between Jews and African Americans. In *How Jews Became White Folks and What That Says about Race in America*, Brodkin suggests that

> the history of Jews in the United States is a history of racial change that provides useful insights on race in America. Prevailing classifications at a particular time have sometimes assigned us to the white race, and at other times have created an off-white race for Jews to inhabit. Those changes in our racial assignment have shaped the ways in which American Jews who grew up in different eras have constructed their ethnoracial identities. (1)[3]

Although the historical record provides important context by which to consider accounts of self-identity by these Jewish jazz autobiographers, it is instructive to listen for the ways in which their individual voices both support and disrupt that record. For example, does Jewishness as a kind of racialized or "probationary" whiteness emerge in their descriptions of their immigrant families or neighborhoods or of themselves as children in the early years of the twentieth century? Do they convey an understanding of Jewishness as ethnicity—that is, as white according to the dominant black-white racial binary of the United States but as culturally distinct from mainstream Protestant whiteness? If so, to what degree might that reflect the mid-twentieth-century perspective from which they were writing and publishing their autobiographies?[4]

Michael Alexander (2001), Jeffrey Melnick (1999), and Eric Goldstein (2006) provide additional ways to consider a number of themes pertinent to this chapter, including relations between Jews and African Americans in large urban centers in the early decades of the twentieth century and the role of popular culture in facilitating and defining those relationships.[5] Yet in certain respects, their studies are at least as important for illuminating the differences between the "jazz age" figures who are their focus and the jazz musicians under discussion here, whose immersion experiences in black jazz culture were of a kind and degree generally unknown to the earlier generation. (Melnick does move into the jazz arena in his examination of Mezzrow and Shaw as white Negroes, a subject I will return to later in this chapter).[6]

It would be an error, however, to view these Jewish jazz musicians as thoroughly assimilated Americans with little or no connection to their Jewish identity. In the first place, the term "assimilation" in this context implies a move into white mainstream society, whereas the accounts of these Jewish jazz autobiographers illustrate as powerful a move into African American musical and cultural spheres. Moreover, as we will see, these musicians retained important, if ambivalent, connections to their Jewish heritage, connections that manifest themselves in their careers and personal lives. The critical point here is that Jewish musicians from the late 1920s and thereafter who were forging careers in "hot" jazz (as opposed to the popular, sweet bands of Paul Whiteman, Jean Goldkette, or Glen Gray's Casa Loma Orchestra, for example) were forced to negotiate African American musical and cultural spaces that the Jewish entertainers of the minstrel and vaudeville eras by and large were not. As a group, then, Jewish jazz autobiographers open a new path for exploration of second-generation Jewish Americans, with particular attention to their experiences in African American cultural environments.

An Unending Search for Identity: Artie Shaw's *The Trouble with Cinderella*

"My background was Russian Jewish," Artie Shaw—formerly known as Arthur Arshawsky—said in a radio interview late in his life. "I think blues has a great deal of affinity with the Jewish experience—as it did with the black experience. A minority group is very hip to what the blues are about" (qtd. in White 206). Shaw's apparent embrace of his Jewish identity here and his acknowledgement of its significance to his development as a musician is in stark contrast to the portrait he constructs in his 1952 autobiography, *The Trouble with Cinderella: An Outline of Identity*; as such, it offers important evidence of the turmoil and confusion that was Shaw's ultimate experience of identity and that is at the heart of his self-representation in his autobiography.

Shaw was an exceptional clarinetist as well as one of the most successful and respected bandleaders of the Swing Era. His 1938 recording of Cole Porter's "Begin the Beguine" catapulted him to the top ranks of popular music celebrity, and through the early 1940s he continued to turn out hit records and to command lucrative contracts. That period also marked the beginning of his close association with Hollywood, both as an actor and composer (he earned two Oscar nominations for Best Score and Best Song on the 1940 Fred Astaire film, *Second Chorus*) and through his tumultuous marriages to movie stars Lana Turner, Ava Gardner, and Evelyn Keyes, among others.[7] Contemptuous of fame and adoring audiences, Shaw walked away from the music business

Portrait of Artie Shaw in New York by William P. Gottlieb, between 1946 and 1948. William P. Gottlieb/Ira and Leonore S. Gershwin Fund Collection, Music Division, Library of Congress.

on several occasions; in 1954 he abandoned his performing career for the last time to dedicate himself to his writing and a wide range of other interests.[8]

Shaw drafted his autobiography between 1950 and 1952 while he was living on a farm in Pine Plains, New York. As an account of a life, *Cinderella* is more impressionistic than factual, with Shaw more concerned with exploring his inner state in the aftermath of his experience with psychoanalysis than with sharing details of his personal life and career. He offers, for example, little insight regarding his own jazz education, his interactions with the musicians in his band, other big band leaders, Billie Holiday (who toured with his band for nine months), or his views on jazz in the various periods about which he writes. Moreover, in contrast to many of the autobiographers in this study, he displays little interest in exploring the African American origins of jazz and his own relationship to that tradition.

Instead, Shaw begins with the story of Cinderella as a useful model for dissecting the failures of twentieth-century American capitalistic striving, in which happiness is a guaranteed consequence of a particular path of social and economic climbing. In personal terms, Shaw's own meteoric rise to fame and fortune as a big-band leader in the late 1930s seems to have had the opposite effect, leaving him both artistically unfulfilled and emotionally unstable; in his words, "the trouble with Cinderella . . . as a working concept for living . . . is that nobody lives happily ever after" (Shaw, *Cinderella* 6–7).[9] In Shaw's experience, success (which he spells $ucce$$—"to spell it the way I think makes more sense in this context") and happiness turn out not to be static concepts, but rather like the experience of "a dog chasing a locomotive" (8). His central concern in his autobiography is to make sense of his "own version of the Cinderella Myth," in which he played "the leading role" (14).

In Shaw's early childhood, his parents ran a small dressmaking business with several employees. After a brief period of prosperity, his family's fortunes took a downward turn; forced to declare bankruptcy, they decided to leave New York City in search of a "new start" (22–23). For Shaw, his family's move from the predominantly immigrant Lower East Side to the mainly "Anglo-Saxon Protestant" community of New Haven, Connecticut, forced him to confront his "otherness," precipitating an existential crisis from which, by his own account, he would never entirely recover (23).[10]

Shaw's introduction to anti-Semitism seems perhaps rather unremarkable: he was teased at school because of his foreign-sounding childhood surname (Arshawsky, which he first reveals in chapter 6) and his astonishment at seeing an anthill for the first time (his previous exposure to the insect world had consisted of a "diagram of an anthill" in his previous school and the cockroaches and bedbugs that cohabited the tenement houses in which his family lived) (27–31). Yet such was Shaw's sensitivity that these and other early experiences with anti-Semitism would leave "a deep and lasting scar" which "had more to do with shaping the course and direction of my entire life than any other single thing that has happened to me, before or since" (24, 26).[11]

As a consequence of these experiences, Shaw suggests that he "underwent certain inner changes resulting in tremendous drives toward conflicting goals" (38). One of these goals returns Shaw to his Cinderella theme, in which he was driven to achieve wealth, public adulation, and social prestige, while at the same time he experienced "an enormous need to *belong*, to have some feeling of roots, to become part of a community" (38, emphasis in original). By the time Shaw began attending New Haven High School, his deep feelings of alienation compelled him to seek refuge in the vaudeville shows at Poli's Palace Theatre in New Haven. He discovered ways to get in without paying and spent hours observing the entertainers on stage; one day a band took the stage, with a saxophonist up front. For Shaw, the saxophonist provided a model for the new life he had been seeking, "the ideal version of any Good Life I could imagine" (52–53, 56). His determination to learn the saxophone and later the clarinet involved a single-minded devotion and discipline over many years in which he practiced many hours every day, stopping only when he could no longer tolerate the aching discomfort in his teeth and lower lip "from the constant pressure of the mouthpiece and reed" (64).

Burton Peretti offers a compelling reading of Shaw's decision to become a musician, suggesting that it "had less to do with musical inspiration . . . than with the general ethnic passion to overcome marginality and to assimilate to what each immigrant's child perceived as being 'America'" (Peretti 90). In Shaw's case, his discomfort with his Jewishness came not only from his experiences of anti-Semitism, but also with the manifestations of Jewish ethnicity within his own family. He remembers his father as "a surly, disgruntled, and, on the whole, miserable man," with his heavy footsteps and strong Russian accent, and his "guttural Yiddish" that both frightened and fascinated him, so that he tried to "imitate the sound of it" (*Cinderella* 136). His father's intimidating physical presence stands in sharp contrast to his memory of his parents' relationship—both in their working and personal lives—as one in which his mother was dominating and capable, while his father seemed powerless and a failure (136). The imbalance in their relationship left Shaw with feelings of resentment toward his father, both for his failure to earn a livelihood and for the consequences of that failure for his mother, who worked day and night in order to support her family (137). As he admits, the move to New Haven only served to highlight "the contrast between [my father] and the fathers of other kids I knew. . . . Not only was he unable to make a living, not only did he not 'go to the office' as most other kids' fathers did, but now he became, by contrast with these other fathers, a 'foreigner'" (137).

The response of Shaw's parents to his music was also divisive: while his mother pushed him to study piano and was later tolerant of his obsessive practice regimen on saxophone (61), his father did not hide his contempt for what he regarded as a frivolous and self-indulgent pursuit, expressing approval only when his son, at age fourteen, won the first prize (and five dollars) at an amateur-night show. This, in Shaw's view, was due to his father's "grudging and cynical respect for anyone who had mastered the knack of picking up a dollar by any means whatsoever" (62). Although he later invited his son to play his "blower" for his cronies at their weekly pinochle game, his invitation seemed as much intended to ridicule his son's achievement as to praise it (136).[12] Over time, Shaw's fear of his father evolved "into a kind of rebellious dislike" that dominated their relationship until one day his father left his wife and son and moved to California (135).[13]

By the time he was fifteen, Shaw was experiencing such a degree of insecurity and shame regarding his Jewish identity that he decided to Americanize his name. His discussion of the implications of this name change is a vivid expression of his feelings of alienation from mainstream American culture and his desperate attempt to resolve those feelings:

> What makes the new personality? Well, take a good look at both those names. Then ask yourself whether a fellow named Art Shaw could possibly grow up to be "the same" as another kid named Arthur Arshawsky. . . . [T]he latter is obviously a Jewish kid, or at any rate some kind of a "foreigner," wouldn't you say?

As for this new kid we'll be dealing with from here on—let's see now.... Art Shaw. Doesn't *sound* very "foreign."... In short, an American kid—may as well let it go at that. (92, emphasis in original)[14]

Yet Shaw's continuing search for belonging remains a central theme of his narrative, even after he has shed the outward markings of his Jewish identity and remade himself as simply "an American kid" (92). When he joined a band of teenagers and discovered their hostility toward Jews, he attempted to pass as "Anglo-Saxon" until his feelings of guilt left the pretense unsustainable (95). In 1930, Shaw went on tour as a member of Irving Aaronson and his Commanders, a nationally recognized dance band. During the band's brief time in Chicago, he was drawn to the jazz world of Chicago's South Side, which he describes as "one of the foremost jazz conservatories in the world" (196). It is striking that this account, which occurs approximately halfway through Shaw's four-hundred-page autobiography, is his first real discussion of jazz, as well as his first mention of African American musicians.[15]

Every night after his job with the Aaronson band had ended, Shaw writes, he "would head for the Negro district to sit in with one of the colored bands" or to take part in sessions with other players who, like himself, "were making their living ... in 'respectable' bands, but who had to get away once in a while and 'play some jazz'" (197). It was these black musicians, as Shaw makes clear, who "were setting the pattern" while "the rest of the jazz musicians in the country were taking their lead" (198). Notably, as Shaw begins to write about himself in relation to the South Side musicians, his own self-identification seems to shift from that of ethnic-Jewish outsider to white American. Yet the shift is implied and indirect for Shaw never mentions his own race or ethnicity here, or that of the other Chicago players with whom he played. Instead, he simply names these players, and the order of his naming suggests that they are being distinguished along a black-white binary. Thus, he places himself—along with Jewish musicians Benny Goodman and Ben Pollack—in the same paragraph as Eddie Condon and Bix Beiderbecke, yet separated from his earlier mention of African American musicians Earl Hines, Louis Armstrong, and Jimmie Noone (196–97). Notably, when Shaw attempts to define what he and these other musicians were playing at these sessions, he emphasizes the national, rather than the racial, origins of the music: "It's a developing, living form of folk music, ... one of the few truly American contributions to music itself" (200).

Another search, when Shaw was barely out of his teens, took him to Harlem, where, in his words, he "found a friend" (223). The friend was Willie "the Lion" Smith, one of Harlem's best-known jazz pianists (see chapter 2 for Bob Wilber's account of his relationship with Smith).[16] In an autobiography that, to this point, has been striking for its sparse reference to the black jazz world, Shaw's lengthy description of his close relationship with Smith is particularly noteworthy.[17] Shaw made nightly trips to Pod's and Jerry's, the well-known

Representations of Identity in Jewish Jazz Autobiography 89

Willie "The Lion" Smith, master musician and teacher, in his Manhattan apartment, ca. Jan. 1947. William P. Gottlieb/Ira and Leonore S. Gershwin Fund Collection, Music Division, Library of Congress.

Harlem club where Smith held court. Although he initially describes Smith as "a Negro player," Shaw thereafter betrays a racial consciousness without explicitly mentioning race, instead referring to Smith's "dark fingers" as they "ran nimbly over the chipped yellow ivories at the keyboard" (224). Here, as earlier, Shaw frames his discussion within a black-white binary, observing that Smith was well-known "in colored musicians' circles" when they first met but relatively unknown to white jazz musicians, an observation clearly intended to illustrate his own insight and cultural hipness (224).

In his description of his musical experience with Smith, Shaw is deferential: Smith is the master, and the nineteen-year-old Shaw is the student who manages "a good bit of fumbling" in the learning process (227). There is an intensity and excitement in Shaw's account here that goes beyond any other musical experience he has described to this point, for not only was Smith a leading innovator of jazz harmony, but Shaw also found in his sessions "at Pod's and Jerry's ... the one thing I needed to fill in the emptiness of my life at that time, a sense of *belonging*—a feeling of being *accepted*" (227, emphasis in original).

Shaw's experience of belonging in a "little cellar joint" in Harlem offers a vivid contrast to his feelings of alienation and rejection, both within his own Jewish community and in the white Gentile world to which he claimed to aspire (223). According to Shaw, Smith admired his playing and would buy him drinks and breakfast when their all-night sessions ended. Occasionally, he even asked Shaw to accompany him to another session, where he would have Shaw take out his clarinet and play along with him, as if he were showing off a prized student to his friends. "Whenever I played something they approved of," Shaw writes, Smith "would look arrogantly over at them and announce, 'Tha's my boy—you hear that?'" (228).[18]

There is considerable irony in Shaw's friendship with Smith, whose biological father, Frank Bertholoff, was "part Jewish" (Nolan 36). As Smith explains in his autobiography, "I favored the Jewish religion all my life and at one time served as a Hebrew cantor in a Harlem synagogue. You could say I am Jewish partly by origin and partly by association" (Smith 12; Nolan 36).[19] Not only does Shaw omit any mention of Smith's connection to Judaism in his account of him in *Cinderella*, but he also maintains in a later interview that "Willie didn't know I was Jewish. I didn't tell him that," a claim that, in my view, ought to be viewed with some skepticism (Hentoff).[20]

Smith's acceptance of Shaw had a reverberating effect, and soon Shaw was meeting other Harlem musicians—experiences that caused a dramatic transformation in how he saw himself. Because of Smith's "sponsorship," he writes, "I was accepted among these Negroes and treated as one of them, and eventually came to feel more like a colored man myself than an 'ofay'" (*Cinderella* 228). His feelings were hardly surprising, Shaw insists, because he was in fact "living the life of a Negro musician, adopting Negro values and attitudes, and accepting the Negro out-group point of view not only about music but life in general. In fact, on the few occasions when I was forced to realize I was a white man, I used to wish I could actually *be* a Negro" (228, emphasis in original).

Shaw's claim—that his experience with Smith and the other black musicians he met in Harlem in 1929 was so powerful that he wanted to be black himself—is remarkable from someone who had previously been unsuccessful, by his own account, in finding comfort in any community to which he aspired to belong. Yet Shaw's flirtation with a black self-identity—at least as he presents it here—is far from convincing; unlike Mezz Mezzrow, for example, who made Harlem his home, Shaw seems to have spent only a brief time immersed in Harlem's jazz community. And although he remembers that time with wistful longing, his own words display the considerable gulf between his world and theirs.[21]

Among the most illuminating descriptions of this gulf is Shaw's anecdote about his relationship with drummer "Chick" Webb, whom he first met in Harlem. Years later, the bandleaders happened to be playing in Boston at the same time, and Webb began to show up to watch Shaw's band rehearse, at times even "sitting in 'just for kicks'" (229). After one rehearsal, according to Shaw,

> [Webb] came ambling over to me and said: "You know somethin', man? Some day I'm gonna be walkin' up the street one way and you gonna be comin' down the other way, and we gonna pass each other and I'm gonna say, 'Hello, best white band in the worl'' and you gonna say, 'Hello, best colored band in the worl'"—you know that?" (230).

The two of them shook hands, Shaw remembers, "almost as if we were entering into a solemn pact—and in a way, I suppose we actually were" (230). In his description here, as in his earlier ones about the South Side jazz musicians and Willie "the Lion" Smith, Shaw has submerged his Jewish identity beneath a generic, "no-name" whiteness—in this case, as the "white" bandleader, Artie Shaw.

But Shaw's search for a consistent presentation of a public "self" continued to elude him, even as he enlisted in the US Navy following the 1941 bombing of Pearl Harbor and in the following year led Navy Band 501—commonly known as Shaw's Navy Rangers—on a lengthy and grueling tour of the South Pacific. He returned to the United States at the end of 1943 suffering from posttraumatic stress disorder (or "combat fatigue," in the military's description)—for which he required hospitalization and received an honorable discharge from the navy (Simosko 103). For his patriotism and service, Shaw was greeted as a war hero, yet his account of his navy experience in *Cinderella* is, like so much of his autobiographical depiction, sketchy and impressionistic at best (14, 372–73).

Shaw's reticence in *Cinderella* is in notable contrast to the glowing accounts of his military service in the press and interviews that Shaw gave to journalists and to his various biographers after his return to the United States and in the decades following the publication of his autobiography (Simosko 99, 102). In these, images of patriotism abound, with descriptions of Shaw as an American eager and willing to serve his country and of the power of his music to comfort thousands of homesick soldiers longing for the familiar sights and sounds of home.[22] Yet these accounts also contain elements that serve as a check against a facile or unambiguous assessment of his military experience, including Shaw's cynical appraisal of upper-level military personnel—the "brass" as he refers to them—as well as his descriptions of the significant mental illness that beset him and other musicians.[23]

In a 1985 interview, Shaw portrays the bombing of Pearl Harbor as a transformational event for him, forcing to the surface previously untapped feelings of duty and patriotism that linked him to American democratic ideals of inclusion and fairness—"a version of American exceptionalism" that David Stowe has outlined as central to the ideology of swing and that emerges in the press coverage of Shaw (Stowe 73; Gross). Yet in May 1953, less than a decade after he returned home a war hero, he found himself forced to defend his patriotism before the House Un-American Activities Committee (HUAC) (Simosko 99). Although Shaw had been anticipating a subpoena during the time he was working on his autobiography, he makes no mention of the subject in the first edition of *Cinderella* (Nolan 275).

He abandons his reticence, however, in the Introduction to a 1979 edition of his autobiography (and reprinted in the 1992 edition that is my source), in which he offers an account of the specific personal circumstances and wider social and political context against which his autobiography took shape. Shaw explains that he was writing *Cinderella* during one of his many hiatuses from the music business when his life was abruptly upended by "the McCarthy plague" (*Cinderella* viii). In his account of these events, Shaw conveys his contempt and cynicism for the United States government from the Cold War through the Vietnam War and beyond. Describing Joe McCarthy as "good old Joe, the sterling Super-American," he reveals his own involvement with McCarthyism as "an invited guest" of HUAC and the dire ramifications of that experience on his life and career (vii–vii). Following his testimony before the committee, Shaw left the United States, spending several years in exile in Spain (viii–ix).

The cynical and defiant Shaw that appears here, as critics have noted, stands in sharp contrast to the patriotic and contrite figure that stood before HUAC in 1953.[24] In his live, televised testimony, Shaw directly linked his own war experience to his support for "leftist causes" in the period following his return home (Nolan 275). When the committee read from sworn statements accusing him of having attended "Communist Party branch meetings" and "Marxist classes," Shaw admitted that he had been—according to biographer Tom Nolan—"'absolutely misled' and 'hoodwinked' into attending some questionable gatherings" and had signed "political petitions and event endorsements" but that he had never knowingly "been a member of the Communist Party" (Nolan 276). On the verge of tears, Shaw professed his deep and abiding loyalty to America, referring to the opportunities it had provided him—"a minority member of a poor family" who had "come a long way" and who had experienced "a lot of love and a lot of affection" (277–78).

As the hearing ended, Shaw reached across the table to shake hands with the committee chairman, Harold H. Velde, a fiercely anti-Communist Republican congressman (White 148). The photograph that captured this moment was printed in *Time* magazine—"to some," according to Nolan, "a portrait of cooperation and reconciliation; to others, a snapshot of collaboration and capitulation" (Nolan 278).[25] John White has suggested that Shaw's dilemma in this period was that he "did not 'belong' in the increasingly conformist America of the early 1950s" (White 148). Yet if Shaw were at ease with his nonconformity, then why did he go to such lengths to prove his patriotism during his HUAC testimony? Beyond the obvious consequences that blacklisting would have had on his life and career, Shaw was deeply torn—as he reveals so clearly in *Cinderella*—between cynicism and nonconformity on the one hand, and a desperate need for success and recognition within mainstream America, on the other.

Indeed, the inherent contradictions and unresolved tensions that emerge in Shaw's accounts of his war experience and trials with McCarthyism are consistent with his autobiographical depiction of his elusive search for a self—for a stable and coherent identity that reflected the many influences that had shaped him. As the title of his autobiography suggests, at the time of publication, he was still searching, and portraits of Shaw that emerge in biographies and other sources suggest that his search continued until the end of his life. Shaw's inability to find a sense of permanence or security within any community—Jewish or Anglo-Protestant or African American; musical, literary, or military—leaves him as a figure of stark contradictions, a loner and outsider who enjoyed remarkable success as a jazz clarinetist and bandleader playing a highly interactive and communicative music.

Black and Jewish Blues: Mezz Mezzrow's *Really the Blues*

Like Shaw's *Cinderella*, Mezz Mezzrow's *Really the Blues* (1946) appears to tell a story of a Jewish jazz musician's attempt to transform his birth identity into something else. But if Shaw's attempt to replace his Jewishness with a "white" or "black" identity proved ultimately unattainable, Mezzrow's transformation to white Negroism has continued to dominate his critical reception. This is perhaps due in part to the claim of Mezzrow's collaborator, Bernard Wolfe, who, in his afterword to a 1972 edition of *Really the Blues*, stated that Mezzrow, after living in Harlem for many years, had actually come to believe that "his lips had developed fuller contours, his hair had thickened and burred, his skin had darkened.... He felt he had scrubbed himself clean ... of every last trace of his origins in the Jewish slums of Chicago ... and pressed himself into ... a pure Black" (Mezzrow 390).[26]

But while critics have interpreted *Really the Blues* as a "passing" narrative and a classic text in the literature of the "white Negro,"[27] they disagree about what Mezzrow claimed (or believed) regarding his quest to achieve the physiological or cultural attributes of blackness, as he defines them in his

Mezz Mezzrow, jamming with Albert Nicholas (clarinet) and Sy Sinclair (tuba) in New York, ca. January 1947. William P. Gottlieb/Ira and Leonore S. Gershwin Fund Collection, Music Division, Library of Congress.

text. Some stress Mezzrow's belief in his actual physical transformation, while others emphasize his displays of black identity beyond skin tone, such as his accent and use of African American vernacular. Others, however, argue that Mezzrow's representation of his transformation was largely metaphorical, symbolic of his close, personal identification with black culture and society.

For many critics, Mezzrow's Jewish identity is a crucial aspect of his white Negro experience; their concern, in other words, is not simply to chart Mezzrow's path from Jewish (or white) to black but to highlight the history of black-Jewish relations and "Jewish racial formation" in the United States during the early decades of the twentieth century as critical background for understanding the "passing" experiences of Mezzrow and other white Negroes (Melnick 95–119; Hersch, "Every Time" 259–82). Emphasizing the role that Jews played in "the history of white Negroism in the American twentieth century" (120), Jeffrey Melnick offers case studies of Mezzrow, Artie Shaw, and George Gershwin, focusing on their respective immersion experiences in "closed social space[s] defined almost exclusively by [their] racialness and maleness" (Melnick 123–24).[28] *Really the Blues*, in his view, holds out "the utopian possibility that Mezzrow's inherited (and usually scorned) Jewishness might harmonize with his acquired Blackness," resulting in what he describes as a "reconciliation of Jewishness and Blackness" (139). Maria Damon offers a more specific view of Mezzrow's relationship to his Jewishness, interpreting his immersion in African American music and society as a reaction to his own middle-class family's upward striving, rather than as an abnegation of his Jewishness, per se (Damon 155, 167).

Although I agree with Melnick's assertion that both Shaw and Mezzrow had "concrete immersion experiences which solidified their felt connections to African American culture," in my view, the differences between them are substantial and not fully explored in his analysis (Melnick 136). Unlike Mezzrow, Shaw never lived among African Americans; in fact, despite his endless musings on the psychological price of fame and fortune, his central associations seem to have been among the wealthy white elite of the American music, literary, and entertainment worlds. Melnick also points to Shaw's and Mezzrow's concern with exhibiting their knowledge of jive talk, yet, for the most part, Shaw aims for a highbrow literary style in *Cinderella* rather than the black vernacular on display in *Really the Blues*.[29] Furthermore, Melnick himself admits that while "Shaw's white Negroism was temporary, Mezz Mezzrow never surrendered his claims on Blackness" (137). Unless one wants to apply the term "white Negro" to all the musicians who describe—as part of their jazz education—some kind of immersion experience in black music and culture, then a more restricted application of the term might preserve its particular resonance.[30]

My own reading of Mezzrow's racial self-representation in *Really the Blues*, while informed by these other perspectives, seeks to makes sense of its fundamental malleability as well as the persistent irony that shapes his accounts of his racial experiences, particularly toward the end of his narrative. While many critics have acknowledged the fluidity of Mezzrow's self-representation (albeit from different perspectives),[31] the ironic aspects of Mezzrow's narrative have generally been overlooked. Although Mezzrow refers frequently to his desire to pass for black and his belief that he had indeed succeeded in that endeavor, there is no evidence in his narrative for the kind of physical transformation that Wolfe describes in his afterword; moreover, a detailed analysis of Mezzrow's self-representation must take into account his many references to himself as white or as Jewish, or as "a link between the races."[32] While Mezzrow's autobiography at times supports a metaphorical, rather than a literal, interpretation of his passing, just as often, he seems intent on disrupting that narrative, and in so doing he throws his entire self-representation into question.

In her trenchant analysis of Mezzrow's white Negro persona, Gayle Wald describes *Really the Blues* as "a passing narrative about the impossibility of passing" (Wald 71). Yet rather than viewing this as evidence of Mezzrow's failure to control his narrative, I want to propose that his unstable and contradictory autobiographical construction is deliberate and controlled and that the contribution of his collaborator, Bernard Wolfe, to this process deserves closer scrutiny. Earlier, I cited Scott Saul's persuasive argument for Wolfe's central role in shaping the text's language and attitudes.[33] Most critics, however, have glossed over Wolfe's contribution, naming him as Mezzrow's collaborator but then focusing almost exclusively on Mezzrow's role in the construction of his autobiographical persona. In her monograph on Wolfe, Carolyn Geduld struggles to make sense of the "literary context" of *Really the Blues*, finding evidence of "its flouting of genre as well as of race: biography and fiction (or, at least, fictive techniques) are combined, as Mezz tells his 'story,' and often it is impossible to distinguish truth from fantasy in the jazzman's recall" (Geduld 19).

What was Wolfe's role, then, in the convoluted narrative construction described by Geduld? If her confusion points to Wolfe's success in narrative disruption—specifically in complicating or embellishing representations of Mezzrow's attempts at (in Wald's words) "crossing the line"—his essays that comprise the afterword mentioned at the beginning of this section have a similarly disruptive effect; for example, when he describes Mezzrow's belief that he had experienced an actual biological transformation. Later in this discussion I will consider Wolfe's response to Mezzrow's tale of racial passing; in the meantime, as we consider Mezzrow's first-person account of his self-representation as Jewish, white, and black, we might pay special attention to the ways his own words contradict, or at least complicate, the very claims he is attempting to make.

"My Kind of People"

Mezzrow, born Milton Mesirow, in 1899, a decade before Shaw, rejected the middle-class respectability of his Jewish family—"loaded with doctors, lawyers, dentists and pharmacists"—for the street life of Chicago's Northwest Side, where he became part of a gang of tough Jewish boys looking for action (Mezzrow 5). In disputes between rival ethnic gangs, he explains, "[i]t took just a whispered 'kike' or 'Jew bastard' from a member of some rival Polish or Irish gang, and fists were flying between us" (6). At the same time, he recounts key childhood experiences that served to heighten his sensitivity toward African Americans. On one occasion, he brought his black friend, Sullivan, with him to his synagogue in Chicago, and, to Mezzrow's delight, the rabbi told Sullivan "that Moses, King Solomon, and the Queen of Sheba were all colored, and maybe the whole world was once colored" (18). He also writes about his experience in the aftermath of the Eastland Disaster of 1915, when he and his Jewish friends "hopped a freight to St. Louis" with photos of the disaster, intending to "pay our way by selling the pictures as we bummed around"

(17).³⁴ By the time they reached Cape Girardeau, Missouri, "dirty from riding the rails and dark-complexioned to begin with," they stopped at a lunch counter, where they were mistaken as African Americans and refused service (17–18). For the rest of their trip, Mezzrow recalls, "whenever we saw a sign saying 'Nigger don't let the sun shine on your head' we knew it meant us too, although we didn't know why" (18).

It would take a life-altering experience—Mezzrow's incarceration at Pontiac Reformatory when he was sixteen, after he was caught joyriding with a friend in a stolen car—for Mezzrow to begin to appreciate the connection between his own status as an often-despised ethnic minority and his intense identification with African Africans and their culture (Wald 65–66; Hersch, "Every Time" 273). At Pontiac, Mezzrow first heard the blues, sung by the black prisoners "in low moanful chants morning, noon and night," and learned to play the saxophone while playing in the reformatory's mixed band (Mezzrow 4). The strictly segregated cells and work details gave him his first taste of Jim Crow, and his account of a race riot between Southern white prisoners and an interracial gang with whom he associated shows his strong identification with the latter (15–16). Shortly afterwards, Mezzrow was hospitalized with dysentery, an illness that he links directly to his emotional response to the riot: "I felt so close to those Negroes, it was just like I'd seen a gang attack on my own family" (16).

As he returned home from Pontiac, Mezzrow found himself reliving his earlier experience in Cape Girardeau, when he and his Jewish friends had been "told we were Negroes. Now, all of a sudden, I realized that I agreed with them. . . . I not only loved those colored boys, but I was one of them . . . and I even got the same treatment they got" (18). At that moment, he decided that he would spend the rest of his life "sticking close to Negroes" and learning to play their music. "I was going to be a musician, a Negro musician, hipping the world about the blues the way only Negroes can." He went into the reformatory "green," he observes, but he "came out chocolate brown" (18).

Mezzrow's dramatic imagery has undoubtedly encouraged the tendency to focus on his subsequent musical and personal associations with African Americans, yet his account in *Really the Blues* shows him returning to his friends from Chicago's Jewish working-class community, "Jewish expressmen, cutters in the garment trade, cab drivers—easygoing guys who spent half their lives playing klabiasch, pinochle, and tarok," while at the same time he observed (at a distance) the more ambitious Jewish bootleggers and gamblers who made their fortunes during Prohibition (20–21). Mezzrow expresses his solidarity for his working-class friends, while the "bigtime gamblers and muscle men" provided him with "kicks" (21). Neither of these Jewish communities, however, provided a life model for Mezzrow, who, following his reformatory experience, had his sights firmly set on the vibrant early jazz and blues scene on Chicago's South Side (Wald 53).

Mezzrow's obsessive pursuit of black music and culture notwithstanding, his identity as a Jew remains an important part of his own self-representation as well as how others view him. In recounting his second incarceration, he describes himself as a target of abuse from the racist and anti-Semitic deputy warden, who remarks that "you Jews and niggers are always duckin' work" before assigning Mezzrow to hard manual labor (Mezzrow 35); later, Red, an African American prisoner whom he befriended, addressed him as "Jew kid": "The 'Jew kid' was me," Mezzrow writes, "and I didn't mind it at all, the way he said it" (42).

This passage seems to illustrate Maria Damon's argument that, in the early decades of the twentieth century, Jewish men frequently "resolved their anxieties about ethnicity and community by bonding with non-Jews of color"; in doing so, they were motivated not by "shame about their outcast status as Jews ... but rather [by] the sense that Jewish American culture, by assimilating upward, was abdicating the special role of critique available to social outsiders" (Damon 155). Mezzrow's identification with Red is one example of such bonding; just as the deputy warden links Jews and African Americans in his racist tirades, Mezzrow links himself with Red in their common struggle against oppression and in their striving for humanity (Mezzrow 35, 42).[35]

Mezzrow also tells stories in which he portrays orthodox Jews listening with empathy and understanding to the music of Blind Lemon Jefferson, Louis Armstrong, and Fats Waller (52, 202), but he rejects the notion that he should support "commercial" Jewish entertainers such as Al Jolson, Eddie Cantor, and Sophie Tucker in the interests of ethnic solidarity (49). "Around the poolroom I defended the guys I felt were my real brothers," he insists, "the colored musicians who made music that sent me" (49).

Certain patterns, then, become apparent in Mezzrow's discussion of his own Jewishness and of his relationship with the various Jewish communities and individuals he encounters along the way. His stories about his Jewish family reflect his critique of their upward assimilation, to borrow Damon's term, or portray them as stereotypically overprotective and emotional, or as unsympathetic toward his interest in music. His mother is the stereotypical "Jewish mother" who "cooked up a big pot of borscht for her returning hero," after Mezzrow had been rejected by the navy in 1918 because of a heart murmur (19). "From the reception she gave me," he adds, "you would have thought I'd come home from the wars with the Kaiser in my vest pocket" (19). She also appears, distraught and weeping, during his first two incarcerations, as Mezzrow describes his exaggerated and notably insincere attempts to reassure her (17, 40).

In the span of a few pages, Mezzrow contrasts his father's disapproval of his playing—a response reminiscent of that of Artie Shaw's father in *Cinderella*— with the warm response of some "shoeshine kids" on Chicago's South Side, where Mezzrow had gone to play, struck by an impulse "to go where people really understand about horns" (30). Much later in his narrative, Mezzrow recalls an encounter he had on the New York subway, when an elderly black man reached out to him when he was in a state of despair: "'Son,' he said to me real soft, 'if you can't make money, make friends,' and with that he stepped out on the platform and drifted away. He saved my life that day" (185). In contrast to this story of idealized interracial friendship is another Mezzrow tells in the same chapter, in which he writes to his family requesting his birth certificate, which he needs in order to obtain a passport for a trip to France. In a note accompanying the birth certificate, his father instructed Mezzrow, "Go anywhere you wish son, ...but always remember, *sei a mensch*," a Yiddish phrase that Mezzrow translates as "be a human being" (188).[36] Although his father's words have the potential for tenderness and caring, they seem remote in comparison to his face-to-face interaction with the old black man on the subway. Significantly, they elicit no comment from Mezzrow; he doesn't tell us how his father's words made him feel or think, or in fact, if they had any effect on him at all.[37]

The contradictions in Mezzrow's racial schema are readily apparent. Although he claims that the response of the orthodox Jews to the music of Armstrong and Waller is further evidence that the "phenomenon of jazz" was capable of reaching people across boundaries of race or class or nationality, the mixed response to jazz among the various groups he observes challenges that claim (202). Moreover, while Mezzrow vehemently rejects uncritical support for Jews in the name of ethnic solidarity, his narrative reveals an increasing tendency toward an essentialist reverence for black people and their culture. In his interactions with them, they are models of goodness and kindness whose abilities—musical, linguistic, and spiritual—far exceed his own or the other white (or Jewish) folks he describes.[38]

And yet between 1923 and 1928, Mezzrow frequently played in white bands or predominantly Jewish bands in which he made no effort to hide from or deny his Jewishness; to the contrary, he recalls experiences involving a variety of Jewish characters with humor and even pride (70). In one incident, Mezzrow describes the anti-Semitism he experienced as a member of an all-Jewish band hired to play at a mainly Gentile resort "across the lake from Chicago" and their defiant decision to set up their own café, where they did brisk business all summer long (86–87). But Mezzrow also devotes considerable space to the consequences of his relationship with Jewish gangsters and drug dealers, most notably in Detroit, where he was introduced to opium by the city's Jewish "sporting people" (96). Years later, Mezzrow would learn that his drug dealers were members of the notorious Purple Gang, a mob composed mostly of Jewish bootleggers that thrived in Detroit during Prohibition.[39]

As noted earlier, critics have focused extensively on Mezzrow's use of African American vernacular, or "jive" talk, as part of his overall strategy to prove his authenticity and belonging within a black jazz world. It is indeed true that jive talk dominates Mezzrow's narrative; his inclusion of an appendix in *Really the Blues* entitled "Translation of the Jive Section" as well as a separate glossary of terms strengthens the impression that Mezzrow believed himself to be an able translator of black speech. Yet here, as elsewhere, Mezzrow juxtaposes boastful claims of authority and authenticity with revelations of his own insecurities and self-doubts, admitting that by the late 1920s he had begun to "use so many of the phrases and intonations of the Negro, I must have sounded like I was *trying to pass for colored*" (111–12, emphasis added). In this instance, Mezzrow's qualified description seems an admission that his jive talk did not always fool the audience for which it was intended.[40]

Mezzrow's portrayal of his own mutable self-identity continues in his depiction of his move to Harlem in the late 1920s, in which he adopts an insider perspective on black culture, with references to African Americans as "they and them" replaced by "we and us" (207). Yet he also recalls that he regularly brought white musicians up to Harlem to hang out and listen to music, and that as a result he began "to be known as the 'link between the races'" (207–8). Here Mezzrow sees his access to both worlds, white and black, as central to his role in New York's jazz community. This dual positioning is apparent in his comments on his role on Harlem's Seventh Avenue, where his self-representations as white and as black seem to converge rather than compete for primacy:

> On The Corner I was to become known as the Reefer King, the Link between the Races, the Philosopher, the Mezz, Poppa Mezz, Mother Mezz, Pop's Boy, the White Mayor of Harlem, . . . I don't mean to boast; that's what the cats really called me, at different times. . . . My education was completed on The Stroll [Seventh Avenue], and I became a Negro. (210)[41]

In August 1940, Mezzrow was arrested at the Gay New Orleans nightclub on Long Island for possession of marijuana (300); following the arrest, the detectives drove him to his apartment in Harlem, where they discovered that he was living openly in an interracial relationship with his African American wife, Johnnie Mae, and their young son, Milton Jr.—a domestic arrangement in clear defiance of the social customs of that time. The detectives responded with predictable antagonism as Mezzrow's own identity became the central focus of their questioning:

> It floored them to find Johnnie Mae there, and little Milton, Jr., and on our way back they began to pop questions at me. Was I colored? No, Russian Jew, American-born. How in hell did I come to be living with a "spade"? Well, I had

this screwy idea that when you loved a girl you married her, without consulting a color chart. (300–301)

For his defiance, Mezzrow eventually received a one-to-three-year sentence in the city jail on Riker's Island for possession of marijuana (300). Although he successfully fought to be housed in the section for black inmates, his attempt to pass was met with discomfort or incomprehension by the black prisoners (305–6, 311–12). In his description of the integrated band he put together when he was transferred to Hart's Island, Mezzrow's self-positioning is that of a black inmate reaching out to the white inmates, as he invites a tough white "two-fisted con" who had heard "some of us colored boys running over some new Basie orchestrations ... to get his bass and join in" (313). As these passages reveal, in his role as a link between the races, Mezzrow felt capable of speaking from either side (313).

The conclusion to Mezzrow's account of his experience on Hart's Island—in which he seems to be parodying his own selective denial of his Jewish origins—offers yet another angle on the complexity of his self-representation in *Really the Blues*:

> Along come the Jewish holidays and with them a weird situation. The Jewish boys, not to be outdone by the Catholics, organize their own choir and ask me, a colored guy, wouldn't I care to lead it. I find out once more how music of different oppressed peoples blends together. Jewish or Hebrew religious music mostly minor, in a simple form, full of wailing and lament. When I add Negro inflections to it they fit so perfect, it thrills me. . . . I just sing "Oh, oh, oh" over and over with the choir because I don't know the Hebrew chants, but I give it a weepy blues inflection and the guys are all happy about it. They can't understand how come a colored guy digs the spirit of their music so good. . . . (315–16)

There are various grounds for concluding that Mezzrow's stance here is facetious, including the passage's concluding ellipsis, Mezzrow's prior references to his Russian Jewish heritage, and his vivid childhood memory of visiting his synagogue with his black friend, Sullivan. His irony resurfaces in a passage later in the chapter, in which Mezzrow recounts pleading his case before a justice in the Bronx Supreme Court, where he offered a critique of state laws that resulted in stiff sentences for marijuana possession and thus prevented a man from supporting his family (319). The judge—seemingly affected by Mezzrow's reference to his family—began to examine the papers detailing his case, which were open before him. "And then he must have come to the line about the prisoner's race," Mezzrow recalls, "because he looked like somebody suddenly hit him in the face. . . . 'Young man,' he said, 'the only trouble is, if I let you go you'll get right out with all the rest of your people and re-elect Roosevelt'" (319). Mezzrow adds that the judge "may have been joking" and that "the whole court kyaw-kyawed, and back to the Island I went" (319). Mezzrow's concluding sentence—"And to think that I never voted in my life"—punctuates the passage's ironic intent.

According to Scott Saul, "irony, paradox, ambiguity, and complexity" are the very tenets of the New York intellectuals with whom he associates Bernard Wolfe (Saul 48). These terms aptly describe Wolfe's afterword in *Really the Blues*, in which he refers to Mezzrow's claim for racial transformation as his "personal mythology" and "his reincarnation myth," suggesting that he found Mezzrow's extreme expression of "Negrophilia" problematic, at the very least (Mezzrow 390). As their collaboration drew to a close, Wolfe recalls that he found himself increasingly drawn to the possibility that Negrophilia and Negrophobia were not "polar opposites" but in fact "dialectically" connected (390).

Wolfe's exploration of this topic was the basis of an essay he wrote in the period following the publication of *Really the Blues*. "Ecstatic in Blackface: The Negro as a Song-and-Dance Man," was originally published in Jean-Paul Sartre's review, *Les Temps Modernes* in 1947, and appended, along with Wolfe's afterword, to the 1972 and later editions of Mezzrow's autobiography. In "Ecstatic in Blackface," Wolfe argues that "despite the claims of many whites to an uncanny sort of racial omniscience, their concept of 'the Negro as he really is' turns out to be a coy fiction, designed to camouflage the Negro as the white world sees him and forces him to behave" (393). According to Wolfe, his decision to write "Ecstatic in Blackface" was a result of his "reaction to the world that Mezzrow was very much a part of" as well as "to the experience of writing the Mezzrow book" (391). Wolfe's explanation here is key, for "Ecstatic in Blackface" must surely be read as a vehement critique of white Negroism and a rejection of the essentialist views of African Americans depicted by Mezzrow in his autobiography, and perhaps a rejection of the very notion of "passing" itself.[42]

To what degree, then, might Wolfe's reservations about Mezzrow's Negrophilia have colored his work as collaborator and contributed to the fanciful and sometimes facetious exploration of Mezzrow's self-representation in *Really the Blues*, which, as we have noted throughout, combines sincere admiration for African American culture with the most extreme stereotyping? I am certainly not suggesting that Wolfe made up the material in *Really the Blues* (I have found no evidence to support such a claim), but rather that his own assertions of authorship (and the other evidence of his influence already noted) suggest his significant contribution to the ironic, complex, and ambiguous text that is before us.

According to Wald, "what distinguishes *Really the Blues* from other autobiographical texts is the degree to which Mezzrow stakes the authenticity of his narrative on his ability to compel the reader's belief in the naturalness of his own performance." At the heart of passing, she explains, is not only "the 'performance' of identity" but also "others' ability or willingness to affirm that this performance is also 'real': that one 'is,' so to speak, the identity that one claims to be" (Wald 72). But who, it seems fair to ask, does Mezzrow *claim* to be? Is he the "voluntary Negro" on whom many critics have focused their analysis, the "Negro musician, hipping the world about the blues the way only Negroes can"? (Mezzrow 18). Or is he, in his own words, a "link between the races" who uses his whiteness (and Jewishness) to mediate between black jazz communities and the music industry in his role as record producer and impresario? Or perhaps the young Jewish man rebelling against his middle-class family but nonetheless finding friends and associates among Chicago's working-class Jews and nightlife characters? Or "the greatest white musician of all time," as a British fan claimed in a letter to him quoted near the end of *Really the Blues*? (329). As should be clear by now, I believe that Mezzrow—at various times and in various interracial and intraethnic communities—is all or some combination of the above, but that none of these identities, in and of themselves, adequately describes the complex depiction of a multiracial self that emerges in *Really the Blues*.

By focusing on Wolfe's role in the creation of the autobiographical subject of *Really the Blues*, I am making a claim about authorial agency in the text that is at odds with that proposed by some of the essays discussed above, in which Mezzrow's failure to be convincing or authentic as a black jazz musician is conflated with a loss of control over the narrative process. As I have attempted to show, *Really the Blues*' exposure of Mezzrow's white Negro identity as inherently flawed and unsustainable was an intentional narrative strategy over which Wolfe, with his powerful editorial strokes, exerted a substantial influence. To be clear, my evaluation is concerned only with the representation of Mezzrow that emerges in his autobiography, rather than with Mezzrow's real-life immersion in black music and culture or his lifelong dedication to traditional jazz, racial equality, and interracial exchange.[43] Whatever truths may be uncovered regarding the latter, in *Really the Blues*, it may be argued that Mezzrow—the "Russian Jew, American-born"—may not have been trying so hard to pass after all.[44]

Beyond Horatio Alger: Benny Goodman's *The Kingdom of Swing*

In stark contrast to Shaw's deeply introspective *The Trouble with Cinderella* and Mezzrow's jive talking and reefer-saturated *Really the Blues*, Benny Goodman's *The Kingdom of Swing* (1939) seems a classic Horatio Alger tale, with Goodman as the industrious, optimistic child of Russian Jewish immigrants who leaves behind the slums of Chicago to become the most successful bandleader of his generation. In contrast to Shaw and Mezzrow, who offer

104   Representations of Identity in Jewish Jazz Autobiography

A contemplative Benny Goodman, posing at 400 Restaurant in New York, ca. July 1946. William P. Gottlieb/Ira and Leonore S. Gershwin Fund Collection, Music Division, Library of Congress.

pointed critiques of America as a land of opportunity and equality for all, Goodman presents himself as the eager recipient of America's beneficence and goodwill. While Shaw and Mezzrow seem eager to display their cultural hipness—and, in the case of Shaw, his powerful intellectual curiosity—Goodman's simple style and modest demeanor suggest that he might have written his autobiography with his young jitterbug fans in mind. And unlike Shaw and Mezzrow, who portray themselves as sharply at odds with their nuclear Jewish families and the larger Jewish community in which they were raised, Goodman emphasizes the closeness of his working-class Jewish family and their contribution to his development as a musician and to his ultimate success as a swing bandleader.[45]

Indeed, Goodman's tendency toward reticence in *The Kingdom of Swing* presents a particular challenge to an analysis of his self-representation, for there is none of the obsessive preoccupation with race and ethnicity found in the autobiographies of Shaw and Mezzrow; moreover, when Goodman approaches these topics, his comments are marked by caution and indirection, as if he is always mindful (and perhaps fearful) of controversy.[46] Nonetheless, a careful reading of his self-representation as a Jew and as the most famous "white" bandleader of the 1930s reveals a complex negotiation of issues of race and ethnicity against the backdrop of the looming Second World War and the ongoing systemic racism and discrimination of the swing music industry.

The Kingdom of Swing begins with Goodman's discussion of his humble beginnings on Chicago's West Side, where he was born in 1909—the ninth of twelve children of David and Dora Goodman, Russian Jewish immigrants who met and married in Baltimore in the 1890s before moving to Chicago in 1902 (Goodman 6). Goodman recalls Chicago's West Side around 1918, when he was nine years old, as "a pretty hopeless neighborhood, the Ghetto of Chicago" (18). His biographer, Ross Firestone, substantiates Goodman's claim, describing the Maxwell Street ghetto ("commonly known as Bloody Maxwell") as "an overcrowded slum near the railroad yards and surrounding factories ... with Jewish, Irish, and Italian gangs roaming within blocks of one another" (Firestone 18, 23).

As William Kenney notes, Goodman seems to have shown little inclination to participate in the tough street life of adolescent gangs that other young Chicago jazz musicians found so alluring; nonetheless, he embraces his poor, working-class origins, as in his description of a popular childhood game called "cops and robbers," in which "the cops always got the worst of it, because in that kind of a neighborhood, the cops represented something that never did much for the poor people" (*Chicago Jazz* 93; Goodman 25). Above any other factor, then, the impoverished circumstances of Goodman's early life planted the seeds for his emerging class-consciousness and for his later political and social affiliations, which I discuss further below.

Goodman credits his father, who worked as a tailor in a factory, for his efforts to steer his children toward a life with opportunities beyond the sweatshop. In contrast to Artie Shaw's portrait of his father's disapproval of his playing, Goodman depicts the prospects of a career as a professional musician as a desirable, even respectable, option for him and his family and a way out of the tough life on Chicago's West Side: "As a matter of fact," he writes, "if it hadn't been for the clarinet I might just as easily have been a gangster" (Goodman 31; Kenney, *Chicago Jazz* 93).

In Goodman's account, the ethos of care within Chicago's West Side Jewish community served as a buffer against the material deprivation of its residents; the local synagogue loaned out instruments to the children, and the band leader provided basic instruction and led rehearsals of the student band, thus providing Goodman and his siblings with their first playing experiences at no cost to the family (Goodman 20). Goodman's father, who had ties to Chicago's Workmen's Circle, a Jewish fraternal organization, would take Goodman to meetings there, where sometimes he would be asked to play (23–24).[47] When the synagogue's funds for the band dried up, David Goodman enrolled several of his children in the boys' band at Hull House, the settlement house founded by Jane Addams (22; Firestone 23–24).

In this period, Goodman began clarinet lessons with the esteemed teacher Franz Schoepp, who not only provided Goodman with an excellent musical foundation but also facilitated Goodman's early social and musical relationships with African Americans: both Buster Bailey and Jimmy Noone, respected black jazz clarinetists of the 1920s and 1930s, were students of Schoepp in the same period as Goodman, who recalls that "we'd play duets, while Schoepp stood over us, counting time and watching that we played correctly" (Goodman 26). Schoepp's apparent lack of racial prejudice made a strong impression on Goodman "because there was plenty of prejudice about such things, even in Chicago" (26).[48]

From the time Goodman joined the American Musicians' Union at the age of thirteen, his jobbing brought him in contact with the black musicians who had settled in Chicago from New Orleans and elsewhere. Accompanied by other West Side Chicago musicians, Goodman began to frequent the South Side cafés such as Lincoln Gardens, where he listened carefully to Bessie Smith, Jimmy Noone, and King Oliver's band with Louis Armstrong. Like Artie Shaw, Goodman is mostly circumspect in his discussion of the black influences on his own development as a musician. In the following passage, he does not refer directly to race; he simply describes Oliver's band with Armstrong as "one of our favorites" and recalls the effect of hearing Bessie Smith for the first time: "Bessie was a great big woman with a voice that was even larger than she was, and a heart that was bigger than both. When she sang the blues, it took you right out" (42).

In 1925, when Goodman was sixteen, he joined Benny Pollack's band, a significant career move for him, he explains, because it was "the first *large* white band that played real jazz" (62, emphasis in original). His model of "real jazz" was the bandleader Fletcher Henderson, who used arrangements but also allowed "some leeway for the soloists"; by contrast, the bands of

Paul Whiteman and Isham Jones gave their musicians little "opportunity to stand up and play a chorus out of their own heads" (63). Thus, in a pattern that Goodman will repeat throughout his narrative, we see him beginning to shape his own image as a jazz musician in relationship to the contemporary black bands he was encountering, either in person or on recordings.

Yet Goodman's description of Pollack's band as a "white band" also reveals a shift to a generic white identity reminiscent of Shaw's and sometimes Mezzrow's. Although Goodman tells an anecdote in which he and the other Jewish members of Pollack's band missed work in order to observe the Jewish high holiday, Yom Kippur, he nonetheless identifies the band, in a broader and perhaps more important sense, as white (69). In his comparison of Pollack's band with Fletcher Henderson's, he and the other Jewish musicians are clearly on the white side of the white-black racial binary; it is worth asking how (or if) the "whiteness" of Pollack's band would change with a comparison to the Casa Loma Band, or the bands of Paul Whiteman or Glenn Miller. At the least, the anecdote suggests that in this period Goodman and his bandmates moved easily between identities as ethnic minority outsiders to members of the white establishment, while at the same time they turned to African American jazz as the model upon which to construct their own musical identities.

Many years would pass before Goodman performed and recorded with African American musicians—chiefly, by his own admission, at the urging of John Hammond, the renowned jazz critic, record producer, and left-wing activist.[49] Goodman's account of his renewed acquaintance with black musicians is rather stiff and formal, focusing mainly on the musical opportunities they provided. For many years, he explains, he had lost touch with them except for hearing them in clubs "or on records"; he recalls that Hammond frequently took him up to Harlem to listen to music and that on one of those visits they came across Billie Holiday singing "in a little dive on 135th Street." Only a handful of jazz recordings prior to this point had featured an integrated band, so that "the idea of working with them had never come my way before" (129). In 1933, Hammond arranged several recordings featuring Goodman with "mixed bands," including a date with Billie Holiday (her first recording) and later dates with Coleman Hawkins, Teddy Wilson, and Bessie Smith (her final recording) (126–28). Although opportunities for performing live with a mixed band remained limited, Goodman stresses the "pleasure" he derived from these mixed-band recordings (129–30).

By 1934, Goodman began taking the first steps toward forming a big band—a big "white band," in his words—that would incorporate the musical conceptions of African American big-band jazz while at the same time establishing its own identity (135). This borrowing would include hiring Fletcher Henderson to arrange for the band and eventually hiring several black instrumentalists. According to Goodman, "no white band had yet gotten together a good rhythm section that would kick out, or jump, or rock, or swing..., using arrangements that fit in with this idea, which would give the men a chance to play solos and express the music in their own individual way" (135).

In this carefully constructed explanation of his ideal band, Goodman situates himself as a white bandleader whose music is modeled on the characteristics of the best black bands of the era—the bands of Henderson, Basie, Webb, and others—whose bands "kick out, or jump, or rock, or swing." In his detailed account of Henderson's wide-ranging abilities as an arranger, Goodman goes out of his way to highlight his debt to him, concluding, "Without Fletcher I probably would have had a pretty good band, but it would have been something quite different from what it eventually turned out to be" (162).[50]

If Goodman's hiring of Henderson represented a significant step toward breaking down racial barriers in jazz, it was, in many respects, an easy step, analogous to the interracialism taking place in that era on radio or in the recording studio, in that Henderson's presence was invisible to the public at large. But Goodman's decision to perform on stage with his mixed trio of Teddy Wilson and Gene Krupa took interracialism in jazz to another, much more public, level, and his description of the audience's response to the trio's first public performance is marked by caution and allusion:

> The thought of a white and colored group playing in a hotel room was pretty revolutionary at the time, but we worked it out so that Teddy played intermission piano (while the band was off the stand) and the trio was made a part of the floor show, spotted separately. After a few days' trial, it was apparent that the thing was a natural from every standpoint, and it has been a part of our organization ever since. (214)

What Goodman only hints at, but does not say directly, is that Wilson's appearance with his *full* big band would have gone beyond what the public or the hotel management would tolerate, or, for that matter, what he himself would seemingly have been willing to demand at that point in his career.

Later, Goodman addresses the controversy created by his mixed bands more directly, noting that "there has been talk about the problems of presenting a band with a mixed group like the trio and the quartet. However, I have found few places where the crowds have not been wonderfully responsive to Lionel [Hampton] and Teddy" (228). Although Goodman refers to a racist encounter during a 1937 tour through the Southwest, he concludes his account on a note of optimism, insisting that the quality of the music was the only thing that mattered, not "what colors or races are represented" (231).[51]

Although Goodman illustrates his determination to challenge overt racism and segregation in recording studios, clubs, and concert halls where jazz was performed, there is more than a hint of paternalism in his suggestion that black musicians had benefited from, and perhaps even required, the assistance of white managers and agents to achieve commercial success. This attitude emerges in his description of Hammond's role in discovering Count Basie, who had been "plugging along in some cellar joint in Kansas City, working for starvation wages, with just about no hope of ever getting anyplace," until Hammond heard Basie on "a radio broadcast from a Kansas City nightclub" and worked to make him "a national success" (236; Stowe 52).

In the end, despite Goodman's efforts to acknowledge the African American influences that shaped his own swing style, he reveals himself torn by conflicting impulses, with his apparent desire to do his part to break down discrimination in jazz tempered by an innate pragmatism and hesitation to push too forcefully against the status quo. Thus, in a passage in which he discusses the epithet "king of swing"—an epithet by which he was increasingly known by the mid-1930s, especially following a glowing article about him that appeared in *Time* magazine in late 1935—he explains that he resisted it "because I didn't know how long this was going to last, and I didn't want to be tied down to something people might say was old-fashioned just because they got tired of the name, in a year or so" (Goodman 209). There is no sense in this passage that Goodman felt undeserving of the epithet, or that Henderson, Basie, or Webb—the African American bandleaders he credits as central influences in his own development—were the real kings of swing.[52]

Benny Goodman, Popular Front "Star" and US Statesman

Earlier, I attempted to read Shaw's terse comments on McCarthyism and its devastating impact on his life and career in the context of his military service and his postwar involvement with leftist- and Communist-linked organizations and campaigns. Efforts to make sense of Goodman's autobiographical depiction of (or silence on) his role in breaking down racial barriers in jazz and his own social and political affiliations require that we go back almost a decade before Shaw's postwar experiences, to consider the role of swing musicians and their audiences in bringing a leftist democratic vision of American culture and society to the forefront of popular entertainment in the United States.

In his comprehensive history of American culture in the 1930s and 1940s, Michael Denning helps to illuminate the connection between swing music and the Popular Front—the loose coalition of left-wing organizations that gathered strength through the 1930s in opposition to the growing threat of European fascism and discriminatory laws and practices within the United States. While Denning acknowledges that Goodman and other swing-era musicians were rarely Popular Front "activists" or "'political' artists," they were motivated by the "social crises" of their time to lend their music and voices in support of the organizations and "campaigns that were mobilizing their popular audiences" (Denning 333).[53] Similarly, David Stowe suggests that the Popular Front provided swing musicians with a platform to express their "commitments to racial equality, antifascism, and other political causes" and that Goodman, John Hammond, and Duke Ellington should be viewed as "fellow travelers" who associated themselves with the Popular Front not because of their devotion to communism but as a way "to pursue their own highly variegated political agendas" (Stowe 72).

But critics are more divided on the strength of Goodman's commitment to these causes. Goodman biographer Ross Firestone insists that "Benny had no discernible politics" and that his involvement with the Popular Front was entirely due to his association with Hammond (Firestone 211).[54] Furthermore, even as he traces Goodman's path from "initial reluctance" to full commitment to integrating his band, he suggests that Goodman's investment in keeping an integrated band over the long term was not as deep or sustained as Hammond's (183, 312).[55]

Other critics, however, are more generous in their assessment of Goodman's role in integrating jazz and his involvement with the Popular Front. Lewis Erenberg credits Goodman with an independent political consciousness, suggesting that his upbringing and early association with black musicians contributed significantly to his progressive attitudes about race and politics. He praises Goodman's willingness to "challenge the color line in music long before this occurred in other areas of American life" and his attempts to connect swing with a vision of American democracy that promoted freedom, inclusion, and pluralism (Erenberg 82, 249–50). Citing contemporary newspapers, he notes that Goodman's mixed bands became "symbols of interracial cooperation in black newspapers and the leftist press" and provided the example for other bands to follow (129–30).

It is important to recognize just how controversial Goodman's decision was to integrate his bands, if only as a guide for interpreting the extreme caution that marks his discussions of his role in countering segregation within the swing community. Both David Stowe and Paul Douglas Lopes have examined the role of *Down Beat* magazine in airing Goodman's mixed-band controversy. Stowe observes that while it was the first American magazine to report regularly on black music, Goodman's move to integrate his bands provoked a passionate and divisive response from its editors and readers (Stowe 75–76). Commenting on *Down Beat*'s October 1937 article, "Can a Negro Play His Best in a White Band?," Lopes notes that the magazine praised Goodman's "integrated ensembles" but nonetheless questioned their purpose. Citing concerns about the contrasting "stylistic qualities between black and white swing musicians and the pressures of performing in an integrated band, *Down Beat* preferred a separate but equal policy in live swing performances" (Lopes 129).[56]

Down Beat's ongoing scrutiny of Goodman's integration of his band continued in 1939, following the bandleader's decision to hire Charlie Christian and Fletcher Henderson for his full big band (Stowe 76). While *Down Beat* had earlier supported Goodman's decision to hire Teddy Wilson for his trio, the magazine appeared doubtful about the idea "of an integrated big band, as opposed to a combo playing between regular sets" (76). Eager to solicit the response of swing musicians to Goodman's decision, *Down Beat* organized the symposium titled Should Negro Musicians Play in White Bands? According to Stowe, "The editors themselves claimed a position of neutrality on the issue, stating their intention to get musicians to '*think* about [the issue] instead of feeling about it,' and noting critically that most musicians opposed to integration refused to give their names" (76, emphasis in original). As *Down Beat* reported, the response to the question posed in the symposium was mixed. "Southern musicians were unanimous in denouncing it as a bad idea, full of trouble." Among the musicians willing to be identified, Jimmy Dorsey, Teddy Wilson, Ella Fitzgerald, and Artie Shaw all expressed their support for integration, and "all gave credit to Goodman for effecting the change" ("Should Negro Musicians" 1, 10, 23).[57]

In this context, it is easier to appreciate the significance of Goodman's veiled remarks quoted earlier regarding his trio with Teddy Wilson, in which he explains that "the trio was made a part of the floor show, spotted separately" in order to appease those hotel patrons who would find Wilson's appearance with Goodman's big band unacceptable. The crucial point here is that Goodman was constructing his explanation of his role in pushing the acceptable limits of integration within jazz at the same time that he was dealing with the responses to his actions in his daily life—the heated response to his mixed bands in the pages of *Down Beat* serving as a prime example.

Erenberg and Stowe identify the period of the late 1930s to mid-1940s—coinciding with or in the years following the preparation and publication of *The Kingdom of Swing*—as Goodman's most active period of involvement with the Left, yet Goodman makes no mention of his activism in his autobiography (Erenberg 129; Stowe 71). Perhaps the most glaring omission is in the context of Goodman's account of his famous Carnegie Hall concert of January 16, 1938, in which he conveys his joy at playing with the greatest jazz musicians of his era in America's most famous concert hall but fails to mention the picket line of "pro-Franco sympathizers" that formed outside the hall "and deluged his radio sponsors with mail" to protest his support for the Loyalists in the Spanish Civil War (Goodman 233; Erenberg 129).[58]

The fallout for Goodman as a result of his public support for the Popular Front should not be minimized. According to Erenberg, Goodman's participation "attracted the FBI, which described Goodman as 'an ardent Communist sympathizer'" (129). As the 1940s drew to a close, Goodman and other prominent bandleaders found themselves under increasing pressure to "cut their ties to the left" or risk losing their lucrative contracts (Denning 335; Erenberg 245). From this perspective, it is easy to see how Goodman's reticence in *The Kingdom of Swing* ultimately served him well. In spite of his leftist affiliations, Goodman would escape the red scare relatively unscathed, certainly in comparison with Shaw and the many other musicians, entertainers, and writers forced to testify before HUAC. In fact, beginning in the early 1940s, the public image that Goodman had cultivated from the beginning of his career—mild-mannered and fatherly, industrious and grateful for the opportunities he had received in his own country—had seemingly begun to bear fruit, as Goodman was appointed to positions befitting his reputation as the leading statesman of jazz, the representative of American democracy through popular music.[59] His other reputation—as a harsh taskmaster whose relentless demand for perfection, frequent and indiscriminate firings of musicians, and odd and sometimes erratic behavior on and off the bandstand—seemed to remain for the most part outside of his public's awareness or concern.

It is perhaps more difficult to understand Goodman's autobiographical reserve regarding his Jewish identity and the ways in which it continued to influence his choice of and approach to his music. In the mid-to-late 1930s, a period in which swing was increasingly incorporating the ethnic music that reflected the origins of many of its practitioners, Goodman made hit recordings of the Yiddish tune "Bei Mir Bist Du Schoen" (1936) and his trumpeter "Ziggy" Elman's klezmer-based melody, "And the Angels Sing" (1939).[60] Absent from his autobiography, however, is any discussion of this material or more significantly, any discussion of what his Jewishness meant to him as the famed bandleader Benny Goodman. Rather, as his childhood in the heart of Chicago's Maxwell Street ghetto receded into the distant past, and as his status as "the king of swing" replaced the earlier images of him and his Jewish bandmates in Pollack's band missing a playing engagement to observe Yom Kippur, he seems to grow progressively "whiter."

But another interpretation is also possible here, one that sees Goodman moving not so much from Jewishness to whiteness but, rather, to something in-between: the Jewish influences that had permeated his childhood in the slums of Chicago would always remain, but they had merged with many others—white Protestant, Irish and Italian Catholic, African American—that were an inevitable part of his jazz journey in urban America. Denning's comments about the "remarkable 'crossover' successes" of "Bei Mir Bist Du Schoen" and other ethnic songs in the late 1930s support this interpretation; in his view, they were not simply "'novelty' hits" but are "better understood as trickster tunes, mediating the social and musical contradictions between the 'national' and apparently 'American' music, swing, and the still vibrant but 'regional' musics of ethnic and racial communities" (Denning 331).

The word "mediating" is key here, a reminder of our earlier discussion of Mezzrow's role as a "link between the races." But if Mezzrow claimed to be a link between black Harlem and the white musicians who traveled to its clubs and dance halls, Goodman's role as mediator (or link) is much broader, as he attempts to bridge the gap between black and white swing communities as well as between the cultural elite of the European art music world and the lowbrow "folk" world of jazz and blues. In this role, Goodman's Jewishness mattered, but it was only one part of a multifaceted identity that allowed him to become the most popular and successful bandleader in America. Gary Giddins notes this in his pithy observation of Goodman's public persona, which might also serve as a summary of Goodman's self-representation in *The Kingdom of Swing*: "The public took comfort in him. . . . He was white, but not too white, which is to say Jewish, but not too Jewish; and serious, but not too serious, which is to say lighthearted, but sober" (Giddins, *Visions* 153).

Ambivalence and Borscht Belt Humor: Max Kaminsky's *Jazz Band: My Life in Jazz*

Although trumpeter Max Kaminsky achieved neither the public acclaim nor wealth of Benny Goodman, Artie Shaw, or many of the other big band leaders of the Swing Era, he earned a reputation as a reliable sideman and exciting hot soloist, working in the big bands of both Goodman and Shaw, as well as in Mezz Mezzrow's short-lived band. In *Jazz Band: My Life in Jazz* (1963), which Kaminsky coauthored with V. E. Hughes, he offers a detailed and candid exploration of his own identity as a Jew and of his involvement with African American and white jazz musicians from the 1920s through the Swing Era and beyond.

Kaminsky was born in 1908 in Brockton, Massachusetts, one of seven children of Jewish immigrants who came to the United States during the 1880s from southern Russia. His large family, like Goodman's, was impoverished; he writes that his father "owned a grocery store most of his life in America, and we were poor most of the time" (Kaminsky 2).[61] Unlike Goodman, Shaw, and Mezzrow, who spent their early years in predominantly European immigrant neighborhoods, Kaminsky's family lived for a time in the mainly black Boston neighborhood of Roxbury, "in an old tenement on William Street in the heart of the colored section" (2). Through this experience, Kaminsky gained an early exposure to black music, recalling that on Sundays his sister Rose would accompany him to the neighborhood black church "to hear the gospel singing, and I still remember the street cries of the Negro pushcart men on summer nights, as they hawked their wagonloads of watermelon or fresh-caught crabs" (2–3). Like Goodman, Kaminsky seems eager to establish his

Max Kaminsky at the National Press Club, Washington, DC, ca. 1939. From left: Tommy Potter, bass; Kaminsky, trumpet; Benny Morton, trombone; Arthur "Zutty" Singleton, drums; Adele Girard, harp; Teddy Wilson, piano; Joe Marsala, clarinet. William P. Gottlieb/Ira and Leonore S. Gershwin Fund Collection, Music Division, Library of Congress.

own origins as poor and working class, while at the same time he illustrates the coming together of two cultures, African American and Jewish, linked by poverty and by their shared engagement with musical expression.[62]

Kaminsky's early exposure to music dominates his account of his childhood in Massachusetts; his sister's husband was an orchestral trumpeter, and Kaminsky was raised "in a house filled with music," so he "just seemed to know instinctively how a band should sound" (2, 5). When he was a teenager, his sister Betty purchased a phonograph player, and for the first time he heard the classic blues and jazz performers "on the 'race' records that came with it as a bonus," and which he remembers his sister singing along to "while she dusted the furniture and mopped the floors" (10–11). Through these memories, Kaminsky conveys not only the general level of musicality in his family, but also their receptiveness to African American music.

Kaminsky devotes considerable attention in *Jazz Band* to exploring his attitudes toward race, religion, and economic and social standing—issues of central concern for him as he struggles with his conflicting desires to be a jazz musician but also to achieve some measure of financial security and social respectability. These conflicting desires seem directly connected to his Jewish immigrant upbringing, in which values of piety and commitment to family compete with a model of upward assimilation and the outward manifestations of material success. For the most part, his immediate family holds to the former values, and Kaminsky portrays them with affection and humor. His mother encouraged his interest in music because she "knew what music meant to me and she understood I wasn't running wild," and even his "very pious" father came to accept his choice of career: "My jobs were a big help to my parents, and when he saw how I loved the music, there was never any argument about it" (14, 57). Kaminsky's poor immigrant family, like Goodman's, did not regard a career as a musician as disreputable but rather as a path toward personal fulfillment and economic security.

Unlike Mezzrow's Jewish mother in *Really the Blues*, Kaminsky's mother is more than a mere stereotype, and he seems eager to show her willingness to embrace new experiences and beliefs, including buying gin for musician Pee Wee Russell during the Prohibition years and accepting her son's relationship with a married woman (54, 104). Nonetheless, in certain respects she represents a particular type of Jewish mother: on the one hand overly proud and boastful about her son's accomplishments while on the other seemingly unaware of what precisely he has accomplished. It is this latter impression of his mother that Kaminsky conveys as he remembers her in the aftermath of her death:

> She had been so proud of my playing, and she had loved to hear the crowds applaud when I played in Boston's Symphony Hall.... I kept remembering how I used to play Louis Armstrong records around the house night and day when I was home in the thirties and how my mother was convinced it was I who was on trumpet...."That's Maxie, but he doesn't want to tell me because he's so modest," she'd say knowingly to Rose, and then turning to me she'd say, "You needn't be ashamed. In fact, it's very good!" (173–74)

Through these anecdotes, Kaminsky represents himself as the quintessential Jewish son, hardworking and dutiful, who by the time he had reached his teens was making an important contribution to his family's finances. In contrast to the middle-class model of upward assimilation, however, Kaminsky was accomplishing this by playing the cornet—and later the trumpet—rather than by going into business or one of the professions available to Jews in that period.[63] Yet, throughout his narrative, Kaminsky struggles with another life model presented to him as a Jewish American male, one based on a particular framework for advancement through economic and social achievement that was beyond his reach as a jazz musician but that he represents in the character of his Jewish friend, Jackie Marshard, who appears in *Jazz Band* at particularly significant moments.

At their first meeting, when the boys are eight, Kaminsky stands up to the bigger and stronger Marshard, who has shown disrespect to an orthodox

Jewish family that had recently moved into the neighborhood. Kaminsky's unexpected victory in a fistfight with Marshard is presented as a moral victory and anticipates the subsequent life paths of the two boys, in which Marshard's striving for financial success and power over others is juxtaposed to Kaminsky's commitment to his music and to his family (4–5). They meet again four years later, when Kaminsky deflects Marshard's demand for a rematch with an offer of a job as a drummer in the band he has formed, dangling the potential of prize money in a contest the band had entered. "He never was able to keep real good time," Kaminsky writes in a blunt assessment of Marshard, "but I soon found out that what he lacked in musical ability he made up for a millionfold in business sense and personality" (6).

Kaminsky runs into him again in 1936, when Marshard, who was "well on his way to success as a society band leader," came to hear him at a club in New York, and after expressing dismay at discovering him playing "in a dive," he offered him a spot in Boston in his society band. In response to Marshard's parting comment to him—"Money is the most important thing in the world"—Kaminsky replies, "I couldn't feel like that, even if he was right, but he was so certain about it that I could find no words to tell him that life ... was for everyone and all things, not just for him and his money" (7).

Yet Marshard's continuing presence in *Jazz Band* underscores Kaminsky's own ambivalence about the path he has chosen. Marshard is symbolic of the type of Jewish male Kaminsky could not himself be but whom he envies—the nonartist who attaches himself to the music business to make money but who lacks the creative impulse and dedication of the artist. As Kaminsky recounts his years of financial and creative insecurity as a jazz musician through the Depression, the decline of small-band New Orleans and Chicago-style ensembles, the rise and fall of the Swing Era, the recording ban during WWII and the rise of bebop, Marshard hovers always in the background, serving to remind him (and the reader) of Kaminsky's dedication to playing jazz in the face of considerable struggles.

Kaminsky and Marshard meet again during the Depression, at a point when Kaminsky was really scuffling and Marshard was playing drums in society bands in Boston and deciding if he should continue to play or become a businessman in the music world. In this story, the tables appear to be reversed: it is Marshard who is doubting the path he has chosen and seeking advice, while Kaminsky appears to recognize that he has made the right choice in pursuing a life as a jazz musician (61). By the late 1940s, however, Kaminsky's confidence was at low ebb; playing opportunities were scarce, and he felt the responsibility of providing for his young family (by that time he was married and had two young children). In desperation, he calls Marshard, who had grown wealthy from his business ventures in the music field, and Marshard promptly invites him to come to Boston to "see what I can work out for you"

(177). Although Kaminsky felt gratitude toward his old friend, the desperate situation that drove him to seek his help made his visit "one of the hardest things I ever had to do" (177).

As earlier, Marshard unburdens himself to Kaminsky, admitting that his success in business has left him unsatisfied and that he has begun to seek fulfillment through religion—a confession clearly intended to contrast once again Kaminsky's own steadfast commitment to his art with Marshard's unfulfilling path toward material wealth (179). And yet even after Marshard's early death in a car crash, Kaminsky seems haunted by what might have been, in terms of his own career, if his friend had not died (182). In some sense, then, he has tied his own success as a jazzman to the success of his lifelong friend; in so doing, he shows himself to be still ambivalent—torn by competing desires to provide a secure and respectable life for his family and to play the music he loves best—jazz. In the end, Kaminsky chooses to compromise; for twelve years he plays in society bands in order to supplement his work as a jazz musician (183).[64]

While Kaminsky's examination of his Jewish identity is a central theme within his narrative, he also highlights his close personal relationships with African American musicians, especially Louis Armstrong and Billie Holiday. Kaminsky recalls seeing Armstrong in a club in Harlem in the late 1920s shortly after Kaminsky had been left stranded by an unscrupulous manager in Binghamton who failed to pay him after a week's engagement. "You just naturally spill your troubles to that warm-hearted man," Kaminsky writes about Armstrong, "but I was completely unprepared for him to put his hand in his pocket and pull out some bills" (48–49). An intricate song-and-dance follows: Kaminsky refuses Armstrong's money, Armstrong insists that he take the money, and Kaminsky finally agrees, with the stipulation that Armstrong will allow him to "pay him back." The following year, when Kaminsky runs into Armstrong again and attempts to pay off his debt, the roles are reversed: "Now it was his turn to refuse and mine to insist, until finally he growled that he'd take it on one condition—'if you autograph it for me, daddy.' I felt as big as Rockefeller as I carefully wrote my name on a ten spot, which Louis gravely tucked away in his wallet" (48–49).

Although on the surface the passage is about Armstrong's generosity, there is also the clear implication that Kaminsky is deserving of that generosity; even though the two had only a passing relationship prior to this encounter, Kaminsky had made a sufficient impression on Armstrong (as a musician or as a human being or as both, Kaminsky does not say) that Armstrong wanted to help him. Much later in *Jazz Band*, Kaminsky recounts his experience of being selected, on Armstrong's recommendation, to tour Europe and the Far East in 1957 as a member of an all-star jazz band (204). The previous summer, he and Armstrong had appeared with different bands at the Carter Barron

Amphitheatre in Washington, DC, where "Louis would listen to our band each day over the speaker in his dressing room while he was getting ready for his own set, and reports came buzzing back to me so thick and fast about how much Louis liked my horn that I stopped in one afternoon to thank him and to return the compliment" (203). Kaminsky's story supports his effort to portray their relationship as mutually respectful and to dispel suspicions that he was a mere copyist of Armstrong's style: as he assures the reader, he was influenced by Armstrong's "feeling" but did not steal "the licks" (203).

Kaminsky's desire to establish his jazz authenticity is perhaps even more evident in his depiction of his relationship with Billie Holiday. At their first meeting at the Famous Door on Fifty-Second Street in the summer of 1936, Kaminsky reminded Holiday that he had met her in Harlem several years earlier when she was "singing and waiting on tables at the Alhambra Grill" (87). "The fact that I had heard her uptown made us good friends, he explains, "because she was a colored girl downtown in the white section and she felt good knowing I knew about Harlem, and when I heard her sing again I knew why I had remembered her name" (87). Later he takes credit for recommending Holiday to Artie Shaw, whose big band he had joined in 1937;[65] yet he also seems intent on showing that his relationship with Holiday was not merely professional, that they were in fact "good friends," as in his description of bringing an ill Holiday to his mother's house when Shaw's band was performing in Boston and the warm welcome his mother gave her (105).[66]

But as we have seen in other depictions of jazz interracialism from white jazz autobiographers, expressions of empathy and genuine rapport can quickly become derailed by paternalistic judgments on black life. Recalling his early experiences in New York, Kaminsky suggests that Harlem during the late 1920s was a place of "hope" for southern blacks who moved north during the Great Migration; although they continued to be "held down, they had the hope of better times. In the twenties, the colored people of Harlem were just glad to be living—never mind for the moment about the freedom" (45). He and other "white folks" were accepted in Harlem, he adds, because black Harlemites were flattered that whites admired black culture and "welcomed the nightly flood of cash customers the music attracted" (46). From his position of entitlement and authority, Kaminsky has managed to reduce a complex, multifaceted argument to generalities and platitudes; yet the passage ends with his image of jazz as a site of interracial harmony that reflected "the innocence and the optimism of the twenties" (46).[67]

If Kaminsky's unreflective remarks about black Harlemites suggest the degree to which he has absorbed the privileges of whiteness, his identification as an ethnic outsider remains central to his worldview, even after he has become a professional musician working within the multicultural world of American popular music. While at times he refers to himself as a white musician working in white bands, he also recalls that through the tough years of the Depression he would find himself reflecting on the fact that he was "just a little guy with a name like Max Kaminsky, living in Boston, the deadest city in the world, and ... maybe someday I can make it and people will like me in spite of my name and how I look" (56). Not surprisingly, his most pointed reflections on his Jewishness occur in his discussion of the impending world war and his memories of staying awake "till dawn to listen to Hitler's speeches over short wave," all the time aware that "in Germany, because of my name and my faith, I would have been in a concentration camp on my way to the gas chamber" (119).[68]

While many white jazz autobiographers highlight their attraction to black street life, Kaminsky shies away from Boston's black neighborhoods, retreating to the comfort and security of his Jewish community and his close relationships with his childhood Jewish friends (58–59). Unlike Mezzrow, the middle-class Jew who cast aside his heritage to embrace a bohemian lifestyle, Kaminsky, the child of poor Jewish immigrants who struggled to make ends meet, displays his longing for middle-class respectability and security.[69]

Mezzrow also serves as a useful foil to Kaminsky much later in *Jazz Band*, in a passage in which Kaminsky describes his friendship with Charlie Parker. Although Kaminsky generally shared Mezzrow's reservations about bebop, he appreciated Parker's skill, even boasting that he "blew the first note" at the opening of Birdland—the club named after Parker—in December 1949 (192). In contrast to Mezzrow's ironic portrayal (discussed earlier) of his involvement with the Chanukah choir during his imprisonment on Hart's Island, Kaminsky explains that the "Torah singing" that he had heard at synagogue during his childhood allowed him to hear Parker's bebop wailing as familiar and even accessible. "When I first started to improvise on the trumpet as a kid," he adds, "I used to go off into those atonal intervals that I had heard in the temple chants simply because they were so familiar to me and so easy to do" (193).[70] In their respective passages, Mezzrow and Kaminsky both acknowledge the link between black music and Jewish music, yet their attitudes toward this connection are, of course, markedly different. While Kaminsky consistently embraces his Jewish heritage and acknowledges its influence on his own development as a jazz musician, Mezzrow, as I have tried to show, depicts a far more complex relationship to his Jewishness.

Among the four Jewish jazz autobiographers, Kaminsky seems most comfortable with wearing his Jewish identity openly and proudly, and seemingly without ambivalence. Unlike Benny Goodman, who admitted to finding his childhood memories of poverty so painful that he resisted discussing them, Kaminsky does not shy away from examining those memories, both good and bad, that force him to examine his own values. Unlike Mezz Mezzrow, whose scorn for his middle-class Jewish background pushes him toward an extreme and unconvincing masquerade as a white Negro, Kaminsky seeks a compromise between middle-class Jewish respectability and creative fulfillment through African American musical traditions. And unlike Artie Shaw, Kaminsky expresses no shame in being Jewish, nor does he attempt to hide his identity, as did Shaw, by Americanizing his name; to the contrary, Kaminsky proudly displays it as evidence of his status as "other" and even as a source for humor.[71]

I began this chapter with a brief outline of some of the central arguments within whiteness scholarship around the response of Jewish Americans to their changing racio-ethnic status over the nineteenth and twentieth century; it is worth noting, however, that other scholars cited in this chapter take issue with some of these interpretations. Michael Alexander rejects the assimilationist model that traces the path of Jews and other European immigrants from racialized outsider to insider within mainstream white America, arguing that "Jews will not fit easily into a larger American tradition of whitening and Americanization based on racism"; instead, he proposes that scholars

> respect the rather pronounced longings among the descendants of Eastern European Jewry for ethnic identity and group feeling in America, rather than impose assimilation, acculturation, whiteness, or any other model that suggests that Jews decided to change into something other than themselves because in America they could. (Alexander 173)

Although Alexander's objections are persuasive in the context of the Jewish Americans who are the subjects of his study, they do not adequately describe the specific conditions of interracial contact and immersion that were central to the development of jazz in the first half of the twentieth century. As Jewish musicians learned to play jazz, they eagerly embraced African American music and culture; theirs, in other words, was an "acculturation" as much into blackness as into whiteness, and one that they undertook with excitement and passion and as central to their jazz experience.

In a related way, Eric Goldstein argues against the tendency within whiteness studies "to posit a fairly uncomplicated embrace of whiteness by immigrant groups" (Goldstein 4). Instead, he focuses on the ambiguous response of Jewish Americans to their shifting racial and ethnic status, describing his book not "as a study of how Jews *became* white, but as one that explores how Jews *negotiated* their place in a complex racial world where Jewishness, whiteness, and blackness have all made significant claims on them" (5, emphasis in original). In particular, he opposes scholarship that stresses "the unmitigated benefits" that whiteness "confers on the holder . . . that are attained primarily by the exclusion of African Americans and other peoples of color," suggesting that the "American Jews' struggle with whiteness" points to a much more complex response to the process of "racial assimilation" (5).[72]

Goldstein's position, in my view, comes much closer to describing the complex depictions of identity found in the accounts of the Jewish autobiographers examined here. As we have seen, their childhood exposure to Jewish musical and cultural traditions were powerful influences on their developing attitudes and worldview, allowing them to see connections and commonalties between themselves as members of a minority group and the black music and culture to which they were attracted. But their accounts also reveal the degree to which whiteness made increasingly "significant claims on them" as they established themselves as successful musicians and bandleaders and thus solidified their place as whites in the dominant black-white binary of American society. Notably, Benny Goodman and Artie Shaw, like many other Jewish entertainers and celebrities of their era, were seen to be strengthening their hold on whiteness through their marriages to non-Jewish women.[73]

And yet the accounts of these Jewish autobiographers also reveal their ongoing negotiations with the "complex racial world" that was their experience as they learned to play music and established careers as jazz musicians. It is perhaps appropriate that the complexity of self-identity revealed in these narratives matches that of the world in which it was shaped. The nuanced and various responses of these autobiographers to the process of "racial assimilation," in other words, seem an accurate reflection of their rich exposure to an urban American immigrant, interracial stew rather than to a wholesale rejection or embrace of any one single identity. In this respect, their autobiographies provide a valuable source for reevaluating concepts of assimilation, ethnic particularity, and relations between Jews and African Americans in the early decades of the twentieth century.

5

Don Asher's Fictional-Real Jazz World

In 1992, nearly twenty years after Don Asher earned notice in the jazz world for his role as collaborator on Hampton Hawes's award-winning autobiography, *Raise Up Off Me*,[1] he published a memoir of his own life in music, *Notes from a Battered Grand: Fifty Years of Music from Honky-Tonk to High Society*. If *Raise Up Off Me* is widely considered one of the most searing accounts of a black musician's jazz life, *Notes* provides a fascinating glimpse from the other side, as Asher, a skilled musician and raconteur, details his own fervid pursuit of a magical but elusive black jazz world.

Since the late 1950s, Asher had maintained busy dual careers as a cabaret pianist at several of San Francisco's best-known nightclubs and as a novelist, short-story writer, and essayist. A striking feature of his writings was his propensity to autobiography and his apparent unconcern with muddying the distinction among literary genres; this included his willingness to publish short stories and novels that were thinly veiled representations of his own real-life experiences and to present as autobiography material that had appeared—sometimes verbatim—in his previously published fiction, essays, or collaboration with Hawes. In other words, while *Notes* may be viewed as his most polished work of self-inscription, it was certainly not his first. In his own wry acknowledgment of this, Asher has said simply, "You got to use what you have, man" (Wasserman, "After Chemistry" 110).

Significantly, Asher offers no disclaimer in *Notes* (or in his other works published as nonfiction) that might alert his readers to his use of pseudonyms and fictional characters alongside the "real" people, bands, and places he describes—even though such practices are common when the author has some motive for protecting the identities of characters or details about historical events or situations.² He offers, for example, lengthy accounts of his experiences with the Hal Harganian band and later with Boston's society bandleader Rudy Yellin, as well as his close friendship with trumpeter Val Catalona. All of these are made-up names, although there is evidence that they are pseudonyms or composites of musicians he played with and bandleaders for whom he worked.³

Asher's unabashed recycling and amendment of material drawn from his own life's experiences allow his readers extraordinary access to the preoccupations and concerns that he felt compelled to put down on paper. In an earlier memoir, *The Eminent Yachtsman and the Whorehouse Piano Player* (1973), and in his first novel, *The Piano Sport* (1966), we find Asher working through his relationship to his Jewish heritage—his homage to that heritage and the rich Jewish American literary influences that shaped him as well as his need to move beyond the narrowness and parochialism of the small New England community in which he was raised.⁴

In other publications, including *Notes* and his novel *The Electric Cotillion* (1970), Asher reveals his enduring and sometimes transgressive fascination with African American music and culture, a fascination that is evident in the thematic material, characterizations, and language on display in these works. Yet the tone that Asher employs in his treatment of this subject is notably contradictory, with his own (and his fictional counterparts') lifelong reverence for and commitment to the black jazz tradition standing alongside descriptions of experiences in African American musical and cultural spaces that evoke the minstrel tradition in their tendency toward essentialism and extreme stereotyping. Why, one might ask, would a white jazz pianist who studied with the great jazz musician Jaki Byard; played in integrated jam sessions in Boston in the early 1950s; and enjoyed a long career as a house pianist at some of the leading West Coast cabarets choose to depict African Americans and their culture with such broad strokes as to reduce them in some of his work to little more than caricature?

In certain respects, Asher's autobiographical and fictional depictions appear to illustrate "the problem with white hipness" described by Monson, or the "love and theft" and "envy . . . of black men" outlined by Lott—and yet it is critical to recognize that his caricatures and stereotypes are aimed not only at African Americans and their world, but also at other ethnic groups—Italians, Irish, Jews—as well as at himself and his fictional counterparts. In his perceptive review of *Notes*, Ted Gioia identifies Asher's employment of humor as a central aspect of his memoir, suggesting that "[h]is wit and irony give much of the book the flavor of parody" ("Gigs from Hell" 151). Gioia's observation may profitably be extended to Asher's literary method in its totality: from his childhood in Worcester to his early career during the 1940s as a journeyman pianist playing throughout the northeast in strip joints, honkytonks, and New England society bands, and finally to his long and stable dual careers as author and musician, Asher was exposed to a rich stew of literary and performance traditions in which he found models for his own satirical, comedic impulses.

During his tenure at San Francisco's legendary hungry i, Asher accompanied or played background music for some of the most successful comedians and social satirists of that era, including Mort Sahl and Jack E. Leonard, as well as for a younger generation who got their first major exposure there, including Lenny Bruce, Woody Allen, and Richard Pryor.[5] Central to the method of these artists was inter- and- intraethnic observation and insult: white-ethnic and African American comedians engaged in barbed and raucous social commentary and satire that was as often directed at their own traditions and manners as at those of others. The influences of this comedic tradition—as I will discuss in greater detail later in the chapter—are readily apparent in the interracial dialogues that are an important feature of Asher's work, as well as in his broad depictions of character "types" of various racial and ethnic backgrounds. In the mid-1960s, Asher also served as accompanist and musical director for the Committee, a groundbreaking San Francisco comedy revue that established improvisatory sketch comedy as *the* go-to formula for upcoming generations of American comedians, influencing the work of *Saturday Night Live* and other comedy troupes.[6]

At the same time, Asher was establishing himself as a writer on the San Francisco scene and publishing short stories, essays, and book reviews for various publications, including *Harper's* magazine and *The San Francisco Chronicle*.[7] In this period, he published three novels, *The Piano Sport* (1966), *Don't the Moon Look Lonesome* (1967), and *The Electric Cotillion* (1970), and sold the movie rights for all three.[8] Over the years, several Hollywood heavyweights expressed interest in the scripts—including Elliott Gould, Jack Lemmon, Sidney Pollack, and Benny Carter—and for a time Asher seemed on the brink of a significant career breakthrough, but financing issues and aesthetic disagreements halted the projects before the filming stage (Wasserman, "After Chemistry" 110). Nonetheless, Asher's close ties to these various West Coast literary, film, and nightclub communities left a deep impression on him, granting him a bird's-eye view of rapidly changing cultural mores in the era of rock and roll, black nationalism, and the violent disintegration of Martin Luther King's vision of "a beloved community." In order to reach a fuller understanding of the depictions of race, ethnicity, and gender that emerge in Asher's writings, we need to consider all of these manifold influences that shaped his worldview and perspectives, beginning with his early years in the parochial Jewish enclave of Worcester, Massachusetts.

Worcester Beginnings and the Search for a Larger World

Asher was born in Worcester—a deeply segregated New England town—in 1926. His father, Daniel Asher, a chemist and close friend of the playwright S. N. Behrman, committed suicide in 1929 at the age of forty-three, leaving his wife to support their two young sons with a modest candy business. In *Notes*, Asher mentions these details only in passing, having treated the subject in considerable detail in *The Eminent Yachtsman*, a highly embellished depiction of his early life and his family's history in Worcester in the first half of the twentieth century.[9] *The Eminent Yachtsman* reveals other details of Asher's early life that receive only parenthetical mention in his later memoir, details that illuminate the early influences of humor and melancholy that permeate his writings, his decision to pursue a life as a musician and writer, and his attraction to jazz culture.

The Eminent Yachtsman devotes considerable attention to Asher's Jewish roots and the harmful effects of his family's insistence on a path to success based on professional and economic standing. When Asher's desire to be "a jazz or cabaret pianist" was met with incomprehension by his family, he agreed to follow the path of his father and older brother, majoring in chemistry and eventually earning an MS in organic chemistry from Cornell (*Eminent Yachtsman* 38). His brief and spectacularly unsuccessful stint as an organic research chemist drove him into a deep and prolonged depression that forced him to examine the parallels between his own struggles with mental illness and those of his father, twenty years earlier. Asher marks his return to playing in the seedy basement rooms, strip joints, and honky-tonks that caused his family such consternation as essential to his recovery, signaling his break from Worcester's insular Jewish community and the beginning of his search for broader cultural vistas (219–33).

Yet Asher also gives a moving account of the famed playwright S. N. Behrman, a Worcester native and his father's best friend, who provided a compelling role model for him, encouraging his early passion for literature and the arts. By Behrman's own account, his success as a writer was largely due to the unflagging support of Dan Asher, whose influence in Behrman's life is reflected in the character Willie Lavin, an obvious stand-in for Dan who appears in Behrman's short stories and in his play, "The Cold Wind and the Warm," a dramatization of Willie's (Dan's) final illness and suicide (Behrman, *The Cold Wind*; Behrman, *Worcester Account*). Asher's detailed exploration of the relationship between his father and Behrman—revealed in the letters the men exchanged in the years before his father's death and reproduced in *The Eminent Yachtsman*—shows Dan Asher's extreme devotion to Behrman, a devotion that existed alongside his apparent suppression of his own search for artistic fulfillment (*Eminent Yachtsman* 136).[10]

Behrman's enduring influence on his best friend's son is clear; Don Asher dedicated *The Eminent Yachtsman* to Sam and to his older brother, H. J. (Hi) Behrman, and the book's final chapter describes a visit Asher and his wife, Poe, paid Sam in New York in the early seventies, near the end of Behrman's life. Asher's offers a moving, respectful portrait of Berman—"[t]he dean of high comedy" (243)—seeking his advice regarding his early ideas for *The Eminent Yachtsman*, which he had begun to imagine as a chronicle of the friendship between his father and Behrman (247). Behrman responded with enthusiasm and followed up with a detailed letter in which he expressed his pride in Asher's accomplishments as a writer, noting his significant improvement since the first efforts Asher had sent him many years earlier (249).[11] Through his genuine engagement with Asher's life and work, Behrman seems to have attempted to fill the paternal vacancy left by his best friend's early and sudden death. And while in most respects Asher's work seems to have little in common with the manner and style of Behrman's "drawing room comedy," it is possible to detect his influence in Asher's tendency to match satire with sentiment in his fictional and real-life characterizations.[12]

Asher's recollection of his childhood in *Notes* is dominated by his family's tenuous financial circumstances and by the attempts of his protective Jewish family to shelter him from Worcester's non-Jewish residents. He was nine before he saw a black person for the first time, on an outing with his family; Asher recalls his aunt's uneasy response—spoken with "an unnerving whispered urgency at odds with the mild sunny day, 'Black as the ace of spades'" (*Notes* 10)—which alerted him to the enormous divide between his closed Jewish community and the mysterious world beyond, a world that he would seek with single-minded purpose in his desire to become a jazz musician:

> Five years later I would find myself on the threshold of a black world, my first step on a frustrating lifelong odyssey to pick the brains, embezzle the rhythms, master the soulful secrets of the race—destined to become a "nigger lover," as the phrase would soon gain currency in political and artistic circles, to the anxiety of my mother, who was too genteel a lady to express her concerns for my physical safety and cultural welfare in any but the most roundabout locutions. *They're very fine people, dear, don't misunderstand me, but they have had a very different background and upbringing* . . . (10, italics in original)

The experience that Asher refers to as marking the beginning of his lifelong commitment to learning and emulating African American jazz practices was his private music lessons with pianist Jackie Byard—also a Worcester native—when Asher was fourteen and Byard a high school senior. Asher first heard Byard at Dominick's Café on Worcester's Green Street and was at once captivated by the older teenager's virtuosity, as well as by his intensity and passion

(Fletcher). In a passage filled with the essentialist language that is a notable feature of his descriptions of black jazz spaces, Asher describes his response to Byard's "sound"—"jubilant" and "cocky"—that stirred in him images of an exotic and intensely desirable black world:

> I can't say how long I stood in the doorway more inside than out, oblivious to the shadowy, questioning faces, washed by echoes of all the music I had ever heard or read about—the Harlem house-rent parties . . . , the strut of southland cakewalks and brass band parades, and endless, linked choruses of pile-driving boogie-woogie that went lickety-split like a night train slamming across prairie tracks. . . . The little room seemed ready to explode, hardly able to contain the cadences pouring out the doorway and into the street, engulfing me in waves of vibration that set my scalp tingling and tripped a wild, grainy current down my backbone. (7)

Asher approached Byard after the set and arranged to take weekly lessons with him (7–8). For the next year, he arrived at Byard's house every Friday in the early afternoon and stayed for hours, often not leaving until dusk (10). Byard charged him seventy-five cents for a lesson, unless Asher stayed for a particularly long time, in which case he "gave him a dollar, which was my entire weekly allowance, and for that he was grateful" (10). Sometimes they would go to play at the nearby Saxtrum Club, a hangout for local musicians as well as for out-of-town bands, where prominent musicians would drop by—among them Roy Eldridge, Anita O'Day, and Frank Sinatra. Although Byard was only eighteen, he was, according to Asher, "the club's resident luminary and official host," known throughout the neighborhood for his all-night practice sessions (10). Asher and other neighborhood kids would gather outside the club's locked door to listen, and Byard, aware that he had an audience, would "slide into some whooping way-back whorehouse piano, a big, pumping, joyous sound, and in our imaginations it was like being present at a spectacular parade, hearing a whole history of the music from the New Orleans cribs and levees on up the river" (10–11).

Notably, Asher says little about Byard's precise teaching methods; rather, his concern is to convey the impact of Byard's playing on him and his awareness of the deep cultural and social divide that these lessons allowed him to cross. With his characteristic humor, he describes the consternation of his classical piano teacher when she "detected something coarse and alien infiltrating the texture of my playing" (11). When Asher finally told her that he was studying with Byard and would no longer be coming for lessons, she was, in his words, "devastated" and called his mother to express her consternation; in a rare reference to his Jewishness in *Notes*, Asher recalls that his "distraught tearful mom all but said Kaddish over my watery grave" (11).

Asher spent only about a year studying with Byard, who had quickly outgrown the musical opportunities of his hometown and moved to Boston, but Asher was convinced that "the legacy had been passed on; his imprint was on me, at least a shallow facsimile of it." By now, he recalls, "I could get through an entire night without repeating tunes, and I was beginning, in a small white way, to swing" (47). Although Asher chooses an image of "whiteness" to highlight the impact of Byard's teaching on him, what he really means is that he was starting to sound "black." In fact, in his next reference to Byard, he notes that his own playing was beginning to display "[a] fresh, rhythmic pulse (the Negro players called it 'snap' or 'dip')," a result of his lessons with Byard and his wider exposure to Worcester's black jazz community (49–50).

Asher's relationship with Byard, in fact, remains an important backdrop to his entire narrative, demonstrating his continuing link to what he believes is *the* authentic, black jazz tradition. At various points in the text, Asher refers to Byard in order to draw attention to their contrasting career paths: while Byard became an influential jazz pianist and educator, Asher scrambled (in part, as he acknowledges, because of his own limitations as a jazz pianist) to put together a more modest career. In his candid observation, "Jackie Byard and I were running roughly parallel courses—on strikingly different levels" (76).

With a novelist's attention to narrative form, Asher has Byard make an appearance at the book's end, when Byard, who had come to San Francisco to play a well-known jazz club in town, accepts Asher's invitation for dinner (299). Noting Byard's recent name change (from Jackie to Jaki) and his slimmed-down appearance and "trim gray beard flecked with white," Asher now describes their relationship as one of father to child, observing with wistful nostalgia that twenty-five years had passed "since he turned me upside down, slapped me on the butt, and pushed me howling into the world" (299). But even though Asher differentiates his own accomplishments and talent from Byard's, he seems most concerned with stressing their bond through the language of jazz. Following their meal, Byard sits down at the piano and plays for Asher, whose response reflects his profound respect for his former teacher as well as his desire to place himself within the elevated ranks of the jazz community to which Byard belongs:

> It isn't often you get to hear a virtuoso of the first rank in your living room. I was awed. . . . A hard act to follow, as they say, but . . . I found the courage to sit down and play some of my things for him. Musicians are always striving to shine for one another, to attain esteem in the other's eyes; envy and admiration, competitiveness and support are complexly linked. . . . In our mutual respect the divisions between former teacher and pupil, between wizardry and mere proficiency, vanish. (300)

If Asher's private lessons with Byard marked the start of his decades-long search for "the soulful secrets of the race" (10), the climax of this search was his participation in interracial jam sessions in New York and Massachusetts beginning in the mid-1940s. Asher's account of these experiences in *Notes* is particularly valuable for the multiple perspectives and angles it reveals. There is Asher's self-representation of himself as an outsider—a Jewish white male in a loud, vibrant, and sometimes-hostile African American cultural space. But his gaze (and judgment) is also directed at the black characters at the center of these experiences just as their gaze (and judgment) is directed at him.

Asher maintains his own essentialist stance with unflinching certainty; he describes a stint as pianist with a white dance band after he graduated from high school that left him musically dissatisfied (60), haunted by a feeling "that there was a secret I wasn't privy to. Now that I had listened extensively to black musicians, I was convinced there was something basic and vital that came easy to them and hard to us" (71). The fundamental difference, he suggests, had to do with "levels of rhythmic charge achieved by whites and blacks," summarizing the style of the former as "more even-keeled, linear, lacking the sudden dips and spurts, the coiled-spring tension-and-release and unexpected displacement of meter that sent the beat slamming and teetering down the tracks like a highballing express, generating incredible excitement" (71–72).[13]

But Asher muddies the waters when he turns to examine the views of the African American musicians he knew on the topic of racial difference. On the one hand, he claims that when he tried to call a tune at an after-hours jam session, a black musician dismissively referred to his selection as "one of your white-boy tunes"; "on the other hand, he acknowledges that some African Americans he knew—including Hampton Hawes—reacted with discomfort to "the whole subject of racial-genetic orientation," protesting that it rekindled worn "stereotypes and images" (72–73). Yet Asher was "unpersuaded" by the latter view and set his own course to learning jazz, which included "pilgrimages in the coming years to the ghetto clubs and after-hours joints . . . , tracking the elusive secret, searching out the passion and sensibility of the black man. Hoping for a miracle of transmutation" (73).

Tension permeates Asher's description of his brief and unsuccessful foray into the world of Harlem's famed jam sessions. His light skin and small stature make him "an easy target for frisky young Harlem bloods" who call out to him, mocking his appearance, as he walks their streets (74). In Asher's view, the unfriendly reception that he experienced in Harlem in the mid-1940s marked the passing of the era in which "affluent whites could pass a flavorful evening slumming in the district's clubs and cafés" (73).[14] Inside the club, where the jam session is underway, the atmosphere of hostility remains, yet Asher responds with passion to the music, describing it as "something fierce,

Don Asher at the Valhalla in Worcester, Massachusetts, ca. early 1940s. From left: Guido Granpietro, clarinet; Tommie Collins, drums; Howie Jefferson, tenor sax; Barney Price, trumpet; unidentified singer; Don Asher, piano. Courtesy of Cynthia Carruthers and the jazzhistorydatabase.com.

uncompromising, and beautiful" (74). Asher's query about "sitting in" serves to heighten the image he has drawn of his own vulnerability; wisely he chooses not to participate, watching instead from the sidelines, while "those without strong wings were cut down [by] schooled, confident musicians" (75).

Recognizing that his search for jazz proficiency required a reboot, Asher moved to Boston, where he studied piano as well as theory and composition with a teacher at Schillinger House (renamed the Berklee College of Music in 1954) (76). But his search also led him to after-hours sessions at black clubs on Boston's Massachusetts Avenue; in *Notes*, he offers a detailed account of one such experience at a club called Coffee John's, where, after returning for a week to listen ("my white friends blanched when I told them where I'd been until four in the morning"), he felt confident enough to ask to sit in (98). This time, he found that the musical level was "within my ken," the tunes familiar, the tempos manageable: "I sensed that one or two of the pianists could play rings around me, but the rings were concentric and not all that wide. I felt I wouldn't be embarrassed as I would have been at the incandescent Harlem sessions" (98).

What Asher does not disclose to his readers is that Coffee John's is a fictional name, likely a composite of the clubs he frequented in Boston during the early 1950s.[15] Furthermore, his account of his experience at Coffee John's in *Notes* is essentially an expanded treatment of his previously published short story, "The Barrier" (1985), described on the jacket blurb in the volume of stories in which it appeared as "the story of an aspiring white musician's exploration of black jazz."[16] In both versions of his experiences at Coffee John's, Asher gives the impression that among the regulars there he was the only white person—not an entirely accurate reflection of Boston's jazz scene in the early 1950s. According to Boston jazz historian Richard Vacca, as early as the 1940s integrated bands were "not an everyday occurrence . . . but not a rare one either," and "everyone sat in at the jam sessions" (Vacca 62, 290).[17] On the other hand, Asher's representation of his lonely pilgrimage to black jazz communities is an effective strategy to bolster the image he is constructing of his own dedication and courage. Although black musicians were the indisputable leaders and innovators within the bebop community, Asher's depiction tends to diminish the contributions of the white jazz musicians who played and recorded with the bebop giants.[18]

Whether viewed through the lens of autobiography or fiction or something in between, Asher's experience at Coffee John's as he describes it in *Notes* is a trial by fire: the pianist whose place he took vacated the piano stool without making eye contact, and he heard "mocking, skeptical voices" as he adjusted it for his short frame (99). As he joined the band in a standard tune, he sensed a different, "looser" rhythmic conception that caused him to feel "the meter sliding out from under my fingers. When this occurred the bass player steadied into a fundamental four-to-the-bar stroll, laying groundwork beneath me" (99). The dancers, though, were less forgiving, "shaking their heads" in response to his unsteady pulse and leaving the dance floor. "I struggled through two more tunes, hands cramping and sweat dropping off my chin onto the keys until the board was slick as an ice rink. The dancers never returned" (99).

After the set, the bass player offered a blunt assessment of Asher's playing, employing imagery that combined the practical and the metaphorical:

> You want a honest critique? . . . The dancers was off balance, that's why they deserted, they couldn't pat their feet right or make their proper moves. You was playing rhythmic enough, don't misapprehend me, but it was too straight-ahead and ricky-tick, if you catch my drift. We're used to a wider beat, space and margin to move around in. It's like a woman sashaying down a wide alleyway swinging her hips and buns, used to plenty of leeway, you picture it? . . . Now that alleyway suddenly *narrows* on her and this fine bitch is getting bruised, *hurting*, so naturally she's going to cut out. What you got to do is listen to me and the iron and skins [drums] more intensely." (99–100, emphasis in original)

The bassist's criticism caused Asher to question his own ability to overcome the disadvantages of his "white upbringing" and his current job as pianist in a society band, in which the music was played with a square feel—a "businessman's bounce" (100). Gradually, however, he began to sense a "a grudging cordiality" as he arrived every night to sit in (100); he relates the good-natured banter—and even praise—that came his way, always accompanied, however, by an intense racial consciousness in which the black musicians and audience signified on racial stereotypes, sometimes happily reversing them (100–101). In musical terms, Asher also felt that he "was starting to get it, . . . assimilating the displaced, driving rhythms and crackling improvisational patterns, sharpening my ear and expanding my repertoire" (102–3). For Asher, his perception of his own growing competence was inextricably linked to his ability to emulate a black jazz aesthetic. "My fondest dream, he confesses, "was that the Coffee John's regulars would one night rise en masse as I came off the stand, shouting, 'The blue-eyed devil plays black!'" (103).

For Asher, a key aspect of playing "black" had to do with playing "time"—in particular, "learning to function at very fast and very slow tempos" (103). This guidance came often in the form of vivid imagery; a bass player taught him that "[a]t slow tempos the beat has to *swell*," before sharing with Asher the advice he had been given by another player: "It's like taking yourself a mouthful of good wine, swishing it around, savoring it before you let it go down; the swallow is that beat finally dropping" (103, emphasis in original). Another pianist instructed Asher on playing up-tempo tunes, showing "me how to stay loose and relaxed by visualizing myself riding a train 'rocketing along at a good clip, ninety miles an hour or more, but it doesn't trouble you 'cause you're sitting there cool and collected, your body swaying and rocking naturally with the train's pulse, which is the drums and bass'" (103). The "supreme lesson," Asher concludes, "is that 'time' should be as natural as a heartbeat pumping pure, fresh blood into a tune" (103).

Although Coffee John's is a world composed primarily of black men, at moments of greatest interracial tension, it is Auraline, the "beautiful tawny-skinned singer," who assumes a leading role (100). Although Asher declares his "infatuation" with her, he stops himself from pursuing what would certainly have been considered a daring relationship for that place and time (105).[19] Nonetheless, Asher cannot hide his disappointment that his sexual desire is not reciprocated; instead, Auraline treats him with a protective, sisterly kindness, viewing him as a curiosity, a young white musician who is either reckless or naive enough to venture into the heart of Boston's black neighborhood. On the bandstand, she urges the audience to applaud Asher "for steppin' across town to do his stuff" (101). She is jocular and familiar with him, even making him the focus of her attention as she engages in light, sexual banter with Coffee John's patrons. "He's sweet an' unspoiled and *ser*-ious," she tells them, "so all you hungry-ass chicks out there with big eyes keep your hands off him, hear?'" (101, emphasis in original). In Asher's telling, Auraline's flirtatious manner is proof of her authority—it is Auraline, not Asher, who controls the manner and extent of their relationship.

Over time, Asher would learn that the cordiality at Coffee John's could quickly turn to hostility, especially when musicians or members of the audience did not know him or his history at the club. He would instantly perceive the tension in the room, the glances no longer friendly but "vigilant and somber. When I sat in, a standard tune would be called in a strange key at a murderous tempo—much faster than the regulars would ever kick it off" (103). He recounts a humiliating session during which he "floundered badly." Auraline again tried to intervene on his behalf, chastising the musicians for their behavior and offering comfort and encouragement to Asher after the set (104). Despite her attempts at kindness, however, the experience was for him " a sobering reminder that despite the previous air of congeniality and counsel, the barrier was still there and always would be—made up of divergent experiences, humor, temper, restraints—a skin-thin membrane tough and impervious as sheet metal" (104).

Even Auraline could lose patience with Asher's attempts at hipness—particularly if the line between respectful emulation and derisive mimicry was less than clear. One night, when Asher tried to tell her that he had played well in the jam session by repeating her own phrase—"I scored a touchdown, baby, you didn't even see the game"—she reproached him for his "nigger talk" and urged him to "be respectful" (104). The experience forced Asher to acknowledge the presumptions he had been making and the need to behave with greater respect or, at the very least, discretion (105).

Expressions of hostility as well as alliance also surface in Asher's account of his first experience with marijuana, which he had tried at the urging of his musician friends at Coffee John's. When the effects of the drug left him unable to drive home, he was forced to return the next day to find his car, only to be confronted by two black youths who demanded money for cigarettes. Asher handed them some change, but when he told them he was a pianist—he instantly realized that this was an ill-advised disclosure—one of them took a switchblade from his pocket and slashed Asher along the knuckles of his right hand (109).

Just then, Everett and Wesley, Asher's friends from Coffee John's, drove by; as Asher explained to Wesley what happened, Everett cut them off, telling them to "[s]top the damn jabbering and let's *go*, . . . we got to get this nigger to a doctor" (109, emphasis in original). In the car, sandwiched between his friends, Asher experienced "[b]ewilderment and wonder that the locus of the music that was my breath and heartbeat should also be the source of animosity and venom. It would take courage to venture to this part of town again; the barrier had been raised a notch, made more forbidding, fortified" (110). Yet, despite the steady throbbing of his hand, Asher was buoyed by Everett's clear reference to him as a brother: "Within the urgency, the humorous play and idiom, was a suggestion of alliance, kinship, acceptance" (109–10, emphasis in original).[20]

Asher's almost identical accounts of his interracial jazz experiences in "The Barrier" and in *Notes* offer proof of their significance to his conception of himself as a jazz musician and demonstrate the ways in which his career as a writer allowed him to reclaim and to validate these experiences. His repeated use of the word "barrier" in these works suggests his recognition of his limited success in bridging the racial divide; the first-person narrator's quest in "The Barrier" to play jazz in black clubs, like Asher's own as he describes it in *Notes*, leads to a measure of grudging cordiality and respect, but to no significant diminishing of the cultural gulf between his own and the black jazz world to which he aspires. And if Everett's affectionate reference to Asher as "nigger" represents what is perhaps the pinnacle of Asher's interracial experiences in 1950s Boston, Asher is quick to acknowledge the limits to his acceptance. "I never scored the big touchdown," he admits, "never made it all the way through to the other side—few of us whiteys do" (*Notes* 110).

"On the Outside Lookin' In": Ross Russell's *The Sound*

Asher's portrayal of the limited success of white jazz musicians to overcome racial and cultural barriers has a notable antecedent in *The Sound* (1961), Ross Russell's fictional treatment of the life and death of Charlie Parker and the interracial band he led in New York following the Second World War.[21] In his analysis of the novel's reception, John Gennari observes that the general focus on Red Travers, the black bebop trumpeter and doomed junkie modeled on Parker, overlooks a central concern of the text—that is, "the drama of the pianist Bernie Rich's anguished struggle with his whiteness: his feelings of sexual and artistic inadequacy" (Gennari 313). Although Russell displays none of Asher's satirical impulses, his attention to the feelings and reactions of a middle-class white pianist to his intense immersion in New York's bebop jazz community and his excessive use of hipster jive talk and racialist imagery provide a convincing model for Asher's depictions of his own jazz experiences.[22]

The Sound opens with Bernie's return to New York following his wartime service as a pianist in the United Service Organizations (USO); although he has extensive European art music credentials, he is a novice to bebop, the revolutionary new music that has usurped the big band jazz that he had earned his living playing before the war (Russell 13). Bernie's new jazz community is a world of hipsters practicing the cult of bebop, replete with its own new language ("*Cool, crazy, hassle—dig, gone, gassed*") that Asher would later attempt to reproduce, with his own variations (8). The stark essentialism of Asher's descriptions of interracial jazz sessions, and his depiction of racial and ethnic "types" more generally, also finds a likeness in Russell's novel. As Red Travers listens to the house band from his dressing room at the club Hi Di Ho, he identifies Bernie as white because of his sense of time ("it wasn't the notes a man played that counted—it was where he played them" [29]). Moreover, Bernie's whiteness is linked to his lack of masculine authority, with Red imagining him as "[o]ne of those pale, taut, overeager grays that seemed drawn in increasing numbers to the new jazz, like moths to the flame" (29). By contrast, Red's black masculinity is incontestable: he is "so male, ugly almost, . . . with an empowering virile odor and primitive genital force" (30).

But when Red joins the band on stage, the focus shifts to Bernie's response to playing with the master bebop musician, his effort to keep up with Red's blinding tempos and challenging rhythmic conceptions reminiscent of Asher's trial-by-fire sessions at Coffee John's. Red's potent physical presence and virtuosic performance leave Bernie euphoric but stunned, in the grips—in Russell's starkly primitivist language—of a "dark, primal force, beyond Bernie's ken; as remote from his own experience as the witch doctor's art lies from the practice of clinical medicine" (36).[23] Yet Bernie, unlike Asher, has sufficient talent to make it to "the other side"—before long he has become the regular pianist, and the only white player, in Red's quintet (37). For a time, this interracial jazz experiment seems to bear fruit; Bernie's former bandleader, Jimmy Vann (modeled on Stan Kenton), incorporates the Red Travers quintet into his big band and organizes a successful mixed-band tour of California. Soon, however, the interracial tensions bubble over, with charges of racist white exploitation and countercharges of Crow Jim that would soon mark the end of Jimmy Vann's mixed-band experiment (37–69).

Briefly, Rich returns to his old job in Travers' quintet, a period marked by Red's rapid emotional disintegration that Russell links directly to the trumpeter's spiraling heroin addiction. Red's desperate need for money to pay his drug dealers fuels his racial resentments; he directs his hostility at Bernie, aiming a toy pistol at him on stage and later demanding that Bernie give him money for his next fix—"You Jew boys always got money stashed"—before assaulting him and emptying his wallet (100, 106). In a crucial scene that highlights the stark racial divide of Russell's jazz world, Bernie writes a complex arrangement for a blues Red has just composed; here, the contrast between Bernie's formal musical training and Red's instinctive (i.e., authentic) genius is illuminated by Bernie's confession that he has always struggled to write good melodies, a skill that comes naturally to Red (see Gennari 315). But Red shows little sympathy for his pianist's confession, instead issuing him a belligerent challenge: "You know your trouble, man?" To Bernie's bewildered reply, "No, tell me," Red exposes the impenetrable barrier (to borrow Asher's word) separating whites and blacks in this postwar jazz world: "You're on the outside lookin' in" (Russell 132).[24]

Bernie's nagging doubts about his suitability for the jazz life lead him back to Jimmy Vann's "symphonic jazz orchestra," with its promise of a steady wage and middle-class respectability (135). Following a New England tour, Vann and Bernie head back to New York, where they decide to check out the Monday jam session at the Harlem club, Cuba Libre, where Red has become the featured soloist. Russell's depiction of the tense mood of late-1940s Harlem is again striking for its resemblance to Asher's. As the men "drove through the bleak streets" searching for the club in Vann's "huge, sleek, powerful, expensive white car," Bernie "sensed an air of hostility surrounding them.... Despite the hour and the cold they saw groups of young men in leather and satin jackets, with club emblems emblazoned on the back. They seemed to be standing watch on those cold, silent corners" (140).

Like Asher and his fictional counterparts, Vann tries to display his hipness by talking jive to the doorman standing at the club's entrance, but, like them, his efforts backfire; in the words of the third-person narrator, "Vann was trying to strike the right note, but it didn't quite come off.... Fashions in jive changed pretty fast" (140). The young man's response is predictably wary, but when Vann offers him money to keep an eye on his expensive car while he and Bernie go inside to hear the music, he quickly agrees to the transaction: "Evil cats 'round here, man. You spoke the right party" (140). As in Asher's interracial jazz world, the black hipsters are in charge. For Russell's doorman, who seemed unaware that he was talking to a world-famous bandleader (and who apparently would not have cared had he known), "[i]t was just a money transaction" (140–41).

By the end of *The Sound*, these various portraits of interracial dissonance have led, painfully and inexorably, to a seemingly insurmountable divide. Bernie's final attempt at immersion in Red's world—including his own brief experience as a junkie—is long behind him. Red Travers is dead, gunned down in the street by "Negro cops" after he stabbed to death his Hispanic lover, who had slashed his face with a razor (182–83). In the novel's final scene, Bernie is living in Hollywood, on his way to being one of its leading musical directors, dining at his beautiful Swiss chalet with Jimmy Vann while the men listen to an old tape of a performance of Travers' quintet "for the Armed Forces Overseas Radio Services" (190). After listening to the tape, Vann observes that Bernie "couldn't play Red's kind of music without living in Red's world" (191). Bernie agrees, adding that he "never quite made it there," to which Vann retorts, "Red never quite made it in our world either" (191). While Vann holds out a glimmer of hope that racial attitudes might someday change, the prevailing mood is one of doubt, the barrier too high.

Dress Rehearsals for an Autobiography: *Raise Up Off Me* (1974)

> *As close as a black and a white come in friendship, as kindred as their tastes, perceptions and temperaments may be, there is that final barrier . . . that usually impedes the total transference of trust and compassion.*
>
> (ASHER, "ABOUT HAMPTON AND ME," 134)

The above quote comes not from *Notes*, "The Barrier," or *The Sound*—although it would not be out of place in any of them—but rather from Asher's 1974 essay, "About Hampton and Me," his candid account of his collaboration with Hampton Hawes on Hawes's autobiography, *Raise Up Off Me*. Nothing else that Asher has published confronts so openly the weighted history of race as he explains his attempts as a privileged white man to capture the voice, beliefs, and worldview of the great African American jazz pianist.

Asher's essay is particularly instructive because his literary depictions of African Americans in his work as a whole—their relationship to him and to his fictional counterparts, his portraits of the simultaneous distance and closeness of interracial relationships, and his treatment of black vernacular forms—cry out for further examination. That Asher was willing to expose the history of his negotiations with Hawes over the portrait of the pianist that emerges in his autobiography provides evidence of Asher's sincerity and genuine commitment to the project; yet in the end, as we will see, it also invites as many questions as it answers.

Asher first heard Hawes in person in 1955, when the pianist, who was then at the height of his career, appeared at Boston's Storyville club. Although Asher had listened to recordings of the bebop pioneers, Hawes was his first opportunity to hear "one of their major disciples" in person. Asher's description of the impact of Hawes's playing on him is uncannily familiar: he "had never heard any pianist crackle and burn up a club like this, utilizing the rise and dip tension-release feel for time that very few white musicians seemed able to get," and that was certainly "beyond my reach" ("About Hampton And Me" 134).

Eleven years would pass before Asher saw Hawes again, in 1966, when Hawes was appearing with a trio at San Francisco's Both/And club. Asher, who was then working as pianist for the Committee, went in the early hours of the morning to catch Hawes's last set, after which he approached the pianist to tell him how deeply his music had moved him on that night in Boston many years ago (134). They had a drink together, and Asher invited him to catch a performance of the Committee on his night off; to Asher's astonishment, several nights later, Hawes showed up, and, following the performance, the men talked for hours. Asher was moved by Hawes's "humor and sadness" and by his remarkable stories about his father (a Presbyterian minister), his life in jazz and association with other jazz greats, his heroin addiction and years of incarceration. As daybreak approached, Asher proposed the book collaboration; Hawes agreed, and in 1967 they began meeting for talks and interviews, sometimes at Hawes's house in East Los Angeles in a neighborhood called "White Fence," after the gang that claimed it as their territory (134).

Asher recognized that his chief responsibility was to learn the black vernacular expressions that were central to Hawes's manner of speech and vocabulary, "to steep myself in his voice, pick up on black street perspective and patois" (134); they met for more than a year before Asher believed that he had captured an authentic version of Hawes's voice and the necessary background that would allow him to provide "transitions" and "additional imagery," as needed (134). Another year passed before Asher sent Hawes a first draft and came to Los Angeles to hear his response; much to his chagrin, Hawes was not impressed, complaining that Asher had represented his speech as "deliberate minority group talk" and insisting that "I didn't mean for you to transcribe stuff directly. . . . it's not dignified enough" (135). As they reviewed the many passages that caused Hawes discomfort, Asher realized that Hawes was calling out his racism, telling him that he "had overdone some inflections, allowed the New England blue-eyed man to creep into certain passages; the glint of unconscious racism had been shimmering below the surface" (135).

A period of intense negotiation continued, at the end of which Asher prepared to return home, armed with notes for a new draft. Yet as he packed his suitcase, he felt deflated, forced to concede that he "hadn't captured the idiom or got beneath Hawes's skin nearly as well as I'd thought" (135). With imagery that pulls us once again to identical passages from *Notes* and "The Barrier," Asher anticipates a long process of revisions that would involve "more visits, tapings, searching out the sensibility and heart of a black man, hoping for a miracle of transmutation" (135).[25] Just then, however, his mood soared, the "barrier" lowering slightly, as he heard Hawes telling his girlfriend, "Come on, Josie, we got to get this nigger to the airport" (135).[26]

In this, Asher's moving account of what was certainly among the most significant interracial relationship of his life, we see him staging a dress rehearsal for the depictions of interracialism that would appear, often verbatim, in later publications for which he received sole credit as author. If the final version of *Raise Up Off Me* tones down some of the expressions of black vernacular that Hawes found particularly offensive, it is indisputably a searing, evocative black voice that speaks from its pages. As Gary Giddins states in his introduction to the 1979 edition of the memoir, "The care put into making the narrative flow, the attention to nuance and rhythmic immediacy, is evident on every page of the finished work. *Raise Up Off Me* is a major contribution to the literature of jazz" (Hawes vi).[27]

Hawes's rich, simile-driven speech is at the heart of his compelling narrative, as when he recalls that he "learned from Bird how to stay loose and relaxed on up tempos, and found out that at very slow tempos the beat has to swell: It's like taking a mouthful of good wine, swishing it around, savoring it before you let it go down; the swallow is that beat finally dropping" (Hawes 34). Hawes also speaks warmly of Chuck Thompson, who played drums in his first trio, describing "his time" as "natural as a heartbeat pumping pure, fresh blood into a tune, his rolls so even it was like hearing a crowd roar during a big play at a football game on the radio with the volume turned down" (35). Once again, we find in these passages a striking resemblance to those examined earlier from *Notes* and "The Barrier"—yet framed within a starkly different context. While Hawes attributes the first idea about tempo to Charlie Parker, and the analogy between "time" and a heartbeat to his drummer, Asher integrates them both into his observations about his *own* progress as a jazz pianist; moreover, he does so without naming Hawes directly, but rather with the descriptor "West Coast bopper," of which Hawes was undoubtedly a leading example.

That Asher made seemingly no effort to disguise the fact that he was claiming the utterances and experiences of the black pianist as his own (or his fictional counterparts') is in itself remarkable, providing clear proof of his desire to lay claim to the cultural markers of blackness. But this observation by itself falls short of addressing the full range of depictions of African Americans and their culture in Asher's work, from the moving accounts of his relationship with Jaki Byard and Hampton Hawes to the extended scenes in both his fiction and nonfiction featuring extreme examples of black character types. For the latter, I turn now to a brief consideration of Asher's third novel, *The Electric Cotillion*—his most explicitly satirical work of quasifiction foregrounding African American culture and interracial relations.

The Electric Cotillion

In *The Electric Cotillion*, Asher's 1970 novel about a forty-year-old struggling jazz pianist from Rhode Island who has settled in San Francisco in the early 1960s, Asher offers a comprehensive fictional version of his own life and career, exploring the themes, characterizations, and language that he would tirelessly revise and recast in his later work. Asher's fictional counterpart in *The Electric Cotillion* is Niles Davey, a musician who has been forced to take long-term employment with a society orchestra because of the scarcity of opportunities to play jazz.[28] Davey, like Asher, has a connection to the hungry i in San Francisco, a significant relationship with a much younger woman, and a close friendship with Hampton Hawes.[29] Several other characters appear in both *Notes* and *The Electric Cotillion*, including the singer Auraline (in *The*

Electric Cotillion, she is Aura). Moreover, the novel's first-person perspective makes a comparison to Asher's autobiographical persona inevitable: at times Asher and Davey sound like the same character writing different versions of a single life and career. Apart from a difference in location—Davey is from Rhode Island, not Worcester, and his jazz education takes place in "the fetid taverns and cellars of Providence . . . and those depressing little surrounding towns" (Asher, *Electric* 69)—in most respects there is little to distinguish Asher's and Davey's experiences with black culture.[30]

And yet in other respects there are substantial and significant differences between the two works, most notably regarding the role of fantasy in them. There are clearly fantastic elements in *Notes*, including Asher's broad construction of racial, ethnic, and gender stereotypes; his proclivity for writing extended dialogue featuring African American and white-ethnic vernacular; and his tendency to present racial types as binaries, as in the "good" and "bad" black characters at the center of his postdrug experience in Boston's Roxbury neighborhood. In *The Electric Cotillion*, however, Asher moves fantasy to the foreground. Early on, the Asherlike character, Davey, admits to being "profoundly addicted to fantasy" (9); later, he comments that he does not need the stimulation of hard drugs because he has his "own built-in fantasy machine" (27). Davey's fantasies are often centered on his career as a musician. He has frequent, extended conversations in his bathroom with such musical luminaries as Art Tatum, Dizzy Gillespie, Arthur Rubinstein, and Norman Granz, during which they compliment his playing or offer him important engagements, treating him as a respected peer and someone deserving of this illustrious company (11, 79, 132, 170–71).

It is easy to interpret Davey's fantasies as Asher's own for Asher grants Davey greater success and recognition as a jazz musician than he ever achieved. We learn that Davey has recorded two LPs with the Fantasy label and that he received notice in *Down Beat* magazine in 1957 for placing "sixth in the 'New Star' division of the International Critics Jazz Poll," this on the heels of his "appearance that summer at the Newport Festival" (8). Much later in the novel, Davey's trumpeter friend Val Catalona reminds him of the night at the famed Boston club "Storeyville" [sic] when Duke Ellington's alto saxophonist Johnny Hodges joined them on the bandstand to perform "I Got It Bad and That Ain't Good": "It was so goddam beautiful no one clapped for about ten seconds, like after the Gettysburg Address" (164).

Fantasy also plays a role in Asher's depiction of interracial sex and sexual attraction in *The Electric Cotillion*. Earlier, I considered Asher's unrequited infatuation in *Notes* with the black jazz singer Auraline, who appears as the character Aura Philips in his novel. In his depiction of their manner, speech, and appearance, Asher was clearly working from a single model. Yet Davey sleeps with Aura, whom he describes as "a big handsome brown queen" (72).

The experience, Davey's "first time with a black woman," was by his own admission not particularly successful. "[T]here was a dimension or two separating us," he recalls, "associations missing, she was too—what? *earthy* for me" (72, emphasis in original).

How then, might we explain the significant changes Asher made in *Notes* to his depiction of the interracial relationship between the young white jazz pianist and the black blues singer? Is Davey's relationship with Aura a fictionalized account of Asher's own real-life experience that he was reticent to reveal in his memoir? Or is Asher perhaps indulging his own unrequited fantasies about black women through his fictional characters, Davey and Aura? Is Davey's description of Aura as "too . . . earthy for me" Asher's satirical commentary on the hypersexualized depictions of black women that have dominated popular culture? It is fair to say that in both versions of this relationship the white man is impotent, incapable of fulfilling the needs of the "big handsome brown queen" (*Electric* 72) or the "beautiful tawny-skinned singer" (*Notes* 100). Asher and Davey's impotence is important evidence, among others offered by Asher, of the limitations of interracial alliance in his fictional-autobiographical world.

In another example of near-identical passages in *The Electric Cotillion* and *Notes*, Asher appears to use the ambiguity of language to convey two starkly contrasting images of interracial relationships. In *The Electric Cotillion*, Davey's sexual fantasies about black women are an important aspect of his recollections of his experiences as a teenager in predominantly black jazz clubs. "[I]n the magical and marvelous dives," he recalls, "young liquid black girls were coming on to me, finding me *cute*, soul-kissing me . . . in sequestered booths, cool hands curling along my limbs like dark spring water" (70, emphasis in original). Davey was aware, however, that the young women were "hoking it up too for the bloods (their soul brothers, if you will) . . . , watching Master Charles get turned on and sanctioning it, tolerant of me because I was just a funny-ass kid and played okay . . . and wasn't too *obvious* a nigger lover" (71, emphasis in original). Here Asher foregrounds the eroticism of Davey's experiences with black women, even if it is a stretch to imagine the "soul brothers" tolerating the sexual advances of their "sisters."

In *Notes*, Asher maintains much of the wording and imagery of this passage but uses it in the context of his account of his jazz education at Coffee John's. More specifically, he wonders why the regulars continued to allow him to sit in, despite his musical limitations, suggesting that "they may have found amusement in the spectacle of Master Charles getting turned on, trying to dwell in their sunshine—tolerant of me because I was just a skinny, earnest, funny-ass kid and not too obvious a nigger lover" (*Notes* 100). In his subtle calibration of the phrase "turned on" here—from explicitly sexual to a more general reference to his response to the music—Asher again shows his tendency to apply greater restraint on his erotic imagination in his autobiography than in his work published as fiction.[31]

In a scene reminiscent of Asher's encounter with the black youth in Roxbury, Davey is confronted by an angry young black man in a San Francisco eatery; once again, the caricature evident in Asher's autobiography is taken to greater extremes. Davey's coffee has just arrived when the man—we learn that his name is Clarence and that he is wearing a "[d]ark beret and immaculate cobalt-blue jump suit"—brushes against Davey's sleeve and shouts out, "You killed my fathuh and raped my mothuh" (*Electric* 90). Davey's response is to attempt to talk "black" and to show his supreme hipness through references to his sorrow over the death of Martin Luther King and his support for Dizzy Gillespie's run for the presidency (90). Yet, like Asher's ill-advised admission to the black youths who accosted him, Davey's words serve only to fuel Clarence's hostility.

With the arrival of Big Brown, a young man who comes over to their table and attempts to calm Clarence, it appears that Asher has introduced a "good" black character, comparable to the role played by Everett and Wesley in *Notes* (91). But this apparent interracial rapprochement quickly dissolves when we learn that Big Brown works as a rock guitarist at the same club where Pope, Davey's young girlfriend, is employed. Davey immediately identifies Big Brown as a sexual threat and, driven by his own insecurities, unleashes a stream of extreme racist commentary. He describes Big Brown variously as a "huge spectacled moon-faced black," "the big spade," and "the massive spade," and at one point he asks Pope, "Who's your big brown friend?" (90–92). Davey's fears about the nature of Pope's relationship with Big Brown turn out to be warranted; after Pope and Davey quarrel, she leaves him to spend the night with Big Brown. When Pope returns, Davey hounds her for details of their sexual experience; his use of graphic and crude imagery here links him to a long history of images and depictions of black men as hypersexualized and frequently reduced simply to the phallus.[32] Moreover, his jealousy of Big Brown reminds us of Lott's reference to the "dangerous power" of the black male body, a power that stokes white fear, which "is difficult to distinguish ... from homosexual fantasies, or at the very least envy, of black men" (*Love and Theft* 126).

In the aftermath of the incident with Clarence, Davey expresses his frustration to Pope, telling her "the son of a bitch ought to be able to sense a blood brother when he sees one" (*Electric* 93). Yet his words and actions only highlight the futility of his attempt to be "a blood brother"; by contrast to Big Brown, who by virtue of his being a real blood brother has the authority to step in and quiet the situation, Davey's attempts to show his hipness leave him looking weak and foolish. As these passages demonstrate, the satirical impulses apparent in *Notes* were already in full evidence in Asher's novel published more than two decades earlier. Reverence for black culture and particularly for the skill and expertise of jazz musicians is combined with extreme racial stereotypes: in both works, African American men have a natural ability to play jazz, but also familiarity and skill with illicit activities such as drugs, burglary, and theft. When Pope goes missing, Big Brown accompanies Davey to Pope's apartment and demonstrates his expertise at breaking locks as he effortlessly opens her door with a wire clothes hanger. In Davey's response to Big Brown—"Glad you're on our side"—Davey's attempt at a black masquerade has evaporated; now he is simply a timid white male standing in fear of the assertiveness (and competence) of a young black male (172).

It is not difficult to find resemblances between Asher's autobiographical and fictional depictions of the interracial experiences of white men and those outlined by Lott and Monson, considered earlier. Asher and Davey evoke Lott's description of the "white obsession with black (male) bodies which underlies white racial dread to our own day," and which has often been expressed through "ridicule and racist lampoon" (*Love and Theft* 4). Similarly, Asher's language and imagery resonate with Monson's observation of "the American cultural tendency to reduce African American cultural values to caricature" ("The Problem" 421). And yet while Monson is concerned with the "presumptions" of white people about African Americans "and their supposedly hip lifestyles" (396), Asher's focus, as I have tried to show, is multidirectional: both angry young black men and foolish and presumptuous white men become, under specific conditions of heightened racial tension, little more than cartoon figures. If Clarence is the stereotypical, angry black militant reduced to caricature, then Davey's response to him is no less caricaturized, with his awkward and failed attempts at hipness. And if Asher's autobiographical persona is less extreme than Davey's, satire is nonetheless evident in his self-representation as well as in his depictions of the black and white ethnic characters at the center of his music experiences; it is also prominent in his portrayal of the dreary conventionalism of the New England society–band world in which he worked for many years.

If Asher made a sincere effort to respond to Hawes's objections to the autobiographical voice that emerged in an early draft of *Raise Up Off Me*, he showed no inclination to abandon the more extreme examples of African American vernacular expression that appear in some of his other work. For these were essential tools for his satirical depictions of American culture more broadly, signaling his rejection of the cultural and political conventions of his early adulthood and his embrace of the 1960s West Coast scene that would provide him with such fertile material for his own literary imagination. The influences of that world—including his immersion in mid-twentieth-century American social satire and leading-edge comedy—is the subject I turn to now.

The hungry i and the 1950s American Comedy Revolution

In *Seriously Funny: The Rebel Comedians of the 1950s and 1960s*, Gerald Nachman considers the centrality of satire in 1950s American comedy and the hungry i's leading role in providing a stage for comedic innovation (Nachman 4). "The hungry i had become by the mid-1950s the Comedy Central of its day," Nachman observes, "the main staging area of the revolutionary movement" (9). As house pianist, Asher writes in *Notes*, he was required to learn "the role of musician as straight man.... We are the comics' perennial fall guys, smiling bravely under our dunce caps—semi-mute and expendable.... No other professional is subject to such public degradation" (*Notes* 247). Asher recalls his experience backing Jack E. Leonard, known as one of the first comedians of insult, who made Asher "an unsuspecting victim of ... his curare-tipped barbs" (247). On another occasion, his piano playing was the target of Professor Irwin Corey's nonsensical putdowns, with Corey asking him, "What key art'st thou in?" before Asher had even begun to play (251). Eventually, Corey ordered Asher and the bass player to leave while he continued with his show unaccompanied. These public humiliations notwithstanding, Asher describes Corey as "a spellbinder [who] delivers his inspired gibberish with a jazzman's timing" (252).[33]

Mort Sahl got his start at the hungry i and quickly became one of the leaders of the comedic revolution, casting aside the safe, suburban, and resolutely apolitical borscht-belt humor of his predecessors in favor of no-holds-barred social commentary that was encapsulated in his refrain to his audiences, "*Are there any groups I haven't offended?*" (Nachman 10; Epstein 169). Both the Left and the Right were the targets of Sahl's commentary as he steered far from anything resembling political correctness (Nachman 77). On Sahl's stance on racial matters, Nachman observes that the comedian "went after blacks with the same abandon as he did whites" (77). Asher's satirical depictions, including his caricatures of extreme black hostility, bear more than passing traces of Sahl's comedic approach.

One night, at the hungry i, Sahl went after Asher, when something about the pianist's rendition of "It's a Grand Old Flag" as Sahl's "play-on" rubbed the comedian the wrong way. In front of the packed hungry i crowd, Asher recalls, Sahl asked him: "Have you ever contemplated an alternate means of livelihood?" Asher replied that he had not, and then, much to his surprise, he threw the question back at Sahl. Almost immediately he realized that his brashness "could have cost me the piano bench; Sahl was as big as they come. But his moods were mercurial, and by the next show all was forgotten" (*Notes* 257–58; Nachman 63).

Of all the comics Asher backed at the hungry i, Lenny Bruce seems to have left the deepest and most lasting impression. With his insistence on challenging limits on free speech and permissible discourse on race, religion, and sexuality, Bruce changed the world of stand-up comedy in ways that are still apparent to this day. According to Nachman, "Bruce was a little too rough for the hungry i," a view supported by the critic Grover Sales, publicist for the hungry i during the 1960s, who observed that Bruce's material, while "fairly tame compared to later on," was at times extremely challenging for the club's "middle-class, Yuppie" audiences (Nachman 404).[34]

In his essay, "*Shpritzing* the *Goyim*/Shocking the Jews," Sanford Pinsker examines one of Bruce's best-known acts that begins with his address to his audience, "By the way, are there any niggers here tonight?" From there, Bruce—"in the guise of a Southern tobacco auctioneer"—would begin to chant, creating a linguistic heap of ethnic slurs—"That's two kikes, and three niggers, . . . and one spic"—and so on (Pinsker 94). In Pinsker's view, Bruce's routine reflected his knowledge "that language is power, and also that the words that hurt can be words defused, exhausted by repetition" (94).[35] Leon Rappoport reaches a similar conclusion, suggesting "that by openly confronting and ridiculing stereotypes and slurs rather than denying them," comedians such as Bruce and Richard Pryor succeeded in weakening them, stripping them of their "emotional poison" and thus finding a way for "laughter to enter" (Rappoport 80).

In *Notes*, Asher describes in some detail another well-known Bruce routine that he performed late one night at the hungry i, in which Bruce disclosed his Jewish identity to the audience as an introduction to his irreverent banter on the subject of responsibility for the death of Christ; from there he segued to the habits and practices of lesbians and "faggots" in small-town America, all the while testing his audience on their knowledge of who did what to whom (*Notes* 253–55). Before Bruce was finished, Asher writes, his audience was "streaming en masse for the exits, a middle-American tide, frozen-faced, demeaned, outraged, some turning to shake a fist, shouting abuse, epithets . . . giving back as good as they got" (255). In vivid contrast to the squares who did not "get" Bruce, Asher was clearly moved, closing the chapter with his elegy to the late comedian, describing him as an "abrasive, tormented man who contained within his slight tummler's frame the voltaic energy to goad, convulse, alienate, and enrage, to empty show rooms and transform minds—who would lift off and burn like a Roman candle for a brief time, and when he came down would leave an electric, bluish afterglow that would remind us of the sparks and scorch and illumination that had been" (256).

Asher's use of the Yiddish "tummler"[36] here suggests the ways in which his own Jewishness provided him with an important link to Bruce and the other Jewish comedians at the hungry i, whose performances revealed important aspects of Jewish cultural, religious, and historical identity. One night, after closing time, Asher writes, Jackie Mason—the ordained-rabbi-turned-comedian—asked him if he was Jewish; when Asher nodded, he recalled "see[ing] the faintest consoling smile cross the cherubic face" (268). Despite their considerable differences in worldview and attitudes, Asher was clearly identifying some common ground as a result of their shared Jewish heritage. In these Jewish entertainers, then, Asher found a fraternity of sorts—one that offered him a range of models of Jewish manhood that had been unavailable to him in Worcester's more conventional Jewish community. And while Asher's Jewish persona is not identical to any of theirs, aspects are readily apparent in his own, including Sahl's staunch secularism, traces of Bruce's *Yiddishkeit*, and the startling rudeness of Corey and Leonard, the masters of comedic insult.[37]

While Asher may not have sought, either consciously or directly, to emulate these comedians in his own work, aspects of their modus operandi—their satirical tone and manner, their exploration of previously taboo subjects such as interracial relations and sexuality, their irreverence toward mainstream values and religion, their use of racial and ethnic dialect and caricature—are clearly discernable in his writings. When Bruce performed his "Are there any niggers in the house routine" or his "send-ups about the Holocaust," he was not only challenging the boundaries of permissible speech but also insisting that through public airing the force of pejorative language and racist thinking would be diminished (Pinsker 95). I have suggested that Asher might have been seeking a similar effect in his depiction of Big Brown and Clarence in *The Electric Cotillion* and that his attempt was at least in part successful: Davey's knee-jerk racism is consistently juxtaposed to Big Brown's thoughtful intelligence, while Clarence's cartoonlike black militancy serves mainly to highlight Davey's exaggerated fears about African American men.

Asher, however, was not a stand-up comedian challenging his audiences with provocative social commentary and biting satire; his public persona—as nightclub pianist and as author—is, in my view, less clearly defined than that of a Mort Sahl or Lenny Bruce. In the end, I continue to struggle most to make sense of Asher's attempt to combine both satire *and* sincerity in his depictions of his experiences with black culture: to demonstrate his authenticity as a jazz pianist who has immersed himself in black jazz traditions while at the same time he reveals the extent of his distance from African American culture through his tendency to reduce it to stereotypes. Earlier, I referred to Asher's moving description in his autobiography of his evening with Jaki Byard during Byard's visit to San Francisco. Asher's passing mention of the interval (twenty-five years) that had passed since he had studied with Byard places their reunion in roughly the same period in which Asher was writing *The Electric Cotillion*—that is, the same period in which Asher was composing his descriptions of Clarence ("*Black as the ace of spades*" [90]) and Big Brown (a "massive spade" [*Electric* 91]); the same period in which he was also composing Davey's response to learning that Pope has been staying with Big Brown: "Gazing tacitly at this gentle purple-glassed spade and brother, I realized that despite Aura, despite Diz, Tatum, Waller and all the storied players and their forebears that it hurt, hurt bad, more than it should have, and that I could hate this kindly spook easily, avidly, with all my heart" (157). While I acknowledge in theory the distinction between the author and his autobiographical personas or fictional representations, Asher's notable tendency to merge fiction and autobiography leaves nagging doubts, in my view, as to where the racist commentary and exaggerated attention to black sexuality resides.

For all of his dedication and hard work, Asher's "lifelong odyssey to pick the brains, embezzle the rhythms, master the soulful secrets of the race" is in the end a disappointing and "frustrating" odyssey (*Notes* 10). Asher admits as much himself in his final assessment of these experiences—"I never scored the big touchdown, never made it all the way through to the other side—few of us whiteys do" (110); his repetition of the word "barrier" to describe his experience at Coffee John's serves as a concise metaphor for the impermeable wall between cultures that is at the heart of his immersion story. In *The Electric Cotillion*, Davey's insistence on proving his credentials as a jazz musician is also ultimately unconvincing; indeed, most of the novel concerns his decidedly unglamorous career as a musician in a society band, with all of the drudgery associated with that work.

Asher seems reluctant to end his story there, but rather to challenge it (both in his autobiography *and* fiction) with repeated references to his success as a white musician in learning and replicating "black" sounds and influences. Asher's account in *Notes* of his experience at Coffee John's ends in such a manner, with him recalling an experience that occurred many years later, when he was working at the hungry i, that appears to show him on "the other side":

> A middle-aged black man approached me in the bar following an entr'acte medley of Duke Ellington tunes. He said he had enjoyed the music and that I must have grown up or spent a lot of time around Harlem to play like that. I told him I had been born and bred in eastern Massachusetts. "Okay," he said, "but somewhere along the line you must've eaten some okra and sweet-potato pie." (*Notes* 110)[38]

A similar mood dominates the ending of *Notes*, with sentiment seemingly prevailing over satire. Depictions of angry young blacks and a frustrated and disappointed middle-aged white piano player fade into the background, replaced by Asher's decidedly misty-eyed optimism over the renewed interest in the music that moves him most—the popular songs and jazz standards from the Great American Songbook (304). A mellow, gentler tone has replaced the fervor and tension that marked his quest for acceptance in African American

Don Asher in 2004 at San Francisco's Moose's restaurant, where he entertained diners with his skillful renditions of the Great American Songbook. Christina Koci Hernandez/ San Francisco Chronicle/ Polaris.

jazz communities, and Asher seems to have embraced his supper-club career with humor and good cheer.

Perhaps the most striking aspect of Asher's overall depiction of his career beyond his early jazz strivings is indeed its whiteness: with the exception of his interracial jazz experiences, Asher, in fact, performed primarily in white society bands or in respectable supper clubs before mostly white audiences. The final scene of *Notes* maintains this impression: the people he mentions—Willie Nelson, Hoagy Carmichael, and the patrons who can afford to dine at the Café Majestic—are all white. There is, however, one notable reference to a black person in this scene—albeit a symbolic one—and that is Asher himself: the young people who ask him to play their favorite songs refer to him as Sam, the black piano player in the movie *Casablanca* (304).[39] Once again, then, Asher invites his readers to imagine his link to the authentic black jazz tradition, specifically to the black pianists whose interpretations of the Great American Songbook were his inspiration and guide.

6
"Straight Life": The Jazz Journey of Art Pepper

The focus of this final chapter is the haunting and often disturbing autobiography of Art Pepper (1925–1982), one of the leading West Coast jazz musicians of the postwar period. In *Straight Life: The Story of Art Pepper* (1979), Pepper describes in painful detail the cruelty and neglect of his early life, his lifelong struggles with drug and alcohol addiction, and his fraught relationships with many of the people closest to him in his personal life and professional career. The motif of the white jazz musician as loner and outsider is at the forefront of Pepper's autobiography, framed by the narrator's early realization of his rare musical ability and its potential to lift him beyond the limited opportunities of the working-class culture in which he was raised. Indeed, it is Pepper's musical gift and vitality that emerge as his salvation, along with Laurie Pepper, his third wife, who was instrumental in his successful return to the jazz scene in the mid-1970s following many years of relative inactivity.

In many respects, Pepper's explanation of the beliefs that drove him to black music and culture provides further opportunity to revisit some of the central themes of this study: among them a white jazzman's early recognition of the black roots of jazz, his desire to belong to that world (as well as his expressed desire to *be* black),[1] and the euphoria of interracialism as well as the crushing discovery of its limits. But as the only jazz autobiography under consideration here coauthored by a woman, *Straight Life* opens significant new pathways for investigation. Laurie Pepper's critical role in the creation, direction, and production of her husband's autobiography is nothing short of a gift, allowing us to consider the authority and influence of a woman in jazz—a rare opportunity in a study of texts in which women's voices are mainly relegated to the sidelines or absent entirely.

As will become clear, Laurie was no mere transcriber or amanuensis, but rather the driving force behind *Straight Life*; without her, it is very likely that there would be no autobiography of Art Pepper, nor would there have been the period of remarkable creative output and critical acclaim that marked the final years of his life. My discussion of Laurie is largely informed by her own words: namely, her afterward for the 1994 edition of *Straight Life* and her own recent, captivating autobiography, *Art: Why I Stuck with a Junkie Jazzman* (2014). While the earlier essay offers an important view of her collaborative method, a much fuller portrait of her role in her husband's life and career emerges in her own autobiography, enabling us to hear and see a woman's experience at the heart of jazz culture.

In addition, *Straight Life* encourages a westward turn in this study's exploration of interracial jazz communities: while the autobiographers examined in earlier chapters have described their experiences in black jazz communities in New Orleans, Chicago's South Side, Harlem, and Boston, the California-born-and-raised Pepper depicts a white musician's midcentury interracial experiences in the heart of Los Angeles's black cultural mecca—Central Avenue. Pepper is a powerful and persuasive narrator, and he drives home his views on race relations in jazz, and in American society more broadly, with a grim and sometimes relentless resolve. In his telling, the friendly and open interracialism that he experienced in the clubs and on the streets of Central Avenue in the late 1930s and 1940s had disappeared by the time he returned to the jazz scene following one of several periods of incarceration for narcotics possession; in its place was a segregationist, aggressively assertive black militancy that left white musicians on the outside looking in. One of the concerns of this chapter is to show how Pepper's response to these deep strains in jazz interracial alliances was both intensely personal (that is, an expression of his own troubled life and the particular interracial experiences that shaped him) and reflective of the wider response of white jazz musicians and critics to the dramatic changes unfolding in the jazz world (and in the nation as a whole) against the charged atmosphere of sit-ins, Freedom Rides, and ongoing violent resistance to civil rights for African Americans.

In the decades since the publication of *Straight Life*, many other portraits of West Coast jazz have emerged, a number of them composed by or focusing on African American jazz musicians and their contributions to the social, political, and musical history of Central Avenue, as well as more general studies of West Coast jazz and its best-known practitioners.[2] Another aim of this chapter, then, is to evaluate Pepper's portrait of his experiences on Central Avenue against these other accounts, to search for those areas of agreement as well as dissonance. If, as Ted Gioia suggests, Pepper's experiences there "contributed to the essentially black aesthetic" that was central to Pepper's own musical expression (*West Coast Jazz* 287), it is worth asking if this "essentially black aesthetic" was expressed only through his music or also in the attitudes and beliefs that guided his extramusical life. One way to approach this question is to ask another: What are the concerns and preoccupations that drive Pepper's narrative, and how do they compare with those articulated by the black voices in these other accounts? More specifically, are his claims for a kind of colorblind interracialism on Central Avenue during the 1940s and a backlash against interracialism in the decades that followed supported by the firsthand accounts of these other African American musicians and by the histories of jazz in Los Angeles in that period?

> "I'd wander around alone, and it seemed that the wind was always blowing and I was always cold" (Pepper and Pepper 9)

In the opening pages of *Straight Life*, Art Pepper offers a wrenching account of his mother's attempts to end her pregnancy while she was carrying him. Mildred Bartold was only fifteen, a recent runaway from the convent life prescribed by her Italian family, in search of good times, drinking, and boyfriends. In a bar in San Pedro, California, she met and began a sexual relationship with Arthur Pepper Sr., a longshoreman and experienced machinist on oil tankers and freighters, a union organizer and world traveler who, at the age of twenty-nine, was thinking about settling down and raising a family (Pepper and Pepper 3–4).[3] When Mildred learned that she was pregnant, she sought advice from her girlfriend about aborting the fetus: "My mother starved herself and took everything anybody had ever heard of that would make you miscarry, but to no avail," Pepper remarks. "I was born. She lost" (3–4).

Through this opening salvo, Pepper establishes the tone of brutal frankness and deep despair that characterizes much of his narrative. His parents' marriage was short-lived, loveless, and marked by explosive episodes of violence. During Pepper's early life, his father continued to work at sea, leaving him and his mother at their home in Watts; frequently, however, his mother would go out drinking and leave her young son home alone. When his parents were together, Pepper recalls, they would drink heavily and fight constantly. On one occasion, he watched as his father beat his mother. "He broke her nose. He broke a couple of ribs. Blood poured all over the floor" (5). In what surely was Pepper's attempt to erase the trauma of witnessing such brutality, he recalls that "the next day I was scrubbing up blood, trying to get the blood up for ages" (5). When he was five, his parents sent him to live with his father's mother on a ranch in Nuevo, California. As if describing a rental agreement, Pepper explains that his move to Nuevo marked "the end of my living with my parents and the beginning of my career with my grandmother." For Pepper, it also signaled the end of any hope for a loving and caring childhood. "I saw my grandmother, and I saw that there was no warmth, no affection. I was terrified and completely alone. And at that time I realized that no one wanted me. There was no love and I wished I could die" (5).

The phobias and obsessions that would remain to varying degrees throughout Pepper's life may be traced to these early childhood experiences. His sexual perversions emerged, he suggests, in response to his grandmother's strong sense of shame about bodily functions. She would lock the door when she went to the bathroom, thus making "the idea of going to the bathroom something that was nasty, that you had to hide" but also "exciting," so that he became drawn "to bathrooms to see what went on in there" (30). Before long, Pepper was a dedicated Peeping Tom, watching the next-door neighbor in her bathroom at night and peering into lit rooms on his walks around the neighborhood. By the tender age of eleven, he had become, in his words, "totally preoccupied by sex" (31). Behind Pepper's detailed accounts of his compulsive masturbation and pursuit of women in search of sexual gratification lies his apparent drive to confess, to put all his anguish and pain before the reader; later in the chapter, I will consider Laurie Pepper's role in encouraging these confessional aspects of her husband's narrative.[4]

At the same time, Pepper was consumed by phobias, "frightened ... beyond words" by thunder and lightning (6). He also feared his father, a tall and handsome man with an authoritative presence "that commanded respect"; it was Pepper who gave him his nickname, "Moses"—"because I felt he had that stature, that strength" (7). Yet his father's strength served mainly to heighten Pepper's sense of his own weakness; in an attempt to prove his toughness and thus "win his [father's] love," Pepper would initiate fights at school, displaying his cuts and bruises to his father "so he would like me" (7). When his father tried to force him to eat the vegetables that his grandmother had prepared, Pepper would gag and vomit; his inability to swallow his food only served to fuel his father's rage and led to frequent strappings (7).[5] In the end, he became convinced that "the things he wanted me to do I just couldn't do" (7). Although Pepper shows little of the probing self-examination of some of the jazz autobiographers we have considered, his stories expose the raw wounds left by these early experiences.

In a childhood marked by distress and upheaval, Pepper quickly discovered that music was a source of joy and light, an opportunity for him to show his talent and to express his deep feelings and emotions. He recalls his excitement at seeing the shiny new horns in music store windows and his powerful desire to "go inside and touch them," until at last he finally approached his father and told him that he "just had to have a musical instrument" (10). His description of his first clarinet lessons when he was nine highlights his innate musicianship and inclination to play by ear, one he shares with many of the other white jazz musicians in this study: "I played what I felt. I didn't want to read anything or play exercises" (11).

Soon, Pepper's father began taking him to the bars lining the waterfront in San Pedro, where he would place him on the bar and instruct him to "play little songs" on his clarinet. Pepper would also take requests from the patrons—"real tough guys; they were my dad's friends"—some of whom had missing fingers or limbs from workplace accidents (11–12). These experiences taught Pepper to view music as an opportunity to escape a life of dangerous and enervating work; more importantly, they provided a rare opportunity for positive interactions with his father: "I always felt scared before I played," Pepper recalls, "but after I did it I was proud and my dad was proud of me" (12).

Pepper's account of his first forays into jazz illustrates his early awareness of the black roots of the music and his attempt to claim, by way of his exceptional musical ability, his own right to play. When he was a student at San Pedro High, he played in a trio with two older white teenagers, guitarist Johnny Martizia and trombonist Jimmy Henson; while Martizia strummed the guitar, he would explain to Pepper that "[t]hese are the chords to the blues, which all jazz emanates from. This is black music, from Africa, from the slave ships that came to America" (40). In a revealing question, Pepper asked him "if he thought that I might have the right to play jazz," to which Martizia replied, "You're very fortunate. You have a gift" (40). In the context of their discussion of the African origins of the blues, their exchange takes on particular significance, granting Pepper legitimacy and the right to cross the racial divide. "I wanted to become the greatest player in the world," Pepper adds in response to the guitarist's encouragement. "I wanted to become a jazz musician" (40).

"Everybody Just Loved Everybody Else, or If They Didn't, I Didn't Know about It": Art Pepper and 1940s Central Avenue

From his early teens, Pepper was a regular on Central Avenue, drawn to the street's music as well as its lifestyle (Pepper and Pepper 42). In his depiction, the Central Avenue of the early 1940s was joyful, idyllic, and inclusive, a vibrant black cultural space in which whites were made to feel welcome and even wanted. Pepper's portrait is a lament of a community lost, as he contrasts the warmth and hospitality that marked his early experiences with the antagonism that he would experience during the 1960s, at the height of black power and black nationalist fervor:

> As soon as evening came people would be out on the streets, and most of the people were black, but nobody was going around in black leather jackets with naturals hating people.... There was no black power. I was sixteen, seventeen years old, white, innocent, and I'd wander around all over the place, ... all night

long, and never once was accosted. I was never threatened. I was never challenged to a fight. I was never called a honkie. And I never saw any violence at all except for an occasional fight over a woman or something like that. It was a whole different trip than it got to be later on. (42)

One of Pepper's earliest friends on Central Avenue was the teenaged saxophonist Dexter Gordon, whose striking appearance and debonair manner made him a popular figure in the community (43). Pepper was undoubtedly drawn to Gordon's confident eccentricity and cool hipness; he remembers standing at a distance and watching as a crowd of "black cats and chicks" would surround Gordon "and pat him on the back, and bullshit with him" (43–44). In this scene, Pepper clearly views himself as a cultural outsider looking in, admiring their speech and facility with "verbal games," yet lacking the confidence to join in (44).[6]

Beyond their shared musical interests, Gordon and Pepper were both eager participants in the free-for-all (and increasingly dangerous) drug culture that was infiltrating Central Avenue in that period. Before he met Gordon, Pepper was already a heavy drinker and had begun his lifelong, indiscriminate use of pills. Together, they "smoked pot and took Dexedrine tablets, and they had inhalers in those days that had little strips of paper in them that said 'poison,' so we'd put these strips in our mouths, behind our teeth. . . . You'd feel as if your whole head was lifting off" (43). But Gordon also aided Pepper's entrance into a very different Central Avenue scene with his suggestion that Pepper audition for a band that drummer Lee Young (Lester's younger brother) was putting together for the Club Alabam, one of the premier jazz clubs on the Avenue (41). Pepper won the alto spot in Young's band—a hot, swinging, bluesy small big band—that accompanied the club's featured black performers, including rising stars Avery Parrish, Wynonie Harris, and comedians Moke and Poke (42–43). Pepper's experience in Young's band "playing these real down-home blues" was both joyful and nurturing: "I'd go in there and play and get so caught up in the feeling that I never had a chance to think about anything bad that might be happening to me or to worry at all. It was such an open, such a free, such a beautifully right time" (43).[7]

In Pepper's telling, Young was solicitous and kind toward him, not only because of his youth and inexperience, but also because of his vulnerability as a cultural outsider. Young was also concerned about Pepper's relationship with Gordon, who had already developed a serious heroin habit, and he sat down with Pepper for a heart-to-heart, warning him that Gordon had "a way to go. . . . But you, man, . . . I'd love to see you not have to pay those dues" (44). Then an opening came up in Benny Carter's big band, and Young used his influence to arrange an audition for Pepper, who realized that the bandleader was trying to find work for him "where he thought I'd be protected" (44).

Although Pepper had become a good reader by then, he still knew nothing about chords or the harmonic structure of the music he was playing (48). Carter went out of his way to help him, initially assigning Pepper the second alto part because he had little experience playing lead alto, although he often provided him with the charts for both (48). On quieter nights at the club, Pepper recalls, "Benny would just get off the stand and let me play his parts. I'd get all his solos. I learned that way how to play lead in a four-man saxophone section. And I learned a lot following Benny, listening to his solos, what he played against the background" (48).

At a time when Young and Carter continued to experience (and bravely challenge) systemic discrimination and racism in their personal and professional lives, their concern for a young, untested white musician was remarkable, demonstrating their individual humanity as well as the potential of jazz communities to foster positive and nurturing relationships among people of different cultural backgrounds.[8] In no way, however, should their mentoring of Pepper be read as evidence of starry-eyed idealism; a consistent refrain in Pepper's accounts of his musical and extra-musical experiences with African Americans is the contrast between the latter's pragmatic understanding of race relations in America (based on their own lived experiences) and his own seemingly willful naiveté.

Pepper's apparent incomprehension about race is, in fact, at the forefront of his responses to situations that occurred during and following his tenure with Carter's band. He had begun, by his account, to feel established and settled with the band when Carter told him that for an upcoming tour through the southern United States, he would have to leave him behind, citing the dangers of taking a mixed band. Pepper's response to Carter's decision—"I couldn't understand why I had to leave the band"—reveals a naiveté about southern racial customs that no black musician could conceivably have held (49). Although Carter held firm to his decision (a wise one, as we will see), he arranged an audition for Pepper with Stan Kenton's new band, thus helping to guide Pepper further along a career path that Young had already opened for him.

During his tenure with Kenton, Pepper became one of the band's featured soloists in live performances and on many recordings, attracting a considerable following and critical acclaim (49–50).[9] And yet, as seemed to happen so often in Pepper's life and career, circumstances and his own personal make-up combined to send him reeling off course. Near the end of 1943, only six months after he had married his high-school girlfriend, Patti, he received his draft notice (52). Despite his extensive efforts to evade service, Pepper passed his draft-board examination, and in early 1944, he "was inducted into Fort MacArthur," an army installation at San Pedro, Los Angeles (53). After basic training, he was sent to Camp Butner in North Carolina, where he was assigned to duty with the combat engineers (58).

One Saturday night, Pepper went into Durham to hear Benny Carter, who was performing there with his band. He was surprised to see the word "loge" on his ticket; when he inquired about it, he was told that he had to sit upstairs. He protested, insisting he had played "with this band: they're old friends of mine and I'd like to be close to the stand, where I can say hello to them" (58). The ticket seller's terse reply—"Whites aren't allowed downstairs"—reminded Pepper of his talk with Carter, when the bandleader had tried, without success, to explain southern racial etiquette to him: "I had been all around Central Avenue for years as a kid. I couldn't understand what he was talking about, and my eyes were still closed at this time" (58). His brief description of the auditorium's seating is in the voice of a child learning about segregation for the first time: "The whole bottom floor was black. The people upstairs were white" (58). Yet his response to his pain was hardly childlike: he began to drink, and, emboldened by the alcohol, he went downstairs, overcome by the feeling that "I had to see them":

> I snuck through the dancefloor. I walked real fast and as I approached the stand I could feel the people staring at me, and then they started moving and all of a sudden they just closed me in. . . . [T]here was a circle of black people around me and they were saying, . . ."What are *you* doing down here, white boy?" I said, "I used to play with this band. I want to say hello." They said, "You get outta here!" And they all started yelling. One guy screamed, "You killed my grandparents, you son-of-a-bitch, you white bastard!" . . . I said, "I didn't kill anybody! I didn't do anything!" (58–59, emphasis in original).

Pepper grew more agitated, even after he was warned to leave. The mob surrounded him, and soon people were grabbing and punching him, and he began to scream and swing back. He called out to Carter, who jumped off the bandstand and directly into the middle of the mob. Pepper's pleading and tearful words to his former bandleader—"What *is* this? . . . I just wanted to say hello!"—serve as a vivid contrast to Carter's wisdom born of experience (59, emphasis in original). "This is what I was talking about before," Carter scolded him. "I thought you knew about these things." When Pepper began to cry, Carter told him that there was nothing he could do and that Pepper would have to wait until after the show to see the band. Pepper realized that if he stayed, he might kill someone or be killed. Instead, he left "and wandered around the town," drinking heavily, overwhelmed by feelings of anger, hurt, and confusion. (59).[10]

It is worth asking here: Could Pepper possibly have been as naïve and unaware of the racial customs of the South as he claimed to be? Or in more general terms, could he have taken his own experience on Central Avenue in the 1940s as reflective of the way white and black folks have gotten along in

America? The short answer is no—within his own account, there are many references to a darker, bleaker racial discourse than the comments above suggest. When he was in Salt Lake City with Carter's band, he recalls having to hail a cab after the gig while trumpeter Freddie Webster "would hide" from view and then quickly get in the back seat once Pepper had opened the door. "Because they wouldn't pick up a black guy. And I was always afraid the cab driver would say something and Freddie would shoot him" (49). Moreover, Pepper notes that his own sense of comfort with the musicians in Carter's band highlighted the gulf between his own attitudes toward race and those of his father, who, he claims, "hated blacks. He hated blacks and policemen and rats, informers; those were the things he raved about all the time, and he was angry that I hung out with 'a bunch of niggers, a bunch of goddamned jigaboos'" (49).

Pepper, in other words, had been exposed to racist attitudes long before he was stationed at Camp Butner, likely as far back as his earliest memories of his father. Is it possible, then, that Pepper might have interpreted the mob's rage as vindication of his father's hateful attitudes toward blacks and a setback for his own search for acceptance in interracial jazz communities? Short of offering a definitive conclusion, I would suggest that patterns emerge in his responses to interracial experiences that replicate those established in his earliest family relationships: among them are his search for love and belonging, his periods of euphoria when he believes that he has found them, and his responses of bewilderment and rage when his hopes are dashed. From this perspective, Pepper's professed astonishment at the behavior of the mob in Durham seems more a result of willful blindness than intellectual ignorance about the customs and laws of segregation and systemic discrimination in the United States. As Pepper's narrative makes abundantly clear, racial discord was profoundly distressing to him, particularly when he had some direct involvement with it.

Loving and Hating: The View from Prison and Beyond: 1950s–1980

I had no prejudice at all until I started into the prison thing, and then the whole thing was changed. The prejudice in prison is beyond description. The hatred is just unbounded.
(ART PEPPER IN A 1979 INTERVIEW, QTD. IN SELBERT 104)

By his own calculations, Pepper spent eleven years "in penal institutions or hospitals or convalescent institutions," a result of his lifelong struggle with drug addiction and his many arrests and convictions for narcotics possession and subsequent parole violations (Selbert 117).[11] He began using heroin in 1950, when he was a member of Stan Kenton's band (Pepper and Pepper 82–86).

His first arrest for heroin possession came two years later, and in 1953 he was busted again and forced to endure the agony of cold turkey withdrawal in the Los Angeles County Jail (130–43). Following his conviction on the heroin charges, Pepper was sentenced to two years at the US Public Health Service Hospital at Fort Worth (144—61). Between 1953 and 1966, Pepper spent a total of about eight years in county or federal prisons for narcotics possession and addiction, including the notorious San Quentin, where he was incarcerated between 1961 and 1964 and again from 1965 through 1966.[12]

The contradictions that we saw in Pepper's account of his experiences of interracialism on Central Avenue are also apparent in his recollections of race relations in prison. He offers a deeply cynical appraisal of the attempt by officials to integrate the prison cells during his incarceration in the Los Angeles County Jail in the mid-1950s, expressing his belief that the motivation was "political" and that the black and Mexican inmates wanted to maintain segregation of prison cells as long as they were guaranteed "the same rights" as the white prisoners (172).[13] Pepper's follow-up to this story—based on a later experience in the Los Angeles County Jail on new charges of heroin possession—is his attempt to expose this mid-1950s attempt at enforced integration as an empty charade, with name cards, color-coded according to race, standing in for the actual integration of human beings (171–72).

Yet in the passage that follows, Pepper offers a moving description of a black prisoner's rendition of "Gloomy Sunday" one Sunday at the LA County Jail. The prisoner was the former child actor Matthew Beard, who played the character "Stymie" in *The Little Rascals* (*Our Gang*) comedy shorts; a few days before the performance, Beard and Pepper had recognized and acknowledged each other from their respective—and still-segregated—"hype tanks," the tanks reserved for "dopefiends" (169, 172–73).[14] In Pepper's experience, Sunday in prison stood apart from any other day:

> Instead of all the anger and brutality . . . , on Sunday everyone becomes quiet, and you feel a presence, like, there *is* a God. . . . So it was Sunday, and all of a sudden I heard a voice. I walked out of my cell and looked down the walkway. I heard a voice and it's singing, "Gloomy Sunday," of all songs, man. It was a voice like usually only the black men have, almost a feminine voice, high, and very, very pretty, very sensual and warm and very much in tune, with a sweet sound and a nice vibrato, and it's Stymie's voice. (173, emphasis in original)

The beautiful tenor voice, Pepper recalls, quieted the prisoners—violent men "who'd done terrible crimes. And everyone was just sitting or standing or leaning on the bars of the tank, looking out the windows, looking out on the parking lot, out at the freeway going toward Hollywood, out at the free people" (174). Pepper was struck by the incongruity of the violence and the beauty together; some of the black prisoners began "humming along with Stymie, and it was so pretty and so sad that all the ugliness was forgotten and all the hatred, and for that short while we were, like, brothers. . . . Everything was wiped away, and we were just human beings sharing a common sadness" (174).

But Pepper's plaintive, even sentimental, memory of interracial accord in the LA County Jail is as brief and fleeting as the moment it describes; by contrast, his memories of San Quentin in the early to mid-1960s come in a different voice—hard-edged, bitter, and increasingly consumed by rage. His descriptions of the various ethnic groups in San Quentin and their responses to the inhumanity of prison life are reductive and stereotyping, his extreme views reflective of the effects of the harsh treatment, including solitary confinement, that he experienced over his many years of incarceration (302–7).

His inability to make alliances with African American prisoners fuels his growing hostility toward them, and he recalls thinking, "'Here I am, a guy that played jazz, had black friends. Why wouldn't they talk to me, help me out? Because I'm white?" (271). During his final years at San Quentin, Pepper experienced their growing militancy, recalling incidents in which he and other white prisoners were taunted and threatened (299–300). Although he makes a gesture at understanding the roots of black anger, he is clearly overwhelmed by the antagonism directed against "whites and Mexicans who have been discriminated against, raised just as badly or worse than they were." Speaking from his own history of trauma and pain, Pepper insists, "*We're* suffering just as much" (306, emphasis in original).

Pepper's hurt and incomprehension turn to fantasies of violence and revenge, reminiscent of his response in the segregated dance hall in Durham (307). In a scene that would not be out of place in Asher's *The Electric Cotillion*, Pepper travels to San Francisco with a prison friend following their release from San Quentin in 1966 and discovers, to his horror, casual and open displays of interracial intimacy in a bar in North Beach (336–37). Pepper, who has been drinking heavily, confronts a young white girl who is sitting at the bar with her black companion—a "real pimp type black guy [who] was slobbering all over her." Pepper's language here is key, for it effectively reduces him to a caricature of the threatened and impotent white male and draws an apt comparison to Davey's ineffectual confrontation with Big Brown (see chapter 5):

> I walked up to the bar and said to her, "What kind of a fuckin' tramp are you?" The guy started to say something. I said, "Oh, shut your mouth, you black punk!" I turned to the chick and said, "You filthy tramp bitch. What are you doing in here with this black motherfucker? Where's your class at." She wigged out: "Oh you white motherfucker! You honkie sons-of-bitches!" (337).

In a moment of self-reflection, Pepper realized that he "had to some way get rid of my hatred or it was going to kill me" (338). Yet three years would pass following Pepper's release from San Quentin—years that saw his jazz career increasingly derailed by the physical and psychological effects of his escalating and extreme use of drugs and alcohol—before a gravely ill Pepper was forced to admit that he would not survive without help.[15] In *Straight Life*, Pepper leaves no doubt that his decision to go to Synanon, the renowned (and controversial) private addiction rehabilitation program in Santa Monica, California, was one predicated on desperation rather than on any notion of redemption or renewal through cult affiliation.[16] And yet he would remain there for almost three years (from 1969 to 1972), a decision that undoubtedly saved his life, not only because of Synanon's strict rules regarding sobriety and nonviolent behavior, but also because it was there that he met Laurie Miller, a young woman with whom he would fall in love and spend the remaining years of his life and who would play such a central role in the good things that happened to him in those final years.

Saving Art, Saving Herself: Why Laurie Pepper "Stuck with a Junkie Jazzman"

A trigger was pulled in me which had been planted by my grandmother who believed that there was no better thing to be (or to serve) than an artist.
(LAURIE PEPPER, "WHY I STUCK" 89)

He gave me himself, as completely as he could, to love and care for. And he gave me a very interesting job.
(LAURIE PEPPER, FROM HER 1994 AFTERWORD IN *STRAIGHT LIFE*, 495)

Shortly after the death of Thelonious Monk's wife, Nellie, historian and Monk biographer Robin D. G. Kelley published a moving tribute to her and to other jazz wives and partners for their immeasurable (and often overlooked) contributions on the domestic front as well as in their husbands' professional and public careers. In "The Jazz Wife: Muse and Manager," Kelley suggests that "[w]omen like Nellie Monk and Lorraine Gillespie [Dizzy Gillespie's wife] were not simply muses who inspired their husbands' creative passions or housewives relegated to the background of their spouses' public lives. Rather, they became a significant social and economic force in the jazz world and thus were ahead of their time" (Kelley 24). After naming other "great couples in jazz," Kelley adds that "stories of such stable, nurturing relationships rarely find a place in the countless movies and books about jazz artists" (24).[17]

Art and Laurie Pepper are notably absent from his list, perhaps in part because Art's self-destructive lifestyle and early death cast a shadow over his remarkable fourteen-year relationship with Laurie, his third and last wife, who indeed gave him the "stable, nurturing relationship" that had previously eluded him and whose diligence and work on his behalf enabled much of the professional success and public recognition that he enjoyed in the final decade of his life. Yet, as Laurie insists in her brief introduction to her own autobiography, her relationship with Art was not one-sided: "I was no angel," she writes, "and we rescued each other" (Pepper xi). Indeed, it is Laurie's compulsion to share both the joy and the pain of her life with Art that gives her work as author and jazz insider particular value, making it an important contribution to the growing list of memoirs penned by spouses of prominent jazz musicians.[18]

But it was Laurie's probing of some of the most problematic of her husband's attitudes and behavior—revealed by him in their countless interview sessions that she edited and held up for public scrutiny in the pages of *Straight Life*—that yield the richest revelations for our purposes; in particular, she insisted (and Art went along with her) that they examine his detailed account of his sexual compulsions and behavior and his overtly racist statements and commentary.[19] As Laurie acknowledges, her "cross-examinations and contradictions could make him angry and defensive. But Art loved honesty—he called it 'Truth'—and he respected me;.... I was single-mindedly oblivious of how cruelly deep I made him dig. I persevered and so did he" (Pepper 67). The results of her perseverance are clear: if Pepper's revelations are at times deeply unsettling, they are also extremely illuminating, and not just for what they say about his own psychic wounds; his comments on interracialism in jazz, as well as Laurie's analysis of them in her own autobiography, offer an important perspective on the very real and escalating racial tensions in the jazz world from the postwar period through the 1960s and beyond.

"A Family of Artists"

Laurie grew up in Los Angeles and New York, an only child of "hardcore Trotskyists" Thelma Babitz and Richard LaPan, from whom she learned "to keep secrets" (Pepper 39, 76). As she recalls, the paraphernalia of their socialist convictions—the family's "little bust of Trotsky" and the "revolutionary books and copies of *The Militant* lying around the house were absolutely not to be seen by outsiders" (76). The hard-drinking socialists who crowded their living room were also suspect, and Laurie came to understand that her home was not a place where she could invite her friends. As a result, she writes, she became a loner who "learned to live in books" (76).

But Laurie developed a broad appreciation for culture and the arts from her mother's family—"a family of artists" (89).[20] When she was in high school, she took an office job at Westlake College of Modern Music in order to cover her piano and vocal lessons (14). Later, she studied folklore and cultural anthropology at the University of California at Berkeley, but she dropped out to study photography with the assistant of her idol, Dorothea Lange (9, 23).

Soon, she was hired as staff photographer for the underground newspaper, the *L.A. Free Press*, where she covered "political demonstrations and museum openings," photographing "rock musicians for album covers and publicity for magazines" (9).[21] By the end of the decade, Laurie's achievements as a photographer were overshadowed by her deteriorating private life and her increasing dependence on drugs and alcohol. Following a suicide attempt in 1968, she checked into Synanon; she was twenty-eight years old, her marriage had recently fallen apart, and she was deeply depressed.[22] She remained at Synanon for over three years; her summary of that experience leaves little doubt that it was for her (as for Art) both life-saving and life-affirming (55).

One night, at Synanon's mandatory weekly gathering, Art came up to her and introduced himself (13). Laurie had heard of him but had never listened to his records; under the influence of the students at the Westlake music school, she had gravitated instead to East Coast jazz musicians—"less melodic, more cerebral, more black" (16). Although Art reminded her of Clark Gable, she admits that she had preferred fair-haired men and that he was "not my type" (17). Still, she found herself attracted by his celebrity and by the way he talked—"like an American"—because it was so different from her own "family's English, which was notably Jewish in that it came from books. Art was 'the people,' the real thing" (23). Their romance developed slowly, following Synanon's strict rules, which included a thirty-day courtship period, after which they were given permission to use the "designated 'guest-rooms,'" where they would make love and then have long talks about themselves (31–32).[23] Laurie was swept away by his keen observations of people and their "predicaments" and his extraordinary skills as a storyteller, likening him to "Othello describing his great battles to Desdemona. That's how he wooed me. Except in Art's tales he was rarely the victor" (33, 52).

When Art left Synanon at the beginning of 1972, Laurie was initially reluctant to follow him, doubting his ability to remain sober in the outside world or her own ability to "save or change him" (52). Yet she had a specific motive for reconnecting with him—her growing conviction that his stories were worthy of publication. In that period, she had fallen under the spell of social anthropologist Oscar Lewis's *The Children of Sanchez* (1961), based on his "oral history of a poor Mexican family," describing it as "the most poetic, personal, revealing, and touching autobiography I'd ever read" (Pepper and Pepper 478). Laurie reread Lewis's book while she was at Synanon and became convinced that its structure—with the oral histories of several members of the Sanchez family providing multiple perspectives on the family's life and interrelationships—would serve as an excellent model for Art's own life story. "He could tell his remarkable life in his own extraordinary language through me," she writes, "and I would interview his friends and family, too. This was something I could do" (Pepper 53).[24]

As Laurie acknowledges, at the root of her decision to participate in Art's autobiography was her own need for "artistic achievement. Put simply, I wanted to be Art. But I lacked the natural ability, the inborn genius" (53). Yet, like Oscar Lewis, Laurie had a deep appreciation for "vivid narrative" and a talent for bringing the stories of others to life. By helping to give Art's story to the world, she would find a path to meaning and purpose in her own life (53). She left Synanon in February 1972, and, in April, she began to interview Art, armed with a notebook and tape recorder as he sat behind his desk in "his office/bedroom" at the organic bakery in Venice Beach where he was working and living at the time (62). Before long, Art had moved in with her, and they were married in 1974.

Although Art had been initially resistant to Laurie's book project, he now blurted out his sense of urgency about putting down his life story, convinced of his own impending mortality. His confession—dramatic and evocative—set Laurie "on fire. I couldn't let him stop talking. I asked him . . . if he believed he was a genius. I'd heard him on this theme before" (63).[25] Art responded by telling her about "his bandstand battle with Sonny Stitt"; as his story ended, they let out an audible gasp: "I hear us on the tape. Then we laughed. I was sitting on his little bed and hollered, 'Wow?' rocking back and hitting my head on the wall" (65). When Art told her to turn off the tape recorder, she did so, but she switched it back on without his knowledge:

> We were both talking at once: His narrative had been like a jazz solo, its repeating theme, its mounting vehemence, its forward movement. And yet it had been history. A social document! This may have been the first time Art was made aware of just how great his storytelling gifts were. As for me, it confirmed my belief that there *could* be a book, and I knew that there *must* be. (65–66, emphasis in original)

That Laurie attached particular significance to Art's story of his bandstand experience with Stitt is clear from her decision to end *Straight Life* with it; later in the chapter, I will return to this passage to examine it in greater detail.

In chapter 1, I noted the difficulty of ascertaining the precise contributions of the collaborators or coauthors of several of the jazz autobiographies examined in this study. By contrast, Laurie's description of her role as author and editor reveals her involvement in every aspect of the text's construction, from coaxer and cheerleader when Art's engagement with the project began to flag, to her instigation of brief "fill-in" sessions to add necessary context and background of particular stories that Art had told her in earlier interviews, to her extensive editing and revising of the manuscript that continued for several years after the completion of the interviews (Pepper 66–67; Pepper and Pepper 479–80).

Laurie's concern was not only with the book's clarity of form and style—*how* Art said what he said—but also with the content of his stories and how they contributed to shaping a fuller and more transparent autobiographical portrait. Some of them, she is quick to admit, disturbed her profoundly, including those that appear in the chapter "Stealing," in which Art "chronicles a spiritual disintegration I had to work hard to understand and convey," ending with his dramatic account of his participation in an armed robbery (Pepper and Pepper 480). In her search for a truthful account of this experience, Laurie convinced Art to tell the story of the robbery over and over as she would interrupt to ask for clarification and explanation, seeking to understand "the ideas, influences, pressures, and acts that brought him to it" (481).

Notably, Laurie comments only indirectly on the most disturbing aspects of Art's narrative of his sexual exploits—for example, his rape of a young English woman when he was a Military Policeman (MP) stationed in England during WWII and his peeping-Tom experiences as a young man. Yet his rape story hovers as the backdrop to Laurie's admission that Art hit her—"on the shoulder and not hard. The only time that ever happened"—following their quarrel over his revelation that he owed his Methadone counselor money for selling him more of the drug than had been prescribed (Pepper 166). After he hit her, Laurie writes, she left briefly but "reconciled" the following day "with a very repentant Art" (166–68). The rape story may also be seen as the subtext to Laurie's frequent references to Art's skill and consideration as a lover: "At first and ever after Art was a wonderful lover, intuitive, generous, enthusiastic" (32).[26]

The publication of *Straight Life* in 1979 would have a transformative effect on their lives together as well as on Art's career. A book tour followed the book's release, with Fantasy Records and their publisher, Schirmer/Macmillan, working alongside their publicists to promote *Straight Life*. In the fall of 1979, they did a whirlwind book tour, appearing on radio and morning television shows and giving interviews "with journalists all over the map" (Pepper 235). But, along with the welcome attention and acclaim, Laurie was forced to confront her own conflicted feelings about her role in the project, feelings she attributed to her indoctrination in 1950s cultural norms that taught girls to stay in their place and avoid competition. "I feared criticism like I feared death," she admits, "and didn't try for praise in case I got its opposite" (235). Also distressing to her were the slights of several prominent male jazz critics whose reviews of *Straight Life* completely overlooked her contribution.[27] Both Laurie's insecurities and the blindness and insensitivities of these critics, are, in my view, flip sides of a related issue, revealing the particular constraints on women in jazz, who have too often been perceived as unlikely contributors as musicians, managers, agents, or critics.

Yet Laurie's contribution is uncontestable. From the mid-1970s until Art's death from a brain hemorrhage in 1982, at the age of fifty-six, Laurie assumed central responsibility for the practical and business ends of his career, organizing recording sessions; signing him to a collection company (BMI) so that he would be eligible to collect "mechanical royalties" (on "record sales") and "performance royalties" (for radio play); and arranging tours and dealing with finances, travel schedules, and hotel bookings when he and his bands were on the road (Pepper 137, 276). Laurie also describes her growing influence over Art's music itself, as he increasingly sought her advice for recording sessions, including the choice of sidemen to accompany him and playlists for concerts and recordings (217, 265, 270). For advice with particular aspects of his career and their personal lives together, she found herself turning to other jazz women, most notably Keiko Jones (the wife of drummer Elvin Jones) and Jill Goodwin (the partner of Phil Woods). Her account of their mentorship and support provides further documentation of the invaluable and frequently overlooked role played by jazz spouses in their partners' lives and careers.[28]

From the publication of *Straight Life* to shortly before his death, Pepper maintained a busy recording and touring schedule, including extended trips to Europe, Australia, Canada, and Japan, as well as frequent appearances in the United States. But if Laurie's steady management enabled him to function as a creative jazz musician and to enjoy the acclaim and recognition that he had sought over his long career, his continuing substance abuse and generally reckless lifestyle continued to erode his physical and emotional health. In her autobiography, Laurie portrays these years with the same attention to candor and honesty that she applied to her role as creator and producer of *Straight Life*, offering a fascinating and sometimes painful glimpse into her own and her husband's drug use, struggles with depression, and fraught relationships with other musicians, agents, and record producers.

"A Digression—Jazz and Race"

In this brief look at Laurie Pepper and her significance to her husband's life and career, I have emphasized her integrity and concern with transparency as a background against which we may now revisit Art's comments on race and his interracial jazz experiences from *her* perspective, as she interprets them in her afterward to *Straight Life* and in her autobiography. As I have tried to show, her judgments deserve serious consideration, not only because she cared about and believed so deeply in her husband and his contributions to jazz, but also because of her insistence that he be revealed to the world with all of his flaws and imperfections, even those that she found most distasteful. Beyond that, Laurie's views on jazz interracialism are valuable to us for what they reveal about *her*, a white woman who was both an observer and a participant in black jazz environments in the 1970s and early 1980s, in which the mood and thrust of black nationalist sentiment remained powerful.

In a brief section of her autobiography entitled "A Digression—Jazz and Race," Laurie makes the following observation:

> In *Straight Life* Art talks about the tensions in the postwar jazz world from an entirely personal point of view (always his only point of view). He talks about rejection by black musicians and his resulting bitterness and pain. When we were working on the book, when Art raged about racism against white jazz musicians (against him, against him!) I didn't disbelieve him, but I didn't really understand its impact on him. And I was able to see what he couldn't or didn't care to see—where that black rage was coming from, and that it wasn't aimed specifically at him. (Pepper 288)

Laurie's suggestion that Art's responses to his interracial experiences was "entirely personal" seems consistent with my earlier efforts to view his stories about those experiences in the context of the pain and trauma of his own life. But then she makes a significant admission, stating that her *own* views on interracialism were altered by her experiences on tours with Art, during which she would spend long hours with the black musicians in Art's bands and other musicians whom she would meet at festivals and concerts. On one occasion, she found herself sitting with a group of musicians who began to say "some awful things about white players" (288). At first, she found their remarks amusing, "but as the insults got more brutal and the ridicule grew nastier," she decided that they were deliberately trying to provoke her. "I was shocked but didn't want to show it," she recalls, "so I kept on laughing like an idiot, playing dumb. I should have walked away. After that I had a better understanding of what Art lived with—working in 'black music.' And I understand that Art, himself, had bought that mindset, though it was unconscious: White guys can't play jazz" (288–89).

Laurie's admission has an immediate and powerful impact, forcing the reader to recognize her own sensitivities to racial matters and the ways in which her responses, like her husband's, were "entirely personal." Moreover, her admission highlights her deep investment in her husband's success in the black jazz world, including the outcome of particular interracial experiences that he recalled during their interview sessions, some of which she witnessed herself. One such experience unfolded in the aftermath of Art's 1978 signing with Fantasy Records (209). For Art's first recording on the label (*Art Pepper Today*), Ed Michel, the producer, decided to use the rhythm section of Stanley Cowell, Cecil McBee, and Roy Haynes, who were then involved with other recording projects for Fantasy. In an attempt to break the ice, Michel invited them all out for Chinese food prior to the recording. According to Laurie, the dinner was a bust, with long and awkward silences at the dinner punctuated with attempts at light conversation from Michel and the recording engineer (210–11).

In their hotel room following the dinner, Art vented his anger over the experience, which had triggered his long-festering resentment toward black musicians for their rejection of him and other white musicians that went back to the 1960s. "Art still reeled from insults he had taken personally," Laurie explains. "In some cases, that dismissive attitude toward white jazz players was still ongoing, so the silence at the dinner table had just increased Art's paranoia. Also, these guys were all New Yorkers. In 'modern' jazz that's always indicated caste: They were important and Art wasn't" (211).

Yet once the recording session got underway, the tension eased. For Laurie, the highlight was the band's recording of "Patricia," a tune that Pepper had written decades earlier for his daughter. In his discussion with his rhythm section before they began to record, Art had proposed "a bluesy sort of coda, a long tag at the end," but Laurie sensed his anxiety that he had failed to explain his wishes to the musicians. Pepper's concerns were unwarranted, as McBee "carried them into a gorgeous, funky, perfect ending" (213). As the musicians gathered around to listen to the take, a hush fell over the room; suddenly, Roy Haynes turned to Pepper and asked him where he was from. To Pepper's reply, "Gardena, California," Haynes retorted, "Is that South Gardena?" The point of Haynes's question was unmistakable and clearly intended as a compliment: Pepper's playing was authentic because it sounded soulful—that is, black. Indeed, Laurie interpreted Haynes's remark as complimentary, noting at the story's conclusion: "We all went out to dinner again and had a pretty good time" (213). The intent of her story, it seems to me, is to illustrate Pepper's black jazz credentials and his ability, through his music, to break down cultural barriers.[29]

The other story concerns Pepper's relationship with George Cables, his regular (and favorite) pianist in the final years of his life. As a respected black jazz musician, Cables was in a position to grant Pepper the legitimacy he craved; his acceptance of Pepper "as a real jazz player" left a deep impression on Pepper, who gave Cables the nickname "Mr. Beautiful" and "cared for [him] in a way he cared for few other musicians. Few other people" (289). Yet even in his relationship with Cables, sensitivities about race would occasionally arise: "One time," Laurie recalls, "when Art was explaining to George how he wanted a tune to sound he kept using a phrase he often used—it meant funky—he said 'down home.' George got irritated, and he finally said, 'What do you mean, "down home," man? I'm from *Brooklyn*!'" (Pepper and Pepper 490, emphasis in original).

From Pepper's perspective, it is easy to see that "down home" described something positive and good in the music and that he intended his instructions to Cables to be interpreted in that spirit, much in the way that Haynes intended his comment to Pepper about South Gardena to be complimentary. And yet, Pepper's intentions are really not the point of this story but, rather, his insensitivity (at that moment) to the cultural impact of the term and the ways in which it might be perceived (and *was* perceived, by Cables) as perpetuating racist stereotypes. If Pepper's responses may be seen as "entirely personal," then we ought to recognize that those of Cables also reflected his experiences as a racialized minority living in a society that had been shaped by the historical legacy of slavery and systemic racism.

One interpretation of Laurie's story might suggest that the potential for misunderstandings was simply a reality of interracial jazz experiences, even among artists who were otherwise capable of playing together with considerable warmth and sympathy. But another might instead focus on Laurie's account of the experience—in which she takes pains to imagine the incident from the perspective of Cables—as evidence of her own thoughtfulness and capacity for cultural sensitivity, attributes that are notably lacking in many of Pepper's accounts of his interracial experiences. As I have already suggested, Pepper's own pain and suffering seem to have left him with little appetite for nuanced reflections on the history and consequences of racial oppression in the United States, even as he spent much of his adult life in the company of African Americans. We need only recall his incomprehension at the antagonism of the black inmates at San Quentin—"*We're* suffering just as much"—to recognize that in his portraits of his interracial experience, his gaze is turned inward, not outward. Pepper's myopia makes it especially instructive for us to compare his views of Central Avenue life and in the jazz world more broadly with those of the black musicians whose lives and careers intersected with his own.

"Central Avenue Was a Place Where My People Lived":[30] African American Experiences of Central Avenue, 1930s–1960s

Many of Pepper's black contemporaries echo his portrait of a before-and-after Central Avenue; that is, that the period leading up to and including the Second World War represented a watershed for jobs, prosperity, and interracial tranquility on the Avenue and that the postwar period marked the beginning of a dramatic downturn in economic fortunes and community spirit. Bandleader Lee Young insists that "Art was just one of the band" during his tenure with Young at the Club Alabam in early 1943, adding, "We didn't know any different down on Central Avenue at that time. It wasn't about 'whitey' this and 'whitey' that. It was about good musicianship and people respecting one another for the talents that they had" (Pepper and Pepper 45). Echoing this sentiment, Gerald Wiggins recalls, "Art Pepper was here. It was no segregated-type thing. Everybody was welcome. If you could play, you were even more welcome" (Bryant et al. 315). And, according to tenor saxophonist William "Brother" Woodman Jr., Central Avenue before the war "was a showcase for talent.... A

Art Pepper on tour with his final quartet, in Europe in the summer of 1981, wearing the new satin band jackets that Laurie Pepper had ordered. From left: Carl Burnett, drums; George Cables, piano; Art Pepper; David Williams, bass. Photo by Laurie Pepper, used with permission of Laurie Pepper.

place of entertainment, ... a melting pot for all races. Things were really nice, and no violence and no crimes" (113).[31]

Despite this apparent consensus, however, the accounts of the black Central Avenue alumni convey a keen social and historical consciousness that is missing from Pepper's stories—a consciousness that they link directly to the effects of systemic racism in their daily lives. Jack Kelson, a multireed instrumentalist born in Los Angeles in 1922 (only three years before Pepper), recalls seeing a minstrel show when he was a child at the Elks Auditorium on Central Avenue; yet he also describes the powerful forces of activism at work on the Avenue with his reference to newspaper publisher and community leader Leon Washington, whose long-running campaign of economic self-empowerment was "defined by the phrase 'Don't spend where you can't work'" (Bryant et al. 205). Later, Kelson remarks on the dignity and bearing of the black men on Central Avenue, manifested in the clothing they wore and also in their physical bearing: "It was a sense of not only black pride, but just pride in being" (217).

From the perspective of these black musicians, then, Central Avenue was their home and community, a black community in which whites were clearly on the periphery. Exemplifying this attitude is bandleader and trumpeter Gerald Wilson's description of the avenue as "a place where my people lived," comparable to "125th Street in New York City, or South Park in Chicago" (Bryant et al. 340). The origins of Central Avenue as a black community were in themselves, of course, the consequence of systemic racism, stemming from the pernicious "restrictive covenants in property deeds in Los Angeles" that over the first decades of the twentieth century forced African Americans into increasingly overcrowded areas of the city whose borders were diligently enforced "by blocks of solid white resistance" (4).[32] In contrast to Pepper's "before," with its focus on Central Avenue as a happy and idyllic black space that extended open arms to people of all racial and ethnic backgrounds, the "before" of these African American musicians acknowledges the warm and embracing interracialism alongside the persistence of systemic discrimination and white control of the economy of Central Avenue, and of the music industry more specifically.

As their accounts illustrate, these black musicians respond to the effects of racism in their lives and careers in a variety of ways. Some use the platform of oral history and autobiography to vent their anger and bitterness at the exploitation and appropriation of black culture by white society. Cecil "Big Jay" McNeely, "one of the original honking saxophonists" and "an early exponent of rhythm and blues," suggests that racism was a factor in the tragic life and career of his close friend, alto saxophonist Sonny Criss (Bryant et al. 179). Roy Porter, a leading West Coast bebop drummer, argues that white musicians appropriated the music of the black bebop pioneers for their own gains (Porter, *There and Back* 55).[33] Many of the interviewees note the persistence of segregation and more covert forms of discrimination in the clubs on Central Avenue and in Southern California more generally (Bryant et al. 17–18).[34]

But other voices in these volumes turn their critique of US society into a proclamation of their own community's strength and resilience, focusing on the role of family, community, and formal education as a social and spiritual buffer against racism. They identify the strong values of discipline and hard work that they learned from their families—as well as black teachers such as Samuel Browne at Jefferson High School and private music teacher Lloyd Reese—as central to both their musical and social development.[35] Horace Tapscott recalls that he was still in junior high when Browne recruited him—as Browne did other talented young players—for his band at Jefferson (Tapscott 26, 31). Tapscott emphasizes Browne's involvement in the community and his insistence on formal music training in order to compete in a "racist society" (34; Bryant et al. 294–96).

A strong social awareness also emerges in the musicians' accounts of the fight to approve or reject amalgamation of the segregated locals of the Los Angeles musicians' union in the 1950s (the proamalgamation side won out, in 1953).[36] Their passionate arguments reveal how much was at stake for them, both in terms of their individual careers and for their sense of cultural solidarity and identity. Tapscott describes this sense of community identity in his moving recollection of himself as a youngster (too young to join the union) hanging out "on the stoop" of the black local 767:

and every cat touched me on my head, my shoulder, and my back and told me something. Every black musician in the world would pass by there, slap you upside the head, and say something smart to you: "What's happening, young blood?" ... How many mentors you'd have in a day was impossible to count. They'd all be telling us about being musicians, about life, about dealing with segregation and racism. (Tapscott 27)[37]

Notably, in *Straight Life*, Pepper makes only one brief reference to his experience with local 767, recalling that his audition for Lee Young's band took place "at the colored union" (Pepper and Pepper 41). Beyond this offhand mention, there is nothing in Pepper's narrative to suggest that the amalgamation battle affected him, either personally or in terms of his career.

If Pepper's portrait of Central Avenue in its heyday seems to miss important aspects of black life that are central to the narratives of the African American interviewees and autobiographers, his "after" portrait—with his repeated refrain of black power and blacks hating whites—is also reductive, for it offers no explanation for the conditions within Los Angeles's postwar black community that fueled these black nationalist impulses. Steven Isoardi provides a succinct history of these changing conditions in his description of the Los Angeles Police Department (LAPD) under William H. Parker, "virulent anticommunist and white supremacist" (Isoardi 45), who became chief of the department in 1950: "Under Parker the LAPD did lose the stigma of corruption, only to have it replaced with that of racism and systematic brutality" (46).[38] Parker's unwavering focus, Isoardi explains, "was to break up the integrated social scene on Central Avenue," with regular patrols by the LAPD targeting "any whites to be found there, routinely harassing and arresting interracial couples" (46).

The accounts of these black musicians support Isoardi's analysis, providing detailed descriptions of the increasingly oppressive measures imposed by Los Angeles's white authorities against the black community in the postwar period. In particular, they identify the police response to interracial mixing between white women and the black musicians and entertainers as a central cause for deteriorating race relations on Central Avenue.[39] The flashpoint for decades of racism and oppression was the 1965 Watts uprising, the causes and effects of which receive close attention in several of these narratives, most famously in Johnny Otis's *Listen to the Lambs* (1968), which includes letters Otis wrote to a friend in the aftermath of the rioting and firsthand accounts of the uprising from Watts' black community.[40] Describing the uprising's effect on an awakened black consciousness, Otis writes that the "'New Negro' burst into full being Phoenix-life, from the flames of 103rd Street" (Otis, *Listen* 119).

An important manifestation of this "New Negro" sensibility had already begun to take shape in Los Angeles in the years leading up to the uprising in the form of African American community-based cultural organizations, among the most vital and enduring of which were the Underground Musicians Association (UGMA)—later renamed the Union of God's Musicians and Artists Ascension (UGMAA)—and the Pan Afrikan Peoples Arkestra (PAPA).[41] These organizations, as Isoardi explains, were among many established in black communities between the 1950s and 1970s in an effort to reclaim "communal values" for people whose lives continued to be shaped by systemic racism "in allegedly postsegregation America" (Isoardi 2).

Tapscott, the central force and spirit behind these organizations, dedicated most of his adult life to their development and growth following his decision to leave Lionel Hampton's orchestra and return to his family and community in South Central Los Angeles (Isoardi 1–2). The strong sense of "comradeship" within UGMA, its unabashed Afrocentrism and bold challenges to societal injustice through its many cultural programs in the community earned it a reputation, according to Tapscott, as a "dangerous commodity" (Tapscott 88). By the late sixties, the Arkestra and UGMA were coming under increasing surveillance from local and federal authorities for their community activities and close association with the Black Panthers and other black radical organizations (117–24).[42]

As Isoardi notes, Pepper was one of a number of "mainstream" musicians receptive to the "new sounds" who would appear occasionally at the performances and rehearsal sessions that were a feature of the UGMA house (Isoardi 59).[43] Yet, except for an acknowledgment that nonblacks were for the most part welcomed in the clubs along Central Avenue, there is relatively little attention paid to him and other white musicians in the accounts of these black musicians (Bryant et al. 402, 277; Collette 65). A notably sympathetic discussion comes from Roy Porter, who mentions "a cooking concert" he played with Pepper in 1977, adding that it "was the last time that I saw Art Pepper alive, a rather forceful reminder that you never really know what dues a person is paying even when you work with them" (Porter, *There and Back* 126).

In *Straight Life*, Pepper makes no mention of Porter, Collette, or Farmer, a significant omission considering they were all prominent black musicians on Central Avenue during the 1940s and 1950s; nor does he mention Tapscott or the community-based organizations with which he was involved. Furthermore, although he recalls hanging out with Charles Mingus and other young black musicians during his early days on Central Avenue, neither he nor Laurie refers to Mingus's astonishing autobiography, *Beneath the Underdog: His World as Composed by Mingus*, published in 1971 to considerable acclaim.[44] Laurie offers a plausible explanation for her husband's reticence with her general observation that he was reluctant to "say anything at all, at least on the record, about other musicians, especially about those still living," yet her explanation seems insufficient to account for his near-complete silence about these renowned black musicians (Pepper 283). We have already found many examples of Pepper's insecurities around particular forms of black cultural expression that he encountered on the streets and in prison; it is possible that the racial pride and assertiveness that were central to Mingus's public persona—as well as to organizations such as UGMA and the Arkestra—were on some level threatening to him, as were the interracial struggles for control of the production of jazz and for employment in a white-dominated music industry.

The Great White Hope: White Critics on Art Pepper (1960s–1970s)

While I have attempted to draw connections between Pepper's personal struggles and his increasingly pessimistic views on race relations, it is also important to see these views as a more general reflection of the escalating interracial tensions in jazz in the postwar period. His hurt and bewilderment, in other words, were not merely a consequence of his own fragile personal makeup; they were consistent with the feelings of many whites in the jazz world at that time who were experiencing a sudden draft in African American jazz spaces in which they had been welcomed, or at least granted admission, in earlier decades.

It is no coincidence that the Los Angeles–based African American cultural organizations discussed above—as well as many others across the country— were established during the 1960s and 1970s, for they were in large part a response to the dramatic social and political upheaval of their time, as African Americans turned to cultural nationalism and demands for economic and social independence from nonblacks as strategies to combat systemic racism, restore self-pride, and seize control of the teaching of black history to upcoming generations of black youth.[45] In Monson's blunt assessment, "[f]reezing out the white people and drawing the racial line was seen as crucial to the promotion of unity against a common enemy" (*Freedom Sounds* 277).

Racial tensions in the jazz world were on full display in several public discussions in the 1960s that brought together interracial panels of musicians, critics, club owners, and record producers to debate, among other topics, the structural racism of the jazz industry.[46] While some of the white participants in these debates professed their sympathies for the segregationist ideologies of particular black musicians and organizations, others directed their grievances, in language and tone reminiscent of Art Pepper's examined earlier, at the "Crow Jim" attitudes of the younger generation of African American jazz musicians, reflected in their hiring practices and public comments about white musicians as well as white critics. The alliance of white jazz musicians and white jazz critics is instructive here; spurred by a shared sense of victimization, they came together to resist (or at least to noisily register their resentment over) the changing mood around interracialism in jazz.

Todd Selbert's collection of essays on Pepper written by white jazz critics during the 1960s and 1970s illuminates this alliance in a striking way. Notably, many of them frame their evaluation of Pepper in racial terms, highlighting his mastery of the black jazz aesthetic and citing his whiteness as an important factor in what they perceived as inadequate attention to his accomplishments as a jazz artist.[47] In so doing, they reprise some of the methods of the authenticating collaborators of white jazz autobiography considered earlier in this study. Even the titles of some of their pieces—T. E. Martin's "Art Pepper: Towards a New White Jazz" (1964); Gary Giddins's "The Whiteness of the Wail" (1977); and Bob Blumenthal's "Baring a White Man's Burdens: Art Pepper Perseveres" (1977)—reveal their preoccupation with Pepper's whiteness at a time when white critics themselves were feeling under attack.

Conveying a sense of their own vulnerability as cultural outsiders, these critics elevate Pepper as the great white hope, the brilliant (but unappreciated) jazz musician who had proved that whites could play as well as (and according to some of them, even better than) the best black players (Selbert 15, 22, 23, 29).[48] By authenticating Pepper, white critics were simultaneously seeking to authenticate themselves, to inch closer to black culture by establishing their ties to a white person who had, in their view, successfully crossed the racial divide. Gary Giddins makes this point with particular clarity in "The Whiteness of the Wail":

> Our fascination with the great white bebopper—of whom there is none greater than Art Pepper—is part envy and part admiration because he got close to the secret world of black culture—that world of genius and fire and bared emotion that promised salvation. He could speak Bird's language: moreover, he could make from it his own language. (Qtd. in Selbert 81)

It is clear that Giddins and these other white male critics had invested heavily in Art Pepper (the man and the musician), finding in him an apt symbol of the potential and the limitations of white jazzmen in the postwar era. As they did so, they often seemed to be echoing his attitudes and worldview, lending credence to his public assertions about the changes in the jazz world that had shattered his image of an earlier time of interracial tranquility.

"What I Said Reached the People"

In the context of the overheated racial rhetoric in which it was framed, Pepper's recollection of his bandstand battle with Sonny Stitt at the conclusion of *Straight Life* holds particular resonance, providing us with a view of Pepper's interaction with a black musician in which his very reputation and authority as a white player were at stake. Earlier I noted that his bandstand story was precipitated by Laurie's question regarding his belief in his own "genius." In *Straight Life*, however, this context is missing; instead, the two-page account consists entirely of Pepper's first-person narration, opening with his brief rumination on his general giftedness, including his musical gifts. By introducing his bandstand battle with Stitt as evidence of these gifts, Pepper establishes a high bar, for Stitt was undoubtedly one of the master practitioners of bebop. Pepper recalls that their battle took place at the Black Hawk, the renowned San Francisco jazz club, and that Stitt approached him and asked "Can I blow?" (Pepper and Pepper 475). That Stitt asks to sit in on Pepper's gig and not the other way around is confirmation of Pepper's status as a world-class saxophonist. Pepper's warm response to Stitt ("Yeah, great") also confirms his collegiality despite the inherent competition of bandstand battles—the famed "cutting contests" of jazz lore.

Indeed, Pepper leaves no doubt about the competitive nature of their bandstand duel; in his words, the fact that he and Stitt both played alto "really makes it a contest. It's a communion, it's a battle, it's an ego trip. It's a testing ground. And that's the beautiful part of it" (475). As further evidence of his magnanimity (and self-confidence), Pepper allowed Stitt to call the tune and to count off the tempo. Stitt called "Cherokee," a challenging tune used frequently at bebop sessions to separate the skilled players from the pretenders. Then Stitt counted it off at a blistering tempo and was the first to solo—playing, according to Pepper, "about forty choruses. He played for an hour, maybe, did everything that could be done on a saxophone. . . . Then he stopped. And he looked at me. Gave me one of those looks, 'All right, sukkah, your turn'" (476).

Having prepared readers for what will surely be the climax of his story, Pepper stops to give a brief summary of his condition at that time, and, in so doing, to lay the groundwork for his own heroism:

> I was strung out. I was hooked. I was drunk. I was having a hassle with my wife, Diane, who'd threatened to kill herself in our hotel room next door. I had marks on my arm. I thought there were narcs in the club, and I all of a sudden realized that it was me. He'd done all those things, and now I had to put up or shut up or get off or forget it or quit or kill myself or do something. (476)

Then Pepper takes a breath before he launches into his final chorus:

> I forgot everything, and everything came out. I played way over my head. I played completely different than he did. I searched and found my own way, and what I said reached the people. . . . I blew and I blew, and when I finally finished I was shaking all over; my heart was pounding; I was soaked in sweat, and the people were screaming; the people were clapping, and I looked at Sonny, but I just kind of nodded, and he went, "All right." And that was it. That's what it's all about. (476)

The multifaceted virtuosity of this passage is striking. There is the musical virtuosity of Pepper and Stitt as well as Pepper's virtuosity as a storyteller. But there is also Laurie's virtuosity as editor—including her insight that Art's first story to her when she began to interview him ("Art's opening salvo," in her words) would provide such a dramatic ending for his autobiography. In her own comments about the passage, she explains that she "edited it and made it the conclusion, his summing up," describing it as "brilliant, touching, rhythmic, evocative, suspenseful, triumphant" (Pepper 63–64).

But what exactly did Laurie find "triumphant" about this passage? Is it, perhaps, the shared triumph of Stitt and Pepper, who demonstrate through their bandstand battle the best of the jazz spirit, in which musicians contribute their own individual stories in order to create something larger than themselves? Or is it the triumph of an individual in the quintessential cutting contest, in which participants blow until there is only one left standing? While Pepper was enthusiastic (here and elsewhere) in his praise of Stitt, in my view, the structure and content of his story pull the reader into his corner and guarantee him a favorable decision.[49] And although Pepper never mentions race directly in his story, its significance cannot be overstated; in his telling, he more than holds his own in his bandstand battle with the legendary black saxophonist.

If this story is, as Laurie claims, Pepper's "summing up," then I would suggest that it is a summary of a white man's personal, rather than collective, jazz journey (Panish, passim). This is not to doubt his accounts of the close and caring relationships he formed with his early mentors on Central Avenue or with the young musicians who were honing their jazz skills along with him in the clubs and dancehalls of 1930s and 1940s Los Angeles. Nor would I dispute Laurie's contention that his final years were his most content and fulfilling, that his views on race softened and became substantially less rancorous, and that he formed strong bonds with the musicians in his later bands (Pepper and Pepper 488). But the burden of Pepper's personal struggles continued to press on him until the very end of his life, and his effort to deal with their physical and emotional consequences forms the central concern and thrust of his narrative. Perhaps for these reasons, there is little *in Straight Life*—or in Laurie Pepper's autobiography, for that matter—to indicate Pepper's belief that his life and music had a larger social purpose or connection to a more embracing cultural community. His largely inward-looking and solitary journey is, in the end, what distinguishes his account from the community-focused portraits of black life of the African American musicians who grew up in Southern California in the early decades of the twentieth century, and who, like Pepper, came of musical age on Central Avenue at midcentury.

CONCLUSION

I began my preface with the suggestion that the Lincoln Center debates on race and jazz illuminate the continuing relevance of issues at the heart of twentieth-century white jazz autobiography, including debates over authenticity, racism, and privilege and claims to cultural authority. Put more bluntly, these debates reveal the tensions, antagonisms, and misunderstandings that surface when people from different backgrounds and life histories find themselves sharing intimate cultural spaces. Yet, in many respects, the social dynamic of the contemporary jazz scene in the United States is dramatically different from that portrayed in the accounts of these earlier jazz musicians; to suggest otherwise would be misleading and even irresponsible.

Clearly, African American musicians in the United States no longer have to organize to amalgamate segregated unions or arrange separate accommodations for sleeping and dining because they are barred from designated "whites-only" spaces. In addition, jazz ensembles today are commonly comprised of people of different nationalities and cultural backgrounds, and while sometimes this diversity is celebrated as evidence of the music's core values, just as often it is taken for granted, understood as a reflection of the contemporary jazz landscape in which musical networks are formed on the basis of shared aesthetic sensibilities rather than on strict ethnic or racial affiliation.

And yet, despite these apparent markers of progress, we are witnessing a period of intense social and political engagement in the contemporary jazz world, as musicians register their alarm at the rising tide of hatred and intolerance in the United States and around the globe and use their art and their voices to bring awareness to the many areas of social justice that remain unresolved. In projects that are reminiscent of the more explicitly political jazz music of the 1960s and 1970s, musicians have taken on issues of gun violence and police brutality, immigration, the African American quest for freedom from slavery times to the present day, and the post-9/11 world from the perspective of communities of color, including veterans of the wars in Iraq and Afghanistan.[1]

While some of these works appear to be aimed at societal injustices more broadly than at the institutions of jazz per se, a growing movement for gender justice in jazz is aimed squarely at the culture of jazz itself, with musicians forming musical and extramusical alliances to combat the sexual harassment and gender discrimination that have been a part of that culture throughout the music's history.[2] From this perspective, negotiations over race and gender justice in the contemporary jazz world must surely be seen as works in progress; while we celebrate the areas of progress made, we need to acknowledge, as Wadada Leo Smith stated so eloquently in a 2018 roundtable discussion of jazz in the Trump era, that "we have taken our eye off the ball for too long" (Blumenfeld 10).

I would like to suggest that the accounts of interracialism in twentieth- and early twenty-first-century white jazz autobiography examined in these pages are also best viewed as works in progress; that is, that the stories and experiences they describe offer the potential for a better and more just society, even as they often fall short. In their accounts of their immersion experiences, white jazz autobiographers illustrate the potential of jazz to encourage intercultural contact and exchange of a kind and degree far beyond that which was typically occurring in the still-segregated US society. Thus, we find moving descriptions of white youngsters learning to play under the guidance of a black mentor, sitting in at interracial jam sessions, or returning night after night to clubs in black neighborhoods to listen to their favorite bands.

In these descriptions, we see the more hopeful and positive aspects of these interracial experiences as well as the sharp boundaries or limits that frequently defined them. The contradictions that emerge in white jazz autobiographers' accounts of these experiences—the countless examples we have seen in which they convey both desire and jealousy, respect and condescension, deference and entitlement—are a central concern of this study, as I have tried to give voice to both the best and the worst aspects of these autobiographers' attraction to, and immersion in, black culture, and to resist (to the best of my ability) conclusions that appear either as outright condemnations or justifications of their sum depiction of these experiences.

In this respect, as I noted earlier, I depart from the more unsparing critiques of white appropriation and theft that seem to leave little room for the positive elements of interracialism in popular culture. I have chosen to do so because I believe that these positive elements are real and important, and that at their best, depictions of interracialism in white jazz autobiography show the ability of people to move beyond or resist cultural barriers imposed by law and custom and to experience deep and sustaining relationships. And yet, on other occasions, the actions and responses of white jazz autobiographers to particular interracial situations not only failed to confound the barriers of race but exacerbated them, bringing to the surface the deep misunderstandings, presumptions, and insensitivities that were proof of the vast social, economic, and cultural gulf between them and the people and cultures on which they made claims. In their accounts of particularly troubling aspects of these experiences of interracial contact, we have seen a range of attitudes—from primitivist or essentializing to colorblind or race-neutral— that demonstrate their inability or unwillingness to recognize the ways in which the systemic racism and discrimination of US society affected their own relationship, as white people, to jazz music and culture.

For a fuller explanation of this point, it is useful to revisit Karen Brodkin's discussion of the terms "ethnoracial assignment" and "ethnoracial identity" (see chapter 4); Brodkin, it is worth recalling, uses them in the specific context of her discussion of the experiences of Jews in the United States over the first half of the twentieth century, during which time they witnessed changes to their ethnoracial classification (how they were classified by the ruling powers) as well as to their own ethnoracial identity (how they perceived themselves as a result of these changing classifications).

Yet the evidence suggests that the immersion experiences in black culture depicted by *most* of the white jazz autobiographers under consideration in *Outside and Inside*—not just those Jewish, Italian, or Irish autobiographers who experienced "in-between" or "not-quite-white" identities in their early lives in America—involve a shift of ethnoracial identity. Furthermore, it is not their extracultural search for meaning and identity that is problematic, but rather their tendency to underestimate the strength of their own ethnoracial classification and its influence on the shape and extent of their interracial experiences. Their relationship to predominantly black jazz communities, in other words, is inevitably marked by their relative positions of power, no matter how sincere or persistent their efforts to cross racial boundaries. Moreover, it is at moments when they seem unable to acknowledge their ethnoracial assignment in relation to the black musicians at the center of their immersion experiences that the strains and tensions of these experiences emerge most clearly.

We see this lack of insight in Art Pepper's profession of bewilderment at the antiwhite backlash he faced in postwar black jazz circles and in his prison experiences, in Bob Wilber's angry denunciation of black studies programs at US universities and the growing demands he faced to hire black musicians, and in Max Kaminsky's presumption that he knew (and had the right to explain) the desires and goals of African Americans who had settled in the north during the Great Migration. Yet these same autobiographers convey other attitudes that appear to contradict, or at least to complicate, the positions suggested above. These include Kaminsky's expression of his own vulnerability as a Jew facing the threat of Hitler's holocaust, Pepper's emotional pleas for racial tolerance and his joyful recollections of his close musical and personal relationships with African Americans, and Wilber's acknowledgment of the hardships faced by African American musicians as a consequence of discrimination.

In many respects, this mixed assessment of the interracial experiences of white jazz autobiographers appears consonant with the analysis of race relations in early and Swing Era jazz communities offered by the social and cultural critics cited throughout this study. In his discussion of 1920s jazz, Burton Peretti finds evidence of both respectful and racist attitudes in "the Chicagoans, the whites who were closest to black musicians," later suggesting that "musical ideas were both exchanged and appropriated between the white and black jazz camps" (Peretti 189, 198). Similarly, William Kenney describes the "shared sensibility" but also acute tensions between whites and blacks in 1920s Chicago jazz communities. He details "the nettling insensitivity" of the white musicians in their experiences in the South Side music halls and their growing awareness of the effects of racism in the lives of the black musicians who were their teachers and peers—an awareness that left them more sympathetic "toward black jazz and deepened their sense of alienation from the white middle class" (*Chicago Jazz* 103, 105–7).

Lewis Erenberg balances the persistence of racism during the Swing Era with the considerable strides made by "swing musicians, fans, and impresarios who challenged racial inequality" by pushing for integration in jam sessions, club performances, and "in concert halls, [where] black and white musicians played together on an equal basis" (Erenberg 178). David Stowe suggests that while swing music "encourage[d] a broader social intimacy between the races than had previously been possible," it "was a profoundly precarious intimacy, requiring an urban environment easily disrupted by hostile forces" (Stowe 167).

And yet I find myself resisting the tone of resignation underlying some of these accounts—a resignation that leads to Peretti's "bittersweet conclusion" "that racial equality in jazz before 1940 could not exist anywhere outside certain individuals' perceptions" because "racism presented the advocates of equality in jazz with too many daunting barriers" (Peretti 209–10). A similar sense of resignation appears to lead John Gennari to conclude that while "personal friendships and individual virtue can help dissolve the color line, they can't quite as easily dismantle the power of systemic, institutional racism in a culture that was founded on white supremacy" (Gennari 384).

My point here is not to challenge the brilliant work of these scholars or even the validity of their conclusions, which are fully supported by their rich and detailed analyses. Rather, I would like to steer my own conclusion in another direction, to propose a reading of jazz autobiography that stresses the importance of "individuals' perceptions" and "personal friendships" in breaking down the social structures upon which racist laws and institutions depend. I would like to use the accounts of these autobiographers, with all the messy and often ugly truths that they reveal, to advance discussions of interracial and intercultural contact at a time when these contacts are so desperately needed. As I write these words, communities around the globe are reeling from the words and actions of cultural and religious extremists who have chosen paths of violence and hatred rather than understanding and peace and who are encouraged by politicians and clerics who use ignorance and fear to promote virulent racism and xenophobia.

In this context, I want to resist the cynicism and despair that come from the belief that individuals are powerless in the face of systems of evil and intolerance. As I have attempted to illustrate throughout this study, the attitudes and perspectives that emerge in jazz autobiographers' depictions of race and identity provide a clear path for resisting these feelings: all of them, in my view, provide at least some evidence of the potential of human beings to demonstrate greater humanity and kindness toward one another. Earlier, I quoted the black drummer Roy Porter's vivid description of the white musicians who followed his West Coast "hard bop" band "with mouth, nose, eyes and ears wide open in the process of what I call 'The Grand Theft of Musical Ideas'" (Porter, *There and Back* 55). It would be possible to leave Porter's comment here as his whole story, a synopsis of his perspective on interracialism in jazz. To do so, however, would leave out his sympathetic remarks about his experience of playing with Art Pepper shortly before Pepper's death and his analysis of the police crackdown on interracialism on Central Avenue: "What these red-neck cops didn't realize was that the bebop and jazz that the black musicians were playing was bringing the races closer together" (67).

It is clear that Porter is no moderate in his views on race, that his assertive expressions of black cultural nationalism aligned him with the growing resistance to white participation in jazz beginning in the late 1950s and increasing through the following decades. Yet in these comments Porter clearly contradicts his "grand theft" view of whites in jazz. This is not to say that he had given up on the latter view, but simply that in the context of his full-length autobiography, he had the opportunity to give a fuller portrait of his perspectives. In a related way, if we consider only those stories of Central Avenue musicians that emphasize the pervasive racism of Los Angeles and the discrimination that black musicians encountered in their careers and personal lives, we drown out drummer William Douglass's moving account of being the only black musician in Benny Goodman's band in the late 1940s, and his description of Benny Goodman as "just the ultimate" for his efforts in breaking down the segregated music scene of the Swing Era (Bryant et al. 248).

In *Outside and Inside*, I have tried to give voice to the many views on race and culture from the perspective of the various participants in these interracial encounters. It is my hope that all of them—from the most embracing to the most virulent—may provide important sources for teaching and studying the history of race in the United States over the twentieth century and may be discussed and shared as tools for resisting the intolerance of our present time.

NOTES

Preface

1. All quotes from the debate follow the transcript in Marsalis et al. "Jazz People." For excellent analysis of the debate and the various controversies surrounding JALC under Marsalis's directorship, see "Jazz People" 142; Gennari 341, 360–68; Porter, *What Is This Thing*: 311–29; Evans: 4–10. For particular attention to the persistent gender bias of JALC and its reliance on corporate sponsorship that reinforces its black masculinist image, see Pellegrinelli; McMullen.

2. Other critical views of Collier's jazz writings include Carner and Morgenstern. On Collier's recent controversy—a pro-Obama opinion piece he wrote in the local New York newspaper, *WestView News*, in July 2014 under the banner, "The N—r in the White House" (the full word appeared in the original)—see Fasick and Italiano.

3. For a prominent early attack on Marsalis, Crouch, and Murray and the politics of JALC, see Terry Teachout's 1995 essay, "The Color of Jazz."

4. Although the transcript does not indicate the audience response, Collier makes several references to it himself, noting the crowd's jeering, applause, and "rudeness" (Marsalis et al. "Jazz People" 152, 156, 160).

5. The video of the conversation may be found at https://wyntonmarsalis.org/videos/view/jazz-and-race-a-conversation-jazz-congress-2018. All quotes from the conversation are from my own transcription.

6. For a thoughtful discussion of jazz and race at the turn of the twenty-first century, see Gerald Early's essay, "White Noise and White Knights: Some Thoughts on Race, Jazz, and the White Jazz Musician" (2000). See also Greg Thomas's fascinating six-part series, "Race and Jazz" (2011–2012), on the website, *All About Jazz*; and Eugene Holley Jr.'s "My Bill Evans Problem: Jaded Visions of Jazz and Race" (2013).

7. In his homage to jazz, *Moving to Higher Ground*, Marsalis recalls his fiercely anti-integrationist stance in his early years on the New York jazz scene and how he remained unconvinced when Dizzy Gillespie tried to explain to him that "[b]ebop was about integration" and that "his and Charlie Parker's objective was to be integrated" (96). In response to this, Ethan Iverson has suggested that "[n]o one has paid heavier dues for being an angry young interviewee than Wynton Marsalis. He has since changed his mind about needing to be integrated" (Iverson, "Do the Math").

8. If JALC has become more racially and ethnically inclusive over the past two decades, its continuing lack of gender diversity, for example, remains deeply problematic. For a discussion of recent steps to counter gender bias at JALC, see the panel "Gender and Jazz" at the Jazz Congress 2018. https://livestream.com/jazz/Jazz-Congress-Day-1-Jazz-and-Race-Gender-and-Jazz/videos/168368468/. Marsalis also remains a deeply polarizing figure for his pronouncements

on rap music and black culture. In 2018, he ignited a firestorm when he argued that rap music was more harmful to black culture than Confederate monuments. For Marsalis's controversial remarks and a sample of the responses they generated, see Capehart, Graham, DeBerry.

Introduction

1. The vagueness of my estimate here is deliberate, in large part because of the imprecise and contestable nature and boundaries of the terms "jazz" and "autobiography." Don Asher, for instance, whom I examine in chapter 5, was not well-known as a jazz musician—he spent most of his career as a working pianist in clubs and society bands—yet he is included here because his accounts of his playing experiences in interracial jazz environments illuminate some of the central concerns of this study. Many other jazz musicians have told their stories to an amanuensis or editor, thus complicating the nature or extending the boundaries of what we recognize as self-inscription. I am aware, in other words, of the inherent subjectivity of any list of "jazz autobiography." The estimate I give above is based on my searches through library catalogues, online bookseller websites, and bibliographies from studies of jazz autobiography; another critic might well make different choices. On issues of categorization, see Gabbard, "The Jazz Canon" 10.

2. Kenney uses the term "autobiographical statements" to describe Armstrong's three published autobiographies and an "autobiographical interview" from 1966 in *Life* magazine ("Negotiating" 38). Harlos's overarching concern is to "track the dynamic at work in a jazz player's transition from a musical to a literary subject" (Harlos 134).

3. See Heble (2000). See also Stein, *Music Is My Life*, in which he offers an expanded treatment of the theory of "autobiographics" in his exploration of Louis Armstrong's books, essays, and letters.

4. Among the white jazz autobiographies that have received some prior scholarly attention are those by Paul Whiteman (1926), Benny Goodman (1939), Artie Shaw (1952), Art Pepper (1979), and especially Mezz Mezzrow (1946).

5. I am not suggesting that Berliner fails to acknowledge the perspective of the non–African American participants in his study or the social implications of their participation in jazz culture, only that these topics are not his primary focus. See Berliner 31–33.

6. In their anthology, *Big Ears: Listening for Gender in Jazz Studies* (2008), Nichole Rustin and Sherrie Tucker have gathered essays that attempt to "integrate marginalized experiences into the story of jazz"; a key concern of the collection is to stress the centrality of women to the music's development "as well as to narratives about jazz history and criticism" (19). Drawing on the critical perspectives of feminist theory and gender and sexuality studies, *Big Ears* builds on the "new jazz studies" of the last two decades that has sought to challenge the narrow focus of traditional jazz historiography. See also *Gender and Identity in Jazz* (Knauer), a collection of conference papers presented at the 2015 Darmstadt Jazzforum.

7. See Billie Holiday with William Dufty; Jeannie Cheatham; Anita O'Day with George Eells; Marian McPartland.

8. Among the autobiographers, only Wingy Manone and Tom Sancton were raised in New Orleans; Bud Freeman, Art Hodes, Benny Goodman, and Mezzrow were all born and raised on Chicago's West Side (Kenney, *Chicago Jazz* 92–93). Eddie Condon grew up in the Midwest; Art Pepper in California; Artie Shaw, Charlie Barnet, and Steve Jordan were born in New York City; Bob Wilber grew up in Scarsdale, New York; Don Asher and Max Kaminsky grew up in Massachusetts (Asher in Worcester and Kaminsky mainly in Boston).

9. I have not included Chet Baker's notably sparse memoir (1997), for example, because Baker offers no serious reflection on his interracial experiences in jazz.

10. See Arthur Rollini, *Thirty Years with the Big Bands* (1987); Drew Page, *Drew's Blues: A Sideman's Life with the Big Bands* (1980); Pee Wee Erwin, *This Horn for Hire* (1987). Rollini was an accomplished multi-instrumentalist whose career included stints with Paul Whiteman, the ABC Symphony, and also with the big bands of Benny Goodman and Bill Bradley and Ray McKinley. The Texan reeds player Page played in territory bands in the Southwest and later in the big band of Harry James and on the NBC staff. And although trumpeter Erwin notes that he was influenced by black jazz trumpeters Roy Eldridge and Red Allen and that he "much preferred the four-beat feel of the black bands," his career was chiefly defined by his work in small Dixieland combos and in several prominent bands of the Swing Era, and as a New York studio musician (Erwin and Vaché 112).

11. My approach to this study has been influenced by two key studies on jazz improvisation—Berliner's *Thinking in Jazz* (cited earlier) and Ingrid Monson's *Saying Something: Jazz Improvisation and Interaction* (1996)—both of which argue that an insider perspective is essential for understanding the process of jazz learning and improvisatory jazz performance. In his response to this approach, Ajay Heble suggests that "the best writing on jazz has to involve a rather tricky balancing act, a complex set of negotiations between on the one hand the teaching of critical theory . . . and, on the other, a recognition of the value and importance of documenting insider perspectives. . . . Just as it would . . . be inappropriate to ignore what musicians have said about their own craft, so too it would be foolish simply to take what they say at face value" (Heble 91).

12. Ruth Frankenberg (1993) describes colorblindness as a kind of "polite" racism that is more accurately viewed "as a double move toward 'color evasiveness' and 'power evasiveness'" and that, in her view, "has had reactionary results through most of the twentieth century" (14, 143). For other critiques of colorblindness, see Panish; Davis 34.

13. See also Teachout; Lees. As Monson points out, the recent examples of this white resentment narrative are reminiscent of "debates that took place in the jazz community during the early 1960s" (*Freedom Sounds* 16). On these earlier debates, see 238–82.

14. Sandke proposes the binary "exclusionary" and "inclusionary" to describe what he sees as opposing approaches to the telling of jazz history since the 1930s (Sandke 1). The exclusionary approach, in his view, represents jazz as "the expression of a distinct and independent African-American culture, isolated by its long history of slavery, segregation, and discrimination"; by contrast, the inclusionary approach allows that jazz, "even when produced by African-Americans (or anyone else for that matter), is more properly understood as the juncture of a wide variety of influences under the broader umbrella of American and indeed world culture" (1). Sandke's claim that most contemporary jazz scholars participate in this "exclusionary" approach is, in my view, a grave misinterpretation of their work. For a detailed and thoughtful critique of Sandke's claim, see Johnson 139, 141.

15. On Sandke, see Gridley 125–36; on Sudhalter, see Sager 509–17; Goodrich 162–66.

16. See Lee Mergner's interview with Randy Sandke in *JazzTimes* (August 5, 2010) and Matt Schudel's obituary on Sudhalter in the *Washington Post* (September 20, 2008).

17. John LaPorta (2001), for example, illustrates the truth that for most jazz and studio musicians of his generation, one's career was spent almost entirely in the company of other men; among the hundreds of personal names in the index to his autobiography, only a few women are included.

18. For analysis of the gender politics of swing culture, see Tucker *Swing Shift*, passim; Erenberg 199; Stowe 168–69.

19. On early jazz, see Peretti; Ogren; Evans. On the Swing Era, see Stowe; Erenberg; Tucker *Swing Shift*; on bebop, see DeVeaux, *Birth of Bebop*; on jazz and its significance to sociopolitical national and transnational discourse before and during the modern Civil Rights Era, see Monson, *Freedom Sounds*; Von Eschen; Saul; and Porter, *What Is This Thing*.

20. See Bjorn with Gallart; Bryant et al.; Burke; Demlinger and Steiner; Driggs and Haddix; Gioia, *West Coast Jazz*; Gordon, *Jazz West Coast*; Hersch, *Subversive Sounds*; Isoardi; Kenney, *Chicago Jazz*; Raeburn, *New Orleans Style* and "Stars of David"; Vacca; Widener; Williams.

21. Brodkin; Jacobson; Roediger; Raeburn, "Stars of David"; Hersch, *Subversive Sounds*.

22. Lott, *Love and Theft*; Monson "The Problem"; Tate; Gabbard, *Black Magic, Jammin'*.

23. Frankenberg; Hill; Jensen; Lipsitz, *Possessive*; Rothenberg.

24. See Goldstein; Alexander; Melnick.

25. For critiques of Mailer's "The White Negro," see Lott, *Love and Theft* 56; Monson, "The Problem" 403–4, 415; Tate, passim; Saul 63–72; Baldwin 171–90; Hentoff 138–42.

26. In his own life, Lipsitz—like many other critical race theorists—has made his own activism central to his career as an academic (*Possessive* xvii–xx). See also Frankenberg; Hill; Jensen; Rothenberg.

27. See Lipsitz, *Midnight* and Lipsitz's introductions in Otis, *Listen* and *Upside Your Head*.

28. Johnny Otis is considered a major influence in early rhythm and blues and rock and roll for his many hit songs, including "Every Beat of My Heart," "The Wallflower," "Willie and the Hand Jive," and "Harlem Nocturne"; for his discovery and promotion of many black artists, including Willie Mae "Big Mama" Thornton, Esther Phillips, Etta James, Little Willie John, Jackie Wilson, and Hank Ballard; and for his work as radio disc jockey and television host, in which capacity he showcased the leading musicians of black popular music whose careers had often been eclipsed by white rock and roll and pop musicians of the 1950s and 1960s. For an excellent overview of Otis's life and career, see Lipsitz, *Midnight* vii–xxxi.

29. Lipsitz suggests that Otis's civil rights activism and fierce denunciation of white supremacy had a significant and detrimental effect on his career (*Midnight* 72, 80–81). In 1960, local white supremacists burned a cross on the lawn of his family home and threatened him with greater violence "if he continued his agitation for Black rights" (71). Lipsitz also praises Otis for the selflessness he exhibited in his business practices and in his musical career, in which he consistently ceded the spotlight to other, younger, African American performers.

Chapter 1

1. All page references to *Really the Blues* are from the 2009 Souvenir Press edition.

2. All page references to *We Called It Music* are from the 1992 Da Capo Press edition. McNulty, who wrote for the *New Yorker* from 1937 to 1955, is featured prominently in Condon's first chapter, "A Pair of English Shoes," and is mentioned in passing on three occasions near the end of the text.

3. Among the white jazz autobiographies referred to in this study, only those by Don Asher, Artie Shaw, Tom Sancton, John LaPorta, and Drew Page do not identify a second author, collaborator, or amanuensis. Among these, Asher and Sancton were professional writers, and Shaw had considerable literary ambitions. LaPorta—who openly acknowledges his shortcomings as an author—seemed chiefly motivated to straighten the record concerning "musical events in my life [that] had been written about contrary to what had occurred" (LaPorta ii). In his preface, Page suggests the extensive role played by his editor, thanking her "for her meticulous attention to detail during the production of the book" (Page ix).

4. For an overview of theoretical perspectives on collaboration in contemporary American autobiography, see Stone, "Collaboration" 151–65. For a specific consideration of the collaborator/autobiographer relationship in African American autobiography since 1945, see Stone, "Two Recreate One" 231–64.

5. In many jazz autobiographies, however, the precise role of the collaborator as distinct from the autobiographical subject is not obvious or apparent for they speak (or write) as one

merged voice. Although the sociohistorical details of these more "seamless" collaborations are clearly worthy of investigation, they are beyond the focus of this study.

6. Chadwick Hansen is the author of a controversial book on the 1692 witchcraft trials, *Witchcraft at Salem* (1969).

7. Thomas Sugrue is probably best known for his 1945 biography of psychic Edgar Cayce (1945). In 1947, he hosted a radio talk show, *Conversations at Eight*, from a Manhattan hotel room.

8. The only autobiography by a white jazz musician that Christopher Harlos analyzes in any detail is Art Pepper's *Straight Life*; he mentions the autobiographies of Art Hodes, Mezz Mezzrow, and Steve Jordan only in passing.

9. Among these voices are an introduction by white bandleader Rudy Vallee and an explanatory chapter that concludes the book by the British musician Horace Gerlach; in addition, almost all of the musicians whose photographs appear alongside transcriptions of solos based on Armstrong's tune "Swing That Music" are white (Kenney, "Negotiating" 40).

10. See especially Ogren's chapter, "Prudes and Primitives: White Americans Debate Jazz," (*Jazz Revolution* 139–61); for critics' embrace or rejection of primitivist attitudes in the 1940s and 1950s, see Gennari 46, 51, 136–44.

11. I thank Sherrie Tucker for suggesting the phrase "white-on-white primitivism" in her comments on an earlier version of this chapter.

12. Among Dance's earlier publications were biographies of Duke Ellington (1970), Earl Hines (1977), Count Basie (1980), and an as-told-to autobiography with jazz trombonist Dicky Wells (1971). For a compelling discussion of the complicated racial dynamics at work in Wells's autobiography, in which several white people (including Dance) speak on behalf of the black autobiographical subject, see Harlos 153–56.

13. For a more critical assessment of Barnet's treatment of the black musicians he employed, see DeVeaux, *Birth of Bebop* 256–59. See also Andrew S. Berish, who praises Barnet's role in breaking down racial barriers during the Swing Era yet maintains that Barnet's essentialist views about musical style actually "reinscribed racial difference" and "reinforced the racial divisions of the music industry that often locked black musicians into specific 'racial' music styles" (Berish 113). In a comment that could have been intended for Stanley Dance, Berish adds, "Jazz critics who celebrated Barnet's 'authentic' jazz further reinforced racial categories and an implicit essentialism about black music and musicians" (113).

14. See Raeburn, "The Storyville Exodus," in which he debunks a popular myth by demonstrating that African American musicians began leaving New Orleans for employment opportunities in Chicago and California in the years preceding, rather than as a result of, the 1917 closing of Storyville.

15. Studs Terkel (1912–2008) published twelve books of oral history based on his interviews with Americans from a diverse range of social, ethnic, and racial backgrounds; among them were his first publication, *Giants of Jazz* (1957), and *Race: How Blacks and Whites Think and Feel about the American Obsession* (1992), published three years after Freeman's *Crazeology*.

16. Steve Philip Jordan (1919–1993)—a jazz guitarist known primarily for his accompanying, or rhythm, style, rather than as a soloist—played in several of the most popular big bands of the Swing Era, including those led by Artie Shaw, Stan Kenton, Boyd Raeburn, and Benny Goodman, and recorded with many well-known jazz musicians, including Vic Dickenson, Buck Clayton, Coleman Hawkins, and Roy Eldridge (Jordan 3).

17. Scanlan notes that Jordan received the first offer to play in Basie's band following Green's death in 1987—adding, as if mindful that some readers might wonder about the interracial makeup of Basie's band, that the bandleader "has had more than a few white players in recent decades, a kind of reverse integration you might say" (Jordan 2).

18. Scanlan also fails to mention the contributions of two black New Orleans guitarists, Lonnie Johnson and Johnny St. Cyr, to the development of the rhythm guitar in early jazz. On Johnson's contribution, see Obrecht 129–88; Schuller 109–12. On St. Cyr's, see Boyd 147–48.

19. In his more extensive explanation, Scanlan proposes a new slant on jazz origins and on concepts of originality. Although he concedes that "[w]ithout the American Negro there would have been no jazz as we know it" and that "most of the great jazz innovators have been black," "jazz artistry" is not synonymous with innovation; in his opinion, "jazz critics . . . have tended to overemphasize innovation [while] the truth is that performance is more important than innovation" (Scanlan 72).

20. See Condon and Gehman, *Treasury of Jazz* xvi; see also *The Eddie Condon Scrapbook of Jazz*, a pictorial history of Condon's jazz world, in which Condon begins a section whimsically entitled "How to Spell" with this description of himself as a writer: "Writing is not what I do best, but I can spell a little and with a patient editor I can usually put a few words together" (unpaginated).

21. Despite Condon's well-documented pronouncements of scorn for jazz critics, there is evidence that he formed close and amicable relationships with many of them, even those whose views he strongly opposed. See, for example, Gilbert Seldes's program notes for Condon's Town Hall concerts and *The Eddie Condon Blotter*, reprinted in *Eddie Condon's Scrapbook of Jazz*, unpaginated.

22. For simplicity's sake, though, I will continue to refer to the narrated chapters as Sugrue's "Narration." Gary Giddins also seems to ascribe dual authorship to *We Called It Music* (see Condon with Sugrue x).

23. Condon's nightclub, Eddie Condon's, opened on West Third Street in Greenwich Village in 1945; in 1958, the club moved uptown to East Fifty-Sixth Street, where it remained until 1967.

24. McNulty's *Third Avenue, New York* was published in 1946, one year before Condon's autobiography.

25. In the essay "This Is Jazz," Condon expresses this latter view in his description of an exchange between a jazz "scholar" and trumpeter Wild Bill Davison: "'Mr. Davison,' the scholar said, 'when you start on a trumpet solo, what do you think about?' 'Man,' said Mr. Davison, 'I don't think about *nothin'*. I just blow'" (Condon and Gehman 21).

26. Compare Hugues Panassié's observation in *The Real Jazz* (1942): "What characterized the extraordinary creative flow produced by the Negroes at the beginning of the twentieth century was that it was spontaneous—unconscious of its novelty, untarnished by the slightest design" (22). For similar views, see also Hobson (1939).

27. A curious distinction between Sugrue's and Condon's jazz histories is their apparent disagreement concerning African musical influences on jazz. While Sugrue emphasizes jazz's connection to African musical traditions, Condon insists that jazz was "first played by Negroes, but it was not, as so many people seem to think, music right out of the heart of Africa; . . . the two kinds of music are as far apart as the clarinets of Benny Goodman and Pee Wee Russell" (Condon and Gehman 27).

28. For a discussion of the complex response of the African American middle class to jazz, see DeVeaux, *Birth of Bebop* 49–54. See also *Blues People: Negro Music in White America* (1963), in which LeRoi Jones (Amiri Baraka) offers a scathing denunciation of the African American middle class, which he accuses of abandoning its cultural traditions in its rush toward assimilation and embrace of materialism (Jones 124, 125, 127).

29. All page references to *The Kingdom of Swing* are from the 1961 Frederick Ungar edition.

30. In his foreword, Kolodin refers to himself as Goodman's collaborator, but, as is the case with many of these jazz collaborations, the precise nature or degree of Kolodin's role is not specified; the only sections directly attributed to him are the book's foreword and two chapters, each of which includes the descriptor, "An interpolation by Irving Kolodin" (Goodman 46, 171).

31. Not surprisingly, Kolodin and Sugrue's jazz histories focus on the styles most closely associated with their respective coauthors; Kolodin is therefore primarily concerned with the evolution of big band swing music, Sugrue with Chicago-style hot jazz ensembles.

32. At the time of his collaboration with Goodman, Kolodin (1908–1988) was classical music critic for the *New York Sun* and had recently published a full-length history of the Metropolitan Opera. Over a long career, he would write more than a dozen books on various aspects of European and American classical music history while also working as music critic for the *New York Sun* (1932–1950) and the *Saturday Review* (1947–1982); he was also "one of the first American critics to give extensive reviews of phonograph records" (Smith, "Kolodin, Irving").

33. As Kathy Ogren notes, there were similar arguments in 1920s jazz criticism suggesting that "jazz was deemed acceptable if it helped young people learn an instrument or become exposed to classical music" (*Jazz Revolution* 158).

34. As Goodman recalls, "John [Hammond] asked me if I had ever played any legitimate clarinet music. I said: 'Well, I used to play cadenzas with the orchestra on the Hoffman Ginger Ale hour.' But John said that wasn't what he meant. He said he was thinking of something like the Mozart clarinet quintet which I don't think, up to that time, I had ever heard, or even knew about" (Goodman 166).

35. Evidence of this skepticism may be found in the promotional flyer prepared by promoter Sol Hurok for Goodman's 1938 concert at Carnegie Hall, which, as Catherine Tackley notes, "demonstrates a careful balance between the obvious tension of swing in the concert hall and reassurance that Goodman's music aspired to the qualities of high art through the presentation of an evolutionary historical narrative for swing that both references and emulates the history of art music" (Tackley 15).

36. The original 1946 publication of *Really the Blues* includes three appendices, all written in Mezzrow's voice, and a glossary of hip slang of unstated authorship. Wolfe's undated afterword, which first appeared in the 1990 edition of *Really the Blues*, is the only portion of the text for which Wolfe receives acknowledgment as sole author.

37. Yet according to Gayle Wald, Mezzrow stated that he "drafted *Really the Blues* in longhand and then submitted the manuscript to Wolfe for editing and revising" (Wald 202, fn. 4). Wald adds that Mezzrow "claimed that 365,000 words were cut from the original manuscript" but that "the material was later lost" (202, fn. 4). Mezzrow's comments here seem suspect in two respects: his claim regarding the length of the manuscript and his reference to a word count (in a precomputer world) rather than to a page count. Carolyn Geduld's monograph on Wolfe also offers little help in untangling the precise nature of the collaboration. Initially, she describes *Really the Blues* as "co-authored by Bernard Wolfe and Mezz Mezzrow"; later she describes it as an "as-told-to" autobiography in which "Mezz responds by talking about himself for a couple of years, while Wolfe, his 'literary pal,' listens and writes" (Geduld 9–20). In later comments, she notes the "popularity of Wolfe's first book" (24); and "for the student of Wolfe, *Really the Blues* is notable because he has not, to date, written another book like it" (35).

38. The reader might justifiably read as ironic Wolfe's remarks to Mezzrow regarding the book's lack of commercial appeal. As Scott Saul notes, Random House published *Really the Blues* in 1946 to considerable hype, with promotional ads that described it as "an upside down success story" about "a man who 'crossed the color line, *backwards*'" (Saul 41, emphasis in original). See also Wald 57–58.

39. Scott Saul cites aspects of Wolfe's biography—his turn to Trotskyist politics and Freudian psychoanalysis in the mid-1930s as the result of the Depression's devastating impact on his family; his year-long position as Trotsky's bodyguard and secretary in Mexico; and his participation in "Greenwich Village bohemia" in the 1940s—as important background for understanding his influence on the crafting of Mezzrow's autobiography (Saul 49–50).

Chapter 2

1. According to Wilber, there were several dozen young musicians playing jazz around Westchester in that period (Wilber 16).

2. Pianist Dick Wellstood, whom Wilber describes as "another guy like me, ... very much of a rebel," would host wild parties at his house in Greenwich, Connecticut, marked by "wild" jam sessions "with people passing out on the lawn. The terrible din would continue until the neighbors called the police" (Wilber 14). His friends Eddie Hubble and Johnny Windhurst had a passion for "foreign cars," and Wilber recalls the wild rides "around the county and into New York" in their "Pierce Arrow convertible with isinglass windows" and "a Rolls with an open cockpit for the chauffeur" (14–15; Balliett, "Westchester Kids" 304).

3. The reception to the Wildcats in the jazz press was mixed. They were compared to early twentieth-century white jazz musicians such as Bix Beiderbecke and Chicago's Austin High School Gang, but more often to black musicians: Wilber to Bechet, Dick Wellstood to Jelly Roll Morton and James P. Johnson, and cornetist Johnny Glasel to Louis Armstrong and Tommy Ladnier (Burke 188–89). As Burke notes, while many of the write-ups were positive, others were more critical of the Wildcats' revivalist aspirations, charging them with "an absence of originality and creativity" (189).

4. See chapter 4 for Artie Shaw's account of himself as an eager young white musician seeking (and finding) a mentor in Smith, whom Gunther Schuller names—with Luckey Roberts, James P. Johnson, and Eubie Blake—"in the vanguard of the Eastern jazz movement by virtue of their harmonic sophistication and increased technical virtuosity" (Schuller 255).

5. While Patrick Burke suggests that these less formal opportunities for interracial contact were an important "step toward more established interracial performances on 52nd Street," he also notes that sometimes white and black bands were hired to compete "against one another," leading him to conclude that even jam sessions "never truly transcended notions of race" (Burke 150–51).

6. Sidney Bechet, however, claims in his autobiography, *Treat It Gentle*, that he "had quite a few scholars, you know; they were all taking lessons. And that's when I had Bob Wilber" (Bechet 185).

7. While Wilber seems primarily interested in describing Bechet's teaching method, the emotional impact of these lessons is clear, from Wilber's opening image of student and teacher sitting down at Bechet's "venerable old upright" piano "with his Brush Soundmirror tape recorder alongside," to his description of Bechet's "approach to song interpretation," harmony, and composition (Wilber 25–27). He ends his description on a note of warm nostalgia, remarking on the wonderful memories stirred by his taped recordings of his lessons with Bechet and offering this summary of the experience: "I was totally absorbed in the man and in his music. Every single day with him taught me more about music than a full year at Eastman could ever have done" (26, 29).

8. In a similar assessment, Dick Wellstood wrote, "Bechet was not prejudiced and he rather enjoyed having young musicians around. For music to him was a skill to be taught, to be learned. There was a right way to play, a right way to breathe, a right set of chords, a right tempo for each tune" (qtd. in Meyer, *Giant Strides* 23).

9. In *Preservation Hall: Music from the Heart* (1991), William Carter notes that the New Orleans traditional jazz bassist Chester Zardis would also address a student as "my scholar" or "my boy" (227).

10. Although Bechet's large family participated in music-making—his father and siblings played instruments and formed small bands for public performances—they maintained the traditional attitudes of their Creole community that viewed music as a hobby and expected that Sidney would eventually follow the path of his father and siblings in learning a skilled trade or profession (Chilton 2–3, 9–10).

11. David Ake notes that Jelly Roll Morton's family also disapproved of his immersion in Uptown culture (Ake 22–23).

12. Near the end of his autobiography, Bechet repeats his explanation that he settled in France in order to be "nearer to Africa" (Bechet 194–95). See also Ake 25.

13. Bechet's comment here is further evidence of the degree to which he had been influenced by an Uptown musical sensibility in which improvising and other skills were more highly prized than was the ability to read music.

14. As Art Hodes opined in *Jazz Record*, "Anyone who has heard Bob Wilber play knows that Bechet has done his job well. It remains for Bob to carry on from there. The real jazz will never die as long as master musicians impart their knowledge to willing youngsters." In a similar vein, Mary Beckwith, writing in *American Jazz Review*, quoted Bechet's remark to an audience about Wilber, "I hope you like him—he's coming and I'm going" (qtd. in Burke 191–92).

15. Wilber describes his search for a way to "be Bob Wilber and no one else.... I was simply looking for my own voice, and I felt that if I found that voice the other things would follow" (Wilber 61). But as Aram "Al" Avakian playfully suggests in a 1947 article about Bechet and Wilber in *Jazz Record*, the direction of the influence was not entirely clear. "How did this green, bespectacled high school student learn and absorb the style of one of the creators of jazz in less than two years and to such a point that a standard gag today on hearing Sidney play is, 'Gee, plays just like Bob Wilber, doesn't he?'" (qtd. in Burke 190).

16. According to John Chilton, Bankhead and Bechet had known each other since the early 1930s; at some point, they began a sexual relationship, in Chilton's description "as durable as it was unpredictable; sometimes years elapsed between their meetings, yet each time they were reunited they picked up the excitement from where they had left off" (Chilton 193).

17. For a sharply contrasting perspective on the teaching of jazz in black studies programs, see Horace Tapscott's account in chapter 6.

18. For a comprehensive review of the history of jazz pedagogy, see Prouty 2010.

19. On Wilber's university teaching, see Dave Helland's piece in *Downbeat* (July 1989), 51.

20. Although Wilber seems unable to recognize the patronizing aspects of his own racialist worldview, he is quick to identify them in Mezz Mezzrow, suggesting that "it was ridiculous to hear this Jewish guy from Chicago coming out with a rich southern drawl." Beyond Mezzrow's black posturing, Wilber charges him with paternalistic impulses, describing him as "the Great White Father looking after his slaves. The black musicians were very conscious of this patronizing attitude, and they resented it" (Wilber 40).

21. See, for example, Wilber's apparent amusement over Jackie Gleason's offensive treatment of Rahsaan Roland Kirk at a rehearsal for Gleason's television show (Wilber 91–92).

22. Wilber would also almost certainly have known that Young and other African American musicians were not drafted to play in black bands (such as Count Basie's) in which they had become famous but instead "were drafted individually like ordinary civilians, and scattered around the country" (Porter, *Lester Young* 24). This is in contrast to the experience of white musicians in the leading big bands who fulfilled their military service in the bands for which they worked in their civilian lives. Young was eventually "dishonorably discharged from the army and sentenced to a year in the disciplinary barracks of Fort Gordon, Georgia" (25).

23. Two of Wilber's closest musical associates, Kenny Davern and Dick Wellstood, showed a similar devotion to and distance from the New Orleans roots of jazz. Davern (1935–2006), born in Huntington, Long Island, and raised in Queens, acknowledged that he "was at odds with my own contemporaries. I thought the real jazz was Louis Armstrong—and I still do" (Meyer, *Life and Music* 9). Later, however, he "abandoned the style because it was 'crippling, like playing with one hand behind my back. I wasn't giving expression to what my full potential could be'" (34). Wellstood (1927–1987), born in Greenwich, Connecticut, was most closely associated with the stride piano tradition of East Coast musician James P. Johnson, but, like

Davern, he had far-ranging and eclectic musical interests (Meyer, *Giant Strides* 19). His combo with Wilber at the Savoy in Boston in the mid-1940s played "New Orleans and Dixieland jazz ... but in rather different and sometimes unsettling ways," refusing to follow precisely the paths of the traditionalists or modernists (29).

24. Crouch credits the phrase "idiomatic nuance" to Marsalis's other prominent mentor, Albert Murray, adding another fascinating thread to the complex relationships between Wilber and Crouch and Wilber and Marsalis (and the Crouch/Murray orbit). See Crouch, "Rotten Club" 57.

25. Pug Horton took her rebuke of Crouch's essentialist argument even further, imagining a world based on his views on musical authenticity in which "[m]usicians will only be allowed to play music indigenous to their background" and audiences would be matched with performers who shared their ethnicity. "In essence," she wrote, "we must segregate culturally, socially, and artistically." Yet her own multicultural background ("East Indian, North African, and English") left her "at a loss as to which musical category I might qualify for" ("Letters" 3). Randy Sandke—whose views on race and jazz I considered earlier and who was one of the musicians hired by Wilber to play on the film soundtrack—also wrote a letter pushing back against Crouch (Wilber 187; "Letters" 3, 39).

26. Crouch observed that since Horton's and Wilber's letters were written "on exactly the same stationery" with the "same address and phone number, I would imagine they are thick as thieves" ("Letters" 39). How Crouch had access to their original letters is not explained.

27. Wilber has appeared as a guest performer, sideman, or musical director with the Lincoln Center Jazz Orchestra (LCJO) on several occasions, including tribute concerts honoring Sidney Bechet (1997 and 2009); Louis Armstrong (2000); Benny Carter (2007); and Benny Goodman (May 2009). An early review of the Wilber/Marsalis collaboration described the "gusto" of their "trumpet and saxophone breaks" (Ratliff E8). In 2008, Wilber served with Marsalis, David Berger, and Reginald Thomas as a judge for the thirteenth annual Essentially Ellington High School Jazz Band Competition and Festival (Thompson).

28. In 1968, Wilber joined the World's Greatest Jazz Band (WGJB), and in 1975, he formed the Soprano Summit with Kenny Davern; these bands focused on early jazz and original music, spurring Wilber's growing interest in jazz repertory work. During the 1970s and 1980s, he became involved with the New York Jazz Repertory Company and Smithsonian Jazz Repertory Ensemble; in 1981, he founded the Bechet Legacy, "a group dedicated to the musical heritage of Sidney Bechet." In 1989, he debuted Ellington's "The Queen's Suite" in a "Royal Ellington concert" for Queen Elizabeth II. See "About Bob Wilber" on the web page "Guide to the Bob Wilber Papers, 1943–2006," https://www.library.unh.edu/find/archives/collections/bob-wilber-papers-1943-2006.

Chapter 3

1. A stage adaptation of *Song for My Fathers* debuted at Tulane University in 2010 and has been performed several times since then, including at Carnegie Hall in 2012.

2. Other white people who figure prominently in Sancton's depiction of the interracial community at Preservation Hall (the center of Sancton's immersion experience) include its owner, Larry Borenstein, and Allan and Sandra Jaffe, the husband-and-wife team who ran it; all three of them moved to New Orleans from elsewhere (Sancton, *Song* 56–61). Sancton's mother and especially his father also had close, enduring relationships with the old musicians.

3. For another perspective on a white musician's immersion in New Orleans early jazz culture in the same period as Sancton's, see Barry Martyn's *Walking with Legends: Barry Martyn's New Orleans Jazz Odyssey* (2007). Martyn, born in England in 1941, was one of many British youngsters of his generation who became infatuated with the New Orleans revival movement

of the 1940s. As a performing musician and through his recordings, interviews, and photographs, Martyn has made an important contribution to documenting and preserving the black jazz traditions of early twentieth-century New Orleans.

4. Sancton witnessed the transformation of Preservation Hall from "a one-room hole-in-the-wall" club whose customers were the most ardent of "traditional jazz fans" to the internationally famed establishment that it remains to this day (*Song* 9, 65). For a comprehensive history of Preservation Hall, see Carter; Bethell 251–55.

5. For more on the life and career of George Lewis, see Bethel; Fairburn; Martyn with Gagliano.

6. Sancton Sr. was born in the Canal Zone in 1915; his father had moved his family there, lured by the prospects of a good job, but within two years he was dead, the result of a work accident (Sancton, *Song* 39). After his death, his wife returned to New Orleans with her two young children and bought a house on Canal Street, where Sancton Sr. spent his childhood (40).

7. See, for example, "Sancton Focuses the Negro Press," *Atlanta Daily World*, May 2, 1943, 6.

8. This view is supported by Lawrence Jackson in his comprehensive and mainly laudatory assessment of Sancton Sr.'s contribution to radical southern liberalism as editor, essayist, and short-story writer. According to Jackson, "Among white southern writers actively publishing who were critical of racism and slavery during the early 1940s, Sancton really had no peer, not excluding Lillian Smith" (Jackson 86).

9. Thomas Sancton Sr. published two novels with Doubleday, *Count Roller Skates* (1956) and *By Starlight* (1960); neither achieved critical or commercial success. For discussion of the novels, see Sancton, *Song* 35–36, 48–49. For discussion of the earlier novel, see Jackson 89–90.

10. Lewis's great-great-grandmother on his mother's side had been stolen as a child by slave traders in Senegal near the end of the eighteenth century and brought to Louisiana, where she was sold into slavery (Bethell 10–12); his grandfather on his father's side was a slave, and his grandmother, a Choctaw Indian (Sancton, *Song* 86; Bethell 16).

11. Lewis biographer Tom Bethell suggests that Lewis and many of the other early New Orleans musicians continued to develop musically and stylistically through the 1940s, but that from about 1950 onward there was a marked "deterioration" in their performance and in the music itself (Bethell 7, 112). In Bethell's view, this decline correlated to the change in the music from serving "a functional role in a social event, usually a dance" to being viewed as art music that was listened to by audiences in night clubs and in concert halls (239).

12. See also Bethell 251–52; Carter 97.

13. Similarly, William Carter notes the influence of New Orleans bassist Chester Zardis "on younger generations of traditional bass players. In this he exemplified the role of Preservation Hall as a catalyst in the worldwide resurgence of New Orleans jazz. Such 'teaching' occurred not only inside the Hall, on the concert stages and on the records, but also in direct, one-to-one encounters, both personal and musical. This passing of the torch flowed naturally from the older musicians, since that was the way they themselves had received the lineage" (227).

14. It is Bethell's suggestion that most early New Orleans jazz musicians, no matter what neighborhood they were from, "played in a relatively legitimate, disciplined style" but that over time "the music became rougher," with increasing emphasis on improvisation over written music (Bethell 23).

15. For a comprehensive treatment of the Robert Charles race riot, see Hair 2008.

16. A. P. Tureaud (1899–1972) was the attorney for the New Orleans chapter of the NAACP and a close friend of Thurgood Marshall. Historian Adam Fairclough describes Tureaud as the "dean of civil rights lawyers in Louisiana" whose "name appeared on virtually every suit filed by the NAACP" over the fifty years he was involved with the organization (Fairclough xii). John Minor Wisdom (1905–1999)—"a well-known liberal jurist and then head of the US

Fifth Circuit Court of Appeals in New Orleans" (Sancton, *Song* 186)—"was the only judge from Louisiana—and probably the only federal judge in the South—to have been actively involved in civil rights before his appointment to the bench" (Fairclough 218). In Fairclough's view, Wisdom's "very Republicanism" was a reaction to Louisiana's "corrupt and undemocratic one-party system" and "[h]is desire to break down that system" (218–19).

17. Sancton writes that he "had a better idea now why the proud Creole trumpet player Peter Bocage had such a precise, almost polite, style of playing ... I realized why Louis Cottrell had such a clean, fluid technique and elegant harmonies, why George Lewis still fumed over the Creole dance halls that wouldn't admit him because he didn't have 'silky hair.' And why George Guesnon always insisted on being called 'Creole George'" (*Song* 188).

18. For the classic account of the legal history of segregation in the United States, see Woodward 1957. For gains and setbacks of the civil rights movement in Louisiana in the early 1960s, see Fairclough, chapters 9–11. For interracial jam sessions in New Orleans's jazz community in the mid-to-late 1950s as a threat to the maintenance of segregation practices, see Carter 116, 120–22.

19. In 1965, Sancton wrote a remarkable essay about his relationship with Punch Miller for an eleventh-grade assignment; his teacher, Charles Suhor, at that time the New Orleans correspondent for *Down Beat* magazine, was so impressed by the essay that he sent it on to *Down Beat* editor Don McMichael, who published the piece in the February 1967 issue. See Sancton, "Portrait" 20–22; Suhor 12–14.

20. In *Walking with Legends*, Barry Martyn also describes visiting black musicians at their homes in New Orleans in the early 1960s, contrasting the indifference of the black police to his presence in black neighborhoods with the mostly vigilant response of the white police (Martyn 25–26).

21. According to Bruce Raeburn, *Jazzmen* was the earliest text to establish "a fully developed cultural and environmental thesis for jazz origins in New Orleans" (*New Orleans Style* 60). Raeburn adds that the various contributors to *Jazzmen* made differing claims regarding the black or multiracial origins of jazz (68, 71).

22. Dora Bliggen's "Blackberries" can be heard on *Classic Sounds of New Orleans*, Smithsonian Folkways Recordings, 2010.

23. Sancton claims that on one occasion his father "saved George Lewis's life," rushing him to the hospital after Lewis collapsed in the throes of "a severe asthma attack." According to the attending physician, Lewis likely would not have survived had Sancton Sr. not taken immediate action (*Song* 194–95).

24. A year before Sancton, Barry Martyn also joined the black local of the American Federation of Music in New Orleans. For his riveting account of this experience, including responses from the black press and the local Ku Klux Klan to his decision, see Martyn 65–66.

25. Israel Gorman (1895–1965) was a regular at Preservation Hall, playing in bands led by Kid Howard and Kid Sheik; he also played in several of New Orleans leading brass bands (Hobbs).

26. From 1992 to 2001 Sancton served as Paris bureau chief and senior European correspondent for *Time*. He has also contributed to many other publications, including *Newsweek*, *Vanity Fair*, *Fortune*, *Le Point*, *Le Monde*, and the *Wall Street Journal*; in addition, he is the author or coauthor of five books, including *The Armageddon Project* (2007); *Death of a Princess: The Investigation* (1998); and *The Bettencourt Affair: The World's Richest Woman and the Scandal that Rocked Paris* (2017).

27. Sancton's recent recordings include "City of a Million Dreams: New Orleans Legacy Band" (2011); "Hymns and Spirituals: Tommy Sancton New Orleans Quartet" (2012).

28. In a footnote, Sancton names Bill Huntington—"a talented New-Orleans-born banjoist and bass player, who played and recorded with many of the old musicians in the 1950s"—as

another local youngster whose experience in black and Creole New Orleans jazz culture was similar to his own (*Song* 108).

29. Like Sancton, Barry Martyn understood the importance of experiencing New Orleans's jazz culture directly from the source. "I knew I wasn't going to learn about it in England—you might as well try to play cricket in New Orleans" (Martyn 12). See also William Carter, who comments on the role of Preservation Hall "as a 'mecca' . . . to help New Orleans-style musicians from around the world tie into the basic lineage of jazz and brass band performance." While many of them had heard recordings of the music, they understood the need for "direct exposure to the living roots" (Carter 205).

30. Yet since his return to New Orleans, Sancton has observed a renewed interest in early jazz among New Orleans's black musicians. While "the mens" are no longer there, "the younger (and not so young) black musicians who have taken their place are products of the same culture. . . . The ethos of the mens' world lives on through them" (Sancton, *Song* 315–16). See also Martyn 122–23; Carter 262–64.

31. My use of the phrase "race and place" is inspired by Hersch's suggestion, in his discussion of the changing status of New Orleans's Creoles noted in chapter 3, that "race rather than place now defined them: to become Americans, Creoles had to become black" (Hersch, *Subversive Sounds* 99). For New Orleanian white jazz musicians, both race (i.e., their proximity to black New Orleans's culture) *and* place clearly mattered in their construction of jazz authenticity.

32. In *Trumpet on the Wing*, Manone states that he was born in February 1904 (10); official sources, however, list his birthdate as February 13, 1900 (Tovey and Kernfeld).

33. All page references to *Trumpet on the Wing* are from the 1964 Doubleday edition.

34. According to Bruce Raeburn, Manone "started out playing for pennies on street corners uptown with his friend Johnny Hyman before embarking on a musical odyssey that took him to Illinois, New York, Alabama, Missouri, Texas, New Mexico, and California before 1926" ("Stars of David" 150).

35. In this respect, Raeburn's argument is consonant with that proposed by Ingrid Monson about a later period of jazz, when she suggests that there was a "blackening of aesthetic standards in jazz during the 1950s and 1960s" (Monson, *Freedom Sounds* 69). In particular, Monson argues that the dominance of "hard bop styles" in this period "represents a blackening of modernist aesthetics, which would ultimately serve as a standard against which any player of jazz would be evaluated" (71).

36. On the Irish Channel's reputation as "a kind of lawless zone where . . . [l]ocal whites fought wars with tough kids from Basin Street, so at times it was dangerous for blacks to set foot in the neighborhood," see Hersch *Subversive Sounds* 83–84. In his autobiography, *Satchmo: My Life in New Orleans*, Louis Armstrong claims that "if you followed a parade out there [to the Irish Channel] you might come home with your head in your hand" (225).

37. The musicians who participated in the recording were Bud Freeman, Artie Shaw, Teddy Wilson, John Kirby, Dickie Wells, Kaiser Marshall, and Jelly Roll Morton (Raeburn, "Stars of David" 150).

38. Hersch frames this in a slightly different way: "Sicilians, who made up the vast majority of Italian immigrants (and Italian jazz musicians) during this period, were particularly despised," in part because of their "willingness to associate with blacks as equals" (*Subversive Sounds* 111–12).

39. The quote "to safely indulge" comes from Burke's specific discussion of Prima, whose dark, wavy hair and reputation for being "well fortified" fit most closely the "stereotypes of black sexuality" and who, according to Burke, was more "directly imitative" of Armstrong than was Manone (Burke 46, 50).

40. Prima's racial "in-betweenness" was perhaps even more evident than Manone's; in fact, a job offer in New York fell through when the club owner mistook him for black. See Boulard 60; Raeburn "Stars of David" 133; Burke 44–45.

41. See Raeburn, "I'll Be Glad" 58–72; Gabbard, *Jammin'* 210–11, 234–35; Giddins, *Satchmo* 36.

42. In 1940, Manone moved to California, where he later became a regular guest on Bing Crosby's radio shows. In the 1950s, he settled in Las Vegas, where he worked as a bandleader into the 1970s; during the 1960s and 1970s, he also performed in Europe and North America as a touring soloist in clubs and at festivals, as well as on television (Tovey and Kernfeld).

Chapter 4

1. Mezzrow was born in 1899, Kaminsky in 1908, Goodman in 1909, and Shaw in 1910.

2. Although Shaw's biographer, Tom Nolan, states that Shaw's mother was "born in Austria and raised in Sambor, near the shifting Polish-Austrian border," in his autobiography Shaw refers only to his father's Russian Jewish heritage (Nolan 1; Shaw 135).

3. Brodkin's study is both historical and sociological as well as a personal record of her own family's experience of living as Jews in America during the twentieth century. She argues that while her generation "grew up as white, middle-class suburbanites, unaffected by the barriers that kept our parents out of certain jobs and neighborhoods," her parents and grandparents "lived in a time when Jews were not white" (Brodkin 2). Her analysis of the latter is particularly helpful in contextualizing the experiences of the Jewish autobiographers in this chapter. Brodkin distinguishes between "ethnoracial assignment"—hegemonic classifications by which racioethnic groups are positioned within society—and "ethnoracial identity"—constructed by individuals under the influence of their particular ethnoracial assignment (3).

4. Goodman's autobiography was published in 1939, Mezzrow's in 1946, Shaw's in 1952, and Kaminsky's in 1963.

5. Eric Goldstein (2006) focuses on groups and individuals most invested in articulating a sense of Jewish particularity; thus, his attention to the cultural sphere is limited mainly to literature, plays, and movies that comment on themes directly related to Jewish identity. Jazz gets only passing mention, and his discussion of Jewish musicians and entertainers in popular music focuses chiefly, as do the studies of Alexander and Melnick, on the earlier generation of Jewish entertainers rather than on the jazz musicians under consideration here.

6. Melnick's focus is primarily on "jazz age" entertainers, publishers, composers, and songwriters—Al Jolson, Irving Berlin, George Gershwin, Fanny Brice, Sophie Tucker, and the Witmark brothers—arguing that they demonstrated "Jewish agility at expressing and disseminating Black sounds and themes as a product of Jewish suffering and as a variant of Jewish cultural nationalism," thus competing "with the Black cultural nationalism of Harlem in the 1920s and 1930s" (Melnick 12–13). Alexander considers the careers of Jolson, gangster Arnold Rothstein, and jurist Felix Frankfurter to exemplify his thesis of "*outsider identification*," that is, the impulse of Eastern European Jewish Americans to identify "themselves with less fortunate individuals and groups . . . by imitating, defending, and actually participating in the group life of marginalized Americans" (Alexander 1). See also Michael Rogin's seminal study (1998), in which he interrogates concepts of "whiteness" and American identity through his examination of Jewish blackface performers in Hollywood films.

7. Shaw married eight times; to the best of my knowledge, only one of his wives—Elizabeth Kern, the daughter of composer Jerome Kern—was Jewish.

8. Shaw published two collections of stories, *I Love You, I Hate You, Drop Dead!* (1966) and *The Best of Intentions and Other Stories* (1989). For a time, he ran a dairy farm; later he became a precision rifleman and a film distributor, as well as a lecturer on the college circuit. See Steyn 139–40; Wilson A24.

9. All quotes from *The Trouble with Cinderella* are from the 1992 Fithian Press edition.

10. In a later interview, however, Shaw described the virulent anti-Semitism he experienced in "Catholic New Haven"; his comments perhaps reflect the influx of Italian, Polish, and French Canadian immigrants to Connecticut in the early twentieth century (Gerber 73).

11. Brodkin describes her family's move in the late 1940s from a Jewish, working-class neighborhood in Brooklyn to the suburbs of Long Island as part of the upward mobility that was central to the history of the Jews in the United States during the twentieth century. In Brodkin's case, however, unlike in Artie Shaw's, her experiences of the city and the suburbs were that both were "community-based cultures" and that the "suburban community was every bit as Jewish in its makeup as the one in which [her parents] had grown up" (Brodkin 8). Shaw's family moved to the suburbs about thirty years earlier than did Brodkin's, in a period in which Jews were far less assimilated into US mainstream culture than they would be by the 1940s.

12. Shaw recalls that his father remarked to his friends in Yiddish, "*America gonniff*"; the literal translation of *gonniff* is "thief," perhaps conveying the elder Shaw's feelings about his newly adopted country. Shaw supplies his own translation of his father's expression: "Very well, then—if people are stupid enough to pay good money to listen to crazy noises coming out of a blower, let them do it, but don't expect me to take it seriously, because I know better" (*Cinderella* 63).

13. Shaw's later "intellectual re-evaluation" of his father was more forgiving, acknowledging his difficulties in adjusting to his new life in America that prevented him from realizing his potential and left him to die alone and "under wretched and poverty-stricken circumstances" (*Cinderella* 136).

14. In his interview with biographer Tom Nolan, Shaw cites economic factors and questions of belief in his decision to change his name (Nolan 11).

15. Shaw's only previous reference to African Americans was in reference to an experience in a whorehouse, when he and another young man—both virgins at the time—set out in search of "one of these joints" to bring an end to the hazing they were enduring from their band members. While the story seems intended to show Shaw's discomfort with a certain form of masculine performance—he in fact did not have sex with the prostitute, but he stayed with her long enough to make the artifice convincing—his description of the African American men in the whorehouse is crude and fantastical. See Shaw, *Cinderella* 158–59; Melnick 137.

16. Shaw's short story, "Snow White in Harlem, 1930"—based on his relationship with Willie "the Lion" Smith—was published in the collection, *The Best of Intentions and Other Stories* (1989).

17. My observation here is in agreement with Jeffrey Melnick, who draws attention to Shaw's dramatic transformation from his restless searching to escape the pain of anti-Semitism to his seemingly complete adoption of black cultural values (Melnick 137).

18. Tom Nolan substantiates the impression given by Shaw that Smith showed particular favoritism toward him: "The Lion, married but childless, had many musical cubs, black and white. None did he favor more than young Shaw, whom he called 'Artie my boy' and escorted to several other clubs" (Nolan 35).

19. For further analysis of Smith's account of his relationship to Judaism and Jewish customs, see Melnick 66–67.

20. From when he was a young child, Smith had close personal interactions with Jews. His mother "took in washing" for "several well-to-do Jewish families" in Newark, New Jersey, while Willie helped with "delivering the finished bundles" (Smith 11–12). Although Smith does not refer to Shaw's Jewishness, it is quite likely that he was aware of it.

21. "I could go on and on," Shaw writes, "remembering all the friends I made during those few months among these people who took me in at a time when my own world had rejected me.... [E]very time I have ever run into one of them, there has been that strange and subtle bond between us, that deep feeling of mutual understanding that exists between human beings who remember a long way back to a time when their life-paths crossed" (*Cinderella* 230–31).

But perhaps Shaw was selling himself short in his "passing-in-the-night" account of his Harlem experience—Albert Murray insisted that Shaw was genuinely engaged, both musically and socially, with Harlem, and Burton Peretti is persuasive in his suggestion that Shaw's experience there influenced his later attitude toward interracial hiring as a famed bandleader (Nolan 103; Peretti 207).

22. For a sympathetic portrait of Shaw's military service, see Simosko 99; for a somewhat more critical assessment, see Nolan 170–82.

23. In his 1962 interview with the *New Yorker*, Shaw claims that at Espiritu Santo, "[t]he brass considered our mission silly, and I heard a lot of 'You're not in Hollywood now'" (qtd. in Simosko 100). In *My Life in Jazz*, Max Kaminsky refers to the "resentment against the band on the part of the other Navy men," attributing the bad feelings to the "ambiguous" status of musicians, who "were in the Navy as regular sailors, and not in Special Services, but we hadn't even gone through boot training" (Kaminsky 151). See also Stowe 149–50.

24. As biographer John White suggests, Shaw's account in his 1979 introduction "is less than candid (or accurate) about either his involvement with or the consequences of his appearance before HUAC," adding that "Shaw's appearance and testimony before HUAC was not his finest hour" (White 151–52).

25. While Tom Nolan and John White view Shaw's testimony as self-serving and capitulatory, Vladimir Simosko and Lewis Erenberg offer a decidedly more sympathetic portrait of his testimony and his connection to the Popular Front. See Nolan 275–78; White 148–52; Erenberg 243, 245; Simosko 127.

26. For further analysis of *Really the Blues* and Mezzrow's racial and ethnic self-representations, see Saul 29–60; Damon 150–75; Wald 53–81; Ross 80; Melnick 134–40.

27. Several critics have cited Mezzrow's text as an important precursor to, and perhaps influence upon, Norman Mailer's controversial 1957 essay, "The White Negro." Scott Saul refers to Mezzrow as "the first white Negro in print" and to Wolfe as the "first highbrow critic of the white Negro" (Saul 48); see also Melnick 50; Kenney, *Chicago Jazz* 113–14; Wald 59; Damon 152.

28. The first part of Melnick's chapter concerns the "blackface Jews" of the teens and twenties. As he observes, the common perception that Jews in that period "were not just really good at sounding 'Black,' but really were Black (or quite close)," left Jewish entertainers defensive about their use of blackface, insisting that it "be understood as professional decisions, made under duress, within the context of Jewish vaudeville" while at the same time "disavowing any special racial sympathy for 'Black' expression" (Melnick 98, 111–12). These attitudes, as should be clear, are markedly different from those expressed by the Jewish American jazz musicians under consideration here. For further analysis of this distinction, see Wald 59.

29. Melnick grants considerable significance to Shaw's use (and explanation) of the word "ofay," arguing that "acts of Blackness" such as "idiomatic fluency" are an important element in the search for authenticity as a white Negro (Melnick 137).

30. Melnick's characterization of George Gershwin as a white Negro seems equally questionable, based as it is on Gershwin's brief visit to the South Carolina sea islands, where he went to research his work, *Porgy and Bess* (Melnick 122). But as he did with Shaw, Melnick qualifies his description of Gershwin, conceding that his "'Blackness' was temporary, detachable and merely functional," and, in a later passage, that "Gershwin's execution of white Negroism . . . was obviously provisional. During his career he more consistently cultivated a high-art cosmopolitanism far removed from Blackness" (122, 128).

31. Gayle Wald, for example, notes the "constant tension in Mezzrow's text between performing and 'being,' a veering between merely imitating 'otherness' and actually becoming 'other'" (71). Similarly, Daniel Stein suggests that Mezzrow is drawn to "black culture but retains the possibility of returning to 'whiteness' or Jewishness'—the performance can be turned on and off" ("Performance" 188, fn. 13).

32. Hersch emphasizes Mezzrow's Jewishness as central to his depiction of himself as a "link between the races" ("Every Time" 270).

33. As Saul observes, Mezzrow's "unassisted publications in Art Hodes's *Record Changer* ... have none of the hip daddy-o acrobatics of *Really the Blues*, even though they were also composed in the mid-forties" (Saul 345, fn. 30). For other examples of Mezzrow's more conventional writing style, see his letter from May 1952 to the British musician and broadcaster Humphrey Lyttelton (Lyttelton) and passages attributed to him in Shapiro and Hentoff 128–29, 167–68.

34. The passenger steamship the SS *Eastland* overturned while docked in the Chicago River, resulting in the deaths of more than eight hundred people.

35. Similarly, Charles Hersch sees Jewish jazz musicians (including Mezz Mezzrow) as embracing "an oppositional identity"—one opposed to mainstream conventions and that allowed them to experiment "with Jewish, white, and black identities in creative ways" ("Every Time" 264).

36. On the term *Menschlichkayt*, see Stein, "Performance" 189, fn. 14.

37. A passage that has received considerable attention from critics—both as an illustration of Mezzrow's critique of his family's middle-class pretensions and also of his troubling embrace of a misogynistic black masculinity—concerns his sister, Helen, who agreed to transcribe the blues lyrics of Bessie Smith as a favor for Mezzrow, who was studying Smith's "unique phrasing" (Mezzrow 53). Mezzrow explains that in the process of doing this, his sister, who was a secretary, "kept 'correcting' Bessie's grammar," which so infuriated him that "I've never felt friendly towards her to this day, on account of how she laid her fancy high-school airs on the immortal Bessie Smith" (54). As an act of retribution, Mezzrow stole Helen's "Hudson-seal fur coat," sold it to "the madam" at a whorehouse, and with the sale bought himself an alto saxophone (54). For compelling readings of this passage, see Wald 68–71; Damon 160–61; Saul 46.

38. The following examples illustrate Mezzrow's essentialist tendencies, revealed throughout *Really the Blues*: "In Pontiac I learned something important—that there aren't many people in the world with as much sensitivity and plain human respect for a guy as the Negroes" (15). "I began to collar that all the evil I ever found came from ounce-brain white men who hated the Negroes and me both, while most all the good things in life came to me from the race" (44). "Their wonderful music was only an expression of something that ran much deeper" (145). For analysis of the primitivist and essentialist attitudes in Mezzrow's white Negro stance, see Kenney, *Chicago Jazz* 112–14; Saul 42–43; Wald, passim.

39. For Mezzrow's account of his harrowing four-year-long struggle with opium addiction, see Mezzrow 238–60; Saul 42.

40. See, for example, Sidney Bechet's comments about Mezzrow in *Treat It Gentle*: "Mezzrow, he'd had his rage of being King of Harlem for a while and that was wearing out some.... [W]hen a man is trying so hard to be something he isn't, when he's trying to be some name he makes up for himself instead of just being what he is, some of that will show in his music, the idea of it will be wrong" (168–69).

41. This passage also introduces imagery that seems to suggest the flexibility of Mezzrow's gender representation—a new and somewhat surprising suggestion that I have not found elsewhere in *Really the Blues*.

42. This point is in agreement with William Kenney, who notes that in "Ecstatic in Blackface," Wolfe "systematically dismantled as 'a coy fiction' Mezzrow's entire story of the spontaneous Negro ... despite his own role as Mezzrow's amanuensis" (*Chicago Jazz* 114). While it is possible to argue that Wolfe's views changed over the period of (or perhaps as a result of) his collaboration with Mezzrow, Carolyn Geduld, in her monograph on Wolfe, suggests otherwise, insisting that the "ideas put forth in *Really the Blues* are misleading at best" precisely because they are so blatantly incompatible with Wolfe's "later work" in which "his concern is rather to *destroy* mythic and stereotyped elements which are often imposed upon a people from the

outside, a view that appropriately applies to his early biography of Mezz" (Geduld 35, emphasis in original). (Note Geduld's description here of *Really the Blues* as "biography.")

43. Other jazz autobiographers express a range of views on Mezzrow as musician, autobiographer, and human being. Art Hodes was "engrossed" by *Really the Blues*, including Mezzrow's fondness for *double entendre*, as in his insistence that he "made arrangements for Louis Armstrong"—"arrangements" being a slang expression used by jazz musicians for marijuana (Hodes 68). In a more serious vein, Hodes and Bud Freeman expressed deep respect for Mezzrow's pioneering effort to integrate jazz and for his desire to seek personal relationships with African Americans at a time when mixed relationships were extremely rare and potentially hazardous (Hodes 68–69; Freeman 20, 33–34). See also Wilber 15. For views of Mezzrow's shortcomings as a musician and bandleader, see Freeman 33–34; Condon with Sugrue 120, 186; Kaminsky 76.

44. In a 2015 interview with the *New York Times*, Mezzrow's son, Milton Mesirow, gave the following intriguing response to a question about his "religious affiliation": "My father put me in a shul, and my mother's side tried to make me a Baptist, . . . So when I'm asked what my religion is, I just say 'jazz'" (Kilgannon).

45. Goodman dedicates his autobiography to the memory of his father, David Goodman, who died in 1926 after being hit by a car, just as his son was establishing himself as a promising young clarinetist playing American popular music. His death was a severe blow to Benny, who recognized "that this had happened just as [my brother] Harry and I were beginning to do well, and could have given the folks some of the things they never had out of life" (Goodman 71). Following his father's death, Goodman assumed an even larger responsibility for his family, with his mother and two younger brothers eventually following him to New York to live with him, an arrangement that seems to have continued up to the end of his narrative.

46. Goodman's reticence is noted early in Ross Firestone's biography of the bandleader, with Goodman's admission (from a 1975 interview) of his reluctance to talk about, or even to think about, his impoverished childhood in Chicago (Firestone 17).

47. Lewis Erenberg describes Goodman's father as "a tailor in a sweatshop and a socialist in his politics" (Erenberg 71; 268, fn. 9). The Workmen's Circle, founded in New York in 1900, had close links to the American labor movement and promoted Yiddish cultural and social programs. As Karen Brodkin explains, it was one of a number of benefit organizations that "were crucial for integrating immigrants into the worlds of waged labor, politics, cultural life, and the neighborhood" (Brodkin 120). In her view, the historical experiences of Jewish immigrants from Eastern Europe left them bound to a communal proletarian Jewishness, no matter what their occupational background (107–9).

48. Firestone and James Lincoln Collier emphasize Franz Schoepp's role in teaching the young Benny Goodman to look beyond racial difference and to focus on his development as a musician. See Collier, *Benny Goodman* 16, 17; Firestone 26.

49. For excellent accounts of Hammond's transformation from "a pampered child of the wealthy Anglo-Saxon elite" (Erenberg 122) to his seminal role during the 1930s and 1940s as critic and activist for jazz and other domestic and international causes associated with racial and working-class justice, see Erenberg 120–49; Stowe 50–72.

50. On Goodman's relationship with Henderson, see Magee 189–232; Erenberg 74–75. Goodman's acknowledgment of African American musical influences goes beyond just Henderson; for example, in order for his band to "find its groove" before it began its weekly broadcasts on "Let's Dance," the musicians went up to the Savoy in Harlem, where they played opposite "Chick" Webb's orchestra, thus getting "a wonderful opportunity to compare our playing with his, to try to match some of the guts he got into the music, without trying to copy him in any other way" (Goodman 158).

51. The incident Goodman refers to here involved a racist Southern cop who prevented a waiter from delivering champagne sent by an admiring fan to Lionel Hampton. According to

Goodman, "we were up against it. We didn't want to complain because the fellow might have gotten some of his boy-friends together and really made trouble for us—and at the same time, we couldn't stand for any jive like this" (Goodman 230). Another policeman, this one "a jazz fan," was enlisted to help straighten out the dispute, offering another illustration of Goodman's strategy toward racial conflict of resolve combined with diplomacy.

52. The suggestion that Goodman had been crowned the "king of swing" because he was white was, of course, not uncommon. In *Crazeology*, for example, Bud Freeman insists that although Goodman "was a super player and had a good band, ... [i]t was primarily on the strength of Henderson's charts that Benny got the title 'King of Swing.' That was ridiculous. If anyone deserved the title it was Henderson" (Freeman 45).

53. Denning lists the "Popular Front events" at which Goodman and other swing musicians performed, including "benefits for the Scottsboro Nine; Harlem political rallies; fundraisers for the Spanish Republicans, the anti-fascist exiles, and Russian War Relief; concerts sponsored by the *New Masses*, as well as dances at left-wing conventions and summer camps" (Denning 332–33).

54. Firestone nonetheless grants the mutual benefits that Hammond and Goodman derived from their relationship, suggesting that Hammond was Goodman's "musical conscience" at a point "when he was in serious danger of losing his way" and that Goodman gave Hammond a more direct connection to the "proletariat" than he derived from "all the petitions he signed and checks that he wrote and articles he published in the *Nation*" (Firestone 85).

55. For jazz producer and writer Helen Oakley's instrumental role in persuading Goodman to perform in public with Teddy Wilson, see Firestone 164. See also Giddins, *Visions of Jazz* 154.

56. Yet the same issue of *Down Beat* featured a review by John Hammond touting the positive response Goodman's integrated band had received in Dallas in September 1937 (Stowe 76).

57. The coincident 1939 publication date of *Down Beat*'s symposium on integration in swing bands and *The Kingdom of Swing* would have likely given Goodman no opportunity to comment on the former; the other *Down Beat* articles on Goodman's integration of his band are from 1936 and 1937—well within the time frame covered in his autobiography, which includes events to the end of 1938—and yet Goodman makes no reference to them either.

58. The background for the protest, Erenberg explains, was Goodman's 1937 donation of $1,000 to the Committee to Aid Spanish Democracy and his leading role as organizer and headliner of Stars for Spain, a benefit for the committee. In response to the protests against Goodman, the *Daily Worker* came to his defense, urging its readers to write letters "upholding the King of Swing" (Erenberg 129).

59. In 1942, Roosevelt appointed Goodman "as the popular music chair of Russian War Relief" (Erenberg 184); in 1947, he assumed "an unsalaried position" as "consulting director of Popular Music for Voice of America" (Stowe 238). Goodman and his orchestra represented the United States on State Department–sponsored jazz tours to Asia in 1956–57 and to the Soviet Union in 1962. For an excellent critique of Goodman as a jazz ambassador, see Von Eschen 43–47, 92–94, 100–120.

60. "Ziggy" Elman, born Harry Aaron Finkelman, was steeped in the Jewish dance tradition of the "frayliches"—"lively dance tunes associated with celebratory events" and derived from klezmer music (Erenberg 90). Elman first recorded his melody under the name "Frailach in Swing" in 1938; Goodman's version of the tune, with the addition of Johnny Mercer's lyrics and recorded as "And the Angels Sing," became the number one hit in the United States in 1939.

61. All page references to *Jazz Band* are from the 1981 Da Capo Press edition.

62. Kaminsky's account illustrates Eric Goldstein's observation that Jews brought with them to America their Eastern European experience "of trading among peoples of different backgrounds" and as a result were comfortable with living and working in black neighborhoods. In their relationships with African Americans, Jewish immigrants "often exhibited little consciousness of themselves as white. As merchants whose very location in black districts

arose from their own marginality in non-Jewish society, they presented themselves as Jews and not as 'white men'" (Goldstein 76).

63. For a discussion of restrictions on employment faced by Jews and other immigrants in the early decades of the twentieth century, see Brodkin 60–64.

64. In Kaminsky's description of his experience playing in society bands, he depicts himself and the other Jewish musicians as outsiders passing in a white Protestant, upper-class world. Typically, these descriptions employ humor, as in his story about "the bandleader who, when asked by a dowager if he was Jewish, smoothly answered, 'Not necessarily, madam,' without his baton losing a beat" (Kaminsky 183).

65. Kaminsky and Shaw had first met in the late 1920s, and, for several years, they were good friends, making trips up "to Harlem together to hear the real thing" (Kaminsky 94). Kaminsky gives a detailed account of his tenure in Shaw's band and their subsequent falling-out, which he attributes to Shaw's jealousy about his prominent position in the band (97–105). According to Kaminsky, "Billie Holiday loved" singing in Shaw's band. "It was a happy band for her. This was the first time a colored vocalist had a full-time, regular job in a white band" (101). There are various other assessments—both positive and negative—of Holiday's relationship with Shaw and of her stay in his band, including mixed reviews from Holiday herself. See Holiday 92; Clarke 140–49; O'Meally 126–28; White 58–64.

66. Kaminsky's account of his mother's kindness to Holiday is corroborated by Holiday herself in *Lady Sings the Blues*, in which she describes the long bus trips with Shaw's band as they drove from one engagement to the next, often through states where she was not allowed to use the facilities or eat in restaurants. Suffering from "nervousness and strain," she went to a doctor, who misdiagnosed her as having gonorrhea. Kaminsky's mother "went to bat" for her, Holiday claims, setting her up with "a woman's specialist" in Boston who diagnosed a bladder infection. "After I'd gone through three months of torture, this specialist had me on my feet in three days" (Holiday 86–87).

67. Kaminsky also emphasizes his own role in breaking down racial barriers in jazz; he takes credit, for example, for introducing black trumpeter Hot Lips Page to Artie Shaw, who hired him for his band in the early 1940s, a decision that Kaminsky claims left Page forever indebted to him (Kaminsky 125).

68. On Kaminsky's military service from 1942 to 1943 as a member of Artie Shaw's Navy band, and his subsequent diagnosis of and recovery from posttraumatic stress disorder, see Kaminsky 131–63.

69. For a brief period in 1933, Kaminsky and other struggling musicians lived with Mezzrow in his one-bedroom apartment in the Bronx, along with Mezzrow's first wife and her son. But Kaminsky's inability to tolerate "the gypsy-caravan life" soon found him moving again, to a nicer room on 144th Street that Mezzrow found for him (Kaminsky 62–63).

70. In his discussion of "the Jewish sacralization of 'Black' music," Melnick argues that the ability of Jews "to depict their involvement in African American music as an outgrowth of their own religious traditions . . . served the dual function of purifying both the Jews and the music in question, and thereby easing the pressures caused by the thorny issue of secularization" (Melnick 168).

71. Kaminsky tells the story about American comic actor Arnold Stang, who, when asked on a radio program if he had heard of Kaminsky, replied, "Why I knew him before he changed his name!" According to Kaminsky, he has "been using that remark ever since when people ask me why I haven't changed my name—a question I am constantly asked. 'But I have changed it,' I say, 'You should have heard what it was before!'" (Kaminsky 158).

72. Charles Hersch makes a similar argument when he suggests that the "multifaceted nature of modern Jewish identity gives Jews the opportunity . . . to construct identities" and, in so doing, to "identify with members of other races" ("Every Time" 262).

73. Critics have suggested that Goodman's 1942 marriage to John Hammond's sister, Alice, signaled his desire for acceptance within elite white society. Goodman and Alice Hammond had two daughters and remained married until Alice's death in 1978. See Firestone 308–10; Collier, *Benny Goodman* 297–303.

Chapter 5

1. In 1975, *Raise Up Off Me* was awarded the prestigious ASCAP-Deems Taylor Award for music writing.

2. Coauthor Laurie Pepper, for example, includes the following disclaimer at the beginning of *Straight Life: The Story of Art Pepper*: "This is a true story, a tape recorded narrative by Art (and those who've known him) which I have transcribed and edited. In order to avoid embarrassing a number of people, some details have been changed and pseudonyms are occasionally used. Attitudes, intentions, and feelings attributed by Art Pepper to anyone besides himself should be understood by the reader to be Art's impressions, not fact" (Pepper and Pepper xvii).

3. My discussion here draws from my June 11, 2015, e-mail correspondence with Richard Vacca, author of an excellent study of Boston jazz history, *The Boston Jazz Chronicles: Faces, Places, and Nightlife 1937–1962* (2012). According to Vacca, Rudy Yellin, for example, is Asher's pseudonym for Ruby Newman, one of the Northeast's most popular society bandleaders during the big band era.

4. The first-person narrator of *The Piano Sport* is Jay Greene, a twenty-one-year-old musician who moves to San Francisco with his older sister from a fictional New England town in order to escape a life of drudgery in his family's clothing business. Asher's satirical and sentimental impulses are on full display in his first novel, with an oddball assortment of characters (overprotective Jewish parents, honkytonk strippers, strong and seductive young Beat women) and preoccupations (anti-Semitism, intermarriage, the dedication to a life as an artist) forming its central structuring elements.

5. Asher's tenure at the hungry i is the subject of his slim volume *honeycomb: ballad of a north beach cabaret* (1979). I have no explanation for Asher's decision to compose his tribute under the guise of fiction (substituting pseudonyms for the club itself and for some of the leading characters) while at the same time he offers portraits of many of the renowned performers who came to prominence at the hungry i (using their real-life names) and dedicates the book to the people most closely associated with the club. In fact, *honeycomb* was the inspiration for the *hungry i Reunion*, a nationally televised documentary of the 1980 reunion concert that featured performers from the hungry i's heyday as well as clips and photographs from the early days of the club (Snider 57, 59).

6. On the Committee comedy revue, see Eichelbaum 31; Wasserman, "Since" 162. The Committee was led by Alan Myerson, former member of Chicago's *The Second City*, perhaps the most influential American improvisational theater of its time.

7. A March 1970 piece in *Holiday* magazine includes a photograph of Asher with "a group of heavy-hitting, high profile, local writers: Jessica Mitford, Paul Jacobs, Evan Connell Jr., Don Carpenter, Barnaby Conrad, and Herbert Gold" (Beyl). In 1985, Asher would publish a collection of short stories with Gold in a volume discussed later in the chapter.

8. Hollywood screenwriters Irving Ravetch and Harriet Frank wrote a script for *The Piano Sport*, Bill Gunn for *Don't the Moon Look Lonesome*, and Asher himself for *The Electric Cotillion* (Wasserman, "After Chemistry" 110).

9. *The Eminent Yachtsman and the Whorehouse Piano Player* has a complex narrative structure, including shifting narrative voices (Asher's first-person account is interspersed with a third-person narration) and reproductions of letters between Dan Asher and author S. N. (Sam) Behrman; it also features frequent leaps in time, from the 1950s to the early years of the

twentieth century to the early 1970s. The "Eminent Yachtsman" was the nickname that Sam Behrman gave to Dan Asher (*Eminent Yachtsman* 46); Asher himself is the whorehouse piano player—a reference to the establishments he played in when he was majoring in chemistry at Cornell during the mid-1940s (15).

10. Asher portrays his father as a frustrated artist whose own ambitions as a writer would go unrealized and who felt compelled to take jobs (as a chemist at Worcester Water Works and in his family's textile business) for which he was clearly unsuited (*Eminent Yachtsman* 59–60). In the years before his death, Dan Asher passed his Massachusetts bar exam and took night classes in commerce and finance but showed no inclination to pursue these skills in a professional setting (144–45, 161).

11. In an interview, Asher recalled that he began writing short stories in 1951 and wrote more than a hundred over the next decade before getting his first publication, noting wryly that beyond "observation and a feel for language, a requirement for writing is perseverance" (Wasserman, "After Chemistry" 110).

12. A review of *The Eminent Yachtsman* notes the presence of "brief dramas, which ever so lightly and, perhaps satirically, echo Behrman" ("The Eminent Yachtsman").

13. In his 2001 autobiography, multi-instrumentalist and jazz educator John LaPorta also distinguishes the stylistic tendencies of white and black players in the jam sessions he frequented in Philadelphia during the late 1930s and early 1940s. Yet LaPorta, who enjoyed considerable success in both the jazz and classical music worlds, appears more confident than Asher in situating himself firmly within the black jazz tradition (LaPorta 18–19).

14. As discussed in chapter 2, Bob Wilber had a much more positive impression of New York's interracial traditional jazz scene in the same period described by Asher. Their contrasting perceptions illuminate different attitudes toward interracialism in the bebop and traditional jazz communities. For analyses of the political implications of bebop, see Lott, "Double V" 597–605; DeVeaux, *Birth of Bebop* 318–63.

15. This suggestion was made by Richard Vacca in my private e-mail correspondence with him on June 11, 2015.

16. "The Barrier" was published by Capra Press in their Back-to-Back Series (there are two stories each by Asher and Herbert Gold). The other Asher story included in the collection, "Angel on my Shoulder," also appears to have a significant autobiographical component. The brief author's bio that appears above the blurb refers to Asher's "two careers . . . as a jazz pianist and as a novelist" and the fact that "much of his writing is enriched by his love for music." Although "enriched by" suggests the resemblance between Asher's real life and his fiction, the relationship is never made explicit.

17. This is not to dispute the grim reality of race relations in Boston in that period. As Richard Vacca notes, "[i]nequality was a fact of life" in Boston, "an overwhelmingly white city that marginalized its small black population" (Vacca 287). Furthermore, Boston's jazz industry was also almost entirely controlled by whites. Until 1947, when Joseph Walcott opened Wally's Paradise, there was no black-owned club in the city, and through the 1960s, club ownership and economic power remained largely in the hands of whites (150, 289–90).

18. Among the best-known white bebop musicians were Al Haig, Red Rodney, Stan Levey, George Wallington, Lee Konitz, Gerry Mulligan, and Lennie Tristano. For a discussion of race and interracialism and bebop, see DeVeaux, *Birth of Bebop* 17–20, 168, 255–60.

19. Interracial mixing in Boston in that period, according to Vacca, was not common and "sometimes had consequences; Boston was one of those places where a mere conversation between a man and a woman of different races could provoke a policeman's interference" (Vacca 288).

20. It is instructive to compare this passage with Sancton's account, considered earlier, of his experience in New Orleans's Tremé neighborhood. See chapter 3.

21. Russell (1909–2000), a native of Los Angeles and owner of the independent West Coast Dial Records, supervised memorable sessions with Parker in 1946 and 1947 and later wrote a biography of the saxophonist, *Bird Lives!* (1973), about which Asher wrote a complimentary review. (See Asher, "Jazz Was" 218, 220). For a comprehensive discussion of Russell as jazz critic, novelist, and biographer, see Gennari 300–38. Jon Panish offers a reading of *The Sound* based on his thesis that white and black authors employed contrasting approaches to representing jazz in the postwar period (Panish 60–66, 106–9). Russell's emphasis on Red Travers "as a victimized artist" rather than as a victim of racism, he suggests, is typical of the dominant representation of jazz musicians by white authors, yet he also identifies ambiguity in Russell's portrait, for Red's role as "victimized artist" "is not unconditionally glorified" (60).

22. Gennari notes the "pulp novel trimmings" of the 1962 paperback edition of *The Sound* (my citations are from this edition) and the "affinity between the tabloid-style back cover and the contents of the novel itself" (Gennari 307–8). In his view, *The Sound* "can be read as an updating of the overlapping hard-boiled and film-noir genres, shifting focus from the Depression-era gangster and private dick to the late-1940s jazz milieu that Russell knew well" (304).

23. Asher uses a similar phrase, "within my ken," to describe the jam session at the fictional Boston club, Coffee John's; the implication here is that the Harlem jazz session had been, like Rich's initial response to Travers, "beyond his ken" (*Notes* 98).

24. There are explicit discussions of racial difference—both innate and learned—throughout *The Sound*, as when Bernie asks Hassan El Benna, the black drummer in Red's quintet, to explain to him "what it is you spades have and us grays are looking for?" (Russell 68). Hassan's answer, with its strong echoes of Norman Mailer, suggests that while "the average gray" is "Hung up. Uncool," African Americans ("spades") respond to racism by looking for "kicks out of common everyday stuff—food, and music, and sex, and even religion" (68). Later, an older white musician offers Bernie a sociological spin on the topic, explaining that black players achieve authenticity through living hard lives, but "you and I came from respectable middle-class homes. We went to school every day with clean collars and full stomachs. We never had to sleep on the floor, or listen to drunken Saturday-night brawls in the next room, or starve, or lie and steal just to live" (138).

25. Compare with Asher *Notes* 73; "The Barrier" 48.

26. Compare with Asher *Notes* 109.

27. Giddins's introduction is reprinted in the 2001 Thunder's Mouth Press edition that is my source.

28. Early on Davey lets the reader in on the truth about his name: "I've been accused of inventing my name to bask by some process of assimilation in the great man's [Miles Davis's] circle of light but it's not true; the name is legally, parentally bestowed, dutifully filed with the Registrar of Births in Woonsocket, R.I." (Asher, *Electric* 8).

29. Davey's girlfriend is eighteen-year-old Pope Jarman, newly arrived to San Francisco from Utah. Asher's real-life wife was Poe Asher, fourteen years his junior.

30. See, for example, Davey's almost-identical recollection of his first memory of seeing an African American while on an outing with his family (Asher *Electric* 69).

31. An interracial sexual relationship involving a white man and black woman is the subject of Asher's second novel, *Don't the Moon Look Lonesome* (1967); Asher's clearly satirical intention, in my view, does little to mitigate deeply disturbing—and seemingly unexamined—misogynistic and racist aspects of the plot and characterizations that are difficult to ascribe simply to comedic effect.

32. Davey says to Pope, "I assume you spent the night with the two-hundred-fifty-pound spade guitar symbolic phallus" (Asher, *Electric* 146). Pope corrects him: "He's Afro-American, not spade. A blood, if you will" (147). They fight, and Pope leaves, but Davey's obsession continues: "I began brooding in earnest, mind's eye inflamed, fixed on an unseen yet nonetheless formidable adversary: Big Brown's Big Brown" (151). See Lott, *Love and Theft* 26.

33. Other critics have also made analogies between the techniques of the new comedians of the fifties and sixties and jazz. According to Gerald Nachman, both Orrin Keepnews and Nat Hentoff stressed the jazz elements of Lenny Bruce's performance style and technique (Nachman 405–6). As Hentoff remarked about Bruce's jazz delivery, "You could really feel his beat, and there was a fair amount of bop in it" (406). Bruce addressed this directly, telling his audiences not to applaud because "it breaks my rhythm" (406). As Lawrence Epstein suggests, "[Mort] Sahl had been deeply influenced by jazz, and the music's free association made its way into Sahl's speech rhythms" (Epstein 166).

34. In his *San Francisco Chronicle* review of Bruce's 1958 appearance at the hungry i, Don Stanley wrote that Bruce "has pushed satire beyond the limits agreed upon by most comics and their audiences" (qtd. in Nachman 405).

35. On the origins of Bruce's use of the word "nigger" onstage, see Epstein 171.

36. "Tummler," from the German "tummeln" ("to stir"), was commonly used to describe a comedian or master of ceremonies, particularly one who encouraged audience participation.

37. Mort Sahl "did not . . . speak of his own Jewishness" and "did not consciously draw on his Jewish heritage for his act" (Epstein 169). Bruce, by contrast, was raised "in a marginally Jewish family" but later immersed himself in *Yiddishkeit* and lower-class Jewish culture to such a degree that "you would think he came from a family of rabbis" (Nachman 396). Jackie Mason, as Nachman adds, did come from such a family (396).

38. "The Barrier" ends with this identical passage (67).

39. Earlier, Asher had explained that all dinner-club pianists since *Casablanca* have at some point been addressed as "Sam." In fact, his first job in San Francisco was at the club Casablanca, where he received countless requests for "As Time Goes By" from patrons who would "call me Sam and command me to—I wince in expectation and silently implore them to desist—'play it again'" (*Notes* 205–6). Asher also reprints a complementary review from the *San Francisco Chronicle* on his engagement there, in which the reviewer suggests that Asher "may not be Sam, . . . but this scribe detected a decided Negro rhythmic influence in his lively excursions" (211).

Chapter 6

1. Pepper made this claim in a 1979 interview, in which he recalled his admiration for saxophonist Willie Smith and his surprise to learn "that he was a seventh-grain negro [sic], and I remember wishing that I was. I wanted to be black because I felt such an affinity to the music" (qtd. in Selbert 104). In another interview from that year, Pepper remarked on his success in mastering a "black" musical vernacular: "It's happened so many times that people think I'm black if they've only heard my records. . . . I learned my music in the same place" (qtd. in Selbert 112).

2. For a remarkable oral history of jazz in Los Angeles from the 1920s to the 1950s, see Bryant et al. For memoirs by African American musicians, see Otis, *Listen*; Porter, *There and Back*; Collette; and Tapscott. For histories of West Coast jazz and culture, see Gordon, *Jazz West Coast*; Gioia, *West Coast Jazz*; Isoardi; and Widener.

3. For many years, Arthur Pepper Sr. was active with the Industrial Workers of the World (IWW, commonly known as "Wobblies") and later worked with Harry Bridges to organize the International Longshore and Warehouse Union (ILWU) (Pepper and Pepper 24).

4. Gary Giddins refers to *Straight Life* as "almost fanatically confessional" (Pepper and Pepper v–vi)

5. His father's beatings seemed to have a permanent effect on Pepper's eating habits; according to Laurie, his "interest in food was minimal. He liked no vegetable, and, because his teeth were bad, few meats." His diet consisted mainly of sweets, soups, and other soft foods that he was able to chew (Pepper 236).

6. Later in *Straight Life*, Pepper admits that he was threatened by the confident air and attitude of the blacks he knew in prison, who would, for example, get under his skin with their signifying while they were playing Ping-Pong with him (Pepper and Pepper 154).

7. In the same period, Pepper also hung out at the nearby Ritz Club, which had after-hours sessions where musicians would sit in, including Jimmy Blanton, Art Tatum, Armstrong, Ben Webster, Coleman Hawkins, and Roy Eldridge. Soon, Pepper became a member of the Ritz Club house band (Pepper and Pepper 43).

8. For Lee Young's pioneering role as a Hollywood studio musician and record company executive, see Bryant et al. 51–73. On Benny Carter, see Crouch, "An Elegant Rebel" 57, 59; Giddins, "Benny Carter."

9. Pepper's experience in Kenton's band was a turning point in his career, for the complexity of Kenton's music forced him "to learn something about chord structure and the theory of music" as he simultaneously gained greater facility and confidence on his instrument (Pepper and Pepper 50).

10. In her afterword in *Straight Life*, Laurie Pepper confirms the lasting impression that the Durham incident made on Pepper, serving to jolt him out of his insular and decidedly utopian views on interracialism based on his own experiences on Central Avenue (488).

11. For a concise summary of Pepper's extensive rap sheet, see Selbert 256–60.

12. In *Straight Life*, Pepper suggests that he was sent to San Quentin—a prison, as Ted Gioia notes, "reserved for the most violent younger prisoners, repeat offenders with serious records"—because he would not "cop out on" his drug connections to the authorities (*West Coast Jazz* 306). This, according to Gioia, was evidence of Pepper's "topsy-turvy sense of values," in which he "prided himself more on this fidelity to his dealers than on almost any other moral decision related in his life story" (306).

13. Policy debates over racial integration of California prison populations continue to the present day. See, for example, Farrell; Lindsey 77–103.

14. There are remarkable resemblances between the lives of Pepper and Matthew "Stymie" Beard (1925–81). Beard was born in Los Angeles in the same year as Pepper, enjoyed early success as a child actor, but became addicted to heroin in his late teens and spent many years in federal prisons for various drug convictions. Beard also spent many years at Synanon (his stay there overlapped with Pepper's), and, like Pepper, he experienced a rejuvenated life and career in his post-Synanon period before dying of complications following a stroke at the age of fifty-six. See "Rites Held for 'Stymie' Beard" 60; "Whatever Happened to Matthew (Stymie) Beard?" 134.

15. In 1968, when Pepper was a member of the Buddy Rich orchestra, he underwent emergency surgery for a ruptured spleen and was also diagnosed with cirrhosis; during his convalescence, he developed a large ventral hernia, which, despite surgical intervention, remained with him to the end of his life (Pepper and Pepper 376–82).

16. Synanon was established by Charles E. Dederich Sr. in 1958 in Santa Monica, California, as a drug rehabilitation program and in the 1960s became a residential community for addicts and others seeking an alternative lifestyle. For Synanon's controversial history, see Janzen 2001. Art and Laurie Pepper offer extensive accounts of their Synanon experiences in their autobiographies. See Pepper and Pepper 392–453; Pepper 6–38, 47–56.

17. On "jazz wives," see Rustin and Tucker 12–13; Wilmer 191–204.

18. See Sue Graham Mingus's *Tonight at Noon: A Love Story* (2002); Chan Parker's *My Life in E-Flat* (1993); Maxine Gordon's *Sophisticated Giant: The Life and Legacy of Dexter Gordon*

(2018). See also Leslie Kenton's memoir, *Love Affair* (2010), in which she offers a wrenching account of her incestuous relationship with her father, the bandleader Stan Kenton.

19. Laurie Pepper explains that Les Koenig (the owner of Contemporary Records and one of Pepper's staunchest supporters) made an early attempt to find a publisher for *Straight Life* by pitching the manuscript to "an editor at a skin magazine" (likely *Penthouse*). Assuming that the magazine's focus would be on Art's "sexual career," Laurie encouraged him to talk about it; her later edits of the material appeared in the chapter "Heroin" (Pepper 100).

20. Laurie Pepper's grandfather, Abram Babitz, was an "actor, essayist, [and] editor of the *California Jewish Voice*"; her aunt, Vera Gordon, was a Hollywood actress who starred in the 1929 film *Humoresque*; her uncle, Sol Babitz, was a violinist and musicologist and the godchild of Igor Stravinsky; and her mother, Thelma Babitz, was a dancer who performed with the Martha Graham dance company in the 1930s (Pepper 91).

21. In her autobiography, Laurie Pepper includes a two-page spread of her photographs of pop and rock stars from 1968, among them Leonard Cohen, Joni Mitchell, and Judy Collins (Pepper 10–11).

22. For Laurie Pepper's account of her family history of mental illness and her own ongoing struggles with depression, see Pepper 3, 136–47; Pepper and Pepper 483.

23. "Synanon had rules for everything including sex," Laurie Pepper explains. "A couple wishing to 'get down' had to first get approval from both their tribe-leaders. They had to be of roughly the same Synanon age, and no one 'younger' than three months could play. I had nine months; Art had three." During the courtship period "mild 'petting' was okay, but nothing further" (Pepper 19).

24. Christopher Harlos examines the function of these other voices in *Straight Life*; describing them as "witnesses," he suggests that their presence "in the ostensibly autobiographical narrative" suggests "the underlying desire to 'authenticate' the subject's perceptions and point of view" (Harlos 144–45). And yet, as Laurie Pepper explains, while some of the additional voices indeed echo and thus "authenticate" Pepper's own perspective, others test some of the more "extreme" aspects of his narrative (Pepper and Pepper 481–82). Harlos, it is worth noting, did his analysis without the benefit of Laurie's explanation of her role that appeared in the 1994 edition. For another interpretation of the extra voices in *Straight Life*, see Gioia, *West Coast Jazz* 284–85.

25. For Laurie's references to Art's "genius," see Pepper 63, 80, 172, 173, 300; Art refers to his own genius in *Straight Life* 192. In Laurie's comments on the documentary film *Art Pepper: Notes from a Jazz Survivor*, released shortly before his death, she states that "what it mainly did . . . [was to affirm] Art's importance as an artist and a man. . . . My favorite moment in the movie is when Art sums up his life: '*I'm right. I'm good. I'm a genius.*' He hesitates, looks into the camera, squints at us, and dares to say it outright. '*I'm a genius. I don't know of anyone who plays better than I do*'" (Pepper 300, emphasis in original).

26. In her discussion of her editorial role on *Straight Life*, Laurie comments on the peeping-Tom stories from Art's perspective rather than her own; she notes that, although he avoided reading the manuscript ("He didn't want to see the truths he'd told"), he expressed concern "about how people would react. But he never asked me to change anything" (Pepper 232).

27. In their sit-down interview with the renowned oral historian Studs Terkel (I discuss him in chapter 1), Terkel directed his attention to Art and ignored Laurie completely, despite Art's insistence that "*Laurie did it all. . . . All I did was talk*" (Pepper 241, emphasis in original). And although Laurie received Whitney Balliett's "long, eloquent, and laudatory," review of *Straight Life* as "a gift," it was brought to her attention that he, too, failed to notice her contribution (242). By contrast, she expresses her gratitude to Gary Giddins, whose praise of her work touched her deeply (242). See also Michael Zwerin, who credits Laurie with "shaping what otherwise might have been just one more boring tragedy into something that can be compared to the novels of Jack Kerouac" (qtd. in Selbert 134).

28. Laurie got to know Keiko Jones during Art's appearance in 1977 at the Village Vanguard in New York, when Elvin Jones played drums. As Laurie writes, "When the student is ready the teacher appears" (Pepper 171). On Keiko Jones's support and mentorship, see 171–72. On Laurie's friendship with Jill Goodwin, see Pepper and Pepper 495.

29. In another telling of this story, Laurie explains that Haynes "couldn't believe a white guy was playing with that much soul" (qtd. in Selbert 108).

30. Gerald Wilson, as quoted in Bryant et al. 340.

31. For a similar perspective on Central Avenue before the war, see Gioia, *West Coast Jazz* 287.

32. Drummer William Douglass describes the resentment within the city's black community over lingering forms of discrimination such as housing covenants: "We didn't have to go to the back of the bus and so on, yet you still knew the areas where you weren't treated quite like other people were" (Bryant et al. 249).

33. Porter played at the Down Beat Club and all over Southern California as a member of Howard McGhee's band, which attracted considerable attention with its new "hard bop" sounds. In his blunt assessment, "A lot of white musicians were there too, with mouth, nose, eyes and ears wide open in the process of what I call 'The Grand Theft of Musical Ideas'" (Porter, *There and Back* 55).

34. William "Brother" Woodman Jr. recalls that many clubs on Central Avenue placed "reserved" signs on tables in order to keep away black patrons (Bryant et al. 110). According to pianist Fletcher Smith, "the white man owned all the clubs" on Central Avenue. "The black man didn't own nothing. So there was no success for the black man on Central Avenue" (87). Yet Steven Isoardi counters this point to a degree, suggesting that the intense concentration of Los Angeles' black population "along Central Avenue was also reflected in the Avenue's status as the community's economic and social center." Although there were many "white-owned" businesses, "a significant number of black enterprises flourished" (9).

35. Among Samuel Browne's students at Jefferson High School were Dexter Gordon, Chico Hamilton, Jackie Kelson, Horace Tapscott, Cecil "Big Jay" McNeely, and Ernie Royal (Bryant et al. 25, 141, 182); on Lloyd Reese, see 236–37.

36. For a brief evaluation of the fight over the integration of locals in the American Federation of Musicians, see Isoardi 12–13. See also Monson, *Freedom Sounds* 42–54.

37. Tapscott offers a thoughtful summary of the consequences of amalgamation, arguing that the best-trained and most versatile of the black musicians—particularly studio players or those wanting studio careers—benefitted as a result of it but that many others were left behind. "It wasn't a racial thing," he concludes. "It was run by cliques" (Tapscott 46–47). Trumpeter Clora Bryant echoes his contention that the black local gave musicians a sense of cultural cohesion (Bryant et al. 364). Yet Buddy Collette and William Woodman Jr., prominent leaders in the amalgamation battle, offer passionate defenses of their fight to desegregate the locals on both musical and social grounds (Bryant et al. 112–13, 158–59).

38. On the entrenched racism of the LAPD, see also Otis, *Listen* 236.

39. In his eloquent summary of the crackdown, Tapscott suggests that "[i]ntegration raised its head and racism snapped it off, as usual" (46). See also Bryant et al. 148, 177; Porter, *There and Back* 66.

40. Otis identifies unemployment, police brutality, and discrimination in education and housing as the "poisons" that created the conditions for the uprising (*Listen* 8). In his autobiography, Tapscott explains that the Arkestra—the community-based African American cultural organization in which he played a leading role—had been "very involved in the Watts community" in 1965 and understood that "it was just a matter of time before it exploded" (Tapscott 109). See also Isoardi 65–88; Lipsitz, *Midnight* vii–xxxi, 80–91.

41. For an extensive history of these organizations, see Isoardi, passim. See also Tapscott 80–124, 136–67. Widener 117–52.

42. Tapscott describes the raid on one of the UGMA houses by the FBI and notes that he was personally "targeted"—put under surveillance and followed by the police—"for about a year" (Tapscott 117–18).

43. For a discussion of the presence of white musicians (including Pepper) in UGMA circles, see Isoardi 59, 91, 285.

44. Over the past several decades, there has been a flowering of scholarship on Mingus as musician, writer, and activist. For an analysis of Mingus's articulations on race, masculinity, and jazz culture, see Rustin-Paschal (2017). Mingus biographies include Priestley (1982); Santoro (2000); and Gabbard (2016).

45. There has been excellent and extensive scholarship on these organizations (I have referenced Isoardi [2006] throughout this chapter). On the Association for the Advancement of Creative Musicians (AACM), see Lewis. For a discussion of the "Black Arts imperative" and the related formation of jazz collectives during the 1960s and 1970s, see Porter, *What Is This Thing*, 191–239; see also Saul 302–36.

46. For analysis of "Racial Prejudice in Jazz" (*Down Beat*, March 1962) and "Point of Contact" (*Down Beat Music '66*), see Monson, *Freedom Sounds* 238–82; see also Porter, *What Is This Thing*, 176–80; and Griffin 161–91. Racial issues in jazz were also discussed in "The Playboy Panel: Jazz Today and Tomorrow," reprinted in Walser 235–62.

47. The critics in Selbert's collection also dwell on Pepper's tragic history of drug abuse and incarceration and his distance from the New York jazz scene as important factors contributing to his relative lack of critical acclaim.

48. Bob Blumenthal recalls Pepper's fond memory of the bebop jazz vocalist Babs Gonzales, who took to the stage of a Los Angeles club and began to chant (à la Lenny Bruce), "Art, you white nigger nigger nigger, you motherfucker you! You the only white nigger who can play jazz, you white nigger nigger, you motherfucker you!" (qtd. in Selbert 86).

49. In her autobiography, Laurie admits that Art was intimidated by Stitt's reputation and talents as a player "and/or competitive nature," and that before a recording session with Stitt, "he got a little crazy, got loaded, accidentally cut his hand, but he performed beautifully, . . . and they did two albums together" (Pepper 217).

Conclusion

1. See, for example, saxophonist Matana Roberts's multipart series, *Coin Coin: Gens de Couleur Libres* (2011); *Mississippi Moonchile* (2013); and *River Run Thee* (2015); Wadada Leo Smith's *Ten Freedom Summers* (2012); Terence Blanchard's *Breathless* (2015); Vijay Iyer and Mike Ladd's *In What Language* (2003), *Still Life with Commentator* (2007), and *Holding It Down: The Veterans' Dreams Project* (2012); and Elder Ones' *From Untruth* (2019).

2. In 2018, Terri Lyne Carrington founded the Berklee Institute of Jazz and Gender Justice at Boston's Berklee College of Music; its mission statement identifies its "focus on equity in the jazz field and the role jazz plays in the larger struggle for gender justice" (Donahue; Lorge). That same year, fourteen female and nonbinary musicians founded the We Have Voice Collective, releasing a Code of Conduct and a written statement outlining their vision for gender justice in jazz and experimental music (Russonello).

WORKS CITED

"About Bob Wilber." *Guide to the Bob Wilber Papers, 1943–2006*, https://www.library.unh.edu/find/archives/collections/bob-wilber-papers-1943-2006.
Ake, David. *Jazz Cultures*. U of California P, 2002.
Alexander, Michael. *Jazz Age Jews*. Princeton UP, 2001.
Aptheker, Herbert, editor. *A Documentary History of the Negro People in the United States: From the Colonial Times through the Civil War*. Citadel P, 1960.
Armstrong, Louis. *Satchmo: My Life in New Orleans*. 1954. Da Capo P, 1986.
———. *Swing That Music*. 1936. Da Capo P, 1993.
Asher, Don. "About Hampton and Me." *San Francisco Examiner*, 7 July 1974, pp. 134–35.
———. "After Chemistry I'll Have to Scramble." *San Francisco Examiner*, 31 May 1970, p. 110.
———. "The Barrier." *Angel on My Shoulder*. Capra P, 1985.
———. *Don't the Moon Look Lonesome*. Atheneum, 1967.
———. *The Electric Cotillion*. Doubleday, 1970.
———. *The Eminent Yachtsman and the Whorehouse Piano Player*. Coward, McCann & Geoghegan, 1973.
———. *honeycomb: ballad of a north beach cabaret*. California Living Books, 1979.
———. "Jazz Was Never the Same Again." *San Francisco Examiner*, 1 April 1973, pp. 218, 220.
———. *Notes from a Battered Grand: Fifty Years of Music, from Honky-Tonk to High Society*. Harcourt Brace Jovanovich, 1992.
———. *The Piano Sport*. Atheneum, 1966.
Avakian, Al. "Sidney Bechet, Musical Father to Bob Wilber." *Jazz Record*, no. 56, June 1947, p. 5.
Baker, Chet. *As Though I Had Wings*. St. Martin's P, 1997.
Baker, Dorothy. *Young Man with a Horn*. Houghton Mifflin, 1938.
Balliett, Whitney. "Straight Life." *New Yorker* 55. 7 Jan. 1980, p. 84.
———. "The Westchester Kids." *American Musicians: Fifty-Six Portraits in Jazz*. Oxford UP, 1986, pp. 301–10.
Barnet, Charlie, with Stanley Dance. *Those Swinging Years: The Autobiography of Charlie Barnet*. Louisiana State UP, 1984.
Bechet, Sidney. *Treat It Gentle*. 1960. Da Capo P, 2002.
Beckwith, Mary. "The Spotlight on Bob Wilber." *American Jazz Review* 3, no. 2 December 1946, p. 3.
Behrman, S. N. *The Cold Wind and the Warm*. New York: Random House, 1959.
———. *The Worcester Account*. Tatnuck Bookseller P, 1996.
Berish, Andrew S. *Lonesome Roads and Streets of Dreams: Place, Mobility, and Race in Jazz of the 1930s and '40s*. U of Chicago P, 2012.
Berliner, Paul. *Thinking in Jazz. The Infinite Art of Improvisation*. U of Chicago P, 1994.

Berry, Jason. "White Men Can Jam." *New York Times Book Review*, 11 July 1999, p. 122.
Bethell, Tom. *George Lewis: A Jazzman from New Orleans*. U of California P, 1977.
Beyl, Earnest. "The Glory Days of Saloon Players in North Beach." *MarinaTimes*, August 2014, www.marinatimes.com/2014/07/the-glory-days-of-saloon-piano-players-in-north-beach/.
Bjorn, Lars, with Jim Gallert. *Before Motown: A History of Jazz in Detroit, 1920–60*. U of Michigan P, 2001.
Blanchard, Terence. *Breathless*. Blue Note, 2015. CD.
Bliggen, Dora. "Blackberries." *Classic Sounds of New Orleans*, Smithsonian Folkways, 2010. CD.
Blumenfeld, Larry, moderator. "Jazz in the Age of Trump: A Roundtable Discussion about Life and Art in America Today." JAZZIZ, www.jazziz.com/free/jazz-in-the-age-of-trump/.
Blumenthal, Bob. "Baring a White Man's Burdens: Art Pepper Perseveres." *The Art Pepper Companion*, pp. 85–94.
Boulard, Garry. "Blacks, Italians, and the Making of New Orleans Jazz." *The Journal of Ethnic Studies* 16, no. 1, Spring 1988, pp. 53–66.
Boyd, Jean A. *The Jazz of the Southwest: An Oral History of Western Swing*. U of Texas P, 1998.
Brodkin, Karen. *How Jews Became White Folks and What That Says about Race in America*. Rutgers UP, 1998.
Bryant, Clora, et al., editors. *Central Avenue Sounds: Jazz in Los Angeles*. U of California P, 1998.
Burke, Patrick. *Come in and Hear the Truth: Jazz and Race on 52nd Street*. U of Chicago P, 2008.
Capehart, Jonathan. "Jazz Artist Wynton Marsalis Says Rap and Hip-Hop Are 'More Damaging Than a Statue of Robert E. Lee.'" *Washington Post*, 22 May 2018. www.washingtonpost.com/podcasts/cape-up/jazz-artist-wynton-marsalis-says-rap-and-hiphop-are-more-damaging-than-a-statue-of-robert-e-lee/.
Carner, Gary. "The Agony and the Agony: James Lincoln Collier's Jazz Writing." *Annual Review of Jazz Studies* 5, 1991, pp. 81–89.
Carter, William. *Preservation Hall: Music from the Heart*. W. W. Norton, 1991.
Cheatham, Jeannie. *Meet Me with Your Black Drawers On: My Life in Music*. U of Texas P, 2006.
Chilton, John. *Sidney Bechet: The Wizard of Jazz*. Macmillan, 1987.
Clarke, Donald. Billie Holiday: *Wishing on the Moon*. Da Capo P, 2002.
Cohen, Thomas A. *hungry i Reunion*. Kultur International Films, 1980. DVD.
Collette, Buddy, with Steven Isoardi. *Jazz Generations: A Life in American Music and Society*. Continuum, 2000.
Collier, James Lincoln. *Benny Goodman and the Swing Era*. Oxford UP, 1989.
———. *Jazz: The American Theme Song*. Oxford UP, 1993.
———. "Jazz Mythology." *New York Times*, 6 Feb. 1994, 90.
———. *Louis Armstrong: An American Genius*. Oxford UP, 1983.
Condon, Eddie. "This Is Jazz." *Eddie Condon's Treasury of Jazz*, pp. 21–32.
Condon, Eddie, and Hank O'Neal. *The Eddie Condon Scrapbook of Jazz*. Galahad Books, 1973.
Condon, Eddie, and Richard Gehman, editors. *Eddie Condon's Treasury of Jazz*. 1956. Greenwood P, 1975.
Condon, Eddie, with Thomas Sugrue. *We Called It Music: A Generation of Jazz*. 1956. Da Capo P, 1992.
Crouch, Stanley. "An Elegant Rebel for His Cause." *New York Daily News*, 17 July 2003, www.nydailynews.com/archives/opinions/elegant-rebel-article-1.519004/.
———. "The Rotten Club." *Village Voice*, 5 Feb. 1985. pp. 57, 59.
Damon, Maria. "Jazz-Jews, Jive, and Gender: The Ethnic Politics of Jazz Argot." *Jews and Other Differences: The New Jewish Cultural Studies*. Jonathan Boyarin and Daniel Boyarin, editors. U of Minnesota P, 1997.
Dance, Stanley. *The World of Count Basie*. C. Scribner's Sons, 1980.
———. *The World of Duke Ellington*. Macmillan, 1970.

———. *The World of Earl Hines*. Scribner, 1977.
———. *The World of Swing*. 1974. Da Capo P, 1979.
Davis, Kimberly Chabot. *Beyond the White Negro: Empathy and Anti-Racist Reading*. U of Illinois P, 2014.
DeBerry, Jarvis. "Wynton Marsalis Is Wrong: Hip Hop Has Value." *Times* (Shreveport, Louisiana), 27 May 2018, p. B4.
Demlinger, Sandor, and John Steiner. *Destination: Chicago Jazz*. Arcadia, 2003.
Denning, Michael. *The Cultural Front: The Laboring of American Culture in the Twentieth Century*. Verso, 1997.
DeVeaux, Scott. 1991. *The Birth of Bebop: A Social and Musical History*. U of California P, 1997.
———. "Constructing the Jazz Tradition: Jazz Historiography." *Black American Literature Forum* 25, no. 3, Autumn, 1991, pp. 525–60.
Donahue, Tori. "Berklee Announces Institute of Jazz and Gender Justice." *Berklee Now*, 3 Oct. 2018, www.berklee.edu/news/berklee-now/berklee-announces-institute-jazz-and-gender-justice/.
Driggs, Frank, and Chuck Haddix. *Kansas City Jazz: From Ragtime to Bebop–A History*. Oxford UP, 2005.
Early, Gerald. "White Noise and White Knights: Some Thoughts on Race, Jazz, and the White Jazz Musician." *Jazz: A History of America's Music*. Geoffrey C. Ward and Ken Burns. Alfred A Knopf, 2000, pp. 324–31.
Eichelbaum, Stanley. "Meet the Committee." *The San Francisco Examiner*, 14 March 1963, p. 31.
Elder Ones. *From Untruth*. Northern Spy Records, 2019. CD.
"The Eminent Yachtsman and the Whorehouse Piano Player." *Kirkus Reviews*, 15 June 1973, www.kirkusreviews.com/book-reviews/don-asher-4/the-eminent-yachtsman-and-the-whorehouse-piano-/.
Epstein, Lawrence. *The Haunted Smile: The Story of Jewish Comedians in America*. Public Affairs, 2001.
Erenberg, Lewis A. *Swingin' the Dream: Big Band Jazz and the Rebirth of American Culture*. U of Chicago P, 1998.
Erwin, Pee Wee, as told to Warren W. Vaché Sr. *This Horn for Hire*. Scarecrow and the Institute of Jazz Studies, 1987.
Evans, Nicholas M. *Writing Jazz: Race, Nationalism, and Modern Culture in the 1920s*. Garland, 2000.
Fairburn, Ann [Dorothy Tait]. *Call Him George: A Biography of George Lewis the Man, His Faith and His Music*. Crown, 1969.
Fairclough, Adam. *Race and Democracy: The Civil Rights Struggle in Louisiana, 1915–1972*. U of Georgia P, 1995.
Farrell, Michael B. "Riot Shows Difficulty of Desegregating California Prisons." *Christian Science Monitor*, 14 Aug. 2009, http://www.csmonitor.com/USA/Justice/2009/0814/p02s04-usju.html/.
Farrington, Holly E. "Narrating the Jazz Life: Three Approaches to Jazz Autobiography." *Popular Music and Society* 29, no. 3, July 2006, pp. 375–86.
Fasick, Kevin, and Laura Italiano. "Obama called the N-word in headline." *New York Post*, 6 July 2014, nypost.com/2014/07/06/obama-called-the-n-word-in-west-village-newspapers-headline/.
Firestone, Ross. *Swing, Swing, Swing: The Life & Times of Benny Goodman*. W. W. Norton, 1993.
Fletcher, Allen. "Don Asher." *Worcester Magazine*, www.worcestermag.com/2007/12/27/don-asher/.
Frankenberg, Ruth. *White Women, Race Matters: The Social Construction of Whiteness*. U of Minnesota P, 1993.
Freeman, Bud, as told to Robert Wolf. *Crazeology: The Autobiography of a Chicago Jazzman*. U of Illinois P, 1989.

Gabbard, Krin. *Better Git It in Your Soul: An Interpretive Biography of Charles Mingus*. U of California P, 2016.

———. *Black Magic: White Hollywood and African American Culture*. Rutgers UP, 2004.

———. *Jammin' at the Margins: Jazz and the American Cinema*. U of Chicago P, 1996.

———. "The Jazz Canon and Its Consequences." *Jazz among the Discourses*, Krin Gabbard editor. Duke UP, 1995.

Geduld, Carolyn. *Bernard Wolfe*. Twayne, 1972.

Gennari, John. *Blowin' Hot and Cool: Jazz and Its Critics*. U of Chicago P, 2006.

Gerber, Michael. *Jazz Jews*. Five Leaves, 2009.

Giddins, Gary. "Art Pepper Talks Straight." *The Village Voice*, 18 Feb. 1980.

———. "Benny Carter, 1907–2003. 'A Gentleman You Didn't Mess With.'" *The Village Voice*, 19 Aug. 2003, www.villagevoice.com/2003/08/19/benny-carter-1907-2003/.

———. *Satchmo*. Doubleday, 1988.

———. *Visions of Jazz: The First Century*. Oxford UP, 1998.

———. "The Whiteness of the Wail," *The Art Pepper Companion*, pp. 79–84.

Gioia, Ted. "Gigs from Hell." Review of *Notes from a Battered Grand*, by Don Asher. *San Francisco Examiner*, 24 May 1992, p. 151.

———. *West Coast Jazz: Modern Jazz in California, 1945–1960*. Oxford UP, 1992.

Goldstein, Eric L. *The Price of Whiteness: Jews, Race, and American Identity*. Princeton UP, 2006.

Goodman, Benny, and Irving Kolodin. *The Kingdom of Swing*. 1939. Frederick Ungar, 1961.

Goodrich, Andrew. "Lost Chords: White Musicians and Their Contributions to Jazz, 1915–1945 by Richard Sudhalter." *Journal of Historical Research in Music Education* 23, no. 2, April 2002, pp. 162–66. JSTOR. Web. 3 Jan. 2014.

Gordon, Maxine. *The Life and Legacy of Dexter Gordon*. U of California P, 2018.

Gordon, Robert. *Jazz West Coast: The Los Angeles Jazz Scene of the 1950s*. Quartet Books, 1986.

Graham, Renée. "Harping on Hip-Hop? Respectability Politics Strikes Again." The Boston Globe, 27 May 2018, p. K1.

Gridley, Mark C. "Where the Dark and Light Folks Meet: Race and the Mythology, Politics and Business of Jazz." *Current Musicology* 92, 2011, pp. 125–36, 163. *ProQuest*, http://ezproxy.library.yorku.ca/login?url=https://search-proquest-com.ezproxy.library.yorku.ca/docview/1289028862?accountid=15182.

Griffin, Farah Jasmine. *If You Can't Be Free, Be a Mystery: In Search of Billie Holiday*. Free Press, 2001.

Gross, Terry. *Fresh Air*. "Interview with Artie Shaw." National Public Radio, 1985, www.npr.org/templates/story/story.php?storyId=126972706/.

Hair, William Ivy. *Carnival of Fury: Robert Charles and the New Orleans Race Riot of 1900*. 1976. Louisiana State UP, 2008.

Hansen, Chadwick. *Witchcraft at Salem*. G. Braziller, 1969.

Harlos, Christopher. "Jazz Autobiography: Theory, Practice, Politics," *Representing Jazz*. Krin Gabbard, editor. Duke UP, 1995, pp. 131–66.

Hart, Peggy. "NYJC Concert Is Best Yet." *American Jazz Review* 3, no. 2, 1946, p. 1.

Hawes, Hampton, and Don Asher. 1979. *Raise Up Off Me: A Portrait of Hampton Hawes*. Da Capo P, 2001.

Heble, Ajay. "Performing Identity: Jazz Autobiography and the Politics of Literary Improvisation." *Landing on the Wrong Note: Jazz, Dissonance and Critical Practice*. Routledge, 2000.

Helland, Dave. "Bob Wilber." *DownBeat* 56, no. 7, July 1989, pp. 50–51.

Hentoff, Nat. "Jews in the Family of Jazz." *JazzTimes*, 1 May 2010. jazztimes.com/columns/final-chorus/jews-in-the-family-of-jazz/.

Hersch, Charles. "'Every Time I Try to Play Black, It Comes Out Sounding Jewish': Jewish Jazz Musicians and Racial Identity." *American Jewish History* 97, no. 3, July 2013, pp. 259–82.

———. *Subversive Sounds: Race and the Birth of Jazz in New Orleans.* U of Chicago P, 2009.
Hill, Mike, editor. *Whiteness: A Critical Reader.* New York UP, 1997.
Hobbs, Holly. "Israel Gorman." *KnowLA Encylopedia of Louisiana.* David Johnson, editor. Louisiana Endowment for the Humanities, 8 Nov. 2013. Web. 22 Apr. 2016.
Hobson, Wilder. *American Jazz Music.* 1939. Da Capo P, 1976.
Hodes, Art, and Chadwick Hansen. *Hot Man.* U of Illinois P, 1992.
Hodes, Art, and Chadwick Hansen, editors. *Selections from the Gutter: Portraits from "The Jazz Record."* U of California P, 1977.
Holiday, Billie, with William Dufty. *Lady Sings the Blues.* 1956. Random House, 2006.
Holley, Eugene, Jr. "My Bill Evans Problem: Jaded Visions of Jazz and Race." *New Music USA*, 26 June 26 2013, nmbx.newmusicusa.org/my-bill-evans-problem-jazz-and-race/.
Horne, Lena, and Richard Schickel. *Lena.* Doubleday, 1965.
Isoardi, Steven L. *The Dark Tree: Jazz and the Community Arts in Los Angeles.* U of California P, 2006.
Iverson, Ethan. (Blog) "Do the Math," 2016, https://ethaniverson.com/the-j-word/.
Iyer, Vijay, and Mike Ladd. *Holding It Down: The Veterans' Dreams Project.* Pi Recordings, 2013. CD.
———. *In What Language.* Pi Recordings, 2003. CD.
———. *Still Life with Commentator.* Savoy Jazz, 2007. CD.
Jackson, Lawrence. "Bucklin Moon and Thomas Sancton in the 1940s: Crusaders for the Racial Left." *The Southern Literary Journal* 40, no. 1 (Fall, 2007), pp. 76–97.
Jacobson, Matthew Frye. *Whiteness of a Different Color: European Immigrants and the Alchemy of Race.* Harvard UP, 1998.
Janzen, Rod. *The Rise and Fall of Synanon: A California Utopia.* Johns Hopkins UP, 2001.
Jensen, Robert. *The Heart of Whiteness: Confronting Race, Racism, and White Privilege.* City Lights, 2005.
Johnson, Aaron J. "Where the Dark and Light Folks Meet: Race and the Mythology, Politics, and Business of Jazz." *Current Musicology* 92 (2011), pp. 137–51, 164. ProQuest. Web. 17 Jan. 2014.
Jones, LeRoi [Amiri Baraka]. *Blues People: Negro Music in White America.* William Morrow, 1963.
Jordan, Steve, with Tom Scanlan. *Rhythm Man: Fifty Years in Jazz.* U of Michigan P, 1991.
Kaminsky, Max, and V. E. Hughes. *Jazz Band: My Life in Jazz.* 1963. Da Capo P, 1981.
Kelley, Robin D. G. "The Jazz Wife: Muse and Manager." New York Times, 21 July 2002, AR24. Expanded Academic ASAP. Web. 18 Oct. 2016.
Kenney, William H., III. *Chicago Jazz: A Cultural History, 1904–1930.* Oxford UP, 1993.
———. "Eddie Condon in Illinois: The Roots of a 'Jazz Personality.'" *Illinois Historical Journal* 77, no. 4 (Winter, 1984), pp. 255–68. JSTOR. Web. 2 Feb. 2014.
———. "Negotiating the Color Line: Louis Armstrong's Autobiographies." *Jazz in Mind.* Reginald T. Buckner and Steven Weiland, editors. Wayne State UP, 1991, pp. 38–59.
Kenton, Leslie. *Love Affair.* St. Martin's P, 2010.
"Kids Crowd Oldtimers with Their Jazz Style," *Down Beat* 13, no. 25, 2 Dec. 1946, p. 2.
Kilgannon, Corey. "Son of Mezz Mezzrow Finds His Father's Legacy Lives in a Jazz Club in the Village." *New York Times*, 10 July 2015. http://nyti.ms/1JVpOq6/.
Knauer, Wolfram, editor. *Gender and Identity in Jazz.* Jazzinstitut Darmstadt, 2016.
Kolodin, Irving. *The Metropolitan Opera, 1883–1966: A Candid History.* 1936. A. A. Knopf, 1966.
———. "Number One Swing Man." *Harper's Magazine*, 1 June 1939, pp. 431–40.
LaPorta, John. *Playing It by Ear: (An Autobiography with Concentration on the Woody Herman Orchestra and the New York Jazz Scene in the '40s and '50s).* Cadence Jazz Books, 2001.
Lees, Gene. *Cats of Any Color: Jazz Black and White.* Oxford UP, 1995.
"Letters." *Village Voice*, 26 Feb. 1985, pp. 3, 39.
Lewis, George E. *A Power Stronger than Itself: The AACM and American Experimental Music.* U of Chicago P, 2008.

Lewis, Oscar. *The Children of Sanchez: Autobiography of a Mexican Family*. Random House, 1961.
Lindsey, Tonya D. "'It'll Never Happen': Racial Integration in California Men's Prisons." *Justice Research and Policy* 11, 2009, pp. 77–103. journals.sagepub.com/doi/pdf/10.3818/JRP.11.2009.77.
Lipsitz, George. *Midnight at the Barrelhouse: The Johnny Otis Story*. U of Minnesota P, 2010.
———. *The Possessive Investment in Whiteness: How White People Profit from Identity Politics*. Temple UP, 2006.
Lopes, Paul Douglas. *The Rise of a Jazz Art World*. Cambridge UP, 2002.
Lorge, Suzanne. "Terri Lyne Carrington Transforms the Culture." *DownBeat* 86, no. 2, 25 Jan. 2019, //downbeat.com/news/detail/terri-lyne-carrington-looks-to-transform-the-culture/.
Lott, Eric. "Double V, Double Time: Bebop's Politics of Style." *Callaloo* 2, no. 3, 1988, pp. 597–605.
———. *Love and Theft: Blackface Minstrelsy and the American Working Class*. 1993. Oxford UP, 2013.
Lyttelton, Humphrey. "Mezz Mezzrow letter to Humphrey Lyttelton," 9 May 1952, http://www.humphreylyttelton.com/part-time-jazz/mezz-mezzrow-letter/.
Magee, Jeffrey. *The Uncrowned King of Swing: Fletcher Henderson and Big Band Jazz*. Oxford UP, 2005.
Mailer, Norman. "The White Negro: Superficial Reflections on the Hipster," *Dissent* 4, no. 3, Fall 1957, pp. 276–93.
Manone, Wingy, and Paul Vandervoort II. *Trumpet on the Wing*. 1948. Doubleday, 1964.
Marsalis, Wynton. Letter to the editor. *New York Times Book Review*, 19 Dec. 1993, p. 31.
———. *Moving to Higher Ground: How Jazz Can Change Your Life*. Random House, 2009.
Marsalis, Wynton, et al. "Jazz People." *Transition*, no. 65, 1995, pp. 140–78. JSTOR, www.jstor.org/stable/2935324.
Martin, T. E. "Art Pepper: Towards a New White Jazz," in *The Art Pepper Companion*, pp. 23–45.
Martyn, Barry. *Walking with Legends: Barry Martyn's New Orleans Jazz Odyssey*. Mick Burns, editor. Louisiana State UP, 2007.
McGlynn, Don. *Art Pepper: Notes from a Jazz Survivor*. Documentary film. 1982. DVD.
McMullen, Tracy. "Identity for Sale: Glenn Miller, Wynton Marsalis, and Cultural Replay in Music." *Big Ears: Listening for Gender in Jazz Studies*, pp. 129–54.
McNulty, John. *Third Avenue*, Little, Brown, 1946.
McPartland, Marian. *Marian McPartland's Jazz World: All in Good Time*. U of Illinois P, 2003.
Melnick, Jeffrey. *A Right to Sing the Blues: African Americans, Jews, and American Popular Song*. Harvard UP, 1999.
Mergner, Lee. "Randy Sandke: Let the Facts Speak." *JazzTimes*, 5 Aug. 2010, jazztimes.com/departments/author/randy-sandke-let-the-facts-speak/.
Meyer, Edward N. *Giant Strides: The Legacy of Dick Wellstood*. Scarecrow P, 1999.
———. *The Life and Music of Kenny Davern: Just Four Bars*. Scarecrow P, 2010.
Mezzrow, Mezz [Milton], and Bernard Wolfe. *Really the Blues*. 1946. Souvenir P, 2009.
Mingus, Charles. *Beneath the Underdog: His World as Composed by Mingus*. Knopf, 1971.
Mingus, Sue Graham. *Tonight at Noon: A Love Story*. Pantheon Books, 2002.
Monson, Ingrid. *Freedom Sounds: Civil Rights Call Out to Jazz and Africa*. Oxford UP, 2007.
———. "The Problem with White Hipness: Race, Gender, and Cultural Conceptions in Jazz Historical Discourse." *Journal of the American Musicological Society* 48, no. 3, Autumn 1995, pp. 396–422.
———. *Saying Something: Jazz Improvisation and Interaction*. U of Chicago P, 1996.
Morgenstern, Dan. "Louis Armstrong: An American Genius." *Reading Jazz: A Gathering of Autobiography, Reportage, and Criticism from 1919 to Now*. Robert Gottlieb, editor. Pantheon Books, 1996, pp. 1034–41.
Nachman, Gerald. *Seriously Funny: The Rebel Comedians of the 1950s and 1960s*. Pantheon Books, 2003.

Nelson, Jim. "Lost Chords: White Musicians and Their Contribution to Jazz, 1915–1945." *All About Jazz*, 4 Mar. 2004, www.allaboutjazz.com/lost-chords—white-musicians-and-their-contribution-to-jazz-1915-1945-by-jim-nelson.php/.
Nolan, Tom. *Three Chords for Beauty's Sake: The Life of Artie Shaw*. W.W. Norton, 2010.
Obrecht, Jas. *Early Blues: The First Stars of Blues Guitar*. U of Minnesota P, 2015.
O'Day, Anita, with George Eells. *High Times Hard Times*. Limelight Editions, 1989.
Ogren, Kathy J. "'Jazz Isn't Just Me': Jazz Autobiographies as Performance Personas." *Jazz in Mind*, Reginald T. Buckner and Steven Weiland, editors. Wayne State UP, 1991, pp. 112–27.
———. *The Jazz Revolution: Twenties America and the Meaning of Jazz*. Oxford UP, 1989.
O'Meally, Robert. *Lady Day: The Many Faces of Billie Holiday*. Da Capo P, 1991.
Otis, Johnny. *Listen to the Lambs*. 1968. U of Minnesota P, 2009.
———. *Upside Your Head: Rhythm and Blues on Central Avenue*. Wesleyan UP, 1993.
Page, Drew. *Drew's Blues: A Sideman's Life with the Big Bands*. Louisiana State UP, 1980.
Panassié, Hugues. *Hot Jazz: The Guide to Swing Music*, 1936. Negro Universities P, 1970.
———. *The Real Jazz*. 1942. Greenwood P, 1973.
Panish, Jon. *The Color of Jazz: Race and Representation in Postwar American Culture*. UP of Mississippi, 1997.
Parker, Chan. *My Life in E-Flat*. U of South Carolina P, 1993.
Pellegrinelli, Lara. "Dig Boy Dig: Jazz at Lincoln Center Breaks New Ground, but Where Are the Women?" *Village Voice*, 7 Nov. 2000, pp. 8–14.
Pepper, Art, and Laurie Pepper. *Straight Life: The Story of Art Pepper*. 1979. Da Capo P, 1994.
Pepper, Laurie. *Art: Why I Stuck with a Junkie Jazzman*. Arthur Pepper Music, 2014.
Peretti, Burton W. *The Creation of Jazz: Music, Race, and Culture in Urban America*. U of Illinois P, 1994.
Pinsker, Sanford. "*Shpritzing* the *Goyim*/Shocking the Jews." *Jewish Wry: Essays on Jewish Humor*. Sarah Blacher Cohen, editor. Indiana UP, 1987, pp. 89–104.
"The Playboy Panel: Jazz—Today and Tomorrow." *Keeping Time: Readings in Jazz History*, Robert Walser, editor. Oxford UP, 1999, pp. 235–62.
Porter, Eric. *What Is This Thing Called Jazz?: African American Musicians as Artists, Critics, and Activists*. U of California P, 2002.
Porter, Lewis. *Lester Young*. Twayne, 1985.
Porter, Roy, with David Keller. *There and Back: The Roy Porter Story*. Louisiana State UP, 1991.
Priestley, Brian. *Mingus: A Critical Biography*. Quartet Books, 1982.
Prouty, Kenneth E., "Toward Jazz's 'Official' History: The Debates and Discourses of Jazz History Textbooks." *Journal of Music History Pedagogy* 1, no. 1, 2010, pp. 19–43.
Raeburn, Bruce Boyd. "'I'll Be Glad When You're Dead': Louis Armstrong's Smack Down with White Authority and His First Films, 1930–1932." *The Southern Quarterly* 51, nos. 1/2, Fall 2013/Winter 2014, pp. 58–72.
———. *New Orleans Style and the Writing of American Jazz History*. U of Michigan P, 2009.
———. "Stars of David and Sons of Sicily: Constellations beyond the Canon in Early New Orleans Jazz." *Jazz Perspectives* 3, no. 2, 2009, pp. 123–52.
———. "The Storyville Exodus Revisited, or Why Louis Armstrong Didn't Leave in November 1917, Like the Movie Said He Did." *The Southern Quarterly* 52, no. 2, Winter 2015, pp. 10–33.
Ramsey, Frederic, Jr., and Charles Edward Smith, editors. *Jazzmen*. 1939. Harcourt Brace Jovanovich, 1967.
Rappoport, Leon. *Punchlines: The Case for Racial, Ethnic, and Gender Humor*. Praeger, 2005.
Ratliff, Ben. "A Tribute to Bechet, with Tunes, of Course." *New York Times*, 22 Nov. 1997, www.nytimes.com/1997/11/22/arts/music-review-a-tribute-to-bechet-with-tunes-of-course.html/.
"Rites Held for 'Stymie' Beard of 'Our Gang.'" *Jet*, 29 Jan. 1981, p. 60.
Roberts, Matana. *Coin Coin Chapter One: Gens de Couleur Libres*. Constellation, 2011. CD.

———. *Coin Coin Chapter Three: River Run Thee*. Constellation, 2015. CD.

———. *Coin Coin Chapter Two: Mississippi Moonchile*. Constellation, 2013. CD.

Roediger, David R. *Working toward Whiteness: How America's Immigrants Became White: The Strange Journey from Ellis Island to the Suburbs*. Basic Books, 2005.

Rogin, Michael Paul. *Blackface, White Noise: Jewish Immigrants in the Hollywood Melting Pot*. U of California P, 1996.

Rollini, Arthur. *Thirty Years with the Big Bands*. Macmillan, 1987.

Ross, Andrew. *No Respect: Intellectuals and Popular Culture*. Routledge, 1989.

Rothenberg, Paula S., editor. *White Privilege: Essential Readings on the Other Side of Racism*. Worth, 2016.

Rowe, Monk. Fillius Jazz Archive (Bob Wilber Interview). 22 May 1998, contentdm6.hamilton.edu/cdm/ref/collection/jazz/id/1373.

Russell, Ross. *Bird Lives!* Charterhouse, 1973.

———. *The Sound*. MacFadden Books, 1962.

Russonello, Giovanni. "Women Fighting Sexism in Jazz Have a Voice. And Now, a Code of Conduct." New York Times, 30 April 2018, www.nytimes.com/2018/04/30/arts/music/we-have-voice-jazz-women-metoo.html/.

Rustin, Nichole T., and Sherrie Tucker, editors. *Big Ears: Listening for Gender in Jazz Studies*. Duke UP, 2008.

Rustin-Paschal, Nichole. *The Kind of Man I Am: Jazzmasculinity and the World of Charles Mingus Jr*. Wesleyan UP, 2017.

Sager, David. (Review) "*Lost Chords: White Musicians and Their Contributions to Jazz, 1915–1945*." Current Musicology 71–73, 2002, pp. 509–17. ProQuest. Web. 3 Jan. 2014.

Sancton, Thomas A. *The Armageddon Project*. Other, 2007.

———. *The Bettencourt Affair: The World's Richest Woman and the Scandal that Rocked Paris*. Dutton, 2017.

———. *Song for My Fathers: A New Orleans Story in Black and White*. Other, 2010.

Sancton, Thomas A., and Lars Edegran. *City of a Million Dreams: New Orleans Legacy Band*. G.H.B. Records, 2011. CD.

———. *Hymns and Spirituals: Tommy Sancton New Orleans Quartet*. New Orleans Legacy Records, 2012. CD.

Sancton, Thomas A., and Scott MacLeod. *Death of a Princess: The Investigation*. St. Martin's P, 1998.

Sancton, Thomas, Jr. "Portrait of a Jazzman." Down Beat, February 9, 1967.

Sancton, Thomas, Sr. *By Starlight*. Doubleday, 1960.

———. *Count Roller Skates*. Doubleday, 1956.

"Sancton Focuses the Negro Press." 2 May 1943, ProQuest Historical Newspapers: *Atlanta Daily World*, p. 6.

Sandke, Randall. *Where the Dark and the Light Folks Meet: Race and the Mythology, Politics, and Business of Jazz*. Scarecrow P, 2010.

Santoro, Gene. *Myself When I Am Real: The Life and Music of Charles Mingus*. Oxford UP, 2000.

Saul, Scott. *Freedom Is, Freedom Ain't: Jazz and the Making of the Sixties*. Harvard UP, 2003.

Scanlan, Tom. *The Joy of Jazz: Swing Era, 1935–1947*. Fulcrum, 1996.

Schudel, Matt. "Musician Richard Sudhalter; Jazz History Left Bitter Note." *Washington Post*, 20 Sept. 2008, washingtonpost.com/wp-dyn/content/article/2008/09/19/AR2008091903832_pf.html/.

Schuller, Gunther. *Early Jazz: Its Roots and Musical Development*. 1968. Oxford UP, 1986.

Selbert, Todd, editor. *The Art Pepper Companion: Writings on a Jazz Original*. Cooper Square P, 2000.

Shapiro, Nat, and Nat Hentoff. *Hear Me Talkin' To Ya: The Story of Jazz as Told by the Men Who Made It*. 1955. Dover, 1966.
Shaw, Artie. *The Best of Intentions and Other Stories*. Daniel and Daniel, 1989.
———. *I Love You, I Hate You, Drop Dead!* Signet Books, 1966.
———. "Snow White in Harlem, 1930." *The Best of Intentions*, 9–28.
———. *The Trouble with Cinderella: An Outline of Identity*. 1952. Fithian, 1992.
"Should Negro Musicians Play in White Bands?" *Down Beat* 6, no. 11, 15 Oct. 1939, pp. 1, 10, 23.
Simosko, Vladimir. *Artie Shaw: A Musical Biography and Discography*. Scarecrow P, 2000.
Smith, Patrick J. "Kolodin, Irving." *Grove Music Online*. 1 Jan. 2001. Oxford UP, www.oxfordmusiconline.com.ezproxy.library.yorku.ca/grovemusic/view/10.1093/gmo/9781561592630.001.0001/omo-9781561592630-e-0000047671/.
Smith, Wadada Leo. *Ten Freedom Summers*. Cuneiform Records, 2012. CD.
Smith, Willie the Lion, with George Hoefer. *Music on My Mind: The Memoirs of An American Pianist*. 1964. Da Capo P, 1978.
Snider, Burr. "the hungry i." *The San Francisco Examiner*, 21 Aug. 1980, pp. 57, 59.
Starling, Edmund William, as told to Thomas Sugrue. *Starling of the White House: The Story of the Man Whose Secret Service Detail Guarded Five Presidents from Woodrow Wilson to Franklin D. Roosevelt*. Simon and Schuster, 1946.
Stein, Daniel. *Music Is My Life: Louis Armstrong, Autobiography, and American Jazz*. U of Michigan P, 2012.
———. "The Performance of Jazz Autobiography." *Blue Notes: Toward a New Jazz Discourse*. Mark Osteen, editor. Special Issue of *Genre: Forms of Discourse and Culture* 37, no. 2, 2004, pp. 173–99.
Stepto, Robert B. *From behind the Veil: A Study of Afro-American Narrative*. U of Illinois P, 1979.
Steyn, Mark. "Ex-Husband of Love Goddesses: Artie Shaw (1910–2004)." *The Atlantic*. March 2005, pp. 138–39.
Stone, Albert E. "Collaboration in Contemporary American Autobiography." *Revue Française D'études Américaines* 14, 1982, pp. 151–65. *JSTOR*, www.jstor.org/stable/20872903.
———. "Two Recreate One: The Act of Collaboration in Recent Black Autobiography—Ossie Guffy, Nate Shaw, Malcolm X." *Autobiographical Occasions and Original Acts: Versions of American Identity from Henry Adams to Nate Shaw*. Philadelphia: U of Pennsylvania P, 1982, pp. 231–64.
Stowe, David W. *Swing Changes: Big Band Jazz and New Deal America*. Harvard UP, 1994.
Sudhalter, Richard M. *Lost Chords: White Musicians and Their Contribution to Jazz, 1915–1945*. Oxford UP, 1999.
Sugrue, Thomas. *There Is a River: The Story of Edgar Cayce*. 1945. Holt, Rinehart and Winston, 1971.
Suhor, Charles. *Jazz in New Orleans: The Postwar Years through 1970*. Scarecrow Press/Institute of Jazz Studies–State U of New Jersey, 2001.
Tackley, Catherine. *Benny Goodman's Famous 1938 Carnegie Hall Jazz Concert*. Oxford UP, 2012.
Tapscott, Horace. *Songs of the Unsung: The Musical and Social Journey of Horace Tapscott*. Steven Isoardi, editor. Duke UP, 2001.
Tate, Greg, editor. *Everything but the Burden: What White People Are Taking from Black Culture*. Broadway Books, 2003.
Teachout, Terry. "The Color of Jazz." *Commentary* 100, Sept. 1995, pp. 50–53.
Terkel, Studs. *Giants of Jazz*. Crowell, 1957.
———. *Race: How Blacks and Whites Think and Feel about the American Obsession*. Anchor Books, 1993.

Thomas, Greg. "BAM or Jazz: Part Two!" *All about Jazz*, 6 Feb. 2012, www.allaboutjazz.com/bam-or-jazz-part-two-by-greg-thomas.php/.

———. "BAM or Jazz: Why It Matters." *All about Jazz*, 12 Jan. 2012, www.allaboutjazz.com/bam-or-jazz-why-it-matters-by-greg-thomas.php/.

———. "Gary Giddins on Ignored Black Jazz Writers." *All about Jazz*, 11 July 2011, www.allaboutjazz.com/gary-giddins-on-ignored-black-jazz-writers-by-greg-thomas.php/.

———. "Jazz vs. Racism." *All about Jazz*, 22 March 2011, www.allaboutjazz.com/jazz-vs-racism-by-greg-thomas.php/.

———. "Race and Jazz Criticism." *All about Jazz*, 3 Oct. 2011, www.allaboutjazz.com/race-and-jazz-criticism-by-greg-thomas.php/.

———. "Race, Culture and a White Boy from Texas." *All about Jazz*, 9 May 2011, www.allaboutjazz.com/race-culture-and-a-white-boy-from-texas-by-greg-thomas.php/.

Thompson, Scott H. "Jazz at Lincoln Center: Duke's Students. *Playbill*, 6 May, 2008, http://www.playbill.com/article/jazz-at-lincoln-center-dukes-students/.

Tovey, Michael, and Barry Kernfeld. "Manone, Wingy [Joseph Matthews]." *Grove Music Online*. 2003, www.oxfordmusiconline.com.ezproxy.library.yorku.ca/grovemusic/view/10.1093/gmo/9781561592630.001.0001/omo-9781561592630-e-2000288000/.

Tucker, Sherrie. *Swing Shift: "All-Girl" Bands of the 1940s*. Duke UP, 2000.

Vacca, Richard. *The Boston Jazz Chronicles: Faces, Places, and Nightlife 1937–1962*. Troy Street, 2012.

Voce, Steve. "Obituary: Stanley Dance." *The Independent*, March 1999, www.independent.co.uk/arts-entertainment/obituary-stanley-dance-1077797.html/.

Von Eschen, Penny M. *Satchmo Blows Up the World: Jazz Ambassadors Play the Cold War*. Harvard UP, 2004.

Wald, Gayle. "Mezz Mezzrow and the Voluntary Negro Blues." *Crossing the Line: Racial Passing in Twentieth-Century U.S. Literature and Culture*. Duke UP, 2000.

Wasserman, John L. "After Chemistry I'll Have to Scramble." *The San Francisco Examiner*, 31 May, 1970, p. 110.

———. "Since the Founding of the Committee, 33 Artists have Worked There: These Are . . ." *The San Francisco Examiner*, 21 Apr. 1968, p. 162.

Wells, Dicky, as told to Stanley Dance. *The Night People: Reminiscences of a Jazzman*. Crescendo, 1971.

"Whatever Happened to Matthew (Stymie) Beard?" *Ebony*, January 1975, 134.

White, John. *Artie Shaw: His Life and Music*. Continuum, 2004.

Whiteman, Paul, and Mary Margaret McBride. *Jazz*. 1926. Arno P, 1974.

Widener, Daniel. *Black Arts West: Culture and Struggle in Postwar Los Angeles*. Duke UP, 2010.

Wilber, Bob, assisted by Derek Webster. *Music Was Not Enough*. Oxford UP, 1987.

"Wildcats." *New Yorker*, 28 Dec. 1946, p. 15.

Williams, David Leander. *Indianapolis Jazz: The Masters, Legends and Legacy of Indiana Avenue*. History P, 2014.

Wilmer, Valerie. *As Serious as Your Life: The Story of the New Jazz*. Quartet Books, 1977.

Wilson, John S. "Artie Shaw, Bandleader, Composer and Wizard of the Clarinet, Is Dead at 94: In the Royalty of Swing." *New York Times*, 31 Dec. 2004, p. A24.

Wolfe, Bernard. "Afterword." *Really the Blues*, pp. 389–91.

———. "Ecstatic in Blackface." *Really the Blues*, pp. 391–404.

Woodward, C. Vann. *The Strange Career of Jim Crow*. Oxford UP, 1957.

INDEX

AACM. *See* Association for the Advancement of Creative Musicians (AACM)
Addams, Jane, 106
Afrocentrism, xxi, 46, 47, 172, 191nn12–13. *See also* black cultural nationalism
Ake, David, 44, 45, 46, 47, 191n11
Alexander, Michael, 83, 120, 196nn5–6
Allen, Red, 185n10
Allen, Woody, 124
"And the Angels Sing," 112, 201n60
Aptheker, Herbert, 64
Armstrong, Louis, 13, 14, 23, 25, 29, 53, 88, 98, 106, 191n23, 200n43, 207n7; as author, xvi, 7, 184n3, 187n9, 204n16; Collier's biography of, vii, viii, ix; as cultural ambassador, 79; Irish Channel and, 78, 195n36; Lincoln Center Jazz Orchestra (LCJO) and, 192n27; *Rhapsody in Black and Blue*, 80
Arshawsky, Arthur. *See* Shaw, Artie
Art Pepper: Notes from a Jazz Survivor (film), 208n25
Asher, Daniel, 125, 203n9
Asher, Don, xviii, xxxii, 184n1, 186n3; as author, 124, 203nn7–8; "The Barrier," 131, 134, 137, 138, 139, 204n16, 206n38; the Committee and, 124, 137, 203n6; *Don't the Moon Look Lonesome*, 124, 203n8, 205n31; *The Electric Cotillion*, 123, 124, 139–43, 146, 147, 159, 203n8, 205n28; *The Eminent Yachtsman*, 123, 125, 126, 203n9; family background of, 123, 125, 126, 204n10; fictional-real elements in writings of, 122, 123, 130, 134, 138, 139–43, 147, 203nn2–3, 204nn15–16, 205n30; Hampton Hawes and, 122, 129, 137–39, 143; *honeycomb*, 203n5; hungry i and, 124, 139, 144–45, 147, 203n5, 206n34; interracial jazz experiences and, 129, 130–34, 140, 204nn13–15, 204n17, 204nn19–20; interracial sexuality and, 132, 133, 140–41, 142, 205n31, 206n32; Jaki Byard and, 126, 127–28; Jewish identity and, 123, 125, 127, 145, 146, 206n37; as nightclub pianist, xxxii, 122, 124, 146, 148, 206n39; *Notes from a Battered Grand*, 122, 123, 125, 126–34, 137, 138–48; *The Piano Sport*, 123, 203n4, 203n8; racial stereotypes and, 123, 126, 129, 133, 138, 140–43; *Raise Up Off Me*, 137–39, 143; Ross Russell and, 134–36, 205n21; as satirist, 123, 124, 126, 143, 144, 146, 147; S. N. Behrman and, 126, 204nn11–12
Asher, Poe, 205n29
Association for the Advancement of Creative Musicians (AACM), 210n45
"As Time Goes By," 206n39
Avakian, Aram "Al," 191n15

Babitz, Abram, 208n20
Babitz, Sol, 208n20
Babitz, Thelma, 161, 208n20
Bailey, Buster, 106
Baker, Chet, 184n9
Baker, Dorothy, 20
Baldwin, James, xxvii
Ballard, Hank, 186n28
Balliett, Whitney, 13, 52, 208n27
Bankhead, Tallulah, 47–49
Barish, Andrew S., 187n13
Barnet, Charlie: background of, xvii; integration and, xxx; Stanley Dance and, xxxi, 5,

9, 12, 13, 16, 187n13; *Those Swinging Years*, 5, 9–10, 31, 35
Basie, Count, 15, 101, 108, 109, 187n12, 187n17, 191n22
Beard, Matthew "Stymie," 158, 207n14
Bechet, Leonard, 46
Bechet, Sidney: Bob Wilber and, xxxii, 46, 47, 53, 54, 56, 190n6; Creole identity of, 44–47, 190n10; Lincoln Center Jazz Orchestra and, 192n27; on Mezz Mezzrow, 199n40; Talullah Bankhead and, 47–49; white jazz revivalists and, 43, 190n8
Beckwith, Mary, 191n14
"Begin the Beguine," 84
Behrman, H. J. (Hi), 126
Behrman, S. N. (Sam), 125, 126, 203n9, 204n12
Beiderbecke, Bix, 20, 29, 88
"Bei Mir Bist Du Schoen," 112
Berger, David, 192n27
Berklee College of Music, 130
Berklee Institute of Jazz and Gender Justice, 210n2
Berliner, Paul, xvi, 184n5, 185n11
Berlin, Irving, 196n6
Bethel, Tom, 63, 193n11, 193n14
Bilbo, Theodore Gilmore, 44
"Blackberries," 194n22
black cultural nationalism, 173, 181, 196n6
Black Hawk (club), 175
black masculinity: Bob Wilber and, 47–49; Charles Mingus and, 210n44; Louis Armstrong and, 80; Mezz Mezzrow and, 199n37; *The Sound* and, 135; white jazz autobiographers and, xxiii; the "white Negro" and, xxvi–xxviii. *See also* Asher, Don; Gabbard, Krin; Lott, Eric; Monson, Ingrid; Russell, Ross
Blanton, Jimmy, 207n7
Bliggen, Dora, 67, 194n22
Blumenthal, Bob, 174, 210n48
Bocage, Peter, 194n17
Borenstein, Larry, 192n2
Bradley, Bill, 185n10
Brice, Fanny, 196n6
Bridges, Harry, 206n3
Brodkin, Karen: on ethnoracial assignments and ethnoracial identities, 83, 179, 196n3; on fluid identity of Jewish Americans, 82, 83; on Jewish upward mobility, 197n11; on Workman's Circle, 200n47

Browne, Samuel, 170, 209n35
Brown v. Board of Education, 45
Bruce, Lenny, 124, 144, 145, 146, 206nn33–35, 206n37, 210n48
Bryant, Clora, 209n37
Burbank, Albert, 70, 71
Burke, Patrick: on Bob Wilber, 53; race and Fifty-Second Street, 40–41, 190n5; racial ambiguity of Italian American musicians, 79, 195n39, 196n40. *See also* Manone, Wingy; Prima, Louis
Burns, Ralph, 56
Byard, Jaki/Jackie, xxxii, 123, 128, 129, 139, 146

Cables, George, 167, 168
California Jewish Voice (newspaper), 208n20
Calloway, Cab, 56
Cantor, Eddie, 98
Capehart, Jonathan, 184n8
Capone, Al, 23
Carmichael, Hoagy, xxviii, 148
Carner, Gary, 183n2
Carpenter, Don, 203n7
Carrington, Terri Lyne, 210n2
Carter, Benny: Art Pepper and, 154, 155–56, 157; Don Asher and, 124; tribute concert to, 56, 192n27
Carter, Ron, ix
Carter, William, 190n9, 193n13, 194n18, 195n29
Casablanca (film), 148, 206n39
Casa Loma Orchestra, 84, 107
Catlett, Sid, 54
Celestin, Papa, 60
Céline, Louis-Ferdinand, 33
Central Avenue: black musicians and, 168–71, 172, 176; discrimination and, 169–70, 171, 181, 209n32, 209n34, 209n39; history of, 150, 169
"Cherokee," 175
Chicago-style ("Condon-style") jazz, 19, 24, 25, 36, 53, 116, 189n31
Chilton, John, 46, 48, 49, 191n16
Christian, Charlie, 111
Clarke, Kenny, 54
Clayton, Buck, 187n16
Club Alabam, 154
Cohen, Leonard, 208n21
collaborators of white jazz autobiography: authenticating strategies of, xxxi, 4, 6; as jazz historians, 34–36; preoccupation with

race, 4, 6; "reverse authentication" and, 8, 13, 35; white-on-white primitivism and, 8, 12, 187n11
Collette, Buddy, 172, 209n37
Collier, James Lincoln: on Benny Goodman, 200n48; debate with Wynton Marsalis, vii–xii, 183n2, 183n4
Collins, Judy, 208n21
colorblindness: Art Pepper and, 151; Bob Wilber and, xxxii, 37, 50, 52, 58, 60; Ruth Frankenberg on, 185n12; Tom Scanlan and, 17; white jazz autobiographers and, 179. *See also* race-neutral perspective; "white resentment narrative"
Committee, the (comedy revue), 124, 137, 203n6
Condon, David, 21, 22
Condon, Eddie, xviii, xxxi; as author and critic, 18, 188nn20–21, 188n25, 188n27; public persona of, 17–18; *We Called It Music*, 3, 5, 17–25, 26, 28, 30, 31; on women, xxiv. *See also* McNulty, John; Sugrue, Thomas
Connell, Evan, Jr., 203n7
Conrad, Barnaby, 203n7
Cook, William Marion, 52
Coppola, Francis Ford, 55, 56, 57
Corey, Irwin, 144, 146, 206n33
Cottrell, Louis, 69, 194n17
Cowell, Stanley, 166
Criss, Sonny, 170
Crosby, Bing, 196n42
Crouch, Stanley: feud with Bob Wilber, 55–58, 192nn24–26, 207n8; influence on Wynton Marsalis, vii, x, 183n3
"Crow Jim" reverse racism, 16, 135, 173

Dabney, Ford, 80
Daily Worker (newspaper), 201n58
Damon, Maria, 95, 98
Damrosch, Walter, 38
Dance, Stanley: authenticating strategy of, 9–10, 12; collaboration with Charlie Barnet, 4, 5, 13, 35, 187nn12–13; and jazz wars, 8, 9
Davern, Kenny: Bob Wilber and, 191n23, 192n28; and New Orleans jazz, 191n23
Davis, Kimberly Chabot, xxviii
Davison, Wild Bill, 188n25
DeBerry, Jarvis, 184n8

Dederich, Charles E., Sr., 207n16
Dejan, Harold, 69
Denning, Michael, 109, 112, 201n53
DeVeaux, Scott, xix, 50, 187n13, 188n28
Dickenson, Vic, 187n16
Dodds, Johnny, 53
Dodds, Warren "Baby," 53
Dorsey, Jimmy, 111
Douglass, William, 181, 209n32
Down Beat (magazine): on Benny Goodman's integrated bands, 110, 111, 201nn56–57; on Benny Goodman's Carnegie Hall concert, 31, 32; and Bob Wilber, 54; on racism in jazz, 210n46; Tom Sancton essay in, 194n19; on Wingy Manone's racial ambiguity, 79
Down Beat Club, 209n33
Du Bois, W. E. B., 61

Early, Gerald, 183n6
Eastland Disaster, 96, 97, 199n34
Eldridge, Roy, 127, 185n10, 187n16, 207n7
Elks Auditorium, 169
Ellington, Duke: Bob Wilber and, 38, 50, 56, 57, 58, 192n27; Charlie Barnet and, 10; Don Asher and, 140, 147; James Lincoln Collier biography of, vii, viii, ix; Popular Front and, 110; Stanley Dance and, 187n12
Ellison, Ralph, 61
Elman, "Ziggy" (Harry Aaron Finkelman), 112, 201n60
Epstein, Lawrence, 206n33
Erenberg, Lewis: on Artie Shaw, 198n25; on Benny Goodman, 31, 32, 110, 111, 200n47; on David Goodman, 200n47, 201n58; on interracialism in the Swing Era, 180
Erwin, Pee Wee, 185n10
Evans, Nicholas M., 183n1, 185n19
"Every Beat of My Heart," 186n28

Fairclough, Adam, 193n16, 194n18
Fantasy Records, 164, 166
Farmer, Art, 172
FBI, 111, 210n42
Firestone, Ross: on Benny Goodman, 105, 110, 200n46, 200n48; on Irving Kolodin, 26, 31; on Goodman and John Hammond, 201n54
Fitzgerald, Ella, 111
Foster, Pops, 7, 39

"Frailach in Swing," 201n60
Frank, Harriet, 203n8
Frankenberg, Ruth, 185n12
Frankfurter, Felix, 196n6
Frazier, George, 19
Freeman, Bud, xviii, xxxi; *Crazeology*, 5, 13–14, 201n52; on Mezz Mezzrow, 200n43; Studs Terkel and, 5, 13–14, 16

Gabbard, Krin, xxvi, xxvii, xxviii, 184n1
Gable, Clark, 162
Gardner, Ava, 84
Geduld, Carolyn, 96, 189n37, 199–200n42
gender justice in jazz, 178, 210n2
Gennari, John: on jazz criticism in the 1930s–1960s, 34–36; on jazz interracialism, 180; on *The Sound*, 134, 205nn21–22; on Stanley Dance, 8, 9. *See also* collaborators of white jazz autobiography
Gerlach, Horace, 187n9
Gershwin, George, 94, 196n6, 198n30
Giddins, Gary: on Art Pepper, 174; on Benny Goodman, 113; on Laurie Pepper, 208n27; on *Raise Up Off Me*, 138, 205n27; on *Straight Life*, 206n4; on *We Called It Swing*, 18, 188n22
Gide, André, 33
Gillespie, Dizzy, 18, 140, 147, 183n7
Gillespie, Lorraine, 160
Gioia, Ted, 123, 150, 207n12
Gleason, Jackie, 191n21
"Gloomy Sunday," 158
Gold, Herbert, 203n7, 204n16
Goldkette, Jean, 84
Goldstein, Eric, 83, 120, 121, 196n5, 201n62
Gonzales, Babs, 210n48
Goodman, Alice Hammond, 121, 203n73
Goodman, Benny, xvii, xviii, xxx, xxxi, xxxii, 5, 9, 38, 56, 113, 184n4, 185n10, 187n16, 188n27; African American musicians and, 106, 181, 200n48; Alice Hammond and, 121, 203n73; black bands as influence on, 106, 107, 108, 109; on career in music, 105, 106; Carnegie Hall concert (1938), 26, 31, 32, 111, 201n58; class-consciousness of, 105; European art music and, 189n34; family and, 82, 105, 200n45; Fletcher Henderson and, 107, 108, 200n50; fluid identity of, 107, 112, 113; Frank Schoepp and, 106, 200n48;
interracial performances and recordings and, 107, 108, 110–11, 201n55; as jazz statesman, 112, 201n59; Jewishness and, 88, 106, 112, 201n60; John Hammond and, 107, 110, 201n54; *Kingdom of Swing*, 26–32, 103–13; as "king of swing," 109, 112, 201n52, 201n58; Lincoln Center Jazz Orchestra and, 58, 192n27; as "link between the races," 113; paternalism of, 108–9; Popular Front and, 109–10, 111, 112, 201n53; reticence of, 105, 106, 112, 119, 200n46; racism on tour and, 108, 200n51
Goodman, David, 105, 106, 200n45, 200n47
Goodman, Dora, 105
Goodman, Harry, 200n45
Goodwin, Jill, 165, 209n28
Gordon, Dexter, 154, 209n35
Gordon, Vera, 208n20
Gorman, Israel, 70, 194n25
Graham, Martha, 208n20
Graham, Renée, 184n8
Granz, Norman, 140
Gray, Glen. *See* Casa Loma Orchestra
Great American Songbook, 147, 148
Green, Freddie, 15, 187n17
Guesnon, George: Creole identity of, 63, 64, 65, 194n17; on systemic racism, 64, 65
Guess, Andre, ix, x, xi, xii
Gould, Elliott, 124
Gunn, Bill, 203n8

Haig, Al, 204n18
Hamilton, Chico, 209n35
Hammond, Alice. *See* Goodman, Alice Hammond
Hammond, John: Benny Goodman and, 30, 110, 189n34, 201n54, 201n56, 203n73; Bob Wilber and, 37, 38; Count Basie and, 109; Irving Kolodin and, 5, social activism of, 110, 200n49
Hampton, Lionel, 108, 172
Handy, W. C., xix
Hansen, Chadwick: authenticating strategy of, 10–13; collaboration with Art Hodes, 5, 16, 187n6
Hardin, Lil, 12
"Harlem Nocturne," 186n28
Harlos, Christopher: on jazz autobiography, xv, xvi, 6, 7, 184n2, 187n8, 187n12, 208n24

Harper's (magazine), 124
Harris, Wyonie, 154
Hart, Billy, ix
Hawes, Hampton: collaboration with Don Asher, 122, 129, 137–39, 143; *Raise Up Off Me*, 122, 143, 203n1
Hawkins, Coleman, 10, 51, 107, 187n16, 207n7
Haynes, Roy, 166, 167, 209n29
Heath, Albert "Tootie," ix
Heble, Ajay, xvi, 184n3, 185n11
Henderson, Fletcher, 106, 107, 108, 109, 111, 201n52
Henson, Jimmy, 153
Hentoff, Nat, 206n33
Hersch, Charles: on Irish Channel, 76; on Jewish identity, 202n72; on Mezz Mezzrow, 199n32, 199n35; on New Orleans race history, 44, 45, 47, 195n31; on "outdoor performance," 77; on Sicilians in early jazz, 195n38
Hines, Earl, 12, 78, 88, 187n12
Hitler, Adolf, 119
Hodes, Art, xvii, xviii, xxxi, 39; on Bob Wilber, 191n14; *Hot Man*, 5, 10–13, 187n8; Louis Armstrong and, 78; on Mezz Mezzrow, 200n43
Hodges, Johnny, 10, 140
Holiday, Billie, xxiv, 85, 107, 118, 202nn65–66
Holiday (magazine), 203n7
Holley, Eugene, Jr., 183n6
Horne, Lena, 9
Horton, Pug, 52, 57, 192nn25–26
Howard, Kid, 194n25
Hughes, Langston, 61
Hull House, 106
Humoresque (film), 208n20
hungry i (club), 124, 139, 144–45, 147, 203n5, 206n34
hungry i Reunion (film), 203n5
Huntington, Bill, 194n28
Hurok, Sol, 189n35

Industrial Workers of the World (IWW), 206n3
International Longshore and Warehouse Union (ILWU), 206n3
interracialism: on Central Avenue, 151, 157, 158, 168–70, 171, 173, 174; Fifty-Second Street and, 41, 190n5; New Orleans early jazz culture and, xxxii, 74–81; New Orleans jazz revival and, xviii, 59, 66–71, 72, 192n2, 194n18; as one-way, xxx; in teacher-student relationships, xxiii, xxvi, xxvii, xxviii, xxxi, 14, 180; triumphs and limitations of, xxiii, xxxi, 178, 181; white jazz autobiographers and, xi, xii, xviii, xxi, xxiii, xxiv, xxv, xxvi, xxix–xxxi, 36, 120, 150, 161, 178–81; white swing bands and, 28, 108, 198n21. *See also under names of specific musicians and critics*
Irving Aaronson and his Commanders, 88
"Isle of Capri, The," 79
Isoardi, Steven, 171, 172, 209n34
"It's a Grand Old Flag," 144
Iverson, Ethan, ix–xii, 183n7
IWW. *See* Industrial Workers of the World (IWW)

Jacobs, Paul, 203n7
Jaffe, Allan, 192n2
Jaffe, Sandra, 192n2
JALC. *See* Jazz at Lincoln Center (JALC)
James, Etta, 186n28
James, Harry, 38, 185n10
jam sessions: Bob Wilber and, 38, 39; Don Asher and, xviii, 123, 129–34; on Fifty-Second Street, 41, 190n5; as integrated, 180; at Preservation Hall, 67, 194n18; white jazz autobiographers and, 178, 204n13. *See also* interracialism
jazz and race debates. *See Down Beat*; "Playboy Panel, The;" Jazz at Lincoln Center (JALC)
jazz and social justice, 177, 210n1. *See also* gender justice in jazz
Jazz at Lincoln Center (JALC): Bob Wilber and, 55; debates on race and jazz, vii, ix, xi, xii; and lack of gender diversity, 183n1, 183n8; Wynton Marsalis and, vii, viii, ix, x, xii, 55, 57, 183n1. *See also* Marsalis, Wynton
jazz autobiography: as performative, xv–xvi; previous studies of, xv–xvi; role of collaborators, 3–36, 163, 174; value of insider perspectives, xix
Jazz Congress (2018), ix
jazz communities: geographical particularity and, xxv
jazz identity: unique "voice" and, xx

Jefferson, Blind Lemon, 98
Jefferson High School, 170, 209n35
Jewish Americans: and black-Jewish relations, 94, 95; fluid racial identity of, 82, 83, 120, 121, 179, 202n72
Jewish jazz autobiographers, xxv, xxxii, 81, 82–121; African American culture and, 83, 84; comparison of, 119, 120; fluid racial identity of, 82–83; as second-generation Americans, xvii, xxxii, 81, 82, 84. *See also names of specific musicians*
Jewish studies, 83
Jim Crow, 45, 64, 66, 74, 97
jive talk: Wingy Manone and, 74, 79; Mezz Mezzrow and, 95, 99, 100, 103; in *The Sound*, 134, 136
John, Little Willie, 186n28
Johnson, Aaron J., 185n14
Johnson, Bunk, 53, 62
Johnson, James P., 191n23
Johnson, Lonnie, 188n18
Jolson, Al, 75, 98, 196n6
Jones, Elvin, 165, 209n28
Jones, Isham, 107
Jones, Keiko, 165, 209n28
Jones, LeRoi, 188n28
Joplin, Scott, xix
Jordan, Steve: collaboration with Thomas Scanlan, 5, 6, 15–17; *Rhythm Man*, xxxi, 5, 15, 16, 17, 35, 187n8, 187nn16–17

Kaminsky, Max, xvii, xviii, xxxii; Artie Shaw and, 202n65; Billie Holiday and, 117, 118, 202n65; black culture and, 113, 114, 120, 201n62; career in music and, 115; Charlie Parker and, 119, 202n69; early music experiences and, 114; family and, 82, 113, 114, 115; friendship with Jackie Marshard, 115–17; jazz authenticity and, 118; *Jazz Band*, 113–20; Jewish identity and, 113, 114, 115, 117, 118, 119, 120, 179, 202n71; Louis Armstrong and, 115, 117, 118; Mezz Mezzrow and, 113, 115, 202n69; military experience of, 198n23, 202n68; models of Jewish manhood and, 115, 116, 202n63; mother's relationship with Billie Holiday, 118, 202n66; paternalism of, 118, 179; racial barriers in jazz, 202n67; as sideman and soloist, 113; society bands and, 117, 202n64; upward assimilation and, 115

Keepnews, Orrin, 206n33
Kelley, Robin D. G., 160
Kelson, Jack, 169, 209n35
Kenney, William H., xv, xvi, 6, 19, 184n2; on Benny Goodman, 105; on Bernard Wolfe, 199n42; on jazz interracialism, 180; on Louis Armstrong, 7
Kenton, Leslie, 208n18
Kenton, Stan, 135, 155, 187n16, 207n9, 208n18
Keppard, Freddie, 65
Kerouac, Jack, 208n27
Keyes, Evelyn, 84
King, Martin Luther, Jr., 124
Kirk, Rahsaan Roland, 191n21
Koenig, Les, 208n19
Kolodin, Irving: Carnegie Hall program notes and, 26, 32; collaboration with Benny Goodman, 4, 26–32, 35, 188n30, 189nn31–32
Konitz, Lee, 204n18
Krupa, Gene, 108

LA County Jail. *See* Los Angeles County Jail
L.A. Free Press (newspaper), 162
Lange, Dorothea, 161
LaPan, Richard, 161
LAPD (Los Angeles Police Department), 171
LaPorta, John, 185n17, 186n3, 204n13
LCJO. *See* Lincoln Center Jazz Orchestra (LCJO)
Lemmon, Jack, 124
Leonard, Jack E., 124, 144, 146
Levey, Stan, 204n18
Lewis, George: New Orleans jazz revival and, 62, 193nn10–11; Thomas Sancton Sr. and, 62, 67, 194n23; Tom Sancton and, 60, 63, 64, 66, 69, 73, 194n17
Lewis, Oscar, 162
Life (magazine), 62, 184n2
Lincoln Center Jazz Orchestra (LCJO), 57, 58, 192n27
"link between the races." *See* Goodman, Benny; Mezzrow, Mezz
Lipsitz, George: on white privilege, xxix–xxx, xxxi, 186n26; Johnny Otis and, xxix, xxx, 186n29
Lomax, Alan, 46
Lopes, Paul Douglas, 110
Lopez, Rosie, 74
Los Angeles County Jail, 158, 159

Los Angeles musicians' union: amalgamation of, 170, 209n37
Lott, Eric, xxvi, xxvii, 123, 142, 143
Lyttelton, Humphrey, 199n33

Mack, Cecil, 80
Mailer, Norman, xxvii, 198n27, 205n24. *See also* "white Negro"
Mannone, Vincent, 74
Manone, Joseph Matthews "Wingy," xvii, xviii, xxv; career of, 80, 196n42; class consciousness of, 78; interracial music experiences and, 77, 78, 195n37; Irish Channel and, 76, 78, 195n36; Louis Armstrong and, 78, 79, 80, 195n39; on musicians' wives, xxiii; New Orleans cultural traditions and, 75, 76, 77, 79, 80; "race and place" and, xxxii, 58, 73, 80; racial ambiguity of, 79, 195n39, 196n40; *Trumpet on the Wing*, 73, 74–81
Marsalis, Wynton: Albert Murray and, vii, x, 183n3, 192n24; Bob Wilber and, 55, 56, 57, 58, 192n27; Ethan Iverson and, ix–xii, 183n1, 183n3, 183n7, 183n8; on integration, 183n7; James Lincoln Collier and, vii–ix, x, xi, xii; Jazz at Lincoln Center and, vii–xii, 183n1; rap music and, 183n8; Stanley Crouch and, vii, x, 55, 192n24
Marshard, Jackie. *See* Kaminsky, Max
Martin, T. E., 174
Martizia, Johnny, 153
Martyn, Barry, and New Orleans jazz revival, 192–93n3, 194n20, 194n24, 195n29
Mason, Jackie, 145, 146, 206n37
McBee, Cecil, 166, 167
McCarthy, Joe, 19, 92, 109
McGhee, Howard, 209n33
McKinley, Ray, 185n10
McMichael, Don, 194n19
McMullen, Tracy, 183n1
McNeely, Cecil "Big Jay," 170, 209n35
McNulty, John, 3, 4, 17, 18, 25, 186n2, 188n24; friendship with Eddie Condon, 19, 20
Melnick, Jeffrey: on Jewish white Negroes, 83, 94, 95, 196nn5–6, 197n17, 198nn28–30, 202n70
Mercer, Johnny, 201n60
Meredith, Burgess, 20
Mesirow, Milton, Jr., 100, 200n44
Mezzrow, Johnnie Mae, 100

Mezzrow, Mezz, (Milton Mesirow), xvii, xviii, xxxi, xxxii, 39, 104, 184n4; collaboration with Bernard Wolfe, 3, 32–34, 93; drugs and, 99, 100, 199n39; essentialist views of, 99, 199n38; family and, 82, 96, 98, 99, 100, 105, 199n37, 200n44; fluid self-representation of, 95, 100–101, 102, 103, 107, 198n31; Harlem and, 90; as hipster, 5, 34; identification with black culture, 96–98, 99, 103, 199n35; and irony, 95, 96; Jewish identity and, 94, 97, 98, 99, 119; "jive" talk and, 99, 100; as "link between the races," 95, 100, 101, 103, 199n32; *Really the Blues*, 32–34, 93–103, 115, 187n8, 189n36, 199n33, 199n38, 199nn41–42; as "white Negro," xxvii, 84, 93, 94, 95, 103, 120, 198n27, 199n42. *See also* Wolfe, Bernard
Michel, Ed, 166
Militant (newspaper), 161
Miller, Glenn, 38, 107
Miller, Henry, 33, 34
Miller, Laurie. *See* Pepper, Laurie
Miller, Punch, 67, 194n19
Mingus, Charles, 172, 173
Mitchell, Joni, 208n21
Mitford, Jessica, 203n7
Moke and Poke (comedians), 154
Monk, Nellie, 160
Monk, Thelonious, 160
Monson, Ingrid: on black cultural nationalism, 173; on "blackening of aesthetic standards," 195n35; and jazz improvisation, 185n11; on white hipness, xxvi, xxvii, 123, 143; on "white resentment narrative," xxi, 185n13
Montgomery, Little Brother, 13
Moore, Bill, xxix, xxx, xxxi
Moore, Patti (Madeleine). *See* Pepper, Pattie Moore
Morgenstern, Dan, 183n2
Morton, Jelly Roll, 44, 191n11
Mulligan, Gerry, 204n18
Murray, Albert, vii, x, xxi, 183n3, 192n24, 198n21
Myerson, Alan, 203n6

Nachman, Gerald, 144, 145, 206n33, 206n37
Nanton, Tricky Sam, 39
Nation (periodical), 201n54
Naundorf, Frank, 70, 71

Nelson, Willie, 148
Newman, Ruby, 203n3
New Masses (magazine), 201n53
New Orleans Times-Picayune (newspaper), 61
Nolan, Tom, 92, 93, 196n2, 197n14, 197n18, 198n25
Noone, Jimmie, 88, 106

Oakley, Helen, 201n55
O'Day, Anita, 127
Ogren, Kathy J., xv, xvi, 6, 189n33
O'Hara, John, 19
Oliver, King, 13, 14, 23, 25, 53, 106
Oliver, Sy, 56
Otis, Johnny, xxix, xxx, xxxi, 171, 186nn28–29, 209n40

Page, Drew, 185n10, 186n3; misogyny of, xxiii–xxiv
Page, Hot Lips, 40, 202n67
Pan Afrikan Peoples Arkestra (PAPA), 172, 173, 209n40
Panassié, Hugues, 188n26
Panish, Jon, 205n21
Parker, Charlie, 18, 119, 134, 139, 174, 183n7, 205n21
Parker, William H., 171
Parrish, Avery, 154
"Patricia," 167
Pavageau, Alcide "Slow Drag," 62
Pellegrinelli, Lara, 183n1
Penthouse (magazine), 208n19
Pepper, Art, xvii, xviii, xxii, xxxii, 184n4, 209n28; black culture and, xxvii, 149, 173, 206n1, 207n6; Central Avenue and, 150, 151, 153–54, 156, 158, 168, 169, 171, 207n7; childhood of, 151–53, 207n5; drug use and, 149, 150, 154, 157, 158, 160, 165, 207n15, 210n47; incarcerations of, 157, 158, 159, 207nn12–13; interracial experiences and, 150, 151, 153, 154–57, 159, 161, 165, 167–68, 172, 179, 181, 210n48; military experience of, 155; relationships with women, xxiv; Sonny Stitt and, 163, 174, 175–76, 210n49; Stan Kenton and, 155, 157, 207n9; *Straight Life*, xvii, xxiv, xxxii, 149–61, 163–66, 171, 172, 174, 175–76, 187n8, 203n2, 206n4, 207n6, 207n10, 207n12, 208n19, 208nn24–27; Synanon and, 160, 162, 207n14, 207n16; white jazz critics and, 173–74
Pepper, Arthur, Sr., 151, 152, 153, 157, 206n3
Pepper, Diane Suriaga, 175
Pepper, Laurie, xvii; Art Pepper's career and, xxxii, 149, 164, 165; *Art: Why I Stuck with a Junkie Jazzman*, 150, 161–68, 175, 176, 207n18, 210n49; background of, 161–62, 208n20–22; on jazz interracialism, 161, 165–68, 209n29; *Straight Life*, 149, 150, 152, 161, 162–64, 165, 166, 203n2, 207n10, 208n19, 208n24, 208nn26–27; Synanon and, 160, 162, 163, 207n16, 208n23; women in jazz and, 165, 209n28
Pepper, Mildred Bartold, 151
Pepper, Pattie Moore, 155
Peretti, Burton W.: on Artie Shaw, 86, 87, 198n21; on interracialism in early jazz, xxiii, 44, 180; on Sidney Bechet, 46
Phillips, Esther, 186n28
Picou, Alphonse, 63, 65
Pinsker, Sanford, 145
"Playboy Panel, The," 210n46
Plessy, Antoine, 45
Plessy, Homer, 45
Plessy v. Ferguson, 45, 65, 66
Pod's and Jerry's (club), 88, 90
Pollack, Ben, 88, 106, 107, 112
Pollack, Sidney, 124
Popular Front, and swing music, 109–10, 111, 201n53
Porter, Eric, 183n1
Porter, Roy, 170, 172, 181, 209n33
Preservation Hall, New Orleans jazz revival and, 63, 193n13
Price, Sammy, 40
Prima, Louis: black culture and, 78–79; Louis Armstrong and, 195n39; racial ambiguity of, 79, 195n39, 196n40
Prouty, Kenneth E., jazz pedagogy, 191n18
Pryor, Richard, 124, 145

race and place. *See* Manone, Wingy; Sancton, Tom
race: debates on jazz and, vii, ix, xi, xii; as a social construct, x, xxv. *See also* interracialism; racial identity; racial stereotypes; racism

race-neutral perspective, xxi, 179. *See also* colorblindness; "white resentment narrative"
racial identity: Artie Shaw and, 88, 90; Benny Goodman and, 107, 108, 112; Central Avenue and, 169–73; Creoles of Color and, 44–47, 64–66; ethnic minorities in New Orleans and, 75, 76–80, 195n31; fluidity of, xx, xxv, 36, 44, 45–47, 78, 79, 83; Jewish Americans and, 83; Jewish jazz autobiographers and, 119, 120–21; Max Kaminsky and, 114, 117–19; Mezz Mezzrow and, 94–96, 99–101, 102–3; structural power as influence on, 179. *See also under names of specific musicians*
racial stereotypes: Art Pepper and, 159, 168; of black culture, viii, xxvi, 195n39; collaborators of white jazz autobiography and, 23, 27; in *Cotton Club*, 56; Don Asher and, 123, 126, 129, 132, 133, 138, 140–43, 146; Mezz Mezzrow and, 98, 102, 115; stand-up comedy and, 145; white jazz autobiographers and, xxvii. *See also* Lott, Eric; Monson, Ingrid
racism: against white musicians, 166; Bob Wilber and, 50, 51, 52, 57; Central Avenue and, 169, 170, 171; in colorblind jazz histories, xxii; Don Asher and, 138, 146; George Guesnon and, 64; jazz and, ix, xii, 105, 177; Louis Armstrong and, 80; Mezz Mezzrow and, xxvii; New Orleans and, 47, 78; Thomas Sancton Sr. as critic of, 193n8; Tom Sancton on, 66, 70, 71; in US society, xxix, xxx, 16, 155, 168, 172, 173, 179, 180, 181; whiteness as based on, 120
Raeburn, Boyd, 187n16
Raeburn, Bruce: on ethnic minorities in New Orleans jazz, 75–76, 77, 78, 79, 80, 195n35; on *Jazzmen*, 76, 77, 194n21; on jazz "voice," xx; on Louis Prima, 79; on "The Storyville Exodus," 187n14; on Wingy Manone, 78, 79, 195n34
Ramsey, Fred, 67, 194n21
Rappoport, Leon, 145
Ravetch, Irving, 203n8
Reagan-Bush era, 14
Reese, Lloyd, 170
"reverse authentication." *See* collaborators of white jazz autobiography

Rhapsody in Black and Blue (film), 80
Rich, Buddy, 207n15
Ritz Club, 207n7
Robert Charles race riot, 64
Robinson, Bill, 38
Robinson, Jim, 62
Rodney, Red, 204n18
Rogin, Michael Paul, 75, 196n6
Rollini, Arthur, 185n10
Roosevelt, Franklin D., 201n59
Ross, Andrew, xxvii
Rothstein, Arnold, 196n6
Royal, Ernie, 209n35
Rubinstein, Arthur, 140
Russell, Bill, 62
Russell, Pee Wee, 115, 188n27
Russell, Ross: background of, 205n21; jazz writings as influence on Don Asher, 134–36; *The Sound*, 134–36, 137, 205nn21–24
Rustin, Nichole, 184n6. *See also* Rustin-Paschal, Nichole
Rustin-Paschal, Nichole, 210n44

Sahl, Mort, 124, 144, 146, 206n33, 206n37
Sampson, Max, 78
Sancton, Thomas, Sr.: Antoine Plessy and, 65; career of, 61–62, 71, 193n9; early life of, 193n6; "the mens" and, 60, 62, 67, 194n23; radicalism of, 61, 193n8
Sancton, Tom, xvii, xviii, xxviii, xxxii, 186n3; black union local and, 69, 194n24; career of, 71, 194n26; father's influence on, 60, 61, 65, 66, 69; George Guesnon and, 63–64, 65, 66; George Lewis and, 60, 62, 63, 66, 67, 69, 73, 194n17; on interracial relationships, 68, 69, 70, 205n20; New Orleans jazz culture and, 60, 72, 73, 194n28, 194n29; on New Orleans's racial history, 59–60, 63–73; Olympia Brass Band and, 69–70; Preservation Hall and, 60, 69, 192n2, 193n4; Punch Miller and, 67, 194n19; "race and place" and, xxxii, 73, 80, 195n31; *Song for My Fathers*, 59–73, 74, 192n1
Sandke, Randall, xxi, xxii, 185n14
San Francisco Chronicle (newspaper), 206n34, 206n39
San Quentin, 158, 159, 168, 207n12
Sartre, Jean-Paul, 102

Saturday Night Live, 124
Saul, Scott, 32, 96, 102, 189nn38–39, 198n27, 199n33
Saxtrum Club, 127
Scanlan, Thomas: collaboration with Steve Jordan, 5; introduction to *Rhythm Man*, 15–16, 187n17, 188n18; on jazz and race, 16–17, 35, 188nn18–19. *See also* "white resentment narrative"
Schillinger House, 130
Schoepp, Franz, 106, 200n48
Second Chorus (film), 84
Second City, The (newspaper), 203n6
Selbert, Todd, 174, 210n47
Seldes, Gilbert, 188n21
Shaw, Artie: anti-Semitism experienced by, 86, 120, 197nn10–11, 197n17; as author, 85, 104, 186n3, 196n8; Billie Holiday and, 202nn65–66; black musicians as models for, 88; "Chick" Webb and, 91; on "Cinderella myth," 85–86; as clarinetist and bandleader, xxx, 9, 84, 113, 187n16, 202n67; family background of, 82, 86, 105, 196n2; House Un-American Activities Committee (HUAC) and, 92, 93, 109, 112, 198nn24–25; on integrated bands, 111; masculinity and, 197n15; military experience of, 91, 92, 198nn22–23; on name change, 87, 88, 197n14; relationship with father, 87, 98, 197nn12–13; search for belonging and, xxxii, 84, 86, 88, 90, 91, 93, 107; as second-generation Jewish American, xvii; *Trouble with Cinderella*, 84–93, 95, 98, 103; white identity and, 88; as white Negro, 84, 90, 94, 95, 197n21, 198nn29–30; Willie "the Lion" Smith and, 88–90, 91, 190n4, 197n16, 197n18, 197n20; wives of, 84, 121, 196n7; on women, xxiv
Sheik, Kid, 194n25
"Shine," 80
Silver, Horace, 13
Simosko, Vladimir, 198n25
Sinatra, Frank, 127
Singleton, Zutty, 28, 78
Smith, Bessie, xxiv, 13, 14, 106, 107, 199n37
Smith, Fletcher, 209n34
Smith, Wadada Leo, 178
Smith, Willie (saxophonist), 206n1
Smith, Willie "the Lion": Artie Shaw and, 88–90, 91, 190n4, 197n16, 197n18; Bob Wilber and, 39, 40, 53, 55, 88; Jewishness of, 90, 197nn19–20
Stang, Arnold, 202n71
Stanley, Don, 206n34
St. Cyr, Johnny, 188n18
Stein, Daniel, xv, xvi, xix, 184n3, 198n31
Steinbeck, John, 19
Stepto, Robert, 7
Stitt, Sonny, 163, 174, 175–76, 210n49
"St. Louis Blues," 70
Stone, Albert E., 186n4
Stowe, David, 92, 110, 111, 180
Stravinsky, Igor, 208n20
Sudhalter, Richard M., xxi, xxii
Sugrue, Thomas: collaboration with Eddie Condon, 3, 5, 19, 187n7; on jazz interracialism, 28; jazz wars and, 22; "Narration," 18, 21–25, 26, 30, 35, 188n22, 188n27, 189n31; white Chicagoans and, 23
Suhor, Charles, 194n19
Synanon. *See* Pepper, Art; Pepper, Laurie
Szigetti, Josef, 30

Tackley, Catherine, 32, 189n35
Tapscott, Horace: African American cultural organizations and, 172, 210n42; on amalgamation of musicians' union, 209n37; black studies programs and, 191n17; Central Avenue and, 209n39; Jefferson High and, 170, 209n35; Pan Afrikan Peoples Arkestra and, 209n40; Watts uprising and, 209n40
Tatum, Art, 54, 140, 147, 207n7
Teachout, Terry, 183n3
Teagarden, Jack, 29, 51
Terkel, Studs, 5, 13–14, 16, 187n15, 208n27
Thomas, Greg, 183n6
Thomas, Reginald, 192n27
Thompson, Chuck, 139
Thomson, Virgil, 13
Thornton, Willie Mae "Big Mama," 186n28
Time (magazine), 71, 93, 109, 194n26
Tio, Lorenzo, Jr., 65
Traven, B., 33
Tristano, Lennie, 204n18
Trotsky, Leon, 161
Tucker, Sherrie, xxiii, 184n6, 187n11
Tucker, Sophie, 98, 196n6
Tureaud, A. P., Sr., 65, 66, 193n16
Turner, Lana, 84

Underground Musicians Association (UGMA), 172, 173, 210nn42–43
Union of God's Musicians and Artists Ascension (UGMAA), 172
United Service Organizations (USO), 134
University of California (Berkeley), 161
US Public Health Service Hospital, 158

Vacca, Richard, 131, 203n3, 204n15, 204n17, 204n19
Vallee, Rudy, 187n9
Velde, Harold H., 92
Veliotes, John. *See* Otis, Johnny
Voce, Steve, 9
Von Eschen, Penny M., 201n59

Walcott, Joseph, 204
Wald, Gayle, on Mezz Mezzrow, 95, 96, 102–3, 189n37, 198n31
Waller, Fats, 98, 147
"Wallflower, The," 186n28
Wallington, Stan, 204n18
Washington, Booker T., 42, 44
Washington, Leon, 169
Watts uprising, 171
Webb, "Chick," 91, 108, 109
Webster, Ben, 207n7
Webster, Freddie, 157
We Have Voice Collective, 210n2
Wein, George, 50
Wells, Dicky, 7, 187n12
Wellstood, Dick: Bob Wilber and, 39; New Orleans jazz and, 191n23
Westlake College of Modern Music, 161, 162
White, John, 93, 198nn24–25
white bebop musicians, 204n18
white fascination with African Americans, xxv–xxix, 38, 123. *See also* Lott, Eric; Monson, Ingrid; names of specific musicians and critics
white jazz autobiographers: black culture as model for, xvi; and black masculinity, xiii; immersion experiences of, xx, xxxii; on Mezz Mezzrow, 200n43; misogyny of, xxiii–xxiv; as outsiders and insiders, xxii–xxiii. *See also* Jewish jazz autobiographers; "white Negro"
white jazz critics: on Art Pepper, 174, 210n47; resemblance to authenticating collaborators, 174

Whiteman, Paul, xv, xviii, xix, 84, 107, 184n4, 185n10
"white Negro": Jews and, 94; and white jazz musicians, xxvii. *See also* Mailer, Norman; Melnick, Jeffrey; Mezzrow, Mezz; Wolfe, Bernard
whiteness: critical race theory and, xxv, xxix, 196n6; as detrimental to establishing jazz authenticity, 128, 134, 135, 174; white ethnic autobiographers and, xvii, 91, 103, 107, 112, 118, 121, 198n31
whiteness studies, 83, 120
white-on-white primitivism. *See under* collaborators of white jazz autobiography
white privilege: concept of, xii, xxv, xxviii; George Lipsitz on, xxix, xxx; white jazz autobiographers and, xxx–xxxi, 37, 38, 39, 52, 54, 55, 70, 118, 137, 177
"white resentment narrative," xi, xxi–xxii, 17, 50. *See also* colorblindness; "Crow Jim" reverse racism; "race-neutral" perspective
Wiggins, Gerald, 168
Wilber, Bob, xvii, xviii, xxii; adolescent behavior of, 39, 190n2; Bechet and, 40, 41–43, 44, 63, 190n7, 191nn14–15, 192n28; on black studies programs, 50–51, 179, 191n19; *Cotton Club* controversy, 55–58, 192n24; Dick Wellstood and, 39, 190nn2–3; insensitivity of, 191n21; jam sessions and, 38, 40; jazz repertory bands and, 192n28; Lincoln Center Jazz Orchestra and, 55, 56, 57, 192n27; on Mezz Mezzrow, 39, 191n20; *Music Was Not Enough*, xxxii, 28, 37–44, 47–52, 53–56, 60; New Orleans jazz and, 37; privileged life of, 37–38, 54–55; sexual experiences of, 47–49; views on race and, xxxii, 40, 50, 51–53, 54, 58, 59, 72, 179–80, 204n14; Willie "the Lion" Smith and, 39, 40. *See also* Crouch, Stanley
Wildcats, 40, 41, 43, 53; reception of, 190n3
"Willie and the Hand Jive," 186n28
Wilson, Gerald, 169
Wilson, Jackie, 186n28
Wilson, John S., 13
Wilson, Teddy, 30, 38, 107, 108, 111, 201n55
Wisdom, John Minor, 193n16
Witmark brothers, 196n6
Wolf, Robert, 13
Wolfe, Bernard: afterword to *Really the Blues*, 95, 96, 102, 189n36; collaboration

with Mezz Mezzrow, xxxi, 3, 5, 32–34, 93, 96, 102, 103, 189nn37–39; "Ecstatic in Blackface," 102, 199n42; as "white Negro" critic, 198n27

women in jazz: as depicted in white jazz autobiography, xxiii–xxiv; Laurie Pepper and, 165, 208n28; marginalization of, xvii, xxiii, 164

Woodman, William "Brother," Jr., 168, 209n34, 209n37

Woods, Phil, 165

Woodward, C. Vann, 194n18

Workmen's Circle, 106, 200n47

Young, Lee, 154, 155, 168, 171, 207n8

Young, Lester, military experience of, 51, 52, 154, 191n22

Zardis, Chester, 190n9, 193n13

Zwerin, Michael, 208n27

ABOUT THE AUTHOR

Photo Credit Matthew Clark

Reva Marin earned her PhD in humanities at York University in 2014. Her previous publications include *Oscar: The Life and Music of Oscar Peterson*—a finalist for the 2004 Norma Fleck Award for Canadian Children's Non-Fiction—and "Representations of Identity in Jewish Jazz Autobiography," published in the *Canadian Review of American Studies*.

www.ingramcontent.com/pod-product-compliance
Lightning Source LLC
Chambersburg PA
CBHW030615230426
43661CB00053B/1999